# PARADOXES OF WAR

STUDIES IN INTERNATIONAL CONFLICT

*Series Editor:* Manus I. Midlarsky, *Moses and Anuta Back Professor of International Peace and Conflict Resolution, Rutgers University*

Volume 1: THE ONSET OF WORLD WAR
by Manus I. Midlarsky

Volume 2: WAR AND STATE MAKING
by Karen A. Rasler and William R. Thompson

Volume 3: PARADOXES OF WAR
by Zeev Maoz

*forthcoming:*

THE PRICE OF POWER
by Alan Lamborn

TERRITORIAL CHANGES AND
INTERNATIONAL CONFLICT
by Paul F. Diehl and Gary Goertz

# PARADOXES OF WAR

## On the Art of National Self-Entrapment

ZEEV MAOZ

Studies in International Conflict,
Volume 3

Boston
UNWIN HYMAN
London    Sydney    Wellington

© 1990 by Unwin Hyman, Inc.
This book is copyright under the Berne Convention. No
reproduction without permission. All rights reserved.

**Unwin Hyman, Inc.**
8 Winchester Place, Winchester, Mass. 01890, USA

Published by the Academic Division of
**Unwin Hyman Ltd**
15/17 Broadwick Street, London W1V 1FP, UK

Allen & Unwin (Australia) Ltd,
8 Napier Street, North Sydney, NSW 2060, Australia

Allen & Unwin (New Zealand) Ltd in association with the
Port Nicholson Press Ltd,
Compusales Building, 75 Ghuznee Street, Wellington 1,
New Zealand

First published in 1990

---

**Library of Congress Cataloging-in-Publication Data**

Maoz, Zeev
    Paradoxes of war : on the art of national self-entrapment / Zeev
Maoz.
            p.        cm. — (Studies in international conflict ; v. 3)
Bibliography: p.
Includes index.
ISBN 0-04-445113-X
1. War. 2. International relations. I. Title. II. Series.
U21.2.M346 1989
327.1′6—dc20                                                        89-32673
                                                                            CIP

---

**British Library Cataloguing in Publication Data**

Maoz, Zeev
Paradoxes of war : on the art of national self-entrapment. (Studies
in international conflict; 3).
1. War. Political aspects
I. Title II. Series
355′. 02
ISBN 0-04-445113-X

---

Typeset in 10 on 12 point Bembo
and printed in Great Britain by
Hartnolls Ltd, Bodmin, Cornwall

*To Inbal and Omry,*
*for asking tough questions*

# Contents

# Preface

This book emerged out of my difficulty in answering a question posed to me by my (then) seven-year-old daughter. In the spring of 1983 I received a letter from the Israeli army informing me that I was called for a tour of duty in Lebanon. My daughter, alarmed by the prospect, asked me what we were doing there, and why we did not go back to our old border. My first inclination was to run by her the official story about terrorist attacks and the need to defend our towns and villages in the north from repeated shelling and infiltration. But I immediately realized that it did not sound very convincing, even to a seven-year-old child. So my second scheme was to try to convince her by explaining that our leaders were pursuing a fairly stupid policy that was leading nowhere. Because they had been elected by a democratic process, there was little we could do other than protest and hope that next time the public would force the government to make smarter choices. This also did not sound terribly convincing.

Whatever answer I tried to devise, I found it difficult to make it stick. If the invasion of Lebanon had been a smart move, how come we were stuck in a deep mess? Why, within a year, had we lost 100 times more soldiers than we had lost in guerrilla operations emanating from Lebanon over the three preceding years combined? And if the invasion had been a mistake, how was it that the reasonably smart people who ran the government failed to realize it and take the appropriate measures to pull the army out of there? More important, why were so many usually intelligent people fooled by a deceptive rhetoric that sounded false and hypocritical even to a seven-year-old?

I am not sure that today I can provide a more convincing explanation of that war to my eight-year-old son, but this book represents a start. It is not a book about the 1982–1985 Lebanon war, though this war will be examined quite thoroughly in the coming pages. It is about those wars, or those aspects of war, that even the most knowledgeable adult will typically find it difficult to explain even to children. And one of the primary reasons for such difficulty, I believe, is that the kind of logic we employ in our everlasting efforts to comprehend the world around us is simply inadequate when it comes to explaining those puzzles.

*Paradoxes of War* addresses two questions: (1) Why do generally smart people drag their nations, sometimes knowingly, into traps of tremendously destructive proportions? (2) Why is it that nations that find themselves in messes of their own doing, and know it, make it difficult for themselves to escape the traps? The approach I adopt in this book is somewhat unconventional. It focuses on the perverse aspects of a perverse human activity, trying to explain why they are sometimes unavoidable rather than what kind of mistakes lead to their emergence. The paradoxes examined in the present study are not necessarily very frequent, but they do recur with some persistence. And when they do, their consequences are fairly severe. So the primary justification for a study of perversities is their significance, not their prevalence.

The book is organized around the various stages of war. The first part focuses on causes of war, particularly on those causes of war that are associated with schemes to prevent it. The second part focuses on the processes of war management, especially those aspects that lead to long and costly wars due to participants' wishes and plans to make them short and decisive. The third part examines those short- and long-term implications of war that turn the notion of war as an instrument of policy on its head. In each chapter I discuss a paradox of war cast as a causally induced contradiction between reasonable expectations and the outcomes of motivated behavior based on them. I attempt to provide alternative explanations to these paradoxes and to document them in wars that have taken place during the twentieth century.

I have made an effort to balance rigor and simplicity of presentation. The idea is to make the book accessible to a wide audience. Though the primary target readership of this study is the serious student of international politics, I believe that it will also be found interesting by a more general readership. Certainly the issues it addresses are of sufficient significance to appeal to concerned citizens who worry about what their governments, knowingly or unknowingly, might be doing to them. This represents what, I believe, is a reasonable blend of theory and history, scientific methods and jargon, and more traditional historical analysis. I have tried to keep more sophisticated analysis to a minimum. Only one chapter contains a brief mathematical appendix that proves a point made in the text. Uninitiated readers can skip this appendix without loss.

Several individuals have read parts of the text. Steven Brams, Dan Felsenthal, Chuck Gochman, and Avner Yaniv have made numerous comments on various chapters. Jack Levy labored through the entire manuscript and has given me exceptionally perceptive and detailed comments. I wish to thank all of them and hope to share the credit for the insights while absolving them of any responsibility for errors and criticism. The final part of the writing was supported by a New York University Presidential Fellowship, for which I am grateful. I wish to thank Lisa Freeman of Unwin Hyman and Manus Midlarsky, the editor of the series, for placing their faith in this manuscript when it was still in the making and for their encouragement.

My family provided the support and psychological shelter that makes life, which at times seems paradoxical, somewhat more livable. Most important, I wish to thank my children, Inbal and Omry, for asking tough questions. My hope is that, when they grow up and have children of their own, they will have a much simpler time answering questions of the sort they keep asking me about war. I hope that, whether or not there exist more convincing answers to these questions at that time, the need for such answers will be far less pressing than it is at present.

—Zeev Maoz
New York, December 1988

# 1

# *On Paradoxes and Wars*

Were insurance companies to infer the risk propensity of the population from the behavior of most soldiers on the battlefield, they would reach the conclusion that this line of business has no chance of ever being profitable. Were military strategists to infer soldiers' willingness to take risks from their insurance policies, their conclusion would be unavoidable: With cautious people like these, it is impossible to run a decent war, let alone win one. Is it possible that the same person who one day carefully looks both ways before crossing the street will the next day never pause to look back while crossing enemy lines?

Yet, governments are capable of performing this magic. They do it all the time and they do it everywhere. Mobilizing a nation for war involves transforming people from cautious human beings who put their personal safety above many other values into fighting animals who put such vague values as honor, patriotism, and glory far above personal safety. When people are called to rally around the flag, even the most alienated and apolitical go without question. They go regardless of what they think of their own government, of their own economic and social condition, and, sometimes, without paying much attention to what the issues of the war are.

Communists had high hopes when World War I broke out. Because it was a war among the principal capitalist powers, they believed that the working classes in those states would realize that their class interests contradicted the propaganda of the regimes. They reasoned that the oppressed workers could not but rebel against their capitalist bosses instead of killing each other on the battlefield while the capitalists sat back and made more profits. The worldwide communist revolution seemed to be just around the corner. How wrong they were! Soon the oppressed Austro-Hungarian proletariat were fighting against the starved Russian peasants, while the German workers were killing their French comrades and being killed by the British coal miners. How the corrupt and decadent governments of the Austro-Hungarian monarchy and the Russian Czar were able to ignite widespread nationalistic fervor that persisted for the four most bloody years in human history up to that point is still a mystery.

And it is not the only puzzle about the conduct of war. There are many such puzzles. Not all are paradoxes in the sense I will use here. Many can be explained with the help of a little imagination, and, once explained, they cease to be puzzling. But many aspects of war seem counterintuitive even after a good explanation has been given. Worse, even if we understand why a seemingly illogical event happens, we cannot prevent its recurrence if the circumstances leading to it arise again, no matter how hard we may try.

This book explores two issues that carry major theoretical and empirical implications: (1) Why do reasonable people sometimes lead their nations into self-made traps of tremendously destructive proportions? (2) Why is it that nations that find themselves in a mess of their own doing—and know it—sometimes deepen their troubles, making it harder to escape the trap? The stories told here are about processes that take place before the outbreak of wars, during their courses, and following their termination. They have one thing in common: all are unintended consequences of intentional human action; they happen despite the will of those involved and because all involved wish to prevent them. But even as unintended consequences, wars are not necessarily the outgrowth of human stupidity, malice, or cognitive fallibility. Some of the most disastrous wars may stem from the application of rational logic or from choices that, on the face of it, seem quite reasonable. Yet, those wars turn out to be the precise opposite of what their participants expected them to be. Worse, this contradiction between expectations and outcomes is a consequence of those "reasonable" choices. And the awareness that one is in trouble does not make escape from war easier; in fact, it may make escape even more difficult.

This chapter sets the stage for a story of perverse aspects of a perverse social behavior. The next section discusses some general approaches to the study of war and places the present approach next to other schools of thought on the topic. The following section discusses the notion of paradox, defining and illustrating it in a social and philosophical context. The methodology of the study is then reviewed, and, finally, the plan of the book is discussed.

## The Study of War

The systematic study of war goes back to ancient China, with the perceptive observations of Sun Tzu in the sixth century B.C. (see Sun Tzu, 1983). Research on the deadly art (or science) is also noted for historical continuity. I have no intention of providing a survey of the writings on this phenomenon;[1] rather, my intention is to characterize the various stages of war and briefly discuss several key approaches to the study of war. These approaches do not cover the full spectrum of perspectives on war, but they are relevant because they bear some relationship to the present approach.

Before continuing, a definition of the term *war* is in 'order. The dictionary definition of *war* is that of a series of sustained combats between the armies of two or more states that involve large-scale violence and result in numerous fatalities. Typically, wars extend for prolonged periods of time, but that is not a general rule. The key characteristics of wars are mass participation, sustained combat, and extensive bloodshed.[2] What distinguishes war from other forms of interstate violence is that it is large scale in terms of the number of people participating and being killed in its violent confrontations. The line separating war from other forms of organized violence seems to be one of magnitude. This gets a concrete meaning in Singer and Small's (1972) definition. But there is also an issue of intensity. The battles that make up a war are intense in that they are separated by relatively short intervals.[3]

While bloodshed is their most important characteristic, wars start long before the spilling of the first drop of blood, and they end long after the guns quiet down (Maoz, 1982a). Even when actual hostilities are intense but brief, wars are dynamic processes. They are dynamic not only because troops move on the battlefield in complex maneuvers, but also because of the political processes that accompany the violence and the interplay of politics and military considerations.

## *The Stages of War*

The process of war is usually taken to consist of three stages, only one of which entails pure fighting. These stages are as follows:

(1) *The initiation stage:* This stage consists of political and diplomatic maneuvers that set the stage for the actual outbreak of military hostilities. The stage ends with the first large-scale confrontation of the war. Because this stage precedes actual fighting, it is here where scholars usually look for the causes of wars. In this context we will be looking at both remote causes of war, such as arms races and deterrence policies, and immediate causes of war, such as international crises.[4]

(2) *The management stage:* This stage features maneuver and manipulation of sustained violence. The focus of studies of war management is on how strategy is used (or misused) in the service of politics. For this stage I will examine paradoxical aspects in

one of the most ancient arts known to humankind: military strategy. Politics of war management are important because they typically involve struggles and trade-offs between political goals and military considerations, often expressed in terms of civil-military disputes. Politics in this context may become a struggle over the limits to be placed on military activity. Generals wish the politicians to define for them clearly the war aims and then let them do their job without interference. However, just as generals prepare for war in times of peace, politics and diplomacy do not lay dormant in times of war.[5] This interplay between military considerations and political ones while the guns are active is what war management is all about.

(3) *The termination stage:* This stage covers the processes by which wars end and the traces they leave on the participants far beyond the termination of hostilities. Just as there are underlying and immediate causes of war, there are short-range and long-range consequences of war. When the guns are silenced it is time for those who are engaged in peaceful endeavors to take over. It is time for the winners to start plucking the fruits of victory, and for the losers to start healing and recovering from their defeat. Theories of war termination deal with how nations decide it is time to stop fighting and how they go about actually ending a war. Explanations of the political and economic consequences of war explore the effects that war has on the societies that participated in it. Analysis of these issues will focus on the paradoxical consequences of war.

Obviously, these stages are interrelated: the factors causing nations to resort to arms also affect the opening move in war. The nature of the opening move has a profound effect on how the war is managed. The management of war shapes its outcome. The end of war defines to a large extent the destiny of the nations that took part in it. However, I shall try to demonstrate throughout the study that this causal chain is anything but straightforward.

## Approaches to the Study of War

War has been studied from every possible angle, hence any classification of the various approaches to war becomes an exercise in reductionism. It must be stated that the approaches discussed in the present section only scratch the surface. They were selected primarily because they are related to the approach used in the present book and provide a more general context within which we can place the paradoxes of war, not because they are more important than other approaches that are not discussed herein.

## The Strategic Approach

Strategy is the art of using military force to accomplish political ends.[6] The strategic approach is one of the oldest and most influential approaches in the study of war in terms of its impact on the practice of war through the ages. The continuity of this approach is significant not only because certain ideas about when, why, and how military force is to be employed seem to have passed the test of time, but also because it has developed a consistent logic of its own and a set of almost universal principles and lawlike maxims. Technology has changed a great deal from the times of Sun Tzu or Thucydides, yet such principles as force economy, envelopment and pincer movement, the importance of surprise and deception, and the advantages and disadvantages of warfare in external lines predate such eternal books as the Bible. Even seemingly novel principles of strategy that many believe are unique to the nuclear age, such as deterrence, are actually very ancient (Luttwak, 1976; Harkabi, 1983).[7]

Traditional strategic approaches assume that the strategist takes over when political elites have decided to take the military route in pursuing their goals. The strategist's tasks are to accomplish the military objectives that will assure politicians the best terms at the bargaining table and to do so at the minimum possible human and material cost. Since the advent of nuclear weapons, the function of the strategic approach has expanded to include the prevention of war through military maneuver, the deployment of armed forces and military hardware, and the development of weapon systems, without actually firing a single shot. This expansion of strategy was influenced to a large extent by the ideas of people from outside the armed forces of the state. Most of the civilian strategists were academics from a variety of disciplines.[8]

The strategic approach is not distinguished by methodological sophistication. It is difficult to find a coherent scientific logic in the array of premises, prescriptions, and lawlike maxims that have developed over the years. It is not clear how they were established, what kind of evidence they rely upon, and what the limits are of generalizability of principles such as the significance of surprise and the advantage of offense versus defense in the conduct of war. In spite of this—perhaps because of this—many of its maxims sound terribly persuasive. Yet, many of these maxims fall apart when examined closely via a systematic logic that differs from the straightforward commonsense logic that characterizes strategic analyses of international politics.

The strategic approach is characterized by its reliance on informal rational logic and by its assumption that states are unitary rational actors that are out to maximize their national interest, often defined in terms of various elements of power. Military actions are the instruments of politics, and they may be resorted to as an extension of diplomacy, as a substitute for diplomacy, or in conjunction with diplomacy. Common criticisms of strategic approaches focus on the validity of the underlying assumptions of unitary rational actors (e.g., Allison, 1971; Green, 1964; Jervis, 1976; Jervis et al., 1985). Only recently have scholars started to assess the internal logic of the approach more closely, and what they have found is enough to raise some eyebrows. Luttwak's (1987) recent work is one of the more important examples. The present study attempts a similar examination of strategic logic, not by offering alternative assumptions to those that strategists have—explicitly or implicitly—espoused, but by accepting the traditional assumptions and exploring their implications in a new way.

The paradoxical study of strategy is significant, especially in a nuclear context, because this domain is replete with counterintuitive realities and with persistent contradictions. Nations spend billions of dollars on weapons whose sole raison d'être is that they are not to be used. States threaten each other that they will respond to an attack by destroying both attacker and defender. All the thinking in nuclear strategy goes into explaining the unthinkable. Most of the evidence we have of the process and outcome of a nuclear war is of a purely speculative and theoretical nature. Yet, strategic paradoxes have characterized wars that *have* taken place. It would be a mistake not to learn from those wars that have been fought about those wars we do not want to have to fight. And it is the continuity of strategic thinking that attests to the relevance of such an exercise.

## The Decision–Making Approach

The decision–making approach examines the initiation, management, and termination of war as a series of problem-solving sessions involving groups of leaders. The study that launched the decision–making approach in world politics was a study of war initiation decisions (Abel, 1941). This approach traces the various fortunes or misfortunes of war to specific decisions. It attempts to examine what factors affect decisions to initiate, escalate, or terminate wars and to what extent decision-related pitfalls cause disasters.

Decision-making theorists view wars as having specific causes: conscious or unconscious, smart or stupid choices of national elites to solve their problems through armed conflict. This approach assumes that the sources of war are to be found within states, or, more precisely, within the individual or collective calculations of national leaders. Wars are human-made products; hence, their origins must be traceable to the men and women who choose that path.[9] It follows that the decision-making approach sees wars as avoidable phenomena. Because wars are consequences of national choices, finding ways to shape or affect these choices is not an insurmountable task. Policies such as deterrence and arms races are designed to do just that.

The decision-making approach is divided into two schools of thought: the rational choice school and the cognitive school. The rational choice school emphasizes the calculated aspects of war initiation, war management, and war termination decisions. Its key contention is that nations resort to force when national leaders believe that this solution is superior to any other strategy available to the state. It also argues that states end war when the cost of fighting outweighs the political or military benefits associated with the continuation of the war.[10]

The cognitive approach stresses the nonrational or extrarational factors involved in war-related choices. It examines the biases, fallacies, and other errors of judgment and estimation involved in war decisions. This school attempts to show just the opposite of what rational choice theories seem to suggest: that war choices were not the best available, and that rational decisions could have averted war. According to this school's proponents, knowledge provides remedy to war. Teaching those who decide on peace- and war-related issues how to make good choices would make for a better world. This would not necessarily be a world without war, but one in which there are fewer wars, and most of those fought would not be the result of miscalculation and incompetence.[11]

As in the case of strategic approaches, decision-making analyses attempt to explain why wars break out, how they are run, and when they end in terms of a fairly straightforward link between national choices and international outcomes. The various schools within this approach differ in terms of the kind of factors or processes they identify as the most instrumental in the explanation. But the fundamental logic is what I will call—following Luttwak (1987)—linear logic. The present study is aimed at identifying and explaining breaks in this basic logic.

## Systemic Approaches

There is something appealing in the assumption that war is an outgrowth of forces that lie outside the immediate control of specific leaders; that the blame for war, and the destruction and misery that come with it, lies with the structure of the international system. Perhaps this is why the claim of "no choice" is often recited by politicians. In contrast to the "bottom-up" approach that sees war as a culmination of national choices, the "top-down" systemic approach sees those national choices as unavoidable because they are made in a setting where structure and rules leave little room for individual states to maneuver.[12] The systemic approach attempts to identify the large picture in history, the broad chessboard of nations and the rules of play in that game. From the description of the nature of the game defined in terms of the configuration of actors (mostly in terms of capability distribution) and the set of rules that define the interaction among them, systemic theorists deduce propositions regarding conditions under which war is more or less likely.[13]

Systemic approaches create an impression that international reality is analogous to a classical Greek tragedy: our fate has been sealed by the gods; life is but a futile effort to fight our predetermined destiny; no matter how hard we try, what has been decided is what happens. The difference between a Greek tragedy and the tragedy of international politics is that in the latter play nobody really knows who is responsible. Just like the free market that guides the behavior of economic agents, international politics has its own hidden hand that guides the decisions of states. This hidden hand is the structure of the international system, often characterized by the number of major powers, their alignments, and the distribution of capabilities among them.

War plays an important role in systemic theories: it is both the big transformer of the international system and its major regulator. Most of the major changes in the structure of the international system over the past three centuries have been attributed to war: the inception of the modern state-system is the result of the Thirty Years' War. The Treaty of Westphalia (1648) created for the first time a system of autonomous sovereign states. The system that emerged survived for nearly 200 years, despite attempts to transform it by Napoleon Bonaparte. Yet, it collapsed in the big bang of 1914. The replacement system survived exactly twenty years and crashed again in 1939. The bipolar system that emerged from the rubble of World War II is still surviving as these lines are being written. During the balance of power system, war was seen as a major mechanism for preserving the structure of the international system. States ganged up against individual states or against coalitions of states that attempted to transform the international system by becoming preponderant (Gilpin, 1981).

The systems approach will not be examined closely in this book for two principal reasons. First, the focus on paradoxes and the specific definition of the term require a choice-oriented perspective. There are serious questions about the latitude of choice that system theories allow to ordinary people. It is not clear that systemic structures leave much room for maneuver, and hence it is not clear that what I characterize as paradoxes of war constitute a puzzle from a systemic perspective.[14]

Second, some aspects of systems theory enter the explanation of various paradoxes as structural constraints on the choices of national leaders. System-level ideas are represented by what will repeatedly be alluded to as "rules of the game," which determine what is permissible or prohibited in a given interaction that forms a paradox of war. Yet, I will show that, even then, choice rather than structure makes for the paradox.

These approaches view the dynamics of wars as straight-forward consequences of some design, be it human-made or system-determined. The trick is to discover that design. Even the cognitive approach, which looks for human fallibility, ineptitude, and short-sightedness, attempts to trace those generalizable human errors that make people believe that they can get something out of war. Common to all three approaches is a functionalist attitude toward war. War is seen to serve a purpose. Whether that purpose is good or bad, justified or malevolent, it does not take place in a vacuum. Underlying war is a set of reasons, a set of aims that war seems to serve, a set of expectations that give rise to the wish (or perceived necessity) to engage in large-scale violence.

In contrast, the paradoxical logic searches for the breaks in those notions that focus on the straightforward connection between causes and outcomes. When this connection does not seem to be working, an aspect of war becomes a candidate for paradoxical analysis. Zinnes (1980b) recommends research that starts out by delineating puzzles, that is, seemingly inexplicable aspects of inter-national politics. In a way, this is what the paradoxical approach starts doing. But, in contrast to the next step in Zinnes's strat-egy—the development of models that would render this puzzle comprehensible, which is what science is all about—the paradoxical approach keeps screening out the puzzles that turn out to have a reasonable explanation. It then focuses only on those puzzles that remain unexplained and attempts to show why ordinary explanations fail. To understand how this approach works and why I think it is a significant supplement to the more conventional methods of explain-ing war, we move on to an exploration of the notion of paradoxes.

## On Paradoxes

The term *paradox* has, in popular use, come to mean simply something seemingly puzzling or curious. This usage strips the term of its original meaning and of its scientific significance. It is important to discuss the term not only because we must use language correctly, but because paradoxes reflect an approach to human thought the importance of which has been recognized by most philosophers and many scholars in other sciences and arts. The centrality of this concept to the present study requires detailed exploration of what paradoxes are, why they are important, and how they contribute to our understanding of the world around us and our ability to survive in it.

## Definition and Classification of Paradoxes

Logic is probably one of the greatest human assets. It allows us to impose reason and order to transform what we capture with our senses into understandable entities. This intangible process of perception and inference, guided by certain rules, is responsible for our ability to master our physical environment and to interact with our social environment. Logic is the foundation of language, of communication, and hence of science and art. Not surprisingly, logic is also the foundation of social knowledge and social activity.

*Webster's Dictionary* (1980: 1064) defines logic as "the science of correct reasoning; the science which deals with the criteria of valid thought." But logic is more than a science; it is an inherent trait of human thought. It is, as *Webster's* tells us, "the system of principles underlying any science or art." Logic is a set of principles by which perception is transformed into mental conclusions. These mental conclusions serve as bases for reaction. Logic is distinguished from reflex in that it represents a set of rules that mediates between perception of a stimulus and reaction to it. This mental mediation introduces uncertainty into the relation between stimulus and reaction. Reflexive behavior is not mediated by rules of perception. It is a physical reaction to a stimulus that an organism performs without either choosing to do so or understanding why it reacts in a certain way.

A logical system is composed of premises and inference rules. Premises are statements of accepted beliefs about a certain domain that are not subject to inquiry, and their validity cannot or need not be established. Rules of inference specify how conclusions can be drawn from these premises. These rules also specify how inferences can be verified or falsified through observation or reasoning. A logical system must satisfy certain principles in order to be considered valid by logicians. One such principle is that of internal consistency. A logical system is internally consistent if none of its elements (premises or inferences based on them) is incompatible with any other element. A contradiction between two principles threatens the validity of the logical system as a whole. Such contradictions create major problems because the implications of the system as a whole tend to become indeterminate to such a degree that it is impossible to tell which inference is a reasonable consequence of the premises and which is not. Breaks in the internal consistency of a logical system are typically seen as paradoxes.

The dictionary definition of paradox is "a contradictory or absurd statement that nonetheless may be true" (Webster's, 1980: 1298). More formally, logicians view paradoxes as "contradictions between two equally valid principles of a logical system" (Brams, 1976: 2), "an embracing of clashing ideas" (Slaatte, 1982: 1), or as "an apparently unacceptable conclusion derived by apparently acceptable reasoning from apparently acceptable premises" (Sainsbury, 1988: 1).[15]

Paradoxes come in all shapes and colors; it is therefore instructive to classify them. Quine (1965) identified three types of paradoxes:

(1)   *Falsidical paradoxes:* These are contradictions between principles of a logical system, the proof of which contains a hidden fallacy. Once the fallacy is uncovered, the paradox disappears.
(2)   *Veridical paradoxes:* These involve a surprising conclusion reached by correct reasoning, but the (correct) proof contains a hidden element; once the hidden element is revealed, the surprise fades and so, usually, does the contradiction.
(3)   *Antinomies:* These are true contradictions that cannot be resolved within the logical systems that give rise to them, no matter how we twist and turn the proof.

Some examples might help at this point. The first example is a famous paradox called the Barber of Seville. The story is about a small village in Seville in which there lives a barber who shaves all and only those who do not shave themselves. Who shaves the barber? If the barber is being shaved by someone other than himself, then he does not shave *all* those who do not shave themselves, and if he does shave himself, then he cannot be shaving *only* those who do not shave themselves. How do we solve this logical knot? The answer is simple. This statement is false. There cannot exist such a barber. Either way we twist this statement, it cannot be proven true (Sainsbury, 1988: 2). The false element in the barber's paradox is that we are led—even for a moment—to believe that such a barber can exist in the first place. This is a case of falsidical paradox.

The second example is a story about an island with two villages. The first village is one whose residents are all truth telling: they never tell a lie. The other village is the liars' village. None of its residents ever tells a single piece of truth. These two villages have good relations with each other; residents of one village are constantly visiting the other village. Hence, at any given point in time, there are some liars in the truth-telling village and some truth-telling people in the liars' village. How would an outside visitor know in which village she is? If she comes to the truth-telling village she might meet a resident or a visiting liar. She does not know whether to expect truthful answers to her questions or false ones. The same applies if she is in the liars' village. Since we are not told about the volume of visits, a sampling of the population may not solve the problem; anyway, it seems too much effort for this little problem. It turns out that this seemingly insoluble problem has a stunningly simple solution. All the visitor must do is ask the first person she meets in the village, Do you live here? If the answer is yes, she is in the truth-telling village; if the answer is no, she is in the liars' village. This must be the case no matter if she meets a resident of the village or a visitor from the other village. (I let the reader work out the proof.)

This is a veridical paradox. The paradox is susceptible to solution using a principle that I shall call *double flip*. This principle converts the seeming contradiction contained in the paradox into a solution by creating a contradiction to the contradiction. It allows one, therefore, to solve an apparent logical contradiction within the same logical system in which it was shown to exist.

The third example is probably the most famous paradox in philosophy. It is called the Liar's Paradox (no relation to the story about the villages). Suppose a statement is either true or false. What is the following statement: What I am saying now is a lie. If the statement is a lie, then it must be true, in which case it cannot be a lie; if it is true, then it must be a lie, in which case it cannot be true.[16] Though philosophers have grappled with this paradox for centuries, no satisfactory solution has been found. Therefore, this is perhaps the classical example of an antinomy: it is impossible to tell whether the statement is true or false within a system that assumes that a statement must be either true or false.

Another example of a philosophical antinomy is the paradox of existence. Let us assume that there is no such thing as the Loch Ness monster. In order to prove the truth of this assumption, we must know how to establish the fact that a Loch Ness monster does not exist, so we must be able to specify the features of something that we are told to assume does not exist. But how can we do so if that something does not exist? In order to specify what does not exist, we have to assume that something exists in order to show that there is no such thing, which is a contradiction (Toms, 1972: 7).[17]

All these examples are semantic. The feature of vicious circularity renders them frustrating or amusing, depending on how seriously one gets involved in efforts to solve them. The paradoxes I will be concerned with in this book may be less frustrating or amusing than the examples given above, because they have a feature that the semantic paradoxes do not have. This is what Kainz (1988: 44) calls *demonstrability*: they can be shown by some criteria of observation to exist. Because these paradoxes are demonstrable, they cease to become stimulants for thought; they become real-life problems. If they can be shown to have analogues in the conduct of war, and if their existence can be a cause of tangible cost of life, equipment, territory, and so forth, then they are problems that require serious consideration. Their implications must be assessed in both the theory and practice of war.

I apply the notion of paradoxes to a behavioral context. This implies a relationship between thought and action. Hence, the notion of paradox must deal with this relationship. While I have no intention of competing with all the learned and wise people who have devoted their lives to the study of paradoxes or to defining the term, I wish to offer a definition of my own. This definition, I believe, preserves much of the various meanings of the term I have discussed above, while adjusting the concept to a behavioral domain that concerns a relationship between thought and action.

My definition of a paradox is as follows: *a causally induced contradiction between expectations and the consequences of behavior resulting from them.* The definition refers to processes that contain a sequence of three elements: expectations, behavior, and consequences. Thus, a behavioral paradox exists when reasonable expectations produce behavior that results in outcomes that are not only different from those expected, but are their precise opposite (Boise, 1977: 2). The notion of causality is meant to stress that the contradictory consequences are a result of this causal chain: had it not been for these expectations, the contradictory consequences would not have arisen.

One may argue that this contradiction between expectations and the consequences of motivated behavior is due to something fundamentally wrong about the expectations. When one develops stupid, unrealistic, or otherwise illogical expectations about the consequences of certain courses of action, contradictions naturally arise, but this can hardly be seen as a paradox. Expectations emanate from theories, that is, from an organized, logically consistent set of premises we have about the world around us. These expectations motivate a certain course of action designed to serve a given set of goals. A paradox arises not when these expectations are flawed or otherwise illogical, for if that were the case, paradoxes could be easily resolved. All it would require is to realize that there is something wrong with the expectations or with the link between expectations and actions, and revise the setup accordingly. What makes paradoxes central to the understanding of behavior is that they are hard to resolve because the setup of expectations-behavior is perfectly reasonable. The premises may be fundamentally valid, and the behavior may be a logical extension of those premises. Yet precisely because the whole setup is reasonable, the unexpected occurs. And because the whole structure of expectations and consequent behavior is reasonable, paradoxes are hard to resolve; changing expectations will not do.

## Significance of Paradoxes

Leinfellner (1986: 135) notes that paradoxes are "unsolvable problems for rational logicians." They create cracks in our normal way of reasoning, in what I call linear logic. The principal features of linear logic are its straightforwardness, its parsimony, and its simplicity. Linear logic is *straightforward* in that its rules of inference are strict and precise. What is allowed or disallowed in the process of inference is clear and unambiguous. Therefore, two people who share the same premises and are aware of the rules of deduction should have no difficulty transforming the same facts into identical conclusions. Moreover, there should be no contradiction between the conclusions derived from the same premises and the same facts if different people use the same rules of inference.

*Parsimony* is a ratio between the number of premises a logical system contains and the number of inferences that can be deduced from them. The more inferences that can be drawn from a small number of premises, the more parsimonious the system.

*Simplicity* refers to the ease with which one can understand certain principles and use them. A logical system may be straightforward and parsimonious, but it might be difficult to understand and even more difficult to apply. For example, systemic theories of international politics are both straightforward and parsimonious but are of very little use to political leaders because they are based on factors that are nonmanipulable politically. One can understand the principles of balance-of-power systems in world politics, but one cannot affect the distribution of capabilities in the international system upon which the balance is based.

Paradoxes are not just interesting philosophical problems; they represent a significant challenge to linear logic because

(1) . . . they arise from implicitly given, hidden dilemmas in the presuppositions and foundations of [theoretical] systems; (2) most of them are immune to rational methods for solving the contradictory statements they generate; (3) because of the contradictions they generate, they make the whole system worthless and are thus a threat to the whole system; (4) in paradoxes, the opposing views are always somehow related or interconnected. (Leinfellner, 1986: 135–136)

Linear logic is probably the smartest invention of humankind because it gave birth to all other inventions. Hence, cracks in that system threaten the order it generates. Popper (1968: 315–324) claims that science—in contrast to dialectics—cannot put up with contradictions. Paradoxes hamper progress not only because they divert attention from knowledge accumulation via the linear logic of straightforward extrapolation, but also because they block it as long as they are not solved. They create indeterminacies and uncertainties that prevent clear-cut conclusions. But, by the same token, paradoxes are significant in that they set limits to our ability to generalize. In other words, they delimit the applicability of a set of conclusions reached by linear logic.

The adverse effects that paradoxes have on progress in science and in human thought did not escape those who have dealt with the dialectic method, in which contradictions take on a prominent place. Hegel's dialectic triad allows for contradictions between thesis and antithesis, but the synthesis provides a solution for these contradictions that is broader than either the one proposed by the thesis or the one proposed by the antithesis. Yet the synthesis of today becomes the thesis of tomorrow and it encounters its own antithesis. Marx's application of dialectical logic to economics and politics also focuses on the internal contradictions that give rise to revolutions and to new social structures (Elster, 1985). A more modern treatment of the evolution of science also views this process in a seemingly dialectical fashion (Kuhn, 1970). Kuhn claims that science evolves in a wavelike fashion. Paradigms rise and fall only to be replaced by other paradigms that rise and fall.[18]

All of these are devices to resolve fundamental contradictions. Hegel's synthesis, Marx's social revolution and Kuhn's scientific revolution all represent radical solutions to paradoxical aspects of thought, social systems, and scientific progress. Paradoxes, according to this approach, are useful in that they stimulate new forces that attempt to resolve them. Initially, attempts to resolve such paradoxes are done from within the logical or social system in which paradoxes have emerged, using its own rules and principles. When this does not work, paradoxes are resolved by breaking the old system and establishing a new one. This kind of approach to solving paradoxes is what I will label the *Alexander method*, following Alexander the Great, king of Macedonia, who solved the famous Gordian knot problem by cutting it with his sword.

In some areas of science and politics it is possible to use this kind of approach to solve paradoxes. When this is possible, paradoxes can be seen as fundamental sources of social or intellectual change. However, if international politics are characterized by numerous paradoxes, and if those paradoxes are due to some fundamental features of the logic of the realm, it is not at all clear that we can break the system within which contradictions arise and replace it with a different one. The significance of paradoxes in this realm may well be to alert us to fundamental problems in the system, but not to direct us to solutions.

## Social Paradoxes

It might be useful to discuss some social paradoxes and how they have affected knowledge in various fields of science.

## The Paradox of Voting

This paradox ranks probably among the most significant social paradoxes that are known to us. First discovered by the French mathematician Marquis de Condorcet in the eighteenth century, it was formally proved by Kenneth Arrow (1951). This paradox claims very simply that there is no democratic (i.e., majority-rule-based) procedure that can convert rational individual wills into a rational social will. Consider the following example. Three committee members must decide on a social policy. Suppose these people—Joe, Mark, and Alice—are rational. That means that each can rank the various proposals from best to worst, and that each has a preference order that is transitive. If Joe prefers proposal *a* over proposal *b* and proposal *b* over proposal *c*, transitivity means that he must prefer proposal *a* over proposal *c*. Now, suppose that the preference orders of the three individuals are as follows:

*Joe*: Views policy *a* as best, and prefers it over policy *b*. He also prefers policy *b* over policy *c* (hence, he prefers *a* over *c*).
*Mark*: Views policy *b* as best, policy *c* as second-best, and policy *a* as the worst (hence, he prefers *b* to *a*).
*Alice*: For her, *c* is the best policy, *a* is the second-best policy, and *b* is the worst (hence, she prefers *c* over *b*).

Arrow (1951) assumed certain things about the properties of a just scheme that is supposed to represent the social will. Two of these properties are of particular importance. The first is what he called *nondictatorship*. In our case this means that no one in that group can impose a certain preference on the others. Majority decides which shall be the social policy or how the three policies ought to be ranked by the group. The other property is what Arrow called *independence of irrelevant alternatives*. By that he meant that if one of the policies is taken out of the decision process, the choice among the remaining policies should not be affected by the absence of the first policy. The paradox of voting is simply that there exists no system that can satisfy simultaneously these seemingly innocuous requirements.

Here is how the paradox of voting works. Suppose that policy *c* is withdrawn from the decision process. The three committee members must now choose between policies *a* and *b*. Since *c* is now an irrelevant alternative, both Joe and Alice prefer *a* over *b*. Only Mark prefers *b* over *a*. Thus, we can say that *a* is preferred to *b* by a majority. Now suppose that *a* is taken out of the race, and the choice is between *b* and *c*. In this case, Joe and Mark vote for *b* and only Alice votes for *c*. Thus, there is a majority in the committee that prefers policy *b* to *c*. Now suppose that *b* is taken out of the race and only *a* and *c* remain. Only Joe supports *a*, while both Mark and Alice prefer *c*. Hence, a majority in the committee prefers *c* to *a*. What we have here is a cycle: *a* is preferred to *b* and *b* is preferred to *c*, but *c* is preferred to *a* rather than what we would expect, given that all three people are rational and have transitive preferences.

This paradox presents a tremendous problem to normative theories of democracy because it states that no majority-rule system can aggregate rational individual preferences into a rational social preference.[19] One may question the importance of this paradox on the ground that it does not happen very often. Indeed, the probability of such a paradox has been shown to be very low when there are few proposals to be voted upon, no matter how many people exist in the voting body. However, as the number of proposals grows larger, the probability of the paradox increases substantially (Brams, 1976: 42–43). But this argument might miss the point. If we are interested in designing a democratic system that works, we want to make it immune to such a paradox, even if the chances of it arising are low.

## The Paradox of Prediction

Suppose you are presented with two boxes, *A* and *B*. You have two alternatives: to open box *B* only, or to open both boxes *A* and *B*. A superior being informs you that he has made predictions about your choice and has acted as follows: (1) He put $1,000 in box *A*. (2) If he predicted that you would open only box *B*, he added $1,000,000 to box *B*. (3) If he predicted that you would open both boxes, he has put nothing in box *B*. Now, you are, no doubt, out to gain as much as possible, and you seem to be in a good position to make some heavy money. But here is the catch. Not surprisingly, you figure that your best choice is to open both boxes; but to your amazement, you discover that all you get is a mere $1,000. To understand why this is so, consider the matrix in Figure 1.1.

Since you do not know what the Predictor did, you ask yourself what is your best choice if he predicted that you would open only box *B* (and hence put a million dollars in it). In that case your best choice is to open both boxes; this will give you both the million in *B* and the thousand in *A*. Now, if you think that the Predictor predicted that you would open both boxes, you are still better off opening both boxes because this way you at least get the thousand in box *A*. Hence, no matter what you do, you

|  | Predictor | |
|---|---|---|
| | Predicts<br>A & B | Predicts<br>B |
| Open<br>A & B | 1,000 | 1,001,000 |
| Open<br>B | 0 | 1,000,000 |

**Figure 1.1**   The Paradox of Prediction

are better off opening both boxes. The Predictor knows that no matter what he does, you will do just that, hence, he will not put the million in box B. Now you are really stuck; since it is rational for you to open both boxes, the Predictor cannot but predict that you would, hence, you cannot but predict that he will not put money in box B. Even if you wanted to open only box B, now you have no choice but to open both boxes.[20]

The paradox of prediction shows that both you and the Predictor are done in, irrespective of what you do. Whether you are greedy or not, the Predictor is going to guess that you are. Therefore, even if you do not want to appear greedy, you have no choice but to behave as if you were greedy because this is the only way for you to avoid being the sucker. In the process, both you and the Predictor lose. This paradox also shows that even if it is in your interest not to behave greedily, there is no reason in the world the Predictor should believe you. And since you know that, your behavior actually confirms his expectations. The result is bad for both of you. It follows that whether or not you are aware of this paradox, there seems nothing in the world that can resolve it within the parameters set by the story. Solutions to this paradox require some changes in the rules or the setup of the problem in order to make it rational for you to choose box B and for the Predictor to believe that you will (Maoz and Felsenthal, 1987).

The Prisoner's Dilemma is probably the most influential and well-known social paradox. I will not discuss it here for two reasons. First, it will serve us later on in the book and hence will be discussed in a real-world context. Second, it is in many ways similar to the paradox of prediction. Indeed, Brams (1976: 203–209) treats this paradox as a Prisoner's Dilemma.

Now that I have shown what paradoxes are and how they can be used as key instruments in the study of social phenomena, I must specify how the study of war is merged with the paradoxical approach in the present study. This is done in the following section.

# Methodology

The methodology of the study consists of two stages. The first stage focuses on the demonstration of the paradoxes in the abstract. The second focuses on the use of case studies to demonstrate these paradoxes in a historical context.

## The Theoretical Demonstration of Paradoxes of War

All the paradoxes I have discussed thus far, and most of the paradoxes I will introduce later on, illustrate quite clearly some fundamental breaks in rational choice theory. This is a theory that essentially states that organisms have goals and that their behavior is designed to maximize their ability to accomplish those goals. It predicts (or prescribes, depending on whether we treat it as a descriptive theory or a normative one) that an organism will always choose the course of action that, on average, promises the accomplishment of the best bundle of goals within a given set of constraints.

To understand why paradoxes are important, we must understand why linear logic is so powerful. First, it is powerful because it has all the makings of a complete system. It has precise predictions, it is capable of applying relatively few principles to a wide variety of problems, and it is usable. Second, these features render it a standard for scientific reasoning, for public policy-making, and for military planning. The trick is to show that paradoxes exist within such a powerful system of logic, because if paradoxes are difficult to resolve there, then less rigorous types of logic will fail as well.

Rational choice portrays action in a complex environment as predicated on systematic criteria of reason, and therefore renders behavior comprehensible and predictable. The key principle of expected utility maximization is both a powerful tool of good choices and a powerful criterion for evaluation of actual choices. If we can show that certain phenomena are paradoxical within a framework that posits that behavior based on rational expectations yields seemingly "irrational" consequences, we have made a fairly convincing case for the existence of a genuine paradox of the antinomical variety. Paradoxes, seen as breaks in the rational logic that is applied routinely to national security problems, suggest that we may have to rethink many of the ideas and fixed notions we have about war. Such paradoxes suggest more than mere academic puzzles; they are real and painful problems that can be neither brushed under the rug nor easily resolved.

To make a convincing case for the existence of a paradox as a

causally induced contradiction between expectations and the consequences of motivated behavior, we must satisfy three conditions:

(1) *Temporal sequence:* Expectations must precede observed behavior,
and behavior must precede the contradictory consequences. Causality cannot be established if the story of the paradox does not
contain a clear temporal order, no matter how puzzling and
inexplicable the issue under analysis appears to be.

(2) *Logical exclusiveness:* The demonstration of the paradox must
establish that the "reasonable" expectations were the only cause
of the observed behavior, and that the observed behavior was the
only cause of the contradictory outcome. The demonstration must
establish controls for all factors that might have caused a given
behavior other than the particular expectations that motivated it.
Further, we must be able to control for all factors that may have
intervened between the actor's behavior and the contradictory
consequences. The only things that are allowed to vary in the
demonstration of the paradox are those variables that are part of
the logical system that is said to give rise to the contradiction. For
example, in the paradox of voting the only thing that was allowed
to vary at each stage of the game was the policy that was rendered
irrelevant (that is, taken out of the race).

(3) *Substantive meaningfulness:* Contradictions between expectations
and the consequences of motivated behavior must have a meaningful logical explanation. We cannot be satisfied with showing
that such contradictions exist; we must understand why they exist.
This entails explication of the processes that give rise to these
contradictions. Such explanations should be understandable even
to those who are not well versed in the jargon and methodology
of science, because they are the ones whose intuition makes up
the conventional wisdom that the paradox seems to defy.

The theoretical analysis must establish that a given paradox exists
in principle, not that it is common or prevalent in practice. Existence
in principle suggests that a practical problem may exist in a real-world
context with circumstances analogous to those established by theory.
But beyond the demonstration of causality, we must show that this
contradiction is a paradox, not merely a problem that can be fixed.
This leads us to a fourth condition.

(4) *Solvability through awareness:* If awareness of the contradiction
between expectations and the consequences of behavior can cause
us either to revise our expectations or to change our behavior
in a manner that eliminates the contradiction, then the paradox
cannot be termed an antinomy. At best it is a veridical paradox.

To show a real paradox, we must demonstrate that awareness of the contradiction cannot cause a change of setup that leads to its solution. Of course, at a certain level each paradox is solvable in the Alexander sense, that is, by demolishing the whole system that gave rise to the paradox. And awareness of a paradox can provide a major incentive for such an operation. But this is beside the point of demonstrating a paradox.

The theoretical analysis of paradoxes focuses on showing that they satisfy these four conditions. Only if the theoretical demonstration of a paradox proves satisfactory can we proceed to an empirical analysis of actual wars that are seen to reflect such paradoxes. The virtue of the theoretical analysis of paradoxes is that the setting can be specified in such a manner that a paradox in a pure sense is formed, and the proof of the paradox can satisfy all these criteria in an unambiguous manner. The theoretical demonstration of paradoxes may be done by reference to an international political problem, or it can be done by analogy. I will use both political setups and interpersonal ones such as bidding games or committee voting. And when attempting to satisfy the substantive meaningfulness requirement, I shall provide the connection to the war-related aspects of the paradoxes.

The substantive meaningfulness criterion serves to connect the logic of the abstract demonstration to the concrete circumstances of the political world. When the paradox is demonstrated through an example taken from a setting other than international politics, the relevance to the international political realm must be established. This requires a convincing argument for the appropriateness of the rules of the theoretical setup to international politics. It also requires making a convincing case that the kind of processes set in motion by actors' expectations in the abstract case are similar to those that might be operating in international politics. The substantive meaningfulness criterion establishes the parameters that have to be satisfied in the empirical analyses in order to illustrate the paradox convincingly.

## Case Studies

The case study approach has a variety of uses in research (Lijphart, 1971; Eckstein, 1975; George, 1979; George and McKeown, 1985), ranging from exploratory functions of a pilot study when the theory is not well specified to confirmatory functions of theory testing. The case studies conducted in this book serve none of these functions. Rather, their role is to illustrate the workings of these paradoxes in history. The major premise of this study is that paradoxes are the exception rather than the rule in war. This is a study of residual cases, not of modal ones. Most wars and most of the aspects of any given war are susceptible to explanations consistent with linear logic. This is so even if a certain aspect of a given war seems puzzling at first glance. But there are some good reasons to believe that those residual aspects of war that resist a linear logic explanation form a pattern in the sense that they constitute real paradoxes.

Consequently, one of the key considerations in correct design of a case study methodology, that of unbiased case selection, is turned on its head in the present study. In other words, case selection is deliberately biased. In a sense, I have ransacked history to find those examples that seem to fit best the paradoxes to be illustrated. A given war becomes a candidate for analysis not if it seems a good representative of a more general class of cases, but only if it seems a bad representative of a general class but a good representative of the specific paradox I wish to demonstrate. My only defense of this peculiar method is that this is a peculiar study to begin with. Bearing in mind that war itself is the exception rather than the norm in international politics,[21] and that this study focuses on the residual cases of war, the issue of regularity seems a bit irrelevant. In fact, I know of no method for unbiased case selection in a study of the residuals of a residual category.

Two limitations have been imposed on case selection. First, the cases must be international wars according to the standard definition (Small and Singer, 1982): there must be at least one sovereign state on each side of the battlefield. Second, the wars must have occurred in the twentieth century. The reason for these limitations is twofold. Because international wars feature two or more governments fighting each other, and each monopolizes the use of force in its own state, it is easier to identify the key actors in each state and to examine the logic of war employed by each of the opposing sides. This allows assessment of the extent to which the paradoxes I have demonstrated in abstract terms shed some light on the historical case. In civil or colonial war, it is sometimes difficult to pinpoint the key actors and the main decisions. Therefore, demonstrations of paradoxes in such cases are open to criticism of the special case type, that is, that the irregular nature of the war is what gives rise to irregular aspects that are supposed to be paradoxical.

The focus on twentieth-century war is intended to show that these paradoxes have immediate relevance, that they are not a characteristic only of wars fought in other times and therefore nothing but interesting historical anecdotes.[22]

There are two basic problems with the case study approach. First, any historical method that illustrates paradoxes, as those were defined here, runs into serious problems when attempting to satisfy the logical exclusiveness criterion. Second, the strength of the case study method is its internal validity; however, its weakness is its generalizability. Even if we are successful in illustrating paradoxes in one or two cases, the question remains about how general these paradoxes are.

It is possible to lay out a theoretical structure that allows proof of a given paradox such that it satisfies the logical exclusiveness criterion, but it is virtually impossible to do that in historical research, certainly not in research that uses the case study method. To satisfy the logical exclusiveness criterion, we must control for all irrelevant factors that may affect the consequences of the "experiment" and vary only those aspects of the problem that are said to give rise to the paradoxical result. We must also show that in the absence of this manipulation, the paradox would not have occurred. Yet history does not afford us such flexibility. Suppose a given paradox identifies a set of expectations that cause a certain behavior, and that behavior leads to consequences that are the opposite of what was expected. Suppose further that the historical case verifies that sequence. We still have not satisfied the logical exclusiveness criterion, because we know what happened, but there is no way of telling what would have happened had expectations differed, or had behavior been different. Since we do not have a way of controlling for those external factors that might also have been responsible for that outcome, it is impossible to ascertain that it was strictly the expectation-behavior-outcome sequence that was responsible for the paradox.

The substantive meaningfulness criterion is helpful in this regard. It establishes a meaningful sequence of facts that explains the occurrence of a paradox, hence, it specifies a series of traces that can be picked up in historical research. The principal function of the substantive meaningfulness criterion is to form a series of expected events that ought to be found in the case under study so that it can be plausibly argued that what was suggested by theory may have taken place in practice. Here we follow the approach described by George and McKeown (1985: 29–34) as the "congruence procedure." The idea is that a theoretical framework postulates a set of expected outcomes in one or more cases, and the fit between the expected and the actual outcomes serves as a basis for the assessment of the framework.

I have no intention of showing that a given paradoxical sequence that is specified in the abstract demonstration is the *only* plausible explanation of a certain historical process. There are probably other plausible interpretations of the wars that will be analyzed in this volume. My aim is to convince the reader that the interpretation of a given war as paradoxical is just that, a plausible depiction of history. In fact, one of the reasons I chose to account for these paradoxes in terms of two explanations, a rational explanation and a cognitive one, is that history is open to a wide variety of interpretations and in many cases it is impossible to single out a "best" one reliably, even with all relevant data at our fingertips. Showing that a paradoxical explanation of a given war cannot be ruled out as a plausible interpretation suggests sufficient reason for reconsidering some of the straightforward linear notions we have both about this specific war and about other wars that might exhibit similar properties.

The generalizability problem is not that severe, for the very simple reason that the kind of generalization I am looking for is very limited. All I want to show through the case studies is that these paradoxes are not a figment of my imagination. The case studies are used in an attempt to establish that such paradoxes have occurred in the past (the not too distant past) and that they may happen again.

I do not claim that these paradoxes are frequent. In fact, this is a study of exceptions. Each of the paradoxes I will be discussing is quite infrequent, and when it is apparently frequent, I shall state so explicitly. The importance of these paradoxes is not that they recur all the time; it is that they have severe ramifications. This alone justifies an extensive study of the topic. This is also what makes the study of war significant. Hence, if I can show that quite a few of the drops of blood spilled in the course of war represent unintended consequences of motivated and seemingly reasonable behavior, then I may have contributed something to the understanding of a phenomenon of tremendous significance in international politics.

## Explanatory Models

Two models will be introduced to explain the various paradoxes of war. Both models are decision related. The rational model attempts to show that these paradoxes are the result of reasonable choices made by reasonable people. Contradictory consequences of such reasonable behavior arise largely because these choices are made within an interdependent system where the consequences of an actor's choices are based on the choices of other actors. Paradoxes arise because actors cannot control the rules of the game, the choices of other actors, or both. This explanation basically extends the theoretical demonstration of the paradoxes as a break in rational logic.

The cognitive model focuses on psychological factors that bias choices and render them suboptimal or otherwise imperfect. The implicit assumption of this model is that there is something wrong with the expectations-behavior system; otherwise it would not have given rise to paradoxical consequences. This model focuses on the biases and heuristics that cause suboptimal behavior that results in contradictory consequences.

The models are seemingly contradictory, yet I will try to show that they are not; in fact, they may complement one another quite nicely. My purpose is not to devise ways to discriminate among these explanations, or to determine which model "best" explains paradoxes of war. Rather, I will present the two explanations side by side. I will draw the implications of these models for the resolution of the paradoxes of war at the end of the book.

## Plan of the Book

The book is organized according to the three stages of war discussed above. The paradoxes go from the more remote causes of war to the remote consequences. Each of the three stages of war has three paradoxes attached to it. The first part focuses on paradoxical causes of war. Two such causes are remote and only indirectly related to the outbreak of war: arms races and deterrence. The fourth chapter discusses the more immediate cause of war: crisis escalation. All of these paradoxes depict wars as stemming not from deliberate aggressive designs, but rather as the culmination of efforts to prevent their outbreak.

The second part examines paradoxes of war management. It shows how wars, once under way, may evolve in a manner that is just the opposite of what had been planned. Two paradoxes, the paradox of attrition and the paradox of surprise, describe a strange relationship between the ways wars start and how they develop. They show that the best planned wars can develop into fine messes. The third paradox describes how allies can do one another in, not because they feel that they cannot trust each other but because they feel they can.

The third part examines paradoxical consequences of war. The paradox of power challenges conventional wisdom regarding the relationship between military capabilities and the outcomes of war. The last two paradoxes trace the fortunes of the winners and the losers following wars. They show that it is not always beneficial to win the war and not always terrible to lose one.

The last chapter ties the pieces together into some general conclusions about paradoxes, wars, and what all this implies for the study of world politics.

## Notes

1 Quincy Wright's *A Study of War* (1965) is still one of the classics on the topic. For more recent surveys of theory and research on war, see Beer (1981) and Luard (1986). Midlarsky's (1989) edited volume offers some recent surveys of key theories and approaches on the subject.
2 These characteristics are common to most definitions of war. The standard definition is that of Singer and Small (1972: 30–39). Their threshold for classification of a violent international exchange as a war is a total of 1,000 battle deaths. The threshold for individual state participation in war is either the active involvement of the state's forces at 1,000 soldiers or more or the misfortune to suffer 100 or more battle deaths.

3    Luard (1986: 6–7) focuses on the *organization* of violence to emphasize the nonaccidental nature of war.

4    The common distinction is between immediate and underlying (remote) causes of war. Immediate causes operate during the period immediately preceding war outbreak. Underlying causes operate long before the conflict of interests is converted into verbal or physical violence (Levy, 1986; Lebow, 1981).

5    The readings in Paret et al. (1986) and Brodie (1973) are good examples of the multitude of writings on this issue.

6    Luttwak (1987: 239–241) contains a brief survey of the definitions of the term. His favorite, congruent with the present study, is Andre Beaufre's definition: "The art of the dialectics of wills that use force to resolve their conflict."

7    Paret et al. (1986) demonstrates the continuity of the strategic approach, though it covers strategic thinking "only" as far back as Machiavelli. Van Creveld (1985) also illustrates some eternal maxims of military command.

8    Some, such as Levy (1982), predate the expansion of strategy to the civilian domain to the late nineteenth century, with the formation of permanent military establishments in peacetime, though his focus on military bureaucracies suggests that civilian strategic thinking did not really exist. Even in the interwar period all the famous civilian strategists—Fuller, Liddel Hart, and Douhet—were actually retired military officers (just like Clausewitz in his time). Herken (1987) provides a fascinating account of the role of strategists and other scientists in shaping the nuclear strategy of the United States.

9    Representatives of this school of thought are Bueno de Mesquita's (1981, 1985) work on a rational theory of war decisions and Lebow's, (1981) on a cognitive theory of crisis and war.

10   See Bueno de Mesquita (1981, 1985) on rational initiation and on the escalation of conflict to war, and Wittman (1979) and Pillar (1983) on rational models of war termination.

11   Representatives of this approach are Lebow (1981), Jervis (1976), and White (1970).

12   I coined the "bottom–up" and "top–down" terms in earlier work (see Maoz, 1989).

13   Representatives of this genre include Kaplan (1957), Singer et al. (1972), Waltz (1979), Organski and Kugler (1980), and Gilpin (1981).

14   The relations between paradoxes of war and systemic theories are discussed in Chapter 11.

15   Sainsbury's (1988) definition of the term indicates his general attitude toward the topic. He qualifies the contradiction by emphasizing its "apparent" nature and goes on to state: "Appearances have to deceive, since the acceptable cannot lead by acceptable steps to the unacceptable. So, generally, we have a choice: Either the conclusion is not really unacceptable, or else the starting point, or the reasoning has some flaw." It quickly becomes obvious that Sainsbury treats paradoxes as mental appetizers: they stimulate the search for solutions and that is why they fascinate philosophers. Slaatte (1982: 3) phrases the same idea in more prosaic terms: "Thus one result of the paradox is its cathartic effect on the smug or sluggish mind."

16   The Liar's Paradox was first introduced, inadvertently, in St. Paul's epistle to Titus. It states: "One of themselves, even a prophet of their own,

[Epimenides, the Cretan prophet] said, The Cretans are always liars, evil beasts, slow bellies" (cited in Sainsbury, 1988: 114; Kainz, 1988: 2).

17 These examples may seem like mental aerobics, having little practical significance beyond the fun of trying to solve them and the subsequent frustration when one realizes that some of them cannot be solved. Yet, virtually anybody working in the hard sciences knows that one must deal with entities that cannot be established in any tangible way (absolute zero temperature, pure matter, point in geometry, which is defined as a geometrical form lacking dimensions, and so forth). Many scientific laws are based on concepts or entities the existence of which can be neither proved or disproved. Moreover, because such entities are abstract, they are useless as far as empirical research is concerned, hence, there is a question of what their purpose is in the first place. This is the "theoretician's dilemma" (Hempel, 1965).

18 Popper (1968: 312–335) draws a parallel between Hegelian dialectics and scientific evolution. He finds a lot of similarities, but ends up dismissing the analogy on the grounds that dialecticians are too willing to put up with contradictions, whereas scientists are not. Elsewhere in the same book, talking about the theoretical social sciences, he argues that the main task of the social sciences is to explore "the unintended social repercussions of intentional human actions" (p. 342).

19 Riker (1982) emerges from a survey of this literature with a very pessimistic conclusion about the ability of democratic theory to resolve this problem in any rational fashion.

20 This discussion is based on Brams (1976: 193–213) and Sainsbury (1988: 51–71). I disagree, however, with both authors' interpretation of Newcomb's problem as a contradiction between the expected utility principle and the dominance principle. The expected utility principle states the same thing that the dominance principle states: open both boxes. Nonetheless, this is a paradox in the same sense that the Prisoner's Dilemma is: behavior that is based on expectations of maximization of gain leads to minimization of gain. (And if we assume that the Predictor is interested in helping you get your hands on the big bucks, it also minimizes his satisfaction.) Also, depending on the kind of motives one attributes to the Predictor, the game may or may not be defined as a Prisoner's Dilemma, which is another central paradox of social behavior. If the Predictor's goals are to be correct and to aid you in making money, then his best outcome is when he guesses *B* and you choose *B* and his worst outcome is when he guesses *A* and *B* and you choose *B*. The second-best outcome is when he guesses *B* and you choose *A* and *B*, and his second-worst outcome is when he guesses *A* and *B* and you choose *A* and *B*, which is what actually happens. This kind of game has been treated by Maoz and Felsenthal (1987) as an example of paradoxes of international cooperation.

21 There were only 67 interstate wars in all of the 1816–1980 period (Small and Singer, 1982).

22 Jack Levy has pointed out to me, correctly, that relevance is a function of theoretical comparability rather than of time. However, there are good reasons to suspect that, in some of the paradoxes, theoretical comparability and time covary.

# PART I

*Paradoxical Causes of War*

# 2
# The Para Bellum Paradox

Students of international politics have spent a great deal of time investigating why nations spend huge amounts of money on armaments when it seems that they have much more important things to do with the money. The arguments made in the vast literature on arms races can be divided into two themes. First, arms races are a mutual trap. To feel secure, a state must be militarily superior to other states it sees as potential adversaries. Being militarily superior does not necessarily mean that one has any aggressive designs against another state; one may simply want to avoid any challenges to one's security by anybody who may have some nasty plans. Arming oneself—in this context—is equivalent to saving money for rainy days. One does not have any clear plans for spending it, but one wants to be sure to have the money in case it might be needed. If everybody follows this marginal security rule, nobody becomes more secure. In fact, chances are that everybody becomes less secure. Since states do not live in a vacuum, the incentives to increase their military arsenals become even stronger when they realize that all other states do the same. This explanation of arms race processes is called the action-reaction model, because each state tends to determine the amount of money it spends on "defense" based on the amount of money spent on "defense" by its adversaries. Once in such a spiral, arms races become a mutually reinforcing process.[1]

The second theme is that arms races are the result of internal dynamics (Organski and Kugler, 1980). According to this view, the so-called arms race process has nothing to do with what other states do. Nor is the pursuit of security a cause of arms races. States arm themselves because important domestic forces stand to gain from high defense spending. The money that goes to defense is used to produce new weapon systems, to increase the number of existing ones, to increase the number of military personnel, and to support research and development. Thus, there is a host of interest groups that benefit from the money spent on defense. These interest groups include weapon industries, research and development centers, the defense bureaucracy, and weapon importers (in states that are not self-sufficient in terms of

weapon systems). Since the defense establishment and weapon industries have tremendous influence in the policy-making process, their
demands for increased military spending become important considerations in political decisions for the division of the national budgetary pie.

Furthermore, weapon production and military growth are part
and parcel of the overall considerations of national economic policies.
In advanced industrial societies, weapon industries employ a lot of
people, funnel funds into state economies, bring in foreign trade and
foreign currency through arms trade, and so forth. Harming these
industries by drastic cuts in their budgets, or by reducing government
contracts, would harm the national economy—or so it seems. What is
good for the weapon industries is good for the country. It follows that
there is no real arms race. Nations do not race each other in weapons
production and other forms of military growth. They just grow in general. And since military growth is intimately connected to economic
and industrial development, there is an appearance of an arms race.[2]

Whether arms races are an action-reaction process or are produced by economic interests and growth dynamics is of secondary
importance if we wish to explore the linkages between military growth
and war. The main question addressed here is this: How do processes
of military growth that are not ignited by aggressive schemes produce the kind of violence they are designed to prevent? Two sets
of studies are relevant here. The first is a statistical analysis of the
relationship between arms races and conflict escalation. Wallace (1979,
1980, 1982) studied a large number of international conflicts in an
attempt to find out whether or not the likelihood of crisis escalation
to a full-blown war increased if the nations involved in the conflict had been engaged in an intensive arms race prior to the crisis.

Wallace developed an elaborate procedure to determine whether
a mutual growth process in terms of military capabilities between
two nations can be described as an arms race. He then examined the
relationship between arms racing and the likelihood that low-level
conflicts would escalate into massive conflagrations. A total of 99
conflicts involving at least one major power was analyzed. The results
showed that 26 of these conflicts escalated into war. Out of the 26 wars,
23 had been preceded by an intensive arms race. Out of the 73 conflicts
that did not escalate to war, 68 were not preceded by an arms race. Likewise, out of 28 cases that could be characterized as intensive arms races,
23 resulted in war, whereas out of the 71 interstate relations that did
not involve arms races, 68 conflicts ended in forms short of war. This
seems pretty convincing evidence of the arms race-war connection.

Wallace's studies evoked quite a controversy in the field. A lot of
people found it difficult to believe that arms races, which are designed
to promote peace and stability by creating a reliable deterrent against

a revisionist opponent, would be related to war. Some of these critics attacked the methodology used by Wallace, particularly the way he measured arms races. They argued that if one were to measure arms races differently, the findings would have displayed a much less convincing picture of the arms race-war connection (Weede, 1980; Diehl, 1983). It is important to note, however, that none of the criticisms of Wallace's studies suggested that arms races lead to peace and stability. At most, it was argued that the relations between arms races and war are not as strong as Wallace would have us believe. Yet, whether or not these findings are valid, they do not give us a causal explanation. The findings suggest that arms races are related to war, but they do not tell us why this is the case. The causal process that yields such a connection is therefore open to a variety of interpretations.

Intrilligator and Brito (1984; Brito and Intrilligator, 1985) attempted to tackle this issue from an analytic perspective, primarily concerned with the causal aspect of this relationship. They approached the arms race-war problem as a two-stage process. In the first stage, they assumed two states competing for the division of a certain homogeneous good such as territory that yields resources, or rights to a market that yields income. This good can be used to produce weapons or for consumption purposes. The choices (weapon production or consumption) of the actors are irreversible; swords cannot be converted into plowshares. In the second period, the good can be redistributed either by war or by negotiation. If war breaks out, its outcome depends on the amount allocated by the two states to arms production in the first period. War produces a "public bad," a common cost to both nations.

Nations are assumed to be rational actors. Hence, they choose to go to war if the expected gains of the war outweigh its potential costs. Intrilligator and Brito (1985) investigated two cases. In the first case, the two nations are assumed to be informed fully of each other's preferences. With full information, whether or not the nations were engaged in an arms race in the first period, redistribution in the second period occurs through negotiation rather than through war. There will always exist a rational exchange of the good that is preferred by each nation individually, and by both collectively, to a redistribution through war. In this case, arms races are seen as stabilizing processes that not only avert war, but also lead to a better bargaining position of each state vis-à-vis the other.

The second case involves an asymmetric knowledge structure. One party is fully informed of the other's preferences and the other state is not. In such a case, war is a rational possibility. War will occur if the uninformed state adopts a strategy in which it commits itself to a positive probability of war to prevent bluffing by the opponent in the negotiation process. The bottom line of this argument is that arms races can lead to war, but the relationship is restricted to situations that are characterized by the absence of reliable information of what the other actors prefer, as well as their specific attitudes toward risk-taking.

This set of studies is extremely complicated. The link between arms races and war is uncovered only through a series of mathematical equations of a highly complex nature. It is doubtful, therefore, that this is an accurate description of how nations that make a choice of a certain arms allocation at one point in time decide to engage in war at another point in time. What does it mean that an uninformed state commits itself to a "positive probability of war" to avoid bluffing by the opponent? When, and under what conditions, would a state prefer one equilibrium strategy over another? How could such a model be tested in real-world cases?

Despite these weaknesses, these studies provide some important insights into the arms race-war connection. For one thing, they suggest that arms races may be causally related to war. Moreover, both studies point out that this connection normally involves some short-of-war conflict that is—under some conditions—apt to escalate into full-blown hostilities. So our task is to examine how a pair of states, both seeking to avert war via ever-growing levels of military prepared-ness, become involved in the very conflict they wished to avoid.

## A Theoretical Demonstration of the Para Bellum Paradox

To represent a rational choice explanation of arms race processes, let us assume, like Intrilligator and Brito, that there are two periods to be considered. The first period can be seen as the one immediately following the acquisition of independence by two states, $i$ and $j$. In this period, each state can either arm itself or spend its budget on welfare projects. Each state can also use some rule to divide its budget into defense and welfare chunks. We start out with a naive formulation of the problem, one in which a state is assumed to allocate some of its budget to defense and the remainder to welfare. Let us examine what the consequences of these choices might be.

If $i$ decides to arm and so does $j$, both end up spending much of their money on defense, gain nothing in terms of increased security (because neither state gains a strategic advantage over the other), and serve none of the welfare-related needs of their societies. If, however, $i$ decides to arm but $j$ decides not to, then $i$'s money can be said to have been wisely spent. Though $i$ might face a lot of pressure from its society because it did not provide the people with a sufficient level of social services, it would gain a much-needed strategic superiority over $j$.

If *i*'s decision makers place a strong priority on security, this outcome is the best they get.

If neither *i* nor *j* arms itself, neither gains a strategic advantage over the other, but neither suffers from a strategic disadvantage. Moreover, both satisfy their societies' welfare needs. So, between spending money on defense without either gaining or losing a strategic advantage and spending money on welfare without gaining or losing a strategic advantage, the latter outcome is preferred to the former. If one cannot improve the strategic balance, one might at least increase domestic welfare. Thus, mutual nonarmament is the second-best outcome, and mutual armament is the second-worst outcome. It follows that for nation *i* the worst possible outcome is not to arm while state *j* does arm. This calculus is reflected in a game matrix that represents the payoffs (or preferences) of the two states in each of these outcomes (see Figure 2.1).

The game illustrated in Figure 2.1 is the infamous Prisoner's Dilemma. In this game, it makes sense to both *i* and *j* to arm themselves because by so doing they are each better off regardless of what the opponent decides to do. The problem is that both states would have been better off had they decided not to arm themselves; they would have spent all their money on welfare and neither would have gained any notable strategic advantage over the other. As it is, each state reasons as follows: if I do not arm and neither does my opponent, I get the next-to-best outcome. Yet, if my opponent decides not to arm, I can do even better by arming myself. The money I shift from welfare projects to defense is wisely spent because it gives me a strategic edge over my opponent. By becoming militarily superior, I can deter my opponent from attacking me in the future. If my opponent is stupid enough to try an attack in the future, the military edge I gain now will be crucial in repelling it and winning the war. Even if my opponent decides to arm itself, I am still better off arming myself than not doing so. If I fail

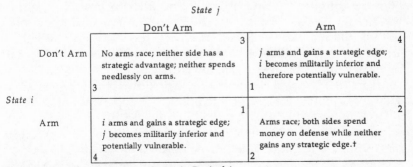

**Figure 2.1**   The Armament Game in Period 1
*Note:* Number in lower-left corner of each cell denotes *i*'s payoffs; number in upper-right corner denotes *j*'s payoffs. Outcomes are ranked from 4 = best to 1 = worst. Payoffs are ordinal preferences, not cardinal utilities.                    † Nash equilibrium.

to arm, my opponent would gain a strategic edge that might tempt it to attack me in the future. Though arming myself when my opponent does the same gives neither of us a strategic edge, it prevents my opponent from entertaining any thought of a quick and easy victory in the event of a war. Since both states use this kind of logic, both end up wasting money on defense without improving their strategic positions.

Arms races could thus be seen as rational outcomes of a strategic environment in which neither side can be identified as the bad guy in terms of its political intentions. But this little exercise captures only the first part of the arms race process. It explains why states are inclined to waste good money for no apparent gain in the first place. The Prisoner's Dilemma model of arms races has been taken to be a single-shot game that shows why states that want peace find it rational to prepare for war. It remains to be seen why this process might end up in war rather than in a continuous arms race. To address this issue, let us take the calculus discussed so far one step further. Since the analysis of the second stage is slightly more complicated, it is useful to depict the strategic dilemma facing the two states by using a game tree. Game theorists call this representation of strategic problems *extensive-form games*. Extensive games are analogous to road maps. They tell an actor where he or she might be at any given stage of the process, and where a given choice of a branch on the tree might lead. Figure 2.2 shows the second stage of the game in extensive form.

In the second period, the choice problem of the actors was expanded via the inclusion of an additional alternative: fighting a war. This alternative was not feasible in the first period because neither state had a war-fighting capability. However, once a state spent money on the purchase or production of weapons (whether or not the other had done the same), it acquired a certain level of war-fighting capability, and the initiation of war becomes a real alternative. Yet, why would a state that has no grudge against its opponent consider this alternative? There are two possible reasons. First, a state, looking forward into the future and anticipating a costly, wasteful, and senseless arms race, may view the initiation of war as a cure for the arms race illness. If this state thinks it has a reasonably good chance of winning the war, it can powerfully disarm the opponent and make sure that it would not pose a strategic threat in the future. After all, "war is a violent act designed to induce the opponent to fulfill our will" (Clausewitz, 1966: 1). Our will, in this case, amounts to having our opponent stay militarily inferior. Since we cannot do it through arms racing, we might be able to accomplish it by winning a war.

Second, a state may suspect that if it does not attack, the opponent, using the same line of reasoning, might. Given the mutual choices of arms racing in the previous period, there is no a priori reason to suspect

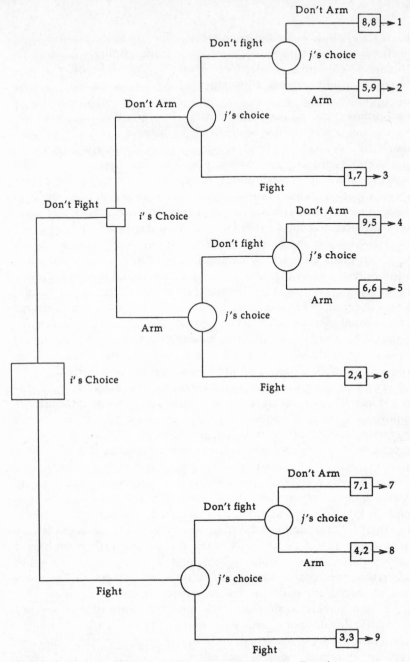

**Figure 2.2** The Armament Game in Period 2 (Extensive Form)

Key: □ = Choice node of state i
     ○ = Choice node of state j
     [i,j] = Payoff for state i and j, respectively
     → = Outcome number

that a state would estimate its chances of victory as excessively high, given that such estimates are based on relative military capabilities (Bueno de Mesquita, 1981). Yet, a first strike might offer a state some important tactical advantages. A first strike might surprise the opponent, and it could wipe out a considerable portion of the opponent's retaliatory capabilities. So, even if a state does not see starting a war as beneficial, it might suspect that an opponent, basing its calculus on the idea that a first strike might increase its chances of victory, would be tempted to strike first. If that is the case, then the focal state should seriously consider striking first itself.[3] Taken together, these points suggest that it is not unreasonable to expect states to start entertaining aggressive strategies once they have some war-fighting capabilities in the second stage of the process.

How the outcomes induced by these strategies are ranked depends on which goals are used by decision makers to evaluate them. It is commonly assumed that the outcomes of national security choices are assessed on at least three goals: (1) security value, defined as the degree of certainty one can place on a state's survivability in an anarchic international environment; (2) human costs of a given policy, defined in terms of the number of casualties incurred by a certain event; and (3) economic cost, defined as the dollar cost of a given event. These values will serve in evaluating and ranking the outcomes of Figure 2.2.

The figure suggests that each state faces a two-stage choice problem. First, it must decide between attacking and not attacking its opponent. If state $i$ decides to attack, the outcome of the war is uncertain. The payoffs of war depend on the circumstances in which it starts. If state $j$ was caught unprepared, in the sense that it decided against fighting and against arming, then $i$ expects to get a payoff of 7 (node 7), which is worse than a mutual cooperation outcome (node 1), and of the strategic advantage due to unilateral armament decision (node 5).[4] If state $i$ attacked, but state $j$ decided to arm, the costs of war for $i$ increase and the probability of victory declines, so $i$'s payoff is 4 (node 8). Finally, if $i$ decides to attack and so does $j$, then we have a "reciprocal initiative" (Maoz, 1985b), that is, a war in which neither side has a strategic or tactical advantage, that is extremely costly for both, and that entails uncertain prospects of victory for each.

If state $i$ decides against an attack, it has two options: to arm or not to arm. If $i$ decides not to arm and $j$ attacks, $i$ faces a possible strategic disaster (node 3). On the other hand, if $i$ arms and $j$ initiates, $i$ still faces a gloomy outcome (node 6), but not as bad as that of node 3. Note that if we eliminate the fighting options of the two states, the game tree reduces to nodes 1, 2, 4, and 5, with a payoff structure identical to the Prisoner's Dilemma game of Figure 2.1. The structure of the original problem was not altered, it was merely adjusted to include an additional alternative that became feasible in the second stage of the game. Since both states choose their strategies simultaneously, we can convert the game tree into a normal-form $3 \times 3$ outcome matrix, as shown in Figure 2.3.

This way of presenting the choices of states is more convenient for solving the game, that is, for trying to figure out logically what the plausible outcomes of such a strategic situation are. We can see clearly that the nonarmament alternative is dominated by the armament alternative for each of the states. The outcomes of an armament policy are strictly better than the respective outcomes of a nonarmament policy, regardless of the opponent's choice. This is not very surprising given that the game is an expansion of the original Prisoner's Dilemma. Now, given that the nonarmament policy is strictly dominated by the armament policy, it is eliminated as a feasible alternative by both states. The arms race-war connection now becomes more apparent because the second stage of the process reduces the choice to one between continuation of the arms race or the starting of a war.

The reduced game is the well-known Stag Hunt problem (used by Jervis, 1978, to interpret Rousseau's famous metaphor of life under the state of nature). In this game, the noncooperative strategy (FIGHT) does not dominate the cooperative one (ARM). No actor has an unequivocally best choice that is independent of the other actor's choice. Yet this game has two possibly stable outcomes: the mutually "cooperative" outcome (ARM-ARM) and the mutually noncooperative one (FIGHT-FIGHT). However, the paradox is this: the mutually best outcome is the nonarmament outcome in the expanded Prisoner's Dilemma-Stag Hunt game, yet it is unstable. Each side has a strong incentive to improve its payoff unilaterally by shifting to another outcome. Hence, both states will wind up in either the ARM-ARM outcome or the FIGHT-FIGHT outcome. Yet these outcomes make each state individually, and both of them collectively, worse off. The FIGHT-FIGHT outcome is truly disastrous for both states, yet it is a distinct possibility in a game played by rational agents. Once in it, neither side has an incentive to depart from it, as it will not improve its lot and might harm itself by doing so.

This game offers a lucid illustration of (1) why rational states seeking to preserve their own security and having no a priori aggressive designs toward one another would get into a wasteful and dangerous arms race, and (2) why, once in the arms race mess, states might find it rational to break the action-reaction chain by fighting it out. Arms races might escalate into races of violence and destruction for two possible reasons. First, stability in a game-theoretic sense implies two things: (1) once in a stable state (equilibrium), no one has an incentive to move to another state, and (2) once the game moves

|  | State j | | |
|---|---|---|---|
|  | Don't Arm | Arm | Fight |
| **Don't Arm** (state i) | 8 \| 8 | 5 \| 9 | 1 \| 7 |
| **Arm** (state i) | 9 \| 5 | 6 \| 6 * | 2 \| 4 |
| **Fight** (state i) | 7 \| 1 | 4 \| 2 | 3 \| 3 * |

*(In each cell: lower-left = i's payoff, upper-right = j's payoff)*

Don't Arm row: Don't Arm (8/8), Arm (9/5), Fight (7/1)
Arm row: Don't Arm (5/9), Arm (6/6)*, Fight (4/2)
Fight row: Don't Arm (1/7), Arm (2/4), Fight (3/3)*

Note: Outcomes are ranked from 9 = best to 1 = worst.
* Nash equilibrium.

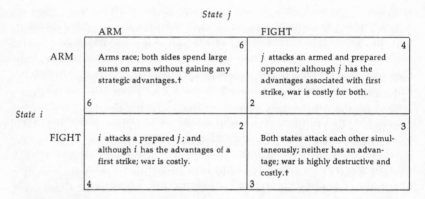

State j

|  | ARM | FIGHT |
|---|---|---|
| **ARM** (State i) | 6 (j) / 6 (i) — Arms race; both sides spend large sums on arms without gaining any strategic advantages.† | 4 (j) / 2 (i) — j attacks an armed and prepared opponent; although j has the advantages associated with first strike, war is costly for both. |
| **FIGHT** (State i) | 2 (j) / 4 (i) — i attacks a prepared j; and although i has the advantages of a first strike; war is costly. | 3 (j) / 3 (i) — Both states attack each other simultaneously; neither has an advantage; war is highly destructive and costly.† |

Note: Number in lower-left corner of each cell denotes i's payoffs; number in upper-right corner denotes j's payoffs. Outcomes are ranked from 6 = best to 2 = worst. Payoffs are ordinal preferences, not cardinal utilities.
† Nash equilibrium.

**Figure 2.3**  The Armament Game in Period 2 (Normal Form)

to another outcome that is unstable, rational calculations lead both actors back to the stable state. The ARM-ARM outcome in the reduced version of the arms race-war game is strictly stable only in the first sense; it is not entirely stable in the second sense. If—for some reason—states depart from the ARM-ARM outcome, there is no absolute guarantee that they would return to it. It is neither theoretically irrational nor practically implausible that they would "stabilize" the game in the FIGHT-FIGHT outcome.

The second reason follows directly from the fact that the game has two stable outcomes, and that neither state has an unequivocally best strategy. In such cases, the behavior of the states is based to a large extent on the expectations they have about the opponent's behavior and on the kind of logic that guides their own behavior under conditions of uncertainty. If the two states realize the kind of game they are playing in the second period, they can decide to play it conservatively. Each state might operate under a worst-case analysis that goes like this: If worse comes to worst, which of the two strategies—ARM or FIGHT—is better? The worst that can happen if I arm is that my opponent attacks; in such a case I get my next-to-worst outcome. On the other hand, if I attack, the worst that can happen is that my opponent also attacks, in which case I get the next-to-next-to-worst outcome. Obviously, the FIGHT strategy assures me at least a payoff of 3 whatever my opponent does and therefore is a better strategy than the ARM (and certainly better than the DON'T ARM strategy).

Prudence, which requires one to avoid the worst possibility, dictates war. Yet, if this is the notion of strategic prudence that guides the behavior of both states, it is prudence that does both of them in. Even if each state would rather arm itself than fight, it cannot safely assume that its opponent will do the same, so fighting it out becomes again a seemingly rational prescription leading to mutual disaster.

The compelling thing about this model of the para bellum paradox is that it shows that arms races can lead to either stability or war, and that neither possibility is an irrational outcome. This duality sheds light on the inconclusiveness of the arms race-war debate in the literature. Theory suggests that both stability and war are logical consequences of a process that starts with states' quest for security and peace. Arms races provide states—at best—peace without security and—at worst—neither security nor peace.

Another interesting feature of this model is that it clearly portrays arms races as underlying causes of war, for, once in the ARM-ARM outcome, no departure should take place, unless something in the relations between the two opponents leads them to change their expectations toward one another. The studies by Wallace and by Intrilligator and Brito are illuminating on precisely this point. They point out that arms races—in and of themselves—are not sufficient to ignite violence. Arms races provide the fuel for the fire, but the spark that ignites it resides in other processes.

## Explanations of the Para Bellum Paradox

### The Rational Explanation

The rational explanation of the para bellum paradox is already evident from the way the model has been set up. It requires, therefore, very little elaboration. The bottom line of this explanation is that starting the arms race in the first place gives birth to a process that requires consideration of a war as a distinctly feasible strategy. Incorporating the FIGHT strategy into the set of feasible policy alternatives makes war a distinctly rational possibility. This is so despite the fact that each state individually and both states collectively view war as a bad solution to their security problems.

The rational model posits an environment that is not necessarily a typical one in terms of the knowledge structure of the opponents. In most real-life situations states may not have complete knowledge as to what their opponents want and how they rank various futures in terms of preference. Moreover, attempts to model arms races in terms of simultaneous choice are somewhat questionable in that most action-reaction processes take on some sort of sequential form. A state acts in response to the previous move or set of moves of its opponent.

There are two reasons for these assumptions. First, it is easier to show the para bellum paradox in its purest form, that is, when we make a set of strict assumptions about the rules of the game. Second, war can be seen as a rational outgrowth of arms races even if we do not attribute to the actors some sort of cognitive imperfection. Contrary to Intrilligator and Brito's findings, the present rational explanation of the para bellum paradox suggests that war can emerge not only when one actor has less-than-complete information about the opponent's preferences, but even if both states are perfectly knowledgeable about each other.

An interesting feature of this explanation is that war may be more likely if the leaders of both states involved are risk-averse than if they are risk-neutral or risk-acceptant. If both states behaved like professional gamblers, arms races would become stable—if mutually costly—outcomes. Risk-acceptant players typically go for the highest gain and are willing to risk high losses. Hence, states in the Stag Hunt game are more likely to select the ARM strategy even if this entails a possibility of the opponent's possible initiation of a war. This is so because the ARM strategy offers the best outcome in the Stag Hunt game.[5] Risk-acceptant actors are likely to use the *maximax* decision rule in games without clear-cut rational solutions. This rule requires choosing the strategy that contains the best outcome, regardless of the value of other outcomes associated with it. In this case, a maximax strategy is not necessarily stupid because it contains an equilibrium outcome at the highest payoff.

On the other hand, actors who typically shy away from high-risk policies even if this entails giving up hope for accomplishing their best outcome might try to revert to strategies that assure them at least an acceptable minimum payoff. The implication is that risk-averse states would adopt a conservative strategy that minimizes the costs of error of judgment. This is the *maximin* strategy, which requires choosing the option containing the best among all worst outcomes. In our case, this means the FIGHT strategy. The lesson of this paradox is that supervigilance may breed disaster.

Robert Axelrod (1984), in a highly influential study of an iterative Prisoner's Dilemma game, argues for the merits of a long-term strategy called TIT-FOR-TAT. This strategy says, essentially, start by cooperating (not arming) on your first move and then do whatever your opponent did in the previous move. Axelrod argues that the property of this strategy is that it can induce cooperation in the most treacherous and exploitative actors (as long as those actors are still rational in the sense that they are out to get the most they can for themselves). Can such a strategy work in the para bellum paradox? I would argue that it probably would not, because TIT-FOR-TAT requires one of the actors to start with cooperation the first time it moves. As long as the game is played simultaneously and as long as it ends when a war breaks out, no actor has the incentive to start by cooperating (not arming), because if one does that, the game will end in a unilateral war initiative by the opponent in the next period.

## The Cognitive Explanation

The rational explanation of the para bellum paradox—however insightful—is an incomplete account of the arms race-war connection. The problem is that the rational explanation assumes too much. Specifically, it tends to leave out important issues by ignoring them or by assuming them away. For example, one may want to know how the decision makers of the opposing states come by the ARM-DON'T ARM policy alternatives in the first period and by the ARM-DON'T ARM-FIGHT combination in the second. Similarly, it is unclear which factors give rise to the specific game-theoretic formulation of the model. Why do we have a Prisoner's Dilemma in the first period and a Prisoner's Dilemma-Stag Hunt combination in the second period? Is it not possible that the outcomes of the various games would be different if the games are different from the ones suggested by the rational explanation?

The cognitive explanation concerns itself primarily with the issues that were swept under the rug by the rational explanation by converting them into assumptions that are seen to be beyond the scope of a rational analysis of the para bellum paradox. The cognitive explanation addresses the following questions: (1) How do states come up with a particular set of policy alternatives in an interactive context? (2) Which factors determine national preferences for these policy alternatives? (3) How do policy preferences interact to produce an arms race-war connection? While these questions are not an exclusive invention of cognitive theories, the kinds of answers these theories offer are what sets the cognitive model apart from the rational model.

In order to invoke the cognitive explanation, we have to consider three general principles of perception of self and others. First, people who express their honest beliefs and intentions generally expect other people to believe that these expressions are honest reflections of truly benign motives. Robert Jervis (1976: 354–355) puts it very succinctly:

> When an actor believes he is not a threat to another, he usually assumes that the other knows he is not hostile. . . . Although [decision makers] are aware of the difficulty of making threats and warnings credible, they usually believe that others are not likely to misinterpret behavior that is compatible with the other's interest.

Jervis mentions several reasons for the failure to realize that other actors might misinterpret statements and actions that are motivated by good intentions:

> lack of understanding of the context in which the other sees one's behavior; the familiarity that one actor has with its own intentions, which makes it harder for him to believe that others might not see them as he does; and the self-righteousness that inhibits the conclusion that the other's undesired behavior was provoked. (p. 354)

The second principle is that the first principle usually does not apply to an actor's perception of the honesty underlying the expressed intentions and motives of other actors. Political leaders usually are not willing to take others' honesty at face value. This is more likely true when interpreting the intentions of foes than when interpreting the intentions of traditional friends, but even friends are not given an unconditional affidavit of honesty in international politics. Holsti (1962) analyzed the belief system of John Foster Dulles, the former U.S. secretary of state, and found that Dulles attributed different causes to different types of behavior of the Soviet Union: conflictual behavior was attributed to the fundamentally malevolent intentions of communist Russia, while cooperative behavior was attributed to

Soviet weakness. The second principle, as it applies to interpretation of intentions among traditional foes, suggests that only expressions of hostility are likely to be perceived as honest reflections of true motives; expressions of goodwill are likely to be viewed with suspicion if not as outrightly deceptive.

What, then, are the sources upon which states rely to infer the "true" intentions of others? Prior expectations states have established toward other states in their past interactions are a major factor that determines how decision makers will tie expressed intentions or actions of another state to its underlying motives. The focus of the second principle is on relations between states that have had some dealings with each other in the past. These dealings serve as a basis for the attitudes decision makers in one state have established toward another state and form a system of expectations concerning the other state's intentions and subsequent behavior. The more experience states have in dealing with one another, the more rooted these beliefs are, and the more difficult it is to change them. Decision makers are more likely to interpret discrepant information in a manner that would render it consistent with their prior expectations than they are to change their beliefs (Janis and Mann, 1977; Jervis, 1976; Nisbett and Ross, 1980).

A rough but useful classification of attitudes divides perceptions of others into friends and foes. If two states share a history of common interests and cooperation, then there is a tendency to accept expressions of goodwill and cooperative actions as honest reflections of benign motives. While decision makers do not give friends a blank check under all circumstances, friends *are* allowed to make mistakes. Thus, if a friendly state does something that is inconsistent with its good image (for example, its policy harms the focal actor in some way), it might still enjoy the benefit of the doubt. Harmful actions of friendly states are therefore unlikely to cause a drastic change of attitude. Such actions might be explained away as stemming from misunderstanding, miscalculation, or other constraints that are not a direct result of the other state's intentions.

The interpretation of the motives and intentions of belligerent states depends on the nature of actions and statements of the opponent. Hostile actions are apt to be perceived as stemming from, and as evidence of, hostile intentions. Such actions (or statements) are linked directly to prior expectations of hostility and are seen as consistent with the image of malevolent intent. This applies even more to verbal expressions of hostility. On the other hand, cooperative actions and statements of goodwill are not normally trusted as such. Here decision makers attempt to break the direct link between intentions and actions that characterizes their perceptions of hostile acts or hostile statements. This is done in one of three ways: (1) These statements or actions

are perceived as deceptive; they are deliberately designed to conceal—rather than reveal—the opponent's true intentions. (2) These
statements or actions are attributed to constraints rather than to
free choice (like Dulles's attribution of Soviet cooperation to weakness). (3) The significance of cooperative actions is downgraded.

The third principle deals with the factors that affect the formation
of initial expectations and attitudes of states toward one another in
the absence of a shared history of interactions. In such cases, a state
cannot base its interpretations of the underlying motives of a certain
act on prior expectations concerning the other state. Therefore, we
must consider ways in which expectations and attitudes are formed.

In general, initial actions and statements form the basis of
new expectations and attitudes of states toward each other. However, new expectations vary according to the compatibility between
statements and actions. If statements and actions are unequivocally
cooperative, the underlying motivations of the other state are seen
as benign and friendly. If both statements and actions are hostile,
they are taken as evidence of underlying malevolent motives. In both
cases, behavior (verbal or physical) is interpreted as a reflection of
true motives. But what if words and deeds conflict? Whatever the
nature of verbal statements and whatever the nature of physical
acts, if they differ, underlying motives are taken to be malevolent.

The reason is a tricky one. In international politics, especially in
national security affairs, where major values are at stake, decision makers tend to be risk-averse. They would rather err in depicting good guys
as bad than in depicting bad guys as good, simply because the consequences of the first type of error are believed to be less damaging than
the consequences of the second type of error. Conflictual behavior
(whether verbal or physical) is seen as more severe than cooperative behavior. Thus, whether statements are cooperative and behavior is conflictual or actions are cooperative and statements are conflictual, decision makers infer hostility from the observed contradiction between
words and deeds. They invoke this interpretation simply because they
cannot afford not to. This initial interpretation causes subsequent interpretations of behavior to be biased by existing expectations of hostility.

Thus, whether or not states are playing a rational game in the
mutual armament process is of secondary importance to the cognitive explanation. What matters is that even if the game turns out
to have a rational choice interpretation in the final analysis, its foundations might well have been an outgrowth of irrational logic. In
order to substantiate this seemingly contradictory argument, it must
be shown that the three principles of inference and attribution put
forth by the cognitive explanation violate the principles of rational
logic.

At a very minimum, rationality requires consistency. It implies adherence to a certain set of logical principles regardless of the kind of problem one is trying to solve. It means that one cannot juggle different logical principles to suit different problems. Now, if rational people must be consistent, then they cannot adhere to the cognitive principles of attribution presented above because these principles are the epitome of inconsistency. Let me illustrate why that is the case. If you expect others to trust your good intentions, it would seem inconsistent not to trust others' good intentions. Given that you are unwilling to grant others an automatic affidavit of goodwill, there is no good reason you should expect others to grant you one. Thus, if the logic concerning how you expect others to perceive your sincere statements of good intentions is based on the first principle, then the logic of interpreting others' intentions cannot be based on the second principle, and vice versa.

The logic of the third principle is even more convoluted. The third principle does not require reference to other principles to prove inconsistency with rational logic, for the contradictions are already built into it. When an actor does not have an a priori basis for forming expectations about the underlying motives of other actors, the general rule is "you trust what you see." Thus, if the acts and deeds of another actor coincide, this general rule would be followed in the sense that the derivation of underlying motives is based on a direct link between intentions and behavior. However, if words and deeds contradict each other, this inferential rule is immediately replaced by another rule that takes into account the potential costs of erroneous inference. Yet, if potential costs of erroneous inference are seen as important, then they should be invoked even more in cases where words and deeds coincide. The cognitive explanation suggests that people juggle different rules about the underlying motives of observed behavior. Sometimes they assume that observed behavior is a true reflection of underlying intentions, and sometimes they assume that it is not (or even that behavior is intended to conceal real intentions). It is this inconsistency that violates rational logic.[6]

How do these principles of inference and attribution explain the arms race–war connection? In the first period, the two states have no clear prior basis for establishing expectations about each other's motives. So they wait and see what the other says or does in the first period. Yet, as far as each state's own policy is concerned, the decision to arm is based on two premises. One is that arms provide a measure of security given that you do not quite know what to expect of the other state. The other is that if you make it clear to the other state that your armament policy is purely defensive, you will be believed. The upshot is that each side views its own armament policy as being both necessary and of a nonthreatening nature.

But this gets us into the second period, in which each state is equipped with the knowledge of what the other state did in the first period. Since each state perceives a discrepancy between verbal statements of goodwill and a hostile armament policy, the third cognitive principle is invoked. Each state interprets the other state's intentions as potentially hostile due to the fact that it chose to arm in the first period. Each state is unwilling to believe the other state's statement that its armament policy is of a purely defensive nature, and the interpretation of the other's armament policy is necessarily hostile. The motives attributed by each state to the other can be summarized by the following argument: since we made it clear to the other state that our armament policy is not designed to threaten others, we expect to be believed. Thus, we cannot accept the opponent's armament policy as a logical defensive reaction to our own defensive posture. Instead, the opponent's decision to arm reveals hostile intentions. The most reasonable explanation of the opponent's behavior is that it must be part of some kind of aggressive design. If that is the case, we have to reformulate our options. We cannot restrict ourselves to a choice between arming and not arming, because the armament policy of the opponent suggests that the opponent is not so restricted. While we certainly prefer not going to war over fighting it out, we prefer to fight under favorable conditions if we have to, and, given the opponent's aggressive intentions, it looks like we will have to fight it out. The upshot of this is the expansion of the range of alternatives in the second period to include the FIGHT alternative, as well as the subsequent structure of preferences given in Figures 2.2 and 2.3. *The rational structure of the game solved by the rational explanation is thus an outgrowth of an illogical application of cognitive rules of inference and attribution.*

But given that an arms race is on, under what conditions would it terminate in a war? Whatever the logic that led the actors into the strategic mess depicted in Figure 2.3, it is not at all evident why arms races would not provide for long-range strategic stability. Although actors might have been lured into this game by a series of logical fallacies concerning the causal links between intentions and behavior, once in the combined Prisoner's Dilemma-Stag Hunt (PD-SH) game, they may well perceive the situation correctly and act to stabilize it. It is not at all implausible to expect actors to realize the existence of a mutually best ARM-ARM outcome and to adopt strategies consistent with its accomplishment. The cognitive model, while admitting this possibility, argues that such behavior is in no way guaranteed. There are several good reasons an arms race may be converted into a violent race. In situations where none of the actors has an unequivocally best strategy, game theory is not of much help. Nor is an analysis of equilibrium outcomes. The concept of equilibrium is useful in predicting whether an outcome, once reached, would be stable or not; yet, it is not necessarily useful in predicting whether it would be reached in the first place. This problem is compounded when a strategic configuration contains more than one stable solution. The question is how actors would actually behave in such situations and what rules guide their choices. The cognitive explanation suggests two rules that might cause a breakdown of stability in an arms race: behavior that is guided by prudence, and expectation of breakdown in stability due to error or other forms of miscalculation.

Prudence is really a worst-case analysis of the strategic configuration. An actor who is unsure how the opponent would react to the combined PD-SH game wishes to find a strategy that is independent of what the opponent might do. Such a strategy is appealing from the perspective of an actor who is basically risk-averse and who has a low tolerance for uncertainty. Such an actor may seek a strategy that is satisfactory rather than optimal, one that would assure a guaranteed minimum payoff that is higher than the minimum payoff associated with any of the other available strategies. In the combined PD-SH game shown in the top part of Figure 2.3, the least of all evils is the FIGHT-FIGHT outcome. Yet, the pursuit of a strategy motivated by a desire to select the least of all evils traps the actors into a situation in which they get just that—but the least of all evils is itself a large calamity.

A worst-case analysis is intended to make one's choice independent of the opponent's choice. However, if the decision makers of one state have some prior expectations regarding the opponent's rationality, or regarding the ability of their counterparts to control the behavior of their subordinates, the policy choices might well be dependent on the courses of behavior attributed to their opponents. Jervis (1976: 319–329) points out that decision makers tend to perceive their opponents' behavior as an outgrowth of careful and unitary planning rather than as a result of bureaucratic maneuvers and internal compromises. Yet, under some circumstances, the possibility of error and miscalculation by the opponent cannot be avoided. Such situations are especially likely to arise when no clear guidelines of optimal behavior can be inferred readily from the value system attributed to the opponent. The combined PD-SH game is a perfect illustration of such a case. An actor analyzing the opponent's payoff structure can easily realize that the latter lacks an unequivocally best strategy. Although it is reasonable to assume that the opponent would adopt a strategy containing the stable ARM-ARM outcome, the costs of an erroneous judgment of the opponent's behavior must be taken into account.

An analysis of the consequences of strategy shifts as a result of various estimates of the probability of attack by an opponent in the combined PD-SH game is given in the appendix to this chapter. The most important point made by this analysis is that there is a basic interdependence between the values an actor places on the various outcomes and the incentives of that actor to fight. An actor who thinks that the costs associated with a first strike by the opponent are very high compared to the costs associated with a reciprocally initiated war must be very confident that the opponent would not strike first to prefer arming over fighting. This is so even if the focal actor thinks that it stands to gain very little in a first strike of its own. On the other hand, an actor who thinks that being attacked is not much worse than engaging in a reciprocally initiated war would be inclined to cooperate (ARM) even if the chances of the opponent cooperating are fairly low. Thus, the way actors assess the advantages of offense and defense in such situations strongly affects their tendency toward cooperation (ARMing) or defection (FIGHT-ing). This argument is similar to Jervis's (1978) contention that an ideology of the offensive need not be a result of aggressive designs.

Actors who place a high value on offense and a low value on defense might still prefer arming over fighting. However, fearing that their opponent is not entirely rational, or that their opponent's decision makers might lose control over their subordinates, they might be tempted to initiate an offensive war, which they perceive as preventive in nature. Harkabi (1964) distinguishes between preventive and preemptive wars on the basis of two factors: certainty and time. A preemptive strike is considered when actors perceive a high probability of imminent attack by an opponent, that is, when they are fairly certain that an attack by an opponent is going to take place in the very near future. This is based on active and intensive preparations for war by an opponent, such as troop movements, mobilization of reserves on a large scale, and an increased level of alert in the opponent's army. A preemptive strike might give the initiator the advantage of surprise, a free choice of the location and nature of the first strike, and an ability to interfere with the opponent's attack plans.

A preventive strike becomes an attractive option if some change in the opponent's behavior or capabilities has taken place suggesting that the opponent might be in a position to launch an effective first strike in the future. In the context of an intensive arms race, such changes are usually associated with expected or actual technological breakthroughs, with the acquisition of new sophisticated arms, with a drastic increase in the opponent's defense expenditures or military personnel, and so forth (Levy, 1987). None of these changes has an immediate impact on the opponent's capabilities: technological breakthroughs require a lot of time to be converted into practical applications on production lines. New weapons require changes in training procedures, logistical adjustments, alterations of doctrines and command and control structures, and so forth. These changes are not seen to constitute an immediate danger, but might pose a major strategic problem in the longer run. Whether or not these technological or quantitative changes in the opponent's capabilities would be used against the actor is also not entirely clear. But there is a possibility that they would, and this might affect a drastic reassessment of the strategic situation.

First, the ordinal structure of the preferences of the actor facing a technological breakthrough by the opponent might remain unchanged, but the magnitude of difference between the values of the various outcomes might change significantly. An actor might increase the valuation of a first strike, as well as the valuation of a reciprocally initiated war. Thus, although the game is the same as before, the inclination of an actor toward fighting may increase sharply.

Second, in the short run, the opponent is expected to be cooperative, that is, to pursue an arms race policy rather than a violent strategy. But the technological breakthrough or the new weapons acquired by the opponent might tempt it to try its luck with a war in the distant future. While it may not want to fight now, it is not inconceivable that the opponent would want to translate its technological or quantitative superiority into political gains. Decision makers feel that the real choice is not between arming and fighting, but between war now and war in the future under worse conditions. It is the shadow of the future that might prompt states to break an arms race by warfare. The tendency of states that feel they lose a strategic advantage or otherwise foresee a gloomy future to initiate conflict has been analyzed and found not to be supported by empirical evidence (Maoz, 1982a: 87–90). But here we are dealing with the exceptions rather than with the rule.

## War Preparations and
## War Outbreaks in History

Because wars are almost always fought over specific substantive issues such as territory, control over people, and even over ideas, establishing a direct link between arms races and war in a historical context is very difficult. The actual relationship between arms races and war is indirect. Something must happen to convert the general hostile and suspicious climate that characterizes the relations between the racing states into an outburst of violence.

Several things need to be established in any kind of historical application of this paradox. First, it must be shown that an intensive arms race has been going on prior to the outbreak of the war. Second, it must be established that the intensity of this arms race somehow transformed the perceptions of the decision makers on at least one side regarding the intentions of the opponent, or regarding the effects of the capabilities of the opponent on its intentions, generally in the direction of increased hostility. Third, if possible, it must be shown that this perception has been instrumental in the calculus of war initiation. Finally, even if the causal connection between arms races and war cannot be established along these lines, indirect evidence for the effects of arms races on war initiation can be found in calculations of timing affected by perceptions of changes in capabilities of the opponents.

The cases discussed below are different in terms of the effect that the arms race had on the perceptions of the participants. In the first case, changes in the magnitude of the arms race created perceptual changes regarding the intentions of the adversary. In the second case, changes in the arms race pattern created change in the perceptions of relative bargaining power, which served as incentives for war.

## The Israeli-Egyptian Arms Race of 1954–1956 and the Sinai War

The tripartite declaration of May 1950 (signed by the United States, Britain, and France) was designed to prevent a dangerous arms race in the Middle East. The three great powers agreed on what amounted to an actual embargo on weapon shipments to the Middle East. The idea was to reduce the likelihood of hostilities in the area by restricting the quality and quantity of the means of destruction available to the indigenous states. Since the British maintained strong influence over Egyptian and Jordanian politics and the French had close ties with the Syrians and the Lebanese, this seemed like a sensible approach. The Israelis, who had received most of their weapons from Czechoslovakia during the 1948 war, also confronted severe difficulties in getting the weapons they felt were essential for their national security (Safran, 1969). In addition, the need to build the Jewish state and to assimilate thousands of new immigrants from all over the world imposed a heavy economic burden on the Israeli leadership. Consequently, severe cuts in Israel's defense budget were required.

A significant process of demobilization took place immediately after the termination of the 1948 war. This process was not entirely planned. A significant portion of the Israeli Defense Forces (IDF) personnel was voluntarily or involuntarily discharged, with the officer corps being the most badly hit. Two factors contributed to this process. First, many people felt that peace with the Arabs was imminent, and that a large army would be an anachronism. Those who were quick to start a civilian career would have an economic advantage over those who stayed in the army. Second, political rivalries among members of ex-underground organizations caused Ben-Gurion (who occupied the posts of prime minister and defense minister) to discharge many members of the Palmach (a leftist underground organization in the pre-1948 period) who had occupied key command roles during the war of independence.

In Egypt, the corrupt constitutional monarchy of King Farouk did not expend many resources on the army, mainly for fear this would only increase the power of radical elements in the Egyptian army who were opposed both to the monarchy and to the excessive British influence in Egyptian politics. This regime was overthrown in a 1952 coup d'état by a group of young army officers led by General Naguib and Colonel Nasser. Safran (1969: 152) points out that mutual suspicions between Naguib and other members of the ruling junta were responsible for a relative freeze on the level of the armed forces during the 1952–1954 period. In addition, the strong British military presence in the Suez canal zone imposed considerable constraints on military policy in general and on defense allocations in particular.

The 1954 Egyptian-British agreement on the evacuation of the British forces from the canal zone, and the emergence of Nasser as the sole leader of the military junta, caused a major change in the region. Two factors pushed Nasser into a more militant posture vis-à-vis Israel. First, the British initiative to join the key Arab states (along with Turkey and Iran) in an anti-Soviet alliance, known as the Baghdad Pact, caused significant concern in Egypt. Nasser felt that the major aims of the Baghdad Pact were to perpetuate Western domination in the Middle East and to hamper any sincere movement toward Arab unity. Egyptian active resistance caused considerable friction with the British (and the United States) as well as with traditional Arab regimes such as Iraq and Jordan. Nasser, who was trying to establish his regime in Egypt, felt highly threatened by repeated pressures on Egypt to join the Baghdad Pact.

Second, the weakness of the Egyptian army was most blatantly revealed on February 28, 1955, during a raid by Israeli paratroopers on an Egyptian army base in Gaza (in which 28 Egyptian soldiers were killed). This raid convinced Nasser that the Egyptian army needed considerable strengthening (SIPRI, 1971: 519). Throughout 1955, Egyptian officials conducted talks with the United States on a large-scale weapons deal. These talks were suspended as a result of unfavorable terms of payment imposed by the U.S. negotiators. On September 27, 1955, it was announced that Egypt had signed a major arms agreement with Czechoslovakia. (It was clear that the Czechs served as a front for the Soviet Union.) Once this deal was announced, the United States offered Egypt a new deal with much lowered terms of payment, but Egypt turned it down (SIPRI, 1971: 520).

In Israel, increased concern with security issues was a result of numerous infiltrations into Israeli territory from its bordering states.

Many of these infiltrations caused significant human and material damage. Israeli reprisal policy shifted in 1953 from hitting civilian villages, known to have been bases and hiding spots of the infiltrators, to hitting military targets in the neighboring Arab states. The object was to compel the Arab governments to put an end to these infiltrations. Direct hostilities between Israel and its neighboring states also intensified, involving relatively large border clashes with Syria and Jordan (Yaniv, 1985; Maoz and Yaniv, 1989). Israel managed, through a variety of means, to acquire about 200 tanks from American and British surpluses through 1953, but it had not managed to improve the size and quality of its air force. In 1954, Israel signed a major arms deal with France, although the major portion of the deal was not put into practice until the following year. Table 2.1 summarizes the quantitative and qualitative arms race between Egypt and Israel during the 1950–1956 period.

Both the monetary expenditures and the changes in the sizes of the two armed forces reflect a rapid process of mobilization. Both sides more than doubled their expenditures on defense as a proportion of their gross national product (in absolute terms, Israel's defense outlays in 1956 were nearly four times the amount they were in 1953, and Egyptian 1956 defense expenditures were more than twice the amount they were in 1953). The amount of military personnel and weapon stockpiles of the two sides also increased markedly over the period. Israel doubled the size of its armed forces, and Egypt increased its armed forces by two-thirds.

The magnitude of the destructive hardware available to both sides reflects the most dramatic increase. By 1956, the number of tanks, planes, and ships available to both armies was either double or triple the amount available to them in 1950. These figures clearly show that an arms race of a highly intensive nature was going on between these two states. Yet, these figures reveal very little of the connection between the arms race and the Sinai war. To do that, we must focus on the calculus of the initiator of that war: Israel.[7]

The intensification of the fedayeen raids and the need to initiate ever larger retaliatory raids suggested that the policy of limited retaliation had exhausted itself. A large-scale attack on a key Arab state, if successful, might act as a precedent for future deterrence of infiltrations. Second, the direct clashes with the Syrian, Jordanian, and Egyptian armies, although limited in scope, were seen as a constant menace that had to be disposed of. Again, a large-scale attack could be seen as a deterrent. Third, Egyptian blockade of the Tiran straits caused heavy damage to Israel's economy, as it prevented trade between Israel and various Asian states. The fact that no major power was willing to do anything to stop what the Israelis regarded as a blatant violation of international law added to their frustration.

**Table 2.1**   The Egyptian-Israeli arms race, 1950–1956

**Military expenditures**

| Year | Israel | | Egypt | |
|---|---|---|---|---|
| | Real defense outlays[a] | Relative defense outlays[b] | Real defense outlays[a] | Relative defense outlays[b] |
| 1951 | 60.3 | 7.8 | 114.2 | 4.3 |
| 1952 | 58.6 | 7.1 | 121.8 | 4.8 |
| 1953 | 49.8 | 6.1 | 116.8 | 4.7 |
| 1954 | 64.8 | 6.7 | 129.0 | 5.2 |
| 1955 | 72.3 | 6.5 | 182.8 | 7.1 |
| 1956 | 161.9 | 13.4 | 217.6 | 8.2 |

**Comparative strength of the Egyptian and Israeli armed forces, 1950–1956**

| | Israel 1949–50 | Egypt 1949–50 | Israel 1956 | Egypt 1956 |
|---|---|---|---|---|
| Total forces | 100,000[c] | 60,000[e] | 200,000[d] | 100,000 |
| Army | 63,000 | 54,000 | 190,000 | 88,000 |
| Armored brigades | 1.5 | 1 | 4 | 3–4 |
| Tanks | 40 | 80 | 360 | 730 |
| Armored personnel carriers | 200 | ? | 400–500 | 200 |
| Air force | 3,000[c] | 2,500 | 7,000 | 6–8,000 |
| Total planes | 67 | 70 | 200 | 400 |
| Combat planes | 40 | 35 | 160 | 275 |
| Transport planes | 12 | 10 | 20 | 60 |
| Other planes | 15 | 25 | 50 | 65 |
| Navy | 1,500 | 2,000 | 4,000 | 3–4,000 |
| Destroyers | 0 | 0 | 2 | 4 |
| Other ships | 5 | 14 | 11 | 37 |

*Source:* Military expenditures, Safran (1969: 199); comparative strength of forces, Safran (1969: 217, 228).

[a] In millions of 1962 U.S. dollars.
[b] As percentage of GNP.
[c] About 30% of Israel's personnel were in the standing army. The remaining 70% were quickly mobilizable reservists.
[d] About 33% of Israel's personnel were in the standing army. The remaining 67% were quickly mobilizable reservists.
[e] About 90% of the Egyptian personnel were in the standing army. The remaining 10% were mobilizable reservists. Egypt had a nominal 100,000 national guardsmen.

Yet, none of these factors can clearly explain the Israeli decision to attack Egypt. Israel could have picked an easier target, such as Jordan or Syria, to prove its deterrence-related point. In fact, an Israeli attack on Jordan was expected both by Middle East observers and by many people in Israel.[8] The blockade of the Tiran straits did not require an all-out attack over the entire Sinai peninsula, nor was such an attack necessary for the termination of the fedayeen raids originating in the Gaza Strip.

The vast increase in the size of the Egyptian army and the sophisticated weapons it acquired in the arms deal of 1955 were seen as a major motivational input for war. The Israeli nightmare was that once these weapons are absorbed into the Egyptian army, Israel would face a formidable enemy that possessed both the capacity and will to launch a devastating military blow that could potentially put an end to the Israeli dream of a national homeland.

The emergence of Nasser as a major unifying force in the Arab world, his fiery anti-Israeli rhetoric, and his overwhelming prestige as a result of the arms deal were seen as indications that this combination of capabilities and intent was bound to be transformed into a lethal attack on Israel in the future. Shortly after the announcement of the Egyptian-Soviet arms deal, Syria and Yemen started negotiations with the Soviet Union on similar arms deals. Israel faced an ominous future. It was therefore seen as imperative to launch a major military campaign that would reduce the Nasserist image to its "true" proportions. This could be done only by taking care of these new arms, and only through a large-scale attack over the entire Sinai peninsula. Moshe Dayan (1976: 180), then chief of staff of the IDF, summarizes the prevailing perception of the implications of the Egyptian-Soviet arms deal for Israel's security:

> It was clear to us in Israel that the primary purpose of this massive Egyptian rearmament was to prepare Egypt for a decisive confrontation with Israel in the near future. The Egyptian blockade, her planning and direction of mounting Palestinian guerrilla activity against Israel, Nasser's own declarations, and now the Czech arms deal left no doubt in our minds that Egypt's purpose was to wipe us out, or at least win a decisive military victory which would leave us in helpless subjugation.

From November 1955, Dayan pressed for decisive action against Egypt. In a memo to Ben-Gurion, Dayan urged a large-scale operation designed to capture Sharm-a-Sheikh in the southern tip of the Sinai peninsula and the Gaza Strip in the northeastern part of the Sinai (Dayan, 1976: 181), knowing very well that such an operation would mean full-scale war.

But, while most of the motivations for a war against Egypt were already present at the end of 1955, the actual outbreak of the war took place a year later. Dayan writes in his diary of the Sinai campaign that his recommendation of a large-scale attack against Egypt was repeatedly turned down. The reason for the delay was Ben-Gurion's conviction that a unilateral Israeli action might subject Israel to considerable pressure by the major powers. Israel already had its share of diplomatic problems with the British, who were deeply involved in Jordanian politics and reacted to Israeli raids into Jordan with growing anger. Initiating a war without the diplomatic backing of one or more major powers was seen by Ben-Gurion as a highly dangerous adventure. He felt, therefore, that an attack on Egypt must be supported, implicitly or explicitly, by a major power.

The opportunity for meeting this condition came in the summer of 1956, when the Suez crisis—precipitated by the Egyptian nationalization of the Suez canal—erupted. France and Britain started contemplating regaining control over the Suez canal by force. Israeli interests fit very well into that scheme, and, consequently, a military agreement involving Israel, France, and Britain was signed in October 1956. Israel was to launch an attack across the Sinai peninsula, and the two major powers were to dispatch their forces to occupy the canal zone in order to reestablish order in the region (Brecher, 1974: 263–274).

The Egyptian-Israeli arms race took place amid an already deeply rooted climate of hostility and mistrust. It transformed this hostility from a primarily rhetorical form, wherein both sides' bark had been worse than their bite, into a level of threat touching—to judge from the prevailing Israeli perception—the issue of national survival. The economic pressure put on Israel by the Egyptian blockade of the Tiran straits was marginal. The fedayeen infiltrations from the Gaza Strip were a menace, but they were an issue of current security. In contrast, the change in the balance of forces due to the Egyptian-Soviet arms deal converted the problem into one of basic security.[9] The intensified arms race transformed the perceptions of stakes involved in the conflict for both parties. The 1955 Israeli raid on Gaza presented a major threat to the Nasserist regime, which needed the support of an army with an image of effectiveness. For the Israelis, the sophisticated weapon systems acquired by Egypt indicated that it was planning to launch a major offensive in the future.

## Arms Races and the Closing of Options: The Indo-Pakistani War, 1965[10]

Paradoxically, India's humiliating defeat by China in the 1962 war solved its arms acquisition problems. The Americans and the British, who up to that point had viewed India's nonaligned status as a camouflage for procommunist inclinations, had embargoed weapon shipments to India while generously providing Pakistan's needs in military hardware. Since the Indians fought a communist state in 1962, the United States and Great Britain concluded, it must be pro-Western, hence, its needs in arms should be filled so it could face up the Chinese in the future, and never mind what Pakistan feels about it (Burke, 1973: 275-277). Curiously, the Soviets, who started to sense the growing rift with the Chinese, began to feel the need to develop some check to Chinese expansionist aims in South Asia, and they also increased their military aid to India (Burke, 1973: 277–278; Barnds, 1972: 182).

Meanwhile, Pakistan, which up to that point had had the most modern army in Southeast Asia, began experiencing problems in acquiring military hardware. It became clear that Pakistan was being placed into a strategic disadvantage vis-à-vis India. This is documented in Table 2.2.

If Pakistan had been at a numerical disadvantage in 1960, it realized that it had a major problem. Its fear was of falling behind India so badly that it would be at India's mercy anytime the latter may want something from it. Worse, Pakistani decision makers realized that any demand they had from India would be made with the contempt that ministates deserve when they are dealing with great powers. The Pakistani leadership was not so threatened by India's increased military might as they

**Table 2.2**    The Indo-Pakistani arms race, 1960–1965

**Military expenditures**

| Year | India | | Pakistan | |
|------|-------|--|----------|--|
| | Real defense outlays[a] | Relative defense outlays[b] | Real defense outlays[a] | Relative defense outlays[b] |
| 1960 | 2,774 | 0.019 | 978 | 0.028 |
| 1961 | 3,046 | 0.019 | 984 | 0.026 |
| 1962 | 4,336 | 0.026 | 938 | 0.024 |
| 1963 | 7,306 | 0.038 | 1,029 | 0.024 |
| 1964 | 8,084 | 0.036 | 1,208 | 0.026 |
| 1965 | 8,651 | 0.036 | 2,059 | 0.040 |

**Comparative strength of the Indian and Pakistani armed forces, 1960–1965**

| | India 1960 | Pakistan 1960 | India 1965 | Pakistan 1965 |
|--|-----------|--------------|-----------|--------------|
| Total forces | 450,000 | 205,000 | 869,000 | 225,000 |
| Army | 423,000 | 193,000 | 825,000 | 198,000 |
| Armored divisions | 1 | 1 | 3 | 2 |
| Tanks | NA[c] | NA | NA | NA |
| Air force | 18,000 | 8,000 | 28,000 | 20,000 |
| Total planes | NA | NA | 599 | 200 |
| Combat planes | NA | NA | 444 | 140 |
| Transport planes | NA | NA | 140 | 55 |
| Navy | 9,000 | 4,000 | 16,000 | 7,000 |
| Destroyers | 1 | 1 | 3 | 5 |
| Other ships | NA | NA | 43[d] | 24 |

*Sources:* Military expenditures, SIPRI (1974); comparative strength of forces, International Institute of Strategic Studies (1966), Feldman (1972), Ganguly (1986), Burke (1973).

[a] In millions of U.S. dollars (1971 prices).
[b] As percentage of GNP.
[c] NA = Not available.
[d] Including one 16,000-ton aircraft carrier.

were feeling that they were about to lose all the bargaining chips they used to have.

The strange friendship between India, on the one hand, and the United States and the Soviet Union, on the other, caused Pakistan to turn to China. The December 26, 1962, provisional Sino-Pakistani agreement on the Kashmir boundary launched a series of treaties and agreements between these states. These agreements strengthened Indian suspicion that the two states were plotting against India. As Barnds (1972: 190) points out: "In Indian eyes the vastly different nature of the Pakistani and Chinese governments—one a radical Communist regime and the other a conservative Muslim one—appeared less important than bitter hostility of both toward India. Thus India became more convinced than ever that it needed military forces capable of holding off Pakistan and China simultaneously."

Kashmir was the principal stake of the 1965 war. This region had been disputed since the establishment of the two states in 1947. Prolonged negotiations did not produce any results. By the early 1960s, the problem was still unresolved. While both India and Pakistan were willing to be flexible on another disputed border area, the Rann of Kutch, both exhibited intransigence on the Kashmir issue. The Pakistanis viewed the uncompromising Indian position as evidence that India felt sufficiently powerful to allow itself to ignore Pakistani claims. They believed that India was intent on using its military advantage to annex Kashmir formally.

Following numerous small skirmishes throughout 1965 in the Rann of Kutch, significant fighting broke out on April 9, 1965. During the brief exchange of hostilities, the "Indian forces were badly mauled . . . by the Pakistani army" (Burke, 1973: 324). Following British intervention, the two parties signed an agreement on arbitration of the dispute, which seems to have terminated problems in that area. However, the Kutch incident did have an important effect on Pakistan's decision to initiate the war in September. The Pakistani leadership faced what it perceived to be increased Indian intention to annex Kashmir. This perception was not without basis, as the Indians increased their pressure on the local Muslim leadership whose wishes were to be annexed to Pakistan. The Pakistanis felt that the rapid increase in the size and technology of the Indian army convinced the Indians that they could present Pakistan with a fait accompli in Kashmir.

Thus, action had to be taken soon. The Pakistani army still had the qualitative edge due to long-term nurturing by the United States and Britain over the decade before. This qualitative edge was proven in the course of the Rann of Kutch incident. However, the balance was shifting rapidly. As Barnds (1972: 201) remarks:

Over the long term, India's defense buildup would leave Pakistan in a weaker position on the subcontinent, and few Pakistanis thought India would deal fairly from a position of strength. Indeed, as India's indigenous defense production capability grew and as it acquired the capacity to produce nuclear weapons, New Delhi would be even less susceptible to the influence of the world community.

The arms race between the two states was fairly asymmetric. By 1965 it became evident that India was outdistancing Pakistan by far. Though Pakistani rhetoric involved statements that India's military buildup was designed to destroy Pakistan, it is obvious that this was not a driving force in the initiation of the war. The arms race created a sense that the future would leave Pakistan without any viable options in Kashmir. India was being dealt aces, and unless something was done, it would soon own the whole casino.

## Conclusion

It is clear that the path from arms race to war goes through crises. Arms races serve primarily as an important motivational factor in the calculus of war initiation. In most cases, it is neither an exclusive motive nor the factor that determines the scope and timing of the initiative. Yet, the intensity of arms competitions is an important cause of war because it reinforces mutual suspicions in an already tense atmosphere of animosity that is ignited by other substantive issues. Arms races may originate in benign search for security in an uncertain world, or in bureaucratic struggles among competing social and political groups within states. They may also be the result of external causes that have little or nothing to do with a given international conflict. Yet, this analysis suggests that if indeed arms races are taken to be a means toward peace, they can turn out to be a major cause of war.

## Appendix

This appendix deals with some technical aspects of the arguments raised in the chapter. It is directed toward scientifically inclined readers who are interested in the mathematical implications of the para bellum paradox.

The issue addressed here is this: How confident should one be that an opponent will refrain from attacking in order to prefer arming over attacking? To answer this question, it is sufficient to focus on the reduced game given in the bottom part of Figure 2.3. Once the game is reduced to a Stag Hunt problem, each side realizes that neither has an unequivocally best strategy. In such a case, one may wish to examine how one's choice might be affected by different expectations regarding the opponent's behavior. Suppose, further, that side $i$ thinks there is some unknown probability $p$ that side $j$ would ARM and a complementary probability $(1 - p)$ that $j$ would FIGHT. To examine the sensitivity of $i$'s choice to different values of $p$, we must examine the *threshold probability of cooperation*. A threshold probability of cooperation is a probability of cooperation (in our case, a probability of the opponent choosing the ARM strategy) that would render an actor indifferent between ARMing and FIGHTing. For any $p > p^\star$, an actor would prefer ARMing over FIGHTing, and for any $p < p^\star$ an actor would prefer FIGHTing over ARMing.

To compute $p^\star$, we transform the ordinal preferences in the Stag Hunt game into cardinal utilities. This is done by transforming the two extreme payoffs (4 and 1) into extreme points on a zero-to-one utility scale (such that $4 = 1$ and $1 = 0$). The two intermediate payoffs are denoted by $u_3$ and $u_2$ for 3 and 2, respectively. The matrix representation of this normalized Stag Hunt game is given in Figure 2.4.

In the figure, $0 < u_{i2} < u_{i3} < 1$ and $0 < u_{j2} < u_{j3} < 1$. (Note that $u_{i2} \neq u_{j2}$ and $u_{i3} \neq u_{j3}$; no interpersonal comparison of utilities.) Actor $i$ knows the values of $u_{i2}$ and $u_{i3}$ (but not the values of $u_{j2}$ and of $u_{j3}$), and actor $j$ knows $u_{j2}$, $u_{j3}$ (but not $u_{i2}$, $u_{i3}$). Now we can examine the sensitivity of each actor to the probability of ARMing by the opponent. This is done in the following calculation.

| | | $j$ | |
| | | ARM | FIGHT |
|---|---|---|---|
| | | 1 | $u_{j3}$ |
| $i$ | ARM | 1 · · · · · · 0 | |
| | | 0 | $u_{j2}$ |
| | FIGHT | $u_{i3}$ · · · · · · $u_{i2}$ | |

**Figure 2.4**  A Generalized Stag Hunt Game with (Normalized) Cardinal Utilities

The expected utility of ARMing for $i$ is given by

$$EV^i_{ARM} = p \times 1 + (1 - p) \times 0 = p \qquad [2.1]$$

and the expected utility of FIGHTing for $i$ is

$$EV^i_{FIGHT} = p \times u_{i3} + (1 - p) \times u_{i2} \qquad [2.2]$$

Actor $i$ will be indifferent between ARMing and FIGHTing if and only if $EV^i_{ARM} = EV^i_{FIGHT}$. This implies,

$$p = p^\star = pu_{i3} + (1 - p) u_{i2} \qquad [2.3]$$

Solving for $p^\star$ in equation 2.3 yields

$$p^\star = \frac{u_{i2}}{1 - u_{i3} + u_{i2}} \qquad [2.4]$$

Thus, actor $i$ would fight if and only if the actual probability he or she assigns to $j$'s choice of the ARM strategy ($p$) is smaller than that of the threshold probability $p^\star$. Otherwise, the only rational choice is to ARM. The same analysis can be performed for the threshold probability of $j$. Since the Stag Hunt game is symmetrical (diagonal payoffs are ranked the same for both actors and off-diagonal payoffs are mirror images of one another; the game can be transposed over actors without changing its structure), the results would be the same. It is also obvious that there is a fundamental interdependence between the utility an actor assigns to the two intermediate outcomes ($u_2$ and

**Table 2.3**    Threshold probabilities as a function of the values assigned to $u_2$ and $u_3$

| $u_3$ | 0.100 | 0.200 | 0.300 | $u_2$ 0.400 | 0.500 | 0.600 | 0.700 | 0.800 |
|---|---|---|---|---|---|---|---|---|
| 0.100 | — | | | | | | | |
| 0.200 | 0.111 | — | | | | | | |
| 0.300 | 0.125 | 0.222 | — | | | | | |
| 0.400 | 0.143 | 0.250 | 0.333 | — | | | | |
| 0.500 | 0.167 | 0.286 | 0.375 | 0.444 | — | | | |
| 0.600 | 0.200 | 0.333 | 0.429 | 0.500 | 0.556 | — | | |
| 0.700 | 0.250 | 0.400 | 0.500 | 0.571 | 0.625 | 0.667 | — | |
| 0.800 | 0.333 | 0.500 | 0.600 | 0.677 | 0.714 | 0.750 | 0.778 | — |
| 0.900 | 0.500 | 0.667 | 0.750 | 0.800 | 0.833 | 0.857 | 0.875 | 0.889 |

*Note:* Entries are threshold probabilities $p^\star = \dfrac{u_2}{1 - u_3 + u_2}$.

$u_3$) and the threshold probability that would render him indifferent between FIGHTing and ARMing. Table 2.3 depicts how the threshold probability $p^\star$ varies as a function of the values associated with these two intermediate outcomes.

# Notes

1  Some authors claim that the marginal superiority rule is not as universal as many think it is. Incentives for superiority exist especially when offensive strategies are thought to have an advantage. If defensive technology dominates offensive ones, security can be preserved even if one is marginally inferior to one's opponents. See Jervis (1978) and Levy (1984) for more elaborate discussions of this issue. The problem with this argument is that perceptions of the kind of strategy that has an advantage may not be the same across states. One state may believe that defensive strategies have an advantage, but once it sees that its opponent is arming it might do the same, because it suspects that its opponent may be planning a trick and it might want to play it safe just in case. Alternatively, defensive strategies may have an advantage, but everybody might think differently. This was the case on the eve of World War I, when most strategists on both sides placed a high premium on offense. See J. S. Snyder (1984) on this issue.

2  Russett (1983) reviews the rich literature on the military-industrial complex and its impact on defense spending of nations. Pierre (1982) is a good source on the economic determinants of arms transfers.

3  Schelling (1963) provides a fascinating discussion of the "reciprocal fear of surprise attack," a topic with which I shall deal in greater depth in the next chapter.

4  The reason for the ranking of this outcome as lower than the mutual nonarmament outcome is that even a war against an unprepared opponent carries some tangible and intangible costs. These costs may make this outcome less preferred than the mutual nonarmament outcome, which is noncostly either in the diplomatic sense or in the military and economic ones.

5  Formally, the notion of risk propensity involves the tendency of people to accept (or reject) uncertain gambles involving higher expected payoffs over sure, but less valued, outcomes. Risk-acceptant people would systematically go for the risky gambles, while risk-averse people would systematically prefer the certain but less valued outcomes (see Coombs et al., 1970, for a concise introduction to these issues). The assessment of risk propensities requires, therefore, some knowledge of the cardinal utilities that players assign to the various outcomes. In the absence of such utilities, it is possible to talk about the use of different decision rules by players with different risk propensities (Lave and March, 1975: ch. 4).

6  For additional discussion of these principles of attribution, the ways they are reflected in the beliefs of elites and masses in conflict situations, see Heradsveidt (1979). George (1980: 58–61) discusses the effects of these attributional biases on effective decision making. In earlier work, I have applied these attributional principles to processes of preference formation and preference change in foreign policy decision making (Maoz, 1989: ch. 9).

7  The Israeli decisions leading to the Sinai war are well documented. Most of the political and military leaders of that time published their memoirs (e.g., Dayan, 1966, 1976; Sharett, 1978; Ben-Gurion, 1968; Peres, 1970). A host of scholarly studies documenting Israeli decisions to initiate the Sinai war are also available (Brecher, 1974; Blechman, 1966).

8    The mobilization of Israeli reserves in early November 1956 was taken to be a sign of active preparation for war against Jordan rather than against Egypt. See Dayan (1966).

9    In the Israeli strategic jargon, there is a distinction between basic security, which involves threats to Israel's survival due to a large-scale Arab attack, and current security, which involves relatively smaller threats due to low-level military harassments and terrorist activities. I believe this distinction was first made by Yigal Allon (1970).

10   This analysis is based on Barnds (1972), Feldman (1972), Ganguly (1986), and Burke (1973).

# 3

# The Threat of Stability and The Stability of Threats: The Paradox of Successful Deterrence

Deterrence is a policy through which one attempts to scare off a would-be attacker by holding out a drawn sword. It works as long as the sword is not being used. When the sword becomes covered with blood, deterrence is said to have failed, no matter whose blood was spilled. Deterrence consists of a threat issued by a state to inflict unacceptable damage on an opponent if the latter violates some specified elements of the status quo. States relying on deterrence hope that these threats will never have to be made good. A threat of retaliation that needs to be translated into actual force stops serving the purpose for which it was devised.

Most analyses of deterrence suggest that defective application of the policy is the principal cause of its failure. When threats are not sufficiently clear, when they are not backed by a credible commitment to carry them out, or when the capabilities to carry out the threats are inadequate, opponents might find it profitable to challenge the status quo. The conventional wisdom is that, if it is designed and implemented with care and caution, deterrence can convert a dangerous tiger into a peace-loving pussycat. Contrary to this conventional wisdom, the paradox of successful deterrence suggests that deterrence may fail *because* it is applied too well, because threats are credible, because they are believable, and because the premises on which such a policy relies are fundamentally sound. There are cases in which an actor (the deterree) chooses to violate the status quo that another (the deterrer) seeks to preserve via deterrence in spite of the fact that the former thinks the latter is willing and able to carry out the threat. And we do not have to assume that an undeterred deterree is irrational or otherwise unaware of the repercussions of his or her act. Perfectly reasonable

people confronted by an effective deterrent threat may find it logical—in fact, may find it imperative—to defy it. The following section
discusses some central issues in deterrence theory that are important
for explaining and illustrating the paradox of successful deterrence.

## Issues in Deterrence Theory

Deterrence has played an important role in interstate relations
throughout history,[1] but it was popularized in the 1950s and 1960s,
when it became the cornerstone of U.S. strategic policy. The
literature on the theory and practice of deterrence before and after
Hiroshima is too vast for me even to start summarizing it here.[2]
However, as a starting point, it might be useful to list some—by
no means all—of the key questions addressed by this literature:

(1)   When should a state contemplate basing its strategic relations with
      an adversary on deterrence?
(2)   What are the differences between deterrence and other forms of
      influence relations among states?
(3)   What are the minimum requirements for a policy of deterrence
      to work?
(4)   How does a policy of deterrence affect the relations between the
      deterrer and the deterree?
(5)   Under what conditions would deterrence fail?

In order to explain the paradox of successful deterrence, it is instructive
to consider the common themes that run through the literature with
respect to these questions.

### When Is Deterrence Applied?

A state will contemplate a deterrence policy if it values some
aspects of a political or strategic status quo and wishes to preserve them.
A state that wishes to alter the status quo will usually resort to other
forms of influence. But the wish to preserve some essential characteristics of the status quo does not necessitate deterrence. The United States
does not need to threaten Canada or Mexico with retaliation if they violate U.S. territorial integrity. Neither Canada nor Mexico is perceived
to be interested in changing the existing hemispheric order. Deterrence
is contemplated if a state feels that other states are dissatisfied with
the existing status quo and are disposed to pursue its revision actively
in a manner that is harmful to the focal actor. Deterrence becomes
appealing when decision makers feel that, unless they clearly commit
themselves to the preservation of the status quo, there is a high

chance that the opponent will alter it in a manner that runs contrary to the national interest.

## Deterrence, Compellence, and Positive Inducement

Two other forms of influence are typically invoked by states in their dealings with other actors in the interstate system. One is a policy of positive inducement, and the other is a policy of compellence. Positive inducement entails influence through the promises of benefits. The object of positive inducement is to increase the inducee's estimate of the benefits associated with a certain behavior, without attempting to affect its estimate of the costs (or benefits) associated with other undesired behaviors. Positive inducement—to put it bluntly—is a form of bribe. It may include provision of economic and military aid with strings attached to it. The 1985 U.S. arms sale to Iran in exchange for a promise of the release of American hostages in Lebanon is a good example of such a policy. The difference between positive inducement and deterrence is that the former relies on promises and the latter relies on threats to influence an actor's behavior. In addition, deterrence policies are designed to induce inaction; their aim is to cause the opponent to refrain from doing what it might otherwise do—violate the status quo. Positive inducement may be aimed both at causing inaction and at causing some desirable action on the part of other states.

Compellence entails *actual* exercise of force and is designed to cause the opponent either to stop doing what it is doing or to do something that it does not want to do on its own. A state promises to *discontinue* using force if and when an opponent does what is expected of it. The ultimate form of compellence is war, as defined by Clausewitz (1966: 1): "War is an act of violence intended to compel our opponent to fulfill our will. Violence, that is to say, physical force . . . is, therefore, the means; the compulsory submission of our enemy is the ultimate object." Similar to positive inducement, compellence has a built-in element of promise: the discontinuation of violence once the opponent does what is required of it. There is no threat of violence, for the exercise of violence is already part of this policy. The major difference between compellence and deterrence is that the former seeks to reestablish the status quo ante, by forcing the opponent either to give up whatever advantages it had acquired through its past actions or to stop whatever it is doing at present, whereas deterrence is designed to prevent an opponent from taking some action before it begins (Schelling, 1966; George et al., 1972).

A state's reliance on one policy does not rule out reliance on another policy. In fact, the effectiveness of deterrence can be greatly enhanced if it is combined with a policy of positive inducement (George and Smoke, 1974; Lebow, 1985; Stein, 1987). The combination of deterrence with compellence is less common, but still possible. A state might use its forces to compel one opponent to increase the credibility of threats targeted at other opponents. Luttwak's (1976) analysis of the Masada siege is a case in point. The Roman empire—endowed only with a small army—had a real problem of dissuading external and internal "aggressors" without overextending itself. The Romans spent so much time and so many resources on capturing Masada, a fort of no strategic or political significance whatsoever, because they wanted to make of Masada an example of what happens to those who rebel and dare to stand up against the Roman empire. The same can be said about the brutal suppression of the subsequent Bar-Kochbah rebellion (Harkabi, 1983).

## Minimum Requirements for Effective Deterrence[3]

Three necessary—but by no means sufficient—requirements must be met by a policy of deterrence: communicability, credibility, and feasibility. *Communicability* means that the opponent should be aware of (1) the existence of a threat, (2) the conditions under which the threat would be carried out (though not necessarily how, when, and where punishment would be inflicted), and (3) the political, economic, and military consequences of carrying out the threat. Deterrence is unlikely to influence an opponent's behavior if the opponent does not know that a certain behavior on its part would result in severe punishment. Likewise, one cannot be deterred if one does not know which kind of actions are apt to invoke this kind of reaction. Finally, if a state does not know or understand the costs associated with a certain action, it is unlikely to be deterred. Communicability requires that the deterrer make these three issues clear to the actor to be deterred.

*Credibility* consists of two elements: capability and intent.[4] One must persuade the deterree that one has the means of carrying out the threat: you cannot persuade a Bedouin that you would throw rocks at him if you encounter him on a dune. Intent means that the opponent must be convinced that the deterrer has the will to carry out the threat. This usually entails one of two things: first, that it is in the interest of the deterrer to carry out its threat if the status quo is violated; second, that once such a violation has taken place, the deterrer's retaliation is automatic, either because it has no other viable response options or because it does not have complete control over its behavior. Credibility is a multiplicative function of capability and intent (Singer, 1984: 56–57). Capability is a tangible and measurable element of credible deterrence, but intent is more elusive and harder to demonstrate. This causes many problems in the design of deterrence and is the cause of potential paradoxes.

*Feasibility* refers to the extent to which a deterrer can respond to a given violation of the status quo in a specified manner. A deterrer may be seen as credible in general, in that it has both the capacity and will to inflict unacceptable damage upon an aggressor. Yet, there may be serious questions as to whether threats would actually be carried out when push comes to shove. The issue here is whether the means of destruction at the deterrer's disposal are suitable for a certain response, whether the domestic or international constraints under which the deterrer operates prohibit a timely response, or whether the violation of the status quo would be seen as sufficiently damaging to justify excess- ive retaliation that entails considerable damage to the deterrer itself. For example, a key criticism of the U.S. reliance on massive retaliation is that it limits the ability to respond to minor challenges of the status quo, namely, those that could not justify a massive nuclear strike on the Soviet Union. The Soviets could resort to tactics that, over time, would have the same effect as all-out aggression. Another case in point involves the ability of the Ford administration to respond in force to the violation of the 1973 Vietnam agreement. When the North Vietnamese invaded Cambodia in 1974 and South Vietnam in 1975, Kissinger and Ford requested Congress to allocate funds and direct military assistance to South Vietnam. The Congress refused this request, hence preventing the United States from meeting its commitment to South Vietnam.

Feasibility differs from credibility in that it is situation-specific rather than a general attribute of a policy of deterrence. While it is relatively easy to establish credibility in a general context, it might be extremely difficult to tailor responses to all possible violations of the status quo (George, 1984).

## Some Broader Implications of Deterrence

Taken together, these three aspects of deterrence render it work- able in principle. But the effects of deterrence on the relations between the deterrer and the deterree go far beyond the rules of the game that this policy purports to establish. Deterrence, in and of itself, does not reduce perceptions of hostility. Indeed, it is not designed to increase friendliness between the deterrer and the deterree. Deterrence is designed to prevent a state of economic, diplomatic, and ideological hostility to spill over to the military level. It is a preventive treatment, not a cure. Resolution of the conflict of interests that necessitates the resort to deterrence must come through some other means. While some maintain that continued stability due to effective deterrence may pacify a would-be aggressor over the long haul, I will try to demonstrate that this is not necessarily the case. In fact, effective deterrence might cause just the opposite: it may enhance and deepen the grievances the deterree has with respect to the status quo.

However, effective and prudent deterrence does stabilize the expectations of both states with respect to each other's future behavior.

The deterrer can reasonably expect that the adversary will refrain from violating the status quo militarily. If one is not fooled by the notion that successful deterrence makes the opponent less hostile over the long haul, then it is also reasonable to expect continued ideological, economic, and political competition in the future. Finally, effective deterrence subsumes that the deterree will attempt to alter the factors that render deterrence stable. Since the opponent cannot easily change the deterrer's commitment, the former will seek ways to reduce the costs of conflict initiation by changing the balance of military capabilities. The deterrer, on its part, is likely to work at maintaining its capabilities at a level that would make retaliation extremely painful to the opponent. Thus, deterrence is closely linked to arms races.

## Factors Affecting Deterrence Failure

The factors that contribute to effective deterrence are not necessarily the opposites of those that make deterrence fail. A well-communicated, credible, and feasible threat may still fail to deter an opponent. The deterrer may fail to understand the opponent's motives and intentions, and thus the threat may not address what the opponent has in mind. For example, a threat may be overly specific in terms of the kind of violation of the status quo that will be seen as constituting a *casus belli*, and this specificity allows for loopholes that the opponent interprets as permissible. On July 24, 1981—following several days of fierce shelling—Israel and the PLO (through U.S. mediation) agreed on a cease-fire along the Lebanon border. Israel threatened that renewed hostilities against Israeli citizens along the border would meet severe punishment. The PLO took this statement seriously, and displayed considerable restraint throughout the following year. Yet, since the PLO considered attacks on Israeli citizens in Europe as falling beyond the scope of the Israeli threat, its actions constituted violations of what Israel considered to be a cause of war.

Second, a deterrer may threaten action that is seen by it as sufficiently costly to the opponent and thereby thinks that the opponent would be deterred. However, although the opponent views the threat as credible, its assessment of the damage caused by the fulfillment of the threat may be seen as an acceptable price. Because the deterrer attempts to assess the cost-benefit calculus of the opponent, what the deterrer views as unacceptable damage to the opponent may be interpreted by the latter as acceptable risk (George and Smoke, 1974).[5]

Research on deterrence failures has taken two forms. The first type is the case study approach (George and Smoke, 1974; Maersheimer, 1983; Jervis et al., 1985). These studies explore in depth the logic underlying a certain deterrence policy, and then compare this logic to the logic and calculations of the opponent. In this manner, generalizations concerning discrepancies among the logic of threats, their implementation, and the decisions to violate the status quo are formed. These studies point out the importance of credible commitments that take into account the value system of the opponent. The second type of research on deterrence is quantitative analyses of multiple cases (Huth and Russett, 1984, 1988). Here, features that are taken to affect deterrence success or failure are systematically related to deterrence outcomes across a large number of cases in order to assess their impact on these outcomes.[6]

## A Theoretical Demonstration of the Paradox of Successful Deterrence

The paradox of successful deterrence assumes a carefully designed and implemented deterrence policy. The threat is communicable, credible, and feasible. The deterrer seems to understand the opponent's value system quite well and to tailor the threats to that value system. Threats are not excessive, nor do they imply overestimation of the opponent's assessment of the damage of war. The paradox of successful deterrence is not based on a critique of the assumption of rationality that is often raised in the literature. In fact, I assume that both the deterrer and the deterree are perfectly rational, that neither has strong suicidal urges, and that neither is an excessive risk-taker. I will show what it means that deterrence is successful from the perspective of the deterree, and why—despite the fact that it is taken seriously—deterrence might fail.[7]

Suppose a state $i$ contemplates some action designed to change a given strategic status quo, such as occupation of a territory, assertion of political control over some population, or support of a guerrilla group devoted to the overthrow of the regime of a neighboring state. Whether or not $i$ would actually initiate this action depends on whether it thinks that initiation is preferred to the uninterrupted continuation of the status quo. A typical analysis of the potential consequences of conflict initiation is given in Figure 3.1.

What is presented here is a situation that exists prior to the issuance of the deterrent threat by one of the actors in this conflict of interests. The calculus of conflict initiation is as follows. If we initiate conflict, our opponent $j$ may or may not retaliate. If it retaliates in force, a war will break out. We may either win the war or lose it. If we win the war, we get what we want, but we pay some price in terms of casualties, damage to our economy, destroyed equipment, and so forth. We also have to take into account some diplomatic damage that may be caused if world public opinion or important friends tag us as aggressors. These costs of war have to be subtracted from the potential political, territorial,

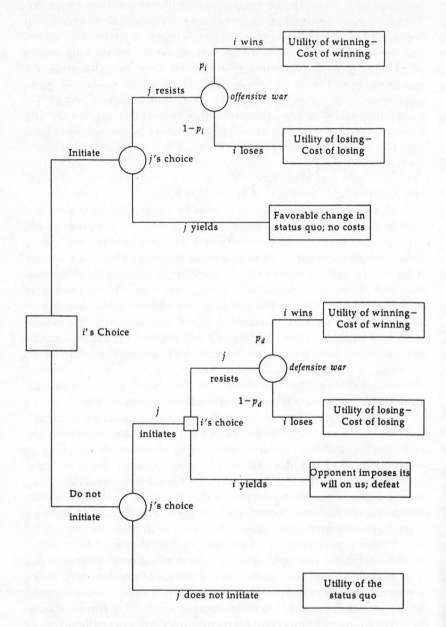

**Figure 3.1** The Initiator's Decision Problem

and economic benefits associated with military victory. However, victory is not guaranteed. If we lose the war, all of the costs mentioned above have to be added to the political damage due to the fact that the opponent will force us to do things that we do not want to do.

There is, however, some chance that once we challenge the opponent, it will back down and will not retaliate. In this case, we score an easy victory. We get what we want without having to fight for it, although we do have to pay some diplomatic price for committing what might be seen as an act of aggression. The probability terms represent the chances of certain events. The term $p_r$ stands for the chances of $j$ resisting our challenge. Of course, the probability that $j$ will not resist our challenge is $1 - p_r$. (The subscript $r$ is for *resist*.) The $p_i$ term stands for the probability that we beat $j$ in the war.

Let us now look at the lower part of Figure 3.1. If we do not attempt to violate the status quo, there is a chance, $p_j$, that $j$ will decide to challenge us. In this case, we will face a choice between defending ourselves and yielding to $j$'s demands. If we decide to resist, we are in war again. Note that this war is somewhat different from the war discussed above: the present war is a *defensive war*; the previous type was an *offensive war*.[8] If we win the defensive war, we gain our political objectives, but we pay the tangible costs of war: casualties, economic costs, and so forth. However, we are not blamed for having started this war. If we lose, we have to submit to $j$'s demands in addition to the tangible costs of war. On the other hand, if we do not initiate and neither does $j$, then the status quo—for whatever it's worth—is maintained. No costs of war are involved because there is no war.

How does deterrence come into this picture? The answer is deceptively simple: largely by the size of the probability and tangible costs terms in this calculus. For deterrence to be effective, the deterrer ($j$) must convince the would-be initiator ($i$) that the probability of resisting a challenge ($p_r$) approaches certainty—this is what is meant by *intent*. But this is not enough; the deterrer must render either the probability of victory for the initiator so low or the costs of victory so high as to make victory meaningless—this is accomplished by capability. Stated generally, effective deterrence is a policy that renders $i$'s initiation alternative far less attractive than the noninitiation alternative.[9]

Effective deterrence implies that $i$ is aware of the deterrent threat of state $j$ and is impressed by its credibility. This affects $i$'s assessment of the values of the various terms in this figure, as follows. We must assume that $j$ will almost certainly respond by force to a military challenge on $i$'s part. This means that $p_r$ approaches unity. Thus, $i$ might as well forget about getting what it wants without actually having to fight for it. Will $i$ win? Given the balance of military capabilities between $i$ and $j$, the answer is probably not. Even if $i$ gets lucky and wins eventually, a war against such a mighty opponent will take an extremely heavy toll. The political objectives do not justify such sacrifices. Thus, the initiation alternative has a negative expected utility, meaning that (1) if $i$ challenges the status quo, a war will erupt, and (2) this war will result in net losses.

However, this is only half of the story, and stopping it here will be extremely misleading. The other half of the initiation calculus—the option not to initiate—also requires close inspection. While the costs of conflict initiation far outweigh its benefits, it is possible that initiation would be seen as the least of all evils for two reasons; both of them constitute the two versions of the paradox of successful deterrence.

Deterrent threats must have an important property, which I will call *nonprovocability*. A sensible deterrence policy must convince the opponent that it will not be converted into compellence. The deterrer must make it clear that the deterree's decision to refrain from initiation will not be taken as a sign of weakness, and that the deterrer has no intention of exploiting the situation by trying to "roll back" the deterree. The deterree must be convinced that the probability of an unprovoked attack by the deterrer is very low (that is, $p_j$ approaches zero). Effective deterrence must be both credible and nonprovocable. But herein lies a paradox. Specifically, in some cases, the more credible the deterrent threat, the more provocable it is. By making war an extremely costly affair for a would-be initiator, deterrence might convince the deterree that because attack is costly for it, it is going to be a cheap and profitable venture for the deterrer. And that is why the deterree may be likely to defy the threat.

The second element of the paradox allows for a nonprovocable threat. The deterree believes that the deterrer will react with disarming force following a challenge, but the deterrer will not attack if the deterree does not. Here the paradox of successful deterrence concerns the value the would-be initiator attaches to the status quo. The calculus of conflict initiation given deterrence forces the deterree to choose between two evils: the present situation and a costly war. Effective deterrence implies that the deterree becomes convinced that a gloomy nonviolent future is preferable to a terrible war. Yet, this implies that the deterree must live within an environment it does not like very much, and that it must accept this environment not only as a temporary low period but as the shape of things in the future. Over time, the deterree will be increasingly frustrated, and threats of defeat that deterred it in the past might not deter it in the future. Here the paradox is that precisely because deterrence is effective, it frustrates an actor whose goals require changing some feature of the status quo. It also makes a deterrer, who thinks that deterrence is doing the job, less likely to understand the implications of increased frustration for the opponent. At some point, the opponent might be willing to fight a war even if it thinks the chances of winning are small and the costs are great. Even a bad war can sometimes be preferable to the perpetuation of a disastrous status quo.

## The Credibility-Provocability Trade-off

Suppose $i$ thinks that the balance of military capabilities is the single most important factor determining war outcomes. Assume that the balance of military capabilities is heavily in $j$'s favor. This could provide a solid basis for the deterree's belief that the chances of winning an offensive war are very low. If that is the case, then a defensive war might as well be a disaster for $i$. In addition to overwhelming military advantage in the first place, the deterrer $j$ will enjoy the advantages that are typically associated with a first strike: surprise, the ability to determine the timing and location of the initial stage of the war, and the ability to destroy a portion of $i$'s military capabilities with the first strike. It follows that if $i$ thinks that its probability of winning an offensive war is low, then it sees its probability of victory in a defensive war as approaching zero. And if $i$ thinks that the costs of an offensive war are enormous, it must see the costs of a defensive war as monumental. Thus, it may make more sense to give in to $j$ if it attempts to compel $i$ without fighting than to fight a losing battle that would probably end in submission to $j$'s demands after having suffered enormous casualties.[10]

As was hinted above, for deterrence to be effective, an actor must put itself in the opponent's shoes in order to determine which threats would deter, what kind of capabilities and what kind of commitments would be interpreted as credible by the opponent, and so forth. The deterree may reason as follows: if the deterrer knows that it can actually compel me to give up assets or other acquisitions without fighting, it would be foolish not to take advantage of its military superiority in order to press for more concessions. The reduced decision problem is given in Figure 3.2.

Here, $i$'s choice problem is considerably simpler than before, but it is a hardly pleasant decision: $i$'s leaders must choose between one kind of costly war and another because they think that if they do not violate the status quo, today's deterrer will become tomorrow's aggressor. And when tomorrow comes, $i$ might be put into a situation where it faces a choice between military and political devastation following war, and submission to $j$'s demands without a war. War now might become an extremely appealing option *even if the deterree is fairly certain that it is going to lose*. Credible deterrence can provoke an opponent by invoking fears that the deterrer will be stupid not to convert its overwhelming capabilities into a compelling challenge. The more effort a deterrer puts into establishing credibility, the more

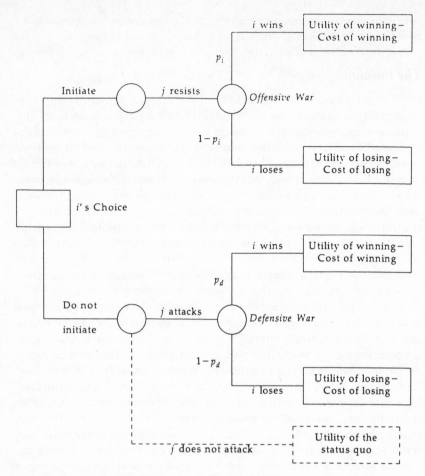

**Figure 3.2**  The Credibility-Provocability Tradeoff

costly an offensive war is going to be perceived by a deterree. But the factors that cause deterrent threats to be credible are those that make the threat more provocable as well. If credibility increases via more capability to inflict damage on a would-be aggressor, then the chances of winning an offensive war are reduced. But the chances of winning a defensive war will also decline because probability estimates of winning or losing a defensive war are based on the same factors as the probability of winning or losing an offensive one.[11] If credibility is established via increased resolve, chances are that the deterree will assign a higher probability estimate also to an attack by the deterrer in the absence of a provocation by the deterree. Since demonstrations of resolve have a built-in element of recklessness (Maoz, 1983), a good show of resolve might increase the deterree's threat perceptions. A preventive war in such cases becomes a real possibility.

## The Frustration Factor

Suppose the deterrer issues the threat in such a manner that it is both credible and nonprovocable. The would-be initiator may not like the status quo, but it likes the idea of losing a war even less. In this case, $i$ knows that a violation of the status quo is certain to invoke a decisive response by $j$, and thus lead to a costly war that is likely to result in $i$'s defeat. On the other hand, not initiating would almost certainly yield the territorial and political status quo that prevails at present. As much as $i$'s decision makers detest the prevailing status quo, they prefer it over the initiation of hostilities. However, what is true for an analysis of such a problem at one point in time is not necessarily true for the same analysis at a later point in time. In fact, assuming that a deterrence policy that worked at one point in time could be extended indefinitely is just as self-defeating as assuming that deterrence is inherently nonprovocable.

An actor who is committed to changing the status quo might become increasingly frustrated by effective deterrence because it is prevented from accomplishing its goals by fear. The more time passes without change in the status quo, the lower the utility such an actor would assign to the present situation.[12] Thus, when the deterrer does nothing to make the status quo more attractive to the would-be initiator, the expected utility of the status quo goes down over time; the status quo becomes less and less attractive. If the deterrer does not make sure that the expected utility of the initiation alternative is also reduced for the initiator, it is possible that a once-effective deterrence will no longer deter an opponent. The failure of deterrence at time $t + n$ is not due to defective application of this policy at the time span between $t$ and $t + (n - 1)$. Nor does deterrence fail *despite* its being effective. Rather, deterrence fails *because* it was effective. This is a no-win situation for the deterrer. If one applies deterrence in a way that is somehow defective, the status quo will be violated because defective deterrence creates loopholes that allow the deterree to do so. If the deterrer applies deterrence effectively, the status quo will be violated by an actor who is increasingly willing to take risks as its frustration with the frozen status quo increases over time.

Effective deterrence suggests that the expected utility of initiation of hostilities is lower than the expected utility that $i$ assigns to the status quo. Now, extending this calculus over a long period of time, assume that each period (month, year) that passes with an actor being in the same situation (status quo) reduces the expected utility of that situation by a certain factor. Let us assume—for the sake of simplicity—that this discount parameter, which we denote by $w$, is fixed. So, at the end of the first period, the utility of the status quo $u_q$ becomes $u_q - w$, while the expected utility of initiation remains $EU_i$. At the end of the second period, the utility of the status quo is $u_q - 2w$, and so forth. And while at the initial stage of deterrence such an actor was genuinely dissuaded from violating the status quo by the deterrent threat, at some later point in time the expected utility of war might become higher than the utility of the status quo. And this may come sooner, the more farsighted an actor is. Farsighted actors can figure out ahead of time how the discount parameter might affect the utility of the status quo before that has happened and incorporate it into their present calculations.

## Possible Objections

One may reasonably argue that what has been presented above does not satisfy the definition of paradoxes as a *causally induced* contradiction between expectations and outcomes. Both cases constitute defective applications of deterrence rather than paradoxes of successful deterrence. The credibility-provocability trade-off suggests that when an actor contemplates deterring an adversary, the possibility that threats will provoke the latter should be taken into account. Thus, one should design threats in a manner that maximizes their credibility and minimizes their provocability. The frustration factor suggests that, to maximize the effectiveness of deterrence, one should supplement it with measures of positive inducement that are designed to make the status quo more tolerable for the adversary. Alternatively, if the depreciation rate in the opponent's valuation of the status quo over time cannot be slowed down, an actor can affect the opponent's valuation of the initiation alternative by increasing the opponent's assessment of the probability of defeat or the opponent's assessment of the costs of defeat over time. Thus, while the utility that the opponent assigns to the status quo declines over time, so does the expected utility of war initiation. If the deterrer is careful not only to maintain the current balance of forces or the current balance of commitments, but actually to increase them in its own favor over time, however frustrated the opponent might become, deterrence will remain instrumental in maintaining the peace.

The question is this: Could deterrence policies be amended in such a way as to render them stable despite the problems raised in this chapter? If they could, then we really do not have a paradox of successful deterrence. However, if we show that a simple patch-up job on how deterrence is applied is not enough to escape these problems, then we do have genuine paradoxes.

To balance credibility and nonprovocability, the deterrer must convince a would-be aggressor that it would react if and *only* if the latter violates the status quo. A violation of the status quo would yield an automatic response, but the deterrer will not attempt to compel the opponent if it preserves the status quo. Some deterrence theorists (e.g., Schelling, 1966) have advocated basing one's credibility on an image of recklessness and irrationality, by convincing an opponent that one is not in full control of what one might do if the opponent chooses to violate the status quo. Response would be somehow automatic; one would be willing to inflict a lot of damage on the opponent, but would also be willing to suffer greatly in the process, for, clearly, war is not harmful only to one party.

But if one shows that one is willing to go to great lengths to deny an opponent victory or to punish it for violating the status quo,[13] is not one—at the same time—trying to convince the opponent that one is willing to fight a war? In effect, is this not telling the opponent that the expected utility of fighting a defensive war is higher than yielding to the opponent's challenge? If that is the case, how can one expect simultaneously to convince an opponent that the expected utility of an offensive war is lower than the expected utility of a defensive war? The more convincing one sounds on the first score, the more convincing one becomes on the second score. Why is that the case? Because the factors that affect the expected utility of war initiation are identical to those that affect the expected utility of retaliation to a first strike by the opponent.

To convince an opponent that deterrence is credible, an actor must show that it is better off fulfilling its threat of retaliation than accepting the change of the status quo.[14] This is typically translated into making the probability of the response high, by making the expected value of response high, or both. Looking at Figure 3.2 from the deterrer's perspective, we try to convince the opponent that the expected value of a defensive war is clearly higher for us than the value of yielding. But if the value of resistance is high, then the value of having the opponent give in to a war that we initiate is also high. And if the probability of our winning a defensive war is high, then the probability of our winning an offensive war is even higher. In short, it is impossible to deter by impressing an opponent that we assign a high expected value to a defensive war without also impressing the opponent that we possess an even higher expected value to war initiation. And vice versa: the minute we reduce the expected value of war initiation, we lower the expected value of deterrence, making it shaky due to low credibility.

Can we design deterrence policies that would reduce the opponent's incentives to violate the status quo without increasing the opponent's frustration? What about supplementing credible threats with positive inducements? If positive inducement could make the deterree value the status quo, there would be no need for deterrence. Substitute threats with bribes, and you accomplish the same goals. Make the status quo more attractive to the opponent and there will be no need to rely on military capabilities to maintain it.

The problem is that states find threats backed by military capabilities necessary because there is a real conflict of interest: the status quo they seek to preserve is seen as harmful by their opponents. The only way the opponent could be satisfied is by a change in the status quo that is seen as highly damaging to the deterrer. The struggle over the structure of the status quo is zero-sum: what is good for deterrer is bad for deterree and vice versa.[15] The need for deterrence arises because there are no real substitutes for threats backed by military capabilities. Had there been a viable compromise that would leave both parties highly satisfied with the status quo, there would have been no need for deterrence. Just as the would-be initiator faces the hard choice between accepting an unpleasant status quo and initiating a disastrous war, the deterrer faces the unpleasant need to preserve peace by threatening an extremely destructive war. Moreover, in some cases, initiating a policy of positive inducement may undermine the very foundations of deterrence. Concessions to some demands of the opponent can be interpreted as a sign that the deterrer is not strongly committed to preservation of the status quo. A revisionist state might conclude that, by growling at the status quo and making frustrated gestures, it can extract significant concessions from the deterrer.

The dilemma here is this: if deterrence must be backed by positive inducement to prevent its violation due to increased frustration, then it might be a bad idea in the first place. If these inducements entail concessions in terms of the structure and form of the status quo that deterrence is designed to preserve, then the most effective deterrence policy would have to be supplemented by the largest concessions, because it is likely to invoke the most frustration and hence generates a strong demand for positive inducement. Anomalously, the most effective deterrence is the one that is least likely to preserve the status quo. If it is supplemented by positive inducements, then the deterrer—of its own free will—gives to the deterree some of what the latter wants, hence rendering the commitment meaningless. If deterrence is not supplemented by positive inducement, the deterree will eventually choose to defy the threat and challenge the status quo due to increased frustration.

Is it possible to prevent the gradual erosion in the effectiveness of deterrence by making sure the initiator's fear of a war increases at the same rate as its frustration with the status quo? The answer is yes. It is definitely possible, at a price. The price is that increasing the magnitude of the promised retaliation makes the threat more provocable. If increased magnitude of retaliation requires more capabilities, then there is another price the deterree must pay: the tangible cost of armament. This raises two additional problems with deterrence; both concern the linkage between deterrence and arms races. First, the increased costs of armaments needed to prevent gradual erosion in credibility make deterrence an increasingly expensive policy for the deterrer. This might increase the deterrer's incentive to substitute deterrence by offense. If the deterree becomes aware of that, deterrence becomes more provocable as it becomes more expensive, and its ability to preserve the status quo decreases with each additional dollar spent on it. Second, deterrence might fail because it is intimately related to arms races. And, as we have seen, arms races can be as much a cause of unintended war as ineffective deterrence.

However one wants to turn it, we have here genuine problems of effective deterrence that are not easily solvable within the same framework in which they arise. It is difficult to devise threats that are both effective and nonprovocable. Likewise, it is not always possible to prevent the gradual erosion of deterrence over time due to the devaluation of the status quo in the eyes of the deterree. Neither positive inducements nor intensification of the threats and whatever makes them credible serve as feasible outlets. It seems that those who attempt to deter run a lot of risks: not only must they worry about how to make threats that will be seen by the opponent as credible and feasible, they also have to worry about how the opponent will react if it thinks that deterrence is effective. Let us see how the paradox of successful deterrence is explained by the rational and cognitive models.

## Explanations of the Paradox of Successful Deterrence

### The Rational Explanation

Why would rational people devise a policy that is designed to preserve peace when this policy might endanger peace? Rational people who rely on a policy of deterrence despite the risks associated with its successful implementation estimate the likelihood of war to be higher in the absence of deterrence than when it is well applied. Moreover, the danger to the status quo seems imminent and certain in the absence of effective deterrence; the risks associated with the violation of the status quo due to the provocability of deterrence or to the frustration of the deterree are remote and uncertain.

A fundamental premise of this theory is that without deterrence, the opponent is very likely to challenge the status quo. With deterrence, the opponent will refrain from challenging the status quo at present and might not challenge it in the future. If the opponent chooses to defy the deterrent threat in the future, the deterrer will have gained some time, at the very least. And to some decision makers, gaining time is a good enough reason for spending money and other resources on a policy. There is nothing irrational about it. Those who devise rational deterrence policies are aware that this policy is prone to a number of paradoxes, not only to the ones discussed in this chapter. Despite these problems, deterrence is seen as the least of all evils. There is, in fact, no real alternative to deterrence in many cases. States cannot guarantee a stable status quo by eliminating all suspects who have plans of changing it in an undesirable fashion. Nor can a state guarantee a status quo by placing its confidence in the good intentions of others. The risks that come with the policy—including those that stem from its successful application—are part of the whole and indivisible package.

In fact, reliance on deterrence is similar to buying a used car. If one had enough money one would have bought a new one, knowing that expenditures on repairs and replacement parts are lower. But because of the lack of funds, one is willing to accept the risks that go with a used car. A careful buyer examines the car before the deal is signed, but the risks and the potential repair expenses associated with a used car are still considerably higher than those associated with a car that has just come off the assembly line.

The paradoxes of successful deterrence tell us that there are risks associated with effective implementation of the policy in addition to the risks associated with its defective implementation. These paradoxes suggest that rational policy planning should take them into account and attempt to minimize them. Yet, much like strategic surprise in wars, deterrence failures are inevitable. The realistic goal of strategic planning should be to minimize the probability of these paradoxes, not to eliminate them.

## *The Cognitive Explanation*

The same logic that was invoked in the cognitive explanation of the para bellum paradox plays a role in the cognitive explanation of the paradox of successful deterrence. This is the idea that if an actor has benevolent intentions vis-à-vis other actors, others are expected to believe him or her. This idea explains why states that rely on deterrence take the nonprovocable nature of their threats for granted. Whether the threatened retaliation is massive or proportional to the severity of the challenge, designers of deterrence policies normally confine assurances of nonprovocability to verbal statements. However, verbal statements are rarely taken as indications of true intentions by opponents, especially if actions (such as excessive military spending) can be interpreted as contradicting those verbal assurances. It is doubtful that policymakers of status quo states are willing to take peaceful statements by opponents as sufficient evidence of intentions not to challenge the status quo. Yet, when an actor states that deterrence is limited only to prevention of challenges toward the status quo, and is not a pretest of a future policy of compellence, the actor expects to be believed.

Alternatively, it may well be that designers of deterrence policies are often very naive about the possible provocability of the deterrent threat.

> Statesmen often believe that they can design and implement a policy that exerts just the right amount of pressure on the other side—enough to restrain but not to lead the other to believe that an all-out conflict is inevitable. If the policy is slightly altered in one direction or the other, the argument goes, it will fail. In fact, such precision is usually beyond our grasp. . . . the impediments to a proper evaluation of the environment often defeat such attempts and, when decision makers are aware of these problems, limit the extent to which they are employed. (Jervis, 1985: 28)

It is interesting to note that these two cognitive principles contradict one another. Being naive about the ability to design just the right amount of threat implies that deterrers are aware of the possible provocability of deterrent threats but think that they can get around the problem through careful design of deterrence policies. The notion that sincere benevolence will be interpreted as such by the opponent suggests that decision makers are oblivious to the possibility that deterrent threats will be provocable. Yet, these principles may be complementary in an additive sense: some people are prone to make the first type of error; those who do not might be prone to the other type of error.

But these principles do not explain why planners of deterrence policy rarely worry about their opponent's frustration under conditions of successful deterrence. Here the cognitive explanation stresses what Jervis (1976, 1985) calls "unmotivated biases." These are inferential rules used by people to facilitate the tasks of interpreting incoming information and making predictions about the future. The opponent's intentions are an integral part of the calculus of deterrence: one must determine how much the opponent is committed to the revision of the status quo in order to design a deterrent threat that works. And this process of assessment of the opponent's intentions must be done on a continuous basis. The difficulty of assessing the opponent's intent forces decision makers to make some inferential leaps. Two of these are worth noting.

The first is the *availability* heuristic (Tversky and Kahneman, 1973). This principle suggests that people tend to overestimate events that they find easy to recall and underestimate events that are difficult to recall. The problem is that the availability of events in one's memory may have little to do with their actual frequency. In fact, some facts are more likely to be remembered because they are less frequent.

The second principle involves trying to infer one thing from another. When it is difficult to use some concept in an operational manner, it is generally useful to try to find some tangible substitutes for this concept. Prediction based on this substitute concept is then facilitated. In the case of deterrence, the estimation of the extent to which the opponent is committed to the change of the status quo is difficult for intelligence analysts, compared to the question of whether the opponent can successfully change the status quo. In the first case, one is trying to predict behavior from intentions; in the second case, prediction is based on the opponent's capabilities. If the deterrer infers the opponent's commitment from the latter's capabilities, substituting them for intentions, then as long as there is no apparent change in the opponent's capability the deterrer need not worry about the opponent's intentions. Whatever they are, if the opponent is rational, it knows that it cannot successfully challenge the status quo.

However, exclusive reliance on capability ratios as an estimate of the opponent's intention can be an extremely misleading practice. It presupposes that the opponent must be irrational to wage a war it cannot win. Thus, as long as the opponent is assumed rational, and as long as its capabilities exhibit marked inferiority, deterrence is taken to be effective. The deterrer assumes that if the opponent evaluates the costs of initiation to outweigh its benefits, then the opponent will stay put. Yet, an alternative that offers net losses to an actor might still be employed if other alternatives offer even higher losses. It is perfectly rational to wage a war that you might lose if the other policies available to you are seen as even more costly.

Another factor that makes reliance on military ratios a faulty basis for assessment of deterrence is that it often overshadows other areas of common interest between deterrer and deterree and tends to worsen hostilities. As mentioned above, the concern with a favorable military balance causes arms races. Arms races increase perceptions of hostility. Crises that break out under conditions of high hostility and mutual suspicion can easily be converted into unintended conflagrations.

Finally, a nation's reliance on deterrence as a major element in its foreign policy makes that nation extremely concerned about its reputation. Everything said or done by such a nation's leaders is determined by its decision makers in terms of how it will affect the nation's image and perceived resolve. Under such conditions, political leaders are reluctant to make concessions because they fear that these will be taken as a sign of weakness and will generate an impression that the risks of defying deterrent threats are not as high as might have been suspected. This preoccupation with an image of resolve makes it difficult to supplement deterrence with positive inducements.

## Failures of Successful Deterrence in History: Pearl Harbor and the 1973 War

The two cases discussed in this section represent, respectively, illustrations of the two types of paradoxes discussed above: the credibility-provocability trade-off and the frustration factor. The historical documentation of these cases is somewhat imbalanced: in each case, the deterrer's calculations and miscalculations are far more documented than the challenger's. In this section, I will attempt to demonstrate the following: (1) that the challenger viewed the deterrent threat as credible and the risks associated with war initiation as very high; (2) that the deterrent threat had a strong impact on the decision to initiate the war—effective deterrence served as a stimulating, rather than a constraining, factor in war decisions; and (3) that there were no major misperceptions involved in the decisions to initiate these wars—those that did take place were not of a nature that would have restrained the challenger's decision makers. Another aspect focuses on how deterrees who attempt to work around a credible deterrent threat overcome a major inferiority in military capabilities.

### The Making of Pearl Harbor[16]

The literature on the Japanese decision to attack the United States on December 7, 1941, is as diverse in its conclusions as it is wide in scope. Theses range from arguments focusing on the personal influence of crazy warmongers taking over the Japanese government to revisionist arguments that the Roosevelt administration provoked the Japanese into an attack in order to justify a war against Nazi Germany in Europe. My own interpretation of the attack on Pearl Harbor rests on evidence suggesting that the Japanese government made careful calculations while planning the attack, and that—in many respects—these calculations seem to have been highly rational (Russett, 1967, 1972: 42–46; Levi and Tetlock, 1980).

But in order to make the case for Pearl Harbor as a consequence of provocative deterrence, three things must be demonstrated: first, that the United States did attempt to deter the Japanese and the Japanese were well aware of this threat; second, that this threat was perceived as credible; and, third, that this threat provoked the Japanese into the attack. The third aspect is the most difficult to demonstrate.

Since 1931, Japan initiated a series of aggressive moves in East Asia, starting with the invasion of Manchuria and continuing with the invasion of China in 1936. There were strong indications that the Japanese intended to invade Indo-China. Whatever the hidden agenda of the Roosevelt administration, there is little doubt that the Japanese acts in the Far East were regarded with disdain. This was particularly the case with respect to the continued Japanese occupation of China. The American embargo on oil and other raw materials to Japan was a clear expression of the pressure the United States attempted to exert on the Japanese. Beyond these acts, the president made it clear that further aggression by the Japanese would be met with force. In his July 24, 1941, meeting with the Japanese ambassador, Nomura, President Roosevelt made the following statement:

> If Japan attempted to seize oil supplies by force in the Netherlands East Indies, the Dutch would, without the shadow of doubt, resist, the British would immediately come to their assistance, and, in view of our policy of assisting Great Britain, an exceedingly serious situation would immediately result. (Langer and Gleason, 1953: 650)

If this statement seems somewhat vague in terms of what kind of actions would be taken by the United States if Japan invaded the East Indies, or if the *casus belli* seems overly specific to make the deterrent attempt obvious, Roosevelt's statement of August 1941 makes this threat more pointed:

> If the Japanese government takes any further steps in pursuance of a policy . . . of military domination by force or threat of force of neighboring countries, the government of the United States will be compelled to take immediately any and all steps which it may deem necessary toward safeguarding the legitimate rights and interests of the United States and American nationals and toward insuring the safety and security of the United States. (Langer and Gleason, 1953: 695)

Both these statements and actions of the United States in the second half of 1941 (including the freezing of Japanese assets in the United States on July 26) made it clear that it was likely to respond in force to a Japanese attack on the East Indies or other initiatives in Southeast Asia. Indeed, this is precisely what the Japanese perceived. Togo Shigenori, the would-be foreign minister in the Tojo cabinet, pointed out following the freezing of the Japanese assets on July 26: "After the embargo, the Navy seemingly became gravely perturbed—not without reason—at the thought that the two-year supply of petroleum which it had accumulated would have to be drawn upon, and would gradually be exhausted. The Japanese-American negotiations now no longer revolved about the China problem alone, but brought the

United States and Japan into direct confrontation" (Shigenori, 1956: 51). From that time on, all the Japanese calculations involving change of the status quo in the region were based on a near certainty of U.S. intervention. The Japanese government, however, attempted to pacify the United States by a series of concessions to previous U.S. demands. On August 28, Japanese Premier Konoye sent a message to President Roosevelt proposing to withdraw all Japanese troops from Indo-China once "the China incident was settled or a 'just peace' was established in East Asia" (Toland, 1970: 94). In addition, this proposal included a complete acceptance of a set of four principles that had been put forth in April 1941 by U.S. Secretary of State Cordell Hall. The Japanese premier proposed a summit meeting with Roosevelt in order to resolve the major differences between the two states.

When the summit meeting fell through, a sense of unavoidable war began to set in on the Japanese government. The pressure of the American embargo on the Japanese army and economy was beginning to become unbearable. Joseph Grew, the American ambassador to Tokyo, sensed that the delaying tactics played in Washington with regard to the summit meeting would have dire consequences. He pointed out that "the Japanese army was capable of sudden and surprise action" and that in Japan "a national psychology of desperation develops into a determination to risk all" (quoted in Toland, 1970: 95). Indeed, on September 3, in a meeting between the chiefs of staff of the Japanese armed forces and the—still civilian—government, the former imposed an October 10 deadline on the successful conclusion of negotiations with the United States.

As it happened, the Japanese government was willing to pursue negotiations with the United States much beyond the October 10 deadline, making additional concessions to the United States. The Roosevelt administration, on the other hand, maintained a noncompromising posture throughout the negotiations. The last set of proposals was approved by the Japanese government on November 3, with the deadline for negotiations extended to December 1. The last Japanese proposal represented marked concessions, but was seen as unsatisfactory from the U.S. perspective. The fact that U.S. intelligence broke the Japanese diplomatic code was not of much help. Bad translations of cables sent by the Japanese government to their Washington representative Nomura served only to deepen the suspicion of the president and secretary of state regarding the sincerity of the Japanese proposals.

The position of the United States was taken by Japan's decision makers to imply that the United States intended to strangle Japan economically by the imposition of the embargo on oil and raw materials. The freezing of Japanese assets in the United States was seen as a direct provocation, representing America's fundamental hostility toward

Japan. Butow (1962: 320) describes the Japanese feelings: "They [the Japanese military commanders] did not deny that war was a gamble; they simply treated it as a gamble that had to be faced. If Japan took the chance, she might be defeated, but if she did not, she would be defeated anyway; therefore Japan should take the chance." When the Japanese submitted their last proposal (and the Americans knew very well that this *was* to be the last proposal) the United States not only rejected it, but presented an alternative proposal that was "far harsher than the American proposal made on June 21" (Toland, 1970: 143). If there had been a glimmer of hope in Japan that the United States was interested in reaching a political solution of the Asian problem, it now disappeared.

But perhaps the problem was not the failure of negotiations. Perhaps the Japanese attacked the United States because they sincerely believed they could get away with it. If that were the case, then the implication would be that deterrence failed because the United States failed to convince the Japanese government that an attack would result in unacceptable damage to Japan. However, the Japanese did not foresee the chances of victory to be particularly appealing. Nor did they entertain naive thoughts of a quick and easy victory. On August 1, the chief of staff of the Japanese navy submitted a position paper on the war option to the emperor. The bottom line was that war now was better than war in the future. He promised victory, but when asked whether Japan could accomplish a quick and decisive victory over the United States, his reply was decidedly negative. The emperor's reaction to this was: "Then, the war will be a desperate one" (Toland, 1970: 86).

Prior to the Japanese call for a summit meeting between Koyone and Roosevelt, the Japanese premier asked for an estimate of the probability of victory. Admiral Isokoro Yamamoto, commander in chief of the combined fleet, said that he foresaw success for a year or so, "but after that I am not at all sure" (quoted in Toland, 1970: 90). Finally, during the imperial conference of December 1, where the final decision to go to war was made, Admiral Nagano, speaking on behalf of both the army and the navy, said that "[regarding the outcome of the war] the real problem, however, was how Japan would fare if the war became a protracted one. There was no way of calculating definitely what the outcome would be, since a great deal would depend on various abstract as well as concrete factors, including the total national strength and developments in the world situation" (quoted in Butow, 1962: 362).

However mistaken the Japanese decision might seem in retrospect, it was not made lightly. Perhaps it was affected by many misperceptions, but it is fairly obvious that a misperception that a quick and easy victory could be accomplished was not one of them. Neither was this decision aided by a misperception regarding the degree to which the United States was committed to defense of the status quo in Southeast Asia. Had the

Japanese government thought it could make further strides in the area without confronting a violent U.S. response, it would have refrained from attacking Pearl Harbor. The fact that the Japanese decision for war was made only after the breakdown of the Hall-Nomura talks suggests that the Japanese government made some sincere effort to reach a peaceful resolution of the problem. The uncompromising position of the United States led the Japanese leaders to believe that war was inevitable, and therefore Japan would gain at least a temporary advantage from initiating it. All this is not meant to suggest that the Japanese made the right choice. It is merely intended to point out that this choice was not motivated by perceptions of opportunity or by illusions of quick and easy victory.

What is puzzling about the whole affair is that, even before making the last proposal to the Japanese, the Americans knew very well that the Japanese proposal (Proposal B) represented the last concession that Japan was willing to make. A rejection of that proposal meant a near certainty of war between the United States and Japan. The American response to Proposal B not only represented a flat rejection, but added fuel to the fire with a set of demands that amounted to a near ultimatum. This renders an interpretation of the whole affair in terms of deterrence theory somewhat tenuous. There are serious questions about rationality —not of the deterree, but of the deterrer. Specifically, it is unclear what purpose was being served by presenting to the Japanese a set of demands that would certainly eliminate any shred of hope of avoiding war.

This makes the revisionist theory of "back door to war" (e.g., Beard, 1948) very appealing. This theory asserts that Roosevelt wanted to involve the United States in the war in Europe but could not do so in the face of strong isolationist sentiments and without a good excuse. Throughout 1940 and 1941, he tried unsuccessfully to provoke Hitler into a naval attack on U.S. vessels that would serve as a pretext for a declaration of war on Germany. Hence, provoking the Japanese into an attack on the United States would have served as such a pretext. This explains the "moralistic" position adopted by the United States (Toland, 1970: 146–148). It also suggests that the intention was not to deter the Japanese. Rather, it was to enrage them, to push them into a corner.

There are many appealing things about this argument. It seems to account for a lot of puzzles in the bargaining process that preceded the outbreak of the war. If the United States had intended to provoke Japan into a "seemingly unprovoked" attack, it certainly succeeded, perhaps beyond its wildest dreams. But this argument serves only to suggest that one can use a deterrence policy in a manner that is clearly provocative. Toland's and Butow's perspectives, which emphasize blunders and misconceptions on the part of both sides, differ from the revisionist perspective focusing on deliberate provocation disguised as deterrence simply in the extent of Machiavellianism or cognitive fallibility they attribute to the decision makers, not in their interpretation of the paradox of deterrence.

## The Unlikely War: October 1973

Most analyses of the joint Egyptian–Syrian attack on Israel on October 6, 1973, focus on the strategic surprise accomplished by the initiators. These studies explore how it was possible for the Egyptians and Syrians to catch the Israelis by surprise. Only recently have scholars begun to explore the 1973 case as an example of colossal deterrence failure (Stein, 1985; Yaniv, 1986).

Nowhere in Israel's history has the reliance on a policy of deterrence been more pronounced than following the victory in the 1967 war. For the first time in its short history, the Israeli leadership felt secure within the new borders that the war had carved. Yaniv (1986: 171) summarizes the prevailing Israeli perception:

> The prevailing belief in Israel immediately after the war was predicated on a somewhat too simple set of assumptions. Egypt, in this view, remained hostile because as long as it continued to believe that Israel could be subdued by the force of arms, it was not adequately deterred. Having been so badly beaten, the Israelis imagined, the Egyptians would at least reappraise their strategic calculus. They would realize that vanquishing the Jewish state was a pipe dream, and they would have no alternative but to enter into meaningful negotiations. In the wistful words of Yigal Allon [then the Israeli minister of education and a leading strategic thinker] a year after the war, "the results of the Six Day War led to a moment of truth [in the Arab world] which may bring leaders, circles, and governments to the thought or even to the conclusion that Israel is an unalterable fact in the region, and that any attempt to assault it is bound to fail and to bring further calamities on the heads of the Arab states [Allon, 1970: 391]."

To a large extent, Israel's attack on June 5, 1967, was a result of what was perceived a deterrence failure. Nasser violated several *casi belli* one after another, and Israel had no choice but to retaliate. The blow they handed the Egyptians, Jordanians, and Syrians was seen by Israeli strategists as having established deterrence by example. Moreover, the fruit of victory, the acquisition of territorial depth all around Israel as a result of the war, was seen to render impossible any effort to eliminate Israel by force. Finally, the Six Day War significantly altered the balance of military capabilities between Israel and her neighbors. The air forces of Egypt, Syria, Jordan, and Iraq had been almost completely wiped out. The armies of these states suffered severe losses in material and personnel. The doctrines on which these armies had relied proved ineffective and strategic levels. Rebuilding the military hardware and software (i.e., reassessing doctrines at the tactical and strategic levels) would take a long time.

The Israelis were, therefore, fairly confident that the victory in 1967 and their continued military superiority would be sufficient to deter their opponents from launching an all-out military campaign. Although Israeli thinkers had no illusion that small-scale warfare could be deterred, they believed that no Arab state would attempt a general attack as long as the military balance had not altered dramatically in their favor. Allon's somewhat naive belief that the Arabs would come to the negotiating table on Israel's terms soon proved to be unfounded. But most Israelis believed that the strategic analysis regarding the impact of the war on Arab strategic calculus was fundamentally sound.

So strongly was this conception rooted in Israeli strategic thinking that it became the paradigm used by the Israeli military intelligence to assess Arab intentions. The so-called conception of the Israeli military intelligence was composed of two fundamental assumptions: (1) Syria would not attack Israel alone, and (2) Egypt would not attack Israel as long as it had not overcome its fundamental inferiority in aerial capability. The implication was simply that—no matter what tactical information suggested about the possibility of an Arab attack—as long as these conditions were not satisfied, the probability of an Arab attack was seen as "extremely low." The irony was that—contrary to conventional wisdom—these assumptions were fundamentally sound.[17] The credibility of Israeli deterrence was based on the seemingly overwhelming military advantage Israel had in general, and on its aerial superiority in particular. In terms of intent, Israel took care to demonstrate repeatedly to Egypt that it intended to take violation of the status quo seriously. And during the period between 1967 and 1970 it had ample opportunities to demonstrate resolve. Probably the clearest demonstration of resolve was the Israeli deep-penetration bombing of Egypt during 1970, which was designed to compel Egypt to accept a cease fire along the Suez canal (Shlaim and Tanter, 1978).

But did the Egyptians view the Israeli deterrent as credible? The answer seems to be an unequivocal yes. Stein's (1985) study of the Egyptian decisions in the 1969–1973 period suggests that Egyptian leaders had considered and rejected the option of a major attack on Israel three times before they finally accepted it. On each of these three occasions, the initiation of a limited war of attrition in 1969, in 1971, and in 1972, the Egyptian military and political leadership was both impressed by Israeli capabilities and convinced of Israel's resolve. In each of these decisions, it was clearly pointed out that nothing dramatic had changed in the balance of forces that might render an attack feasible from a military point of view.

What, then, had changed in 1973 that made Sadat change his mind about an attack? Before answering this question, it is important to examine why the Egyptian leadership repeatedly reconsidered the attack option over this period. The answer was the frustration with the outcome of the Six Day War and its fundamental ramifications for all aspects of life in Egypt.[18] With each passing day, Sadat felt that the Israeli occupation of the Sinai became more difficult to terminate. Israel's investment in military and civilian projects in the Sinai (including an increasingly important economic interest in the oil fields on the southwest end of the peninsula) intensified, and thus its resistance to returning it to Egypt became more pronounced. Egyptian passivity made it the laughingstock of the Arab world. Internally, the Egyptian economy was on the verge of bankruptcy. In 1969, military planners felt that they could put pressure on Israel through a war of attrition. Although the war proved very costly to Egypt, it was not without its accomplishments.[19] A major implication of the war was a realization that Egypt could use regional instability as a stimulant for superpower activity. Another implication was that antiaircraft missiles could be a good defensive substitute for a large and effective air force. Finally, the war demonstrated that the Egyptian society was able to incur high costs and was willing to accept modest achievements in warfare against Israel as a sign of progress. In fact, the war of attrition set an important precedent: it was the first Arab-Israeli war in which an Arab state was not flatly defeated by Israel.

While these achievements were significant, Sadat was not fooled into believing that Egypt could launch an effective attack on Israel. However, as time went by, Egyptian frustration increased markedly. And two events acted to increase significantly Sadat's determination to change the status quo. The first was the outright rejection, by the Israeli government, of his 1971 initiative for a limited settlement along the canal. This was seen by Sadat as a sign that Israel, on its own, has little or no incentive to make any concessions involving the Sinai. If it could be persuaded to make concessions, it would be due only to significant external pressure, especially from the United States. The other event was the intensification of détente, as evidenced by the 1972 SALT I treaty, Nixon's trip to China, and the 1973 peace agreement on Vietnam. This change in the relations between the superpowers suggested that it was unlikely that the United States would be motivated to exert any pressure on Israel, unless it was convinced that the lack of a settlement in the Middle East created a potentially explosive situation likely to endanger détente and to create a major superpower crisis. What détente had in store for Egypt was a promise of perpetuating the Israeli hold over the Sinai, and its legitimization by default. Détente implied that the superpowers had implicitly agreed not only to recognize each other's spheres of influence, but also to do their utmost to prevent the escalation of regional conflicts in "gray" areas into a superpower crisis. The implication was that both the United States and the Soviet Union had agreed not to awake the dormant conflict in the Middle East.

Wars—especially those that result from careful calculations—are fought to accomplish several goals, not just one. However, there is almost always one goal that becomes central enough to make decision makers think that it is worthwhile to risk all on it. From Sadat's perspective, this goal was not to regain Egyptian honor, nor was it the return of the Sinai. Rather, the major goal of the war was "to catch détente by its tail" (Heikal, 1975: 210). Sadat initiated the war not because he thought he could lead Egypt to a major military victory, but because he wanted to spark a superpower crisis that would lead to a greater and more effective superpower involvement in a Mideast settlement. In 1973 Sadat felt that Egypt was running out of time, and if something drastic was not done to lead to intense U.S. pressure on Israel, the Sinai would be lost forever. For that purpose he was willing to risk a great deal, by going to war against military odds that suggested that the likelihood of success was very low.

It was the increase in Egyptian frustration, not a change in their estimates of capabilities, as Stein (1985: 58) would have us believe, that tipped the balance toward war. There was no significant—qualitative or quantitative—change in the military balance in the Middle East in 1973 compared to the previous two years. The decision for war was made despite the overwhelming Israeli military superiority, not because of a sudden belief that Egypt had found a magic formula for victory.[20] Once Sadat came to the conclusion that war was the best way to bring about diplomatic movement, the operational problem was how to overcome Egypt's fundamental inferiority in military capabilities. This was a tactical problem, to which the Egyptian military command found a threefold solution: limited military objectives for the war, devising countermeasures for the superior Israeli air and armored forces, and attempting to strike by surprise (Shazli, 1980: 17–19).

The limited military objective (occupation of a narrow—seven to eight miles—strip east of the Suez canal by Egypt, and occupation of a similar strip in the Golan Heights by the Syrians) was designed to assure a short war that would not enable the Israelis to recover and counterattack while Egypt and Syria faced extended lines of defense. It also maximized the chances that the war could be presented internally as a major military achievement worthy of the enormous sacrifice.[21] To have a shot at a successful crossing of the canal, the Egyptians had to overcome the Israeli aerial superiority, and they had to be assured that their forces east of the Suez canal would not be wiped out by the Israeli armor.

Instead of trying to beat the Israelis at their own game, Egyptian strategists devised a new one. Instead of more or better planes, the

Egyptians relied on antiaircraft missile defense. The response to Israel's superior armored force was a dense line of antitank missiles that would be launched by infantry. Failing to see these developments in Egyptian tactical thinking, Israel's estimate of the balance of forces—which was a key component in its belief that Egypt was not ready for an attack—remained unchanged. Finally, a surprise attack was the best of all worlds from the Egyptian perspective, and Egypt certainly mounted a major deception campaign (Handel, 1976). Tactics, as Clausewitz (1966) and, more recently, Luttwak (1987: 179) have pointed out, are strongly affected by strategic choices. In this case the strategy of war was fundamentally political.

Yaniv's (1986: 183) analysis of the Israeli calculus suggests that

> the 1967 war and its outcome put to the test two principal Israeli theses: first, that if only Israel had a chance to deliver a decisive defeat to the Arabs, the latter would come round to the idea that peace was in their interest; and second, that Israel's main source of weakness (in addition to its small demographic size) was the lack of strategic depth. If only Israel had natural—that is, tactically defensible—boundaries, and if only it had enough strategic depth to ensure that no Arab surprise attack could ever deal it an irremediable defeat, the Arabs' incentive for starting wars would be so greatly diminished that peace would again become a realistic proposition.

By 1971, the Israelis must have recognized the growing Egyptian frustration with the prevailing status quo. Sadat made several heroic speeches in which he argued that 1971 (and then 1972) would be the "year of decision." Why did the Israelis resist Sadat's initiative of a partial settlement? The Israeli government interpreted Sadat's proposal as a diplomatic maneuver lacking any sincerity. Its main aim was to get around Israeli conditions for peace: direct negotiations and full peace in exchange for territories. Giving in to such a proposal, or even seriously considering it, would have meant relinquishing a commitment to a set of principles that was seen as very reasonable. It would have been interpreted as a sign of weakness, and, as it was seen by the Golda Meir cabinet, abandoning the principle of direct negotiation would invite increased external pressures on Israel (Dayan, 1976; Gazit, 1986).[22]

The frustration variant of the paradox of successful deterrence requires that we observe four things in the empirical case: first, that deterrence was in effect and that the deterree knew that; second, that the deterree had no doubt that the deterrer was both willing to inflict and capable of inflicting a heavy blow if the status quo were violated; third, that the deterree was willing to take risks at time $t$ that it had been unwilling to take at $t - 1$, $t - 2$, and so forth; and, fourth, that the deterree's decision process was not inconsistent with some rational calculation. We have seen that the first three conditions were clearly satisfied in this case. The question is whether Sadat's decision to violate the status quo despite the seemingly insurmountable risks was indeed a rational one. According to Stein (1985), both the decisions to preserve the status quo in 1971 and 1972 and the decision for war in 1973 were inconsistent with a rational model. Since the present interpretation differs from Stein's analysis, it is instructive to explain why I think that Sadat's decision to initiate the 1973 war was fundamentally rational.[23]

Stein's analysis of the Israeli and Egyptian decisions is based on an implicit premise that, had the deterrer and deterree been rational, deterrence should have worked. However, the problem was that deterrence failed precisely *because* the deterree was fundamentally rational. When assessing the costs and benefits associated with action versus inaction in 1971, Sadat felt that the chances of actually getting the United States to put pressure on Israel to move toward a diplomatic settlement were low. Sadat knew that Nixon could not afford to withhold support from Israel if he was going to secure the Jewish vote in the 1972 election. The Vietnam negotiations were still taking place, with the United States involved in massive bombing of North Vietnam. Getting it to invest in another negotiation process would be very difficult. Détente was not an obvious process at that point in time. Sadat also had some hope for a limited settlement along the Suez canal. Thus, the status quo was not that terrifying and the attack option was seen as potentially disastrous. It was only obvious that, in making political argumentation, Sadat would state the drawbacks of the attack option (all of which were military in nature) while emphasizing both the drawback and least-of-all-evils nature of the status quo option. However, Sadat had to deal with a reluctant general staff that was very much against the idea of war (Sadat, 1978; Heikal, 1975).

In 1972, not much had changed in the military capabilities sphere, but two changes had taken place: the reshuffling of the military command in Egypt, and the intensification of détente. The decision process at that point was not as simple as a dichotomous choice between some form of attack and lack of action. There were serious deliberations on whether to attack now or to attack later. The decision made at that point was to postpone an attack until 1973. It was predicated on two factors. The first was that such an attack required a general staff that had more than a few months' experience. The other was that the July decision regarding the dismissal of the Soviet advisers in Egypt created logistical problems with weapon systems (especially with heavy bridging equipment that was required for the canal crossing). In addition, considerable planning was required in terms of defining the operational details of the attack, coordination with the Syrians, and so forth. The 1973 decision was, to a large extent, an operational decision that entailed an approval of a well-defined and well-calculated plan. That misestimation did occur (especially overestimation of the costs of attack) is true. It does not follow, however, that the decision to attack was not a rational one. Thus, the fourth characteristic of the paradox of deterrence has been demonstrated.

## Conclusion:
## Some Possible Escapes from the Paradoxes

Schelling (1963, 1966) discusses another problem inherent in deterrence. Actors who feel that the credibility of their commitment to defend some status quo is not all that high might irrevocably commit themselves to a policy that—on the face of it—appears quite irrational. If this irrevocable commitment is taken seriously by the opponent, the latter might be deterred. Hence, an irrational action, voluntary commitment to a course of action that seems inferior, and surrender of options yields results that are superior to those that would have been accomplished if the rational option were employed. Schelling's commitment strategy requires an automated response to a specific violation of a status quo by the opponent. This presumably creates reputation of resolve. But, as noted above, this might be a cause of deterrence failure because of its inherent provocative implications.

However, self-binding commitments can work both ways. More recently, it was shown that self-binding commitments can be used to induce cooperative responses by creating incentives for agreement for both actors (Maoz and Felsenthal, 1987). One of the possible outlets from the credibility-provocability trade-off is precisely of that sort. An actor can willingly surrender not only the option of nonretaliation if the opponent violates the status quo; it can also surrender the option of attacking the opponent if the latter does not attack. This can be done in a variety of ways, none of which affects the credibility of the deterrent threat. One way is that of increasing the intangible costs of aggression by using third-party actors as a buffer between the deterrer's and the deterree's forces. This was the arrangement that characterized the diplomatic settlement of the Sinai war of 1956 in the Middle East, as well as the arrangement that was implemented in the Sinai desert and the Golan Heights following the 1973 war. In both cases, the unintended implication of this setup was to render the Israeli deterrent threat clearly nonprovocable.

To convert deterrence into compellence, one would have to use force. To use force, one must be willing to accept diplomatic or other sanctions by third parties. Sanctions may be seen as more or less acceptable depending on how severe they are, who takes part in applying them, how widespread they are, and how dependent one is on those third parties. Putting an international force between a deterrer and a deterree means that if deterrer wishes to attack the deterree, it may have to make sure that these forces are first removed, or run the risk of hurting people of friendly states. If the deterrer is dependent on the goodwill and other amenities supplied by these good states, a convincing case can be made that the presence of the international force acts as a deterrent to the deterrer. Even if the deterrer wanted to use its military advantage to roll back the deterree, it cannot do so without suffering tremendously in the process.[24]

The advantage of using international forces as a buffer between deterrer and deterree is that they reduce the possibility of deterrence failure due to miscommunication and miscalculation. Such forces might reduce the possibility that the deterree would resort to aggression because of a belief that it can surprise the deterrer. They also impose an additional cost on violation of the status quo by the deterree. Finally, international buffer forces create a clear notion of what would constitute a violation of the status quo. By placing them in a geographically defined buffer zone, it is implied that any infringement of this zone would lead to a clash with the international force. This makes for a well-defined *casus belli* not only for the protagonists but also for the third-party nations whose forces are part of the international buffer force.

But, as we have seen in the case studies, this does not resolve the other type of paradox of deterrence. In fact, the imposition of international buffer forces on the deterree might lead to a more rapid deterioration of the effectiveness of deterrence by increasing the perception of helplessness of the deterree. The problem of making the status quo more acceptable to the deterree requires going beyond military solutions of the conflict of interests. It requires finding some ways of actively changing the valuation of the status quo by the deterree. The notion of reassurance (Stein, 1987) comes to mind. Reassurance could be interpreted in two ways. One is to reassure the deterree that deterrence will not be converted into compellence. One way of accomplishing reassurance in this sense was discussed above. Another way of reassuring the opponent is to apply some form of positive inducement that would increase its willingness to live with the status quo. For example, critics of Israeli policies in the 1970–1973 period argued that had Israel been willing to negotiate with Sadat in 1971, it is possible that Sadat would not have been pushed to war in 1973. The 1973 case study suggests that this argument is not altogether naive.

Such an argument of reassurance presupposes that a cooperative solution exists that renders deterrence a policy that is necessary only on the margin. There exists an implicit notion that the conflict of interests could be resolved if parties were to search hard enough for political solutions. If that is the case, then presumably the parties can find a status quo that is mutually acceptable, one that both parties are actually willing to live with, one that represents for both more than the least of all evils. Deterrence is required in such a case only to add punch and an aura of credibility to a political settlement, but it is not seen as the primary motivator of the relations among actors.

Of course, the difficulty with this prescription is twofold. First, if actors were rational, then the resort to deterrence would come only if and when it is realized that no further concessions on the status quo could be made without seriously endangering the deterrer's interests. The typical argument is this: "We have gone as far as we could in attempting to pacify the opponent. Any further concession will directly damage us. If the opponent is unwilling to live with what we offer, our only alternative is to force it to live with it out of fear of the consequences of violating the status quo." Second, concessions on the status quo are not independent of perceptions of commitments. If one is willing to make concessions on the status quo, then one's willingness to defend it might be questioned. Concessions might be interpreted as a sign of weak resolve. Seen in such a light, a deterrer might be reluctant to make concessions not because there is nothing to talk about, but because it fears that concessions would be taken as a sign of weakness, thereby endangering deterrence.

I can see no quick and easy way out of the paradox of successful deterrence when the deterrer thinks that it cannot afford to negotiate over the status quo because it represents a minimum that it can live with. That was pretty much the Israeli position prior to 1967. The Israelis believed that they could not afford to make any territorial compromises, because they had already gone as far as they could. The only thing to point out in such a case is that actors relying on deterrence must be aware that the opponent will become increasingly dissatisfied with the status quo, and deterrence will fail at some point in the future no matter how well it is applied. The only beneficial side effect of this is that such an awareness might make an actor more attuned to new political solutions of the conflict of interests that arise as time goes by. In the other case, there are ways to reduce the deterrer's fears that concessions would be taken as a sign of weakening commitment. An actor can make a concession on an issue it considers important while simultaneously tying itself to the new status quo by, for example, surrendering its option of more concessions or nonresistance. Again, the principle seems feasible; operational manifestations are more difficult to apply.

The bottom line of this chapter is that one need not challenge the fundamental assumptions of deterrence theory (principally the rationality assumption) in order to find problems with the policy. Likewise, one need not invoke rationality or reasonableness in order to escape the seemingly self-defeating nature of this policy. Deterrence, like other forms of international influence, is a policy that has its balance sheet of pros and cons. Like other forms of influence strategies, deterrence has its limits and inherent difficulties. And finally, deterrence is susceptible to paradoxes. Since it is based on linear reasoning, deterrence might be defeated by the very same logic it seeks to promote.

## Notes

1   See, for example, Luttwak's (1976) analysis of the practice of deterrence by the Roman empire. For more recent cases of conventional deterrence, see Quester (1966), Huth and Russett (1984), Maersheimer (1983), and Yaniv (1986).

2   Some good reviews of the theory can be found in Morgan (1977), George and Smoke (1974), and Jervis (1979, 1984, 1985). For studies that focus on conventional deterrence and on how it differs from the nuclear version, see Maersheimer (1983) and Yaniv (1986). For studies focusing on the conditions for deterrence failure, see George and Smoke (1974), Huth and Russett (1984), and Jervis et al., 1985).

3   It must be noted that it is extremely difficult—if not impossible—to develop a falsifiable statement on such factors. The success of deterrence is measured in negative terms: whether the opponent refrained from a given action. This requires one to determine whether the lack of action was indeed a consequence of successful deterrence or of the fact that the opponent had no intention of violating the status quo anyway. Even states that refrain from action by effective deterrence are unlikely to admit it because they think they would appear weak in the eyes of some other actors as well as in the eyes of the deterrer.

4   One may wish to call these guns and guts, respectively.

5   The opposite is also possible. That is, the deterrer inflates the promised punishment so as to be sure that the damage to the opponent will be excessive. This is intended to prevent violation of the status quo due to perceptions of low risks. However, inflation of threats may invoke fears that deterrence will be transformed to compellence, thereby creating incentives for preventive strikes.

6   See Levy (1988b) for a review of quantitative studies of deterrence. Achen and Snidal (1989) provide a review and critique of the case studies of deterrence.

7   A more technical treatment of these issues is given in Maoz (1984a, 1985b).

8   As Jervis (1978) and J. S. Snyder (1984) have argued, both politicians and generals make a lot of distinctions between offense and defense in world politics. Sometimes technology and/or strategy may suggest that offense has the advantage; in other cases, defense is seen to have the advantage. Paret et al. (1986) review the main ideas of military strategists on these issues over the last 200 years. In the original paper, I have assumed that decision makers generally favor offensive over defensive postures (Maoz, 1985b). This implies that strategists view the probability of victory in a war that they initiate as higher than the probability of victory in wars initiated by their opponents. The reasons for this perception are discussed at length in that paper (especially pp. 88-97). It is, however,

very difficult to distinguish between offensive and defensive strategies or between technologies that provide clear advantages to offensive strategies or to defensive ones (Levy, 1984).

9   Obviously, effective deterrence implies rendering the *expected utility* of initiation lower than the *expected utility* of noninitiation. Since expected utility is a sum of products of probabilities and utilities, this can be accomplished in several ways. The deterrer can render the costs of war for a deterree high and the deterree's probability of winning a war very low. In that case, even if $p_r$ is relatively low, deterrence might still be effective. Or, alternatively, if $p_i$ is not very low, then deterrer must make $p_r$ sufficiently high to accomplish the same thing.

10  See Maoz (1985b: 80–82) for a formal proof of the proposition that yielding without war might be preferred to yielding with war regardless of whether or not the opponent prefers fighting over the status quo.

11  This is particularly true when strategists believe that offense has a clear advantage over defense. Then, the deterree can be deterred only if it believes that, despite this advantage, the deterrer can repel an attack while inflicting unacceptable damage on the initiator. This can happen only if the deterrer's capabilities allow it to overcome any temporary inferiority caused by its becoming the target of an offensive by the deterree. But offensive advantages might work both ways. If the deterrer's capabilities were so formidable as to enable it to recover from a first strike and defeat the deterree, then surely they would be more than sufficient for an effective first strike, leading to a quick and easy victory.

12  The analogy is what economists refer to as "depreciation of usable resources." For example, a car that is driven extensively loses its value at a faster rate than a car that is rarely driven.

13  Snyder (1961) distinguishes between two types of deterrence: deterrence by denial and deterrence by punishment. The former consists of attempting to deter the opponent through a threat to deny the attainment of its goals. The latter consists of a threat of punishing aggression in addition to denial of goal attainment. See also Yaniv (1986: 9–11).

14  A related deterrence paradox deals with the trade-off between the magnitude of the threatened action and its believability. See Brams (1985) for an analysis and resolution of this trade-off and Maydole (1987) for a logical discussion. This, however, is not part of the paradoxes discussed herein.

15  This is not to suggest that the entire deterrence game is zero-sum. It is not. In fact, the reason that deterrence is even contemplated is that the deterrer reasons that both parties find war a bad idea, and that both stand to gain from the status quo more than they stand to gain from war. Game theorists who have studied superpower deterrence have disagreed on the nature of the deterrence game, but this disagreement reflects only the ranking of the war outcome relative to the unilateral violation of deterrence. See Brams (1985) and Zagare (1987).

16  The analysis of deterrence in 1941 is based on Feis (1950), Russett (1967, 1972), Toland (1970), Butow (1962), and Borg and Okamoto (1973).

17  Virtually everyone who wrote on the surprise of 1973 singles out this conception as being flawed (e.g., Handel, 1976; Ben-Zvi, 1976; Shlaim, 1976; Lanir, 1983; Brecher, 1980; Stein, 1985; Yaniv, 1986). The fact of the matter is that the Israeli intelligence analysts were not misled by the conception. Rather, they failed to see that these two conditions were met in October of 1973.

18  See, for example, Ajami (1981) and Harkabi (1969), on how Arab intel-
    lectuals interpreted the implications of the 1967 defeat for Arab society.

19  The present analysis differs with Stein's (1985: 44–45) interpretation of
    the rationality of the Egyptian decisions. In the case of the 1969 decision
    to initiate the war of attrition, Stein takes the overestimates of Israeli
    casualties and the logical inconsistencies in the analysis of costs and
    benefits to provide evidence of wishful thinking. This, she claims, was
    a result of consistency maintenance in the face of acute value conflict.
    However, it seems more plausible that this was a result of a determination
    to face and to accept hard value trade-offs—which is one of the most
    potent indicators of rational decision making. The Egyptian leadership
    was strongly motivated to put pressure on Israel in order to change the
    status quo, but was aware that it could not do so via a frontal attack. The
    calculus of the war of attrition was fundamentally rooted in the Egyptian
    goals: Egypt calculated correctly that Israel could not afford to change
    the stationary war of attrition into a mobile war in which they had an
    advantage, and that a war of attrition would hurt domestic morale in Israel
    and would lead to diplomatic and domestic pressure on Israel to make
    concessions. For that purpose, they were willing to incur high costs. Stein
    points out correctly that Egyptian planners underestimated Israel's ability
    to escalate warfare into the air, but once this did happen, they realized that
    they could convert this into a diplomatic gain. Indeed, the escalation of
    the warfare is what brought about active diplomacy by the superpowers to
    terminate hostilities (Shlaim and Tanter, 1978; Brecher, 1974: 454–517).

20  Incidentally, this is acknowledged by Stein (1987: 8), contrary to her
    previous argument that what made Sadat decide on an attack in 1973
    was a change in the Egyptian perception of capabilities. She does assert,
    however, that Sadat estimated the Egyptian capabilities to have peaked
    in 1973 and expected them to decline in the future (p. 9). This might be
    relevant information in that it may account for the timing of the Egyptian
    attack, not for why it was decided upon.

21  Sadat (1978) writes that he had expected 50,000 Egyptian casualties only
    during the canal crossing.

22  The Israelis were not completely unaware of the growing level of frustra-
    tion with the status quo experienced by Egypt. Dayan had been virtually
    the only cabinet member who advocated serious consideration of Sadat's
    1971 offer. His argument was based on Sadat's growing impatience with
    the status quo and the belief that Israel could, at little cost, reach some
    sort of *modus vivendi* with Egypt short of a full-scale peace.

23  A more detailed analysis of the Egyptian calculus of war initiation is given
    in Maoz (1989: ch. 8).

24  Another resolution of the paradox is through the creation of domestic
    sanctions on compellence. An actor might persuade an opponent that
    it will not initiate because initiation would automatically lead to the
    overthrow of the government. However, the obvious problem with this
    strategy is that it does affect the credibility of deterrence. The opponent
    might be led to believe that the domestic constraints on aggression extend
    to domestic constraints on violent resistance to minor violations of the
    status quo, hence resulting in deterrence failure.

# 4

# Wars That Nobody Wanted and Everybody Tried to Prevent: The Paradox of Crisis Escalation

What a strange game! The only winning move is not to play.
(From the movie *War Games*.)

Many of us have been in situations in which we have confronted an opponent and, although both wanted to avoid a fight, each wanted the other to be the first to blink. In many cases, such confrontations end in fights that the parties involved wanted to avoid but could not prevent because no one wanted to be the first to back down. This, in a nutshell, is the paradox of crisis escalation. This chapter is about nations that get into confrontations because they believe they can control the course as well as the consequences of their actions. However, once a crisis is under way, it turns out that both parties lose control, not only over their opponents' actions, but over their own as well. The irony is that even though each party is aware of its eroding ability to control the escalatory sequence, they find it difficult, if not impossible, to prevent the final crossing of what Deutsch (1969) calls "the point of no return in the progression toward war."

Obviously, the first reaction to such encounters is that something has gone terribly wrong in the national decision-making process. Temporary insanity is invoked as a typical explanation. Other explanations about organizational inertia (Levy, 1986) and primacy of military planning over political discretion (J. S. Snyder, 1984) suggest that such crises start as political duels of will, but are converted into struggles between bureaucratic organizations that assume lives of their own. The paradox of crisis escalation is not the product of organizations gone wild, nor is it the consequence of politicians gone mad or stupid. Rather, crises may escalate precisely because politicians are reasonable and prudent and precisely because they do all in their power to avoid confrontation. In a system of interactions where what one gets depends as much on what other actors do as on what one does, things may get out of hand precisely *because* each side tries to prevent them from getting out of hand.

Previous chapters examined some of the underlying causes of war. Both arms races and deterrence policies serve to set the stage for violent conflagrations, but they do not accompany the troops to the battlefield (Choucri and North, 1975). The present chapter explores the relationships between crises and war. Both arms races and deterrence define important aspects of the calculations of states during international crises. They reside in people's minds when crisis decisions are made. They can render crises among states more hostile and more intense than crises that do not erupt in an environment of intense hostility and fundamental suspicion and mistrust. But deterrence and arms races—in and of themselves—do not determine the likelihood that a crisis, once it erupts, will lead to war. Lebow (1981: 334) puts it as follows:

> Our investigation of acute international crisis has demonstrated that immediate causes of war can exercise an important and even decisive influence on the course of a conflict. Acute international crises were found to be significant in two respects. They can determine whether war breaks out or peace is maintained. They can also intensify or ameliorate the underlying sources of conflict in cases where war is avoided.

Crises arise over issues that are largely operational, if not tangible. Each party in a crisis makes specific demands of its opponent, and the opponents respond to these demands with demands of their own. It is the conduct of crisis that has the most immediate bearing on its outcome. While speeding and failure to observe pertinent road signs increase the likelihood of a traffic accident, it is the ability of the reckless driver to observe an imminent catastrophe and react to this situation in a proper fashion that determines—in the final analysis—if he or she will avert a head-on collision. Indeed, one of the common analogies used to describe these situations is the game of Chicken, which was a favorite test of courage among teenagers in the late 1950s. This game captures some of the major dilemmas that confront decision makers during crises. Before going into the paradox, a brief discussion of the extensive literature on international crises and crisis management is in order.

## Research on International Crisis

Crises are crucial turning points in the relations among states, those points that determine if subsequent relations will be more or less hostile than before. About 89 percent of all wars in the 1816–1987 period erupted after an exchange of threats and other (violent or nonviolent) shows of military force. During that period, each of the participants had been well aware (or should have been aware, given the information available to it at the time) that there was a distinct possibility of war (Maoz, 1982a: 62).[1] There are many definitions of crisis. A reasonable working definition views crises as crucial periods in international conflict characterized by intense interactions among states and an objective or subjective increase in the probability of war.[2] Research on crisis has been very diverse, ranging from attempts to explain decision-making processes under conditions of stress (Holsti, 1972; Hermann, 1969; Brecher, 1980) through attempts to map interaction patterns during the various phases of crises (McClelland, 1968; Azar, 1972), and up to examinations of the effects of crises on the international system (Brecher and James, 1986). Snyder and Diesing (1977) view crises as "a microcosm of international politics" because they represent important turning points in the relations among states. Hence, crises bring out most of the aspects of international interactions that are of interest to scholars, such as decision making and information processing, bargaining, and systemic constraints.

Two aspects of crisis research are of interest in the analysis of crisis escalation: crisis decision making and crisis management. Research on crisis decision making centers on how political leaders react to problems arising in a setting characterized by high stress. Stress is defined as a combination of threats to basic values, short time for decision, and high (collectively or subjectively) perceived probability of military hostilities (Brecher, 1979, 1980).[3] A substantial body of literature claims that decision making under crisis conditions entails fundamental pathologies that spell disaster. Both motivated and unmotivated biases serve to make crisis decision making suboptimal. Decision makers ignore significant portions of relevant information available to them, distort the meaning of other information, and engage in only limited effort to explore multiple alternatives, and their evaluation of the alternatives explored is only partial and biased. The result is that crises may escalate to war not because states decide that this is what they want, but because they fail to realize that their actions make war likely or even inevitable. And when war breaks out, it comes as a big surprise to everybody.

Another body of research finds that decision makers can behave very rationally even under the most stressful conditions. Due to the critical nature of issues at stake and to the acute possibility of war, decision makers weigh their actions carefully, taking into account the opponent's behavior and the possibility that their actions might be misunderstood by the opponent, and hence crisis behavior is—in many cases—characterized by considerable prudence.[4] The evidence points to a curvilinear relationship between stress and decision performance: decision makers do a lousy job under both very low and very high levels of stress, but perform generally well under medium stress (Holsti, 1979; Brecher, 1980; Stein and Tanter, 1980; Maoz, 1989).

*Crisis management* refers, fundamentally, to a process by which nations interact with one another in a setting wherein each tries to accomplish its objectives without losing control over the unfolding of the crisis. It entails a fundamental trade-off between risks of unintended escalation and the benefits of coercive diplomacy (George et al., 1972; Maoz, 1982b). Good decision making is essential: the smallest error may spell disaster. The fundamental idea of crisis management literature is that words and deeds in a crisis have a dual meaning: they are intended to demonstrate resolve and determination. At the same time, they are meant to restrain the opponent from going over the brink by signaling that it is possible to resolve the conflict of interests without resorting to war (Jervis, 1970). Schelling (1966) discusses the problem of crisis management in terms of a legal analogy. Guilt in car accidents is determined by establishing who had the last clear chance to avoid collision. In crisis, each actor wants the other to be the one with the last clear chance. Thus, the purpose of actions in crisis is to pass the buck to the opponent. This is nicely illustrated by two games, called Hero and Leader. These games are illustrated in Figure 4.1.

In Hero, each actor wants to be the first to commit to the defection strategy. If players were allowed to move sequentially, each in turn, each actor would want to be given the first move. Once an actor gets the first move, the game ends in his or her victory. The actor with the first move gets the best outcome because the opponent has no choice but to cooperate. In Leader, the situation is just the opposite: each wants the other to be given the first move. The actor who moves first solves the game by cooperating, but in the process he or she gets the second-best outcome, while the opponent gets the best outcome. The leader is a reluctant one under these circumstances. The point of the game of Leader is that an actor attempts in a crisis to get the other to a point where the last chance to avoid a major conflagration is by making

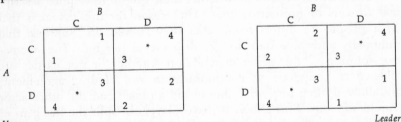

Hero

Leader

**Figure 4.1** Leader and Hero as Games of Commitment

Key:

*Note:* C = cooperate; D = defect. Outcomes are ranked from best = 4 to worst = 1. Outcomes in the lower-left corner of each cell are row's (*A*'s) payoffs; outcomes in the upper-right corner are column's (*B*) payoffs.

* Nash equilibrium.

a major concession. This concession makes the follower look great. He or she has been able to accomplish his or her goals while avoiding war. Obviously, failing to see a last clear chance when one exists can lead to disaster. Here is why both the art of sending signals and the art of deciphering them are so important in international crises (Jervis, 1970). The theoretical and empirical focus of this literature has traditionally been on when and what signals and bargaining techniques work or are successful in avoiding war, and on the main factors associated with the escalation of crises to war (Leng, 1980; Leng and Wheeler, 1975).

## The Chicken Trap:
## Crises as Escalation Ladders

The theoretical illustration of the paradox of crisis escalation focuses on two different models. I will start with a model that makes rather simple but highly restrictive assumptions. But given these assumptions, the model suggests a frightening process of compound escalation. This process is represented by the Dollar Auction game. The second model reflects unintended escalation in setting where choices are made under uncertainty, but the setting in which this game is played renders the incentives of the actors much more cooperative. Hence, the message of the second game seems to be that cooperative intentions are a less than perfect guarantee of the avoidance of disaster.

### The Dollar Auction Game

Players are offered a dollar in an auction-type sale. The dollar goes to the highest bidder, no matter how high or how low this bid is. The winner pays the amount of his or her bid to the seller and gets the dollar. However, unlike a typical auction, the second-highest bidder also pays the amount of his or her bid, and gets nothing. How should this game be played? Who is the winner? What is the optimal sale price of the dollar? What is the price paid by the second-highest bidder?

The answers depend on whether these questions require descriptive answers or normative ones. The reason for this caveat is that what people do differs from what they should do. Suppose that minimally allowable bids are set to a nickel per bid. The normative solution to this game depends on whether or not parties are allowed to cooperate. If communication and binding agreements are allowed, then one actor should bid a nickel and the other actor should stay out. This allows the two players to split the net gain of 95 cents. However, suppose that parties are not allowed to communicate, or that there exist no mechanisms to enforce an agreement. In such a case the optimal strategy appears to be for the player who has the first move to make a certain bid that is lower than a dollar (how much lower will become clear in a moment) and for the second player to stay out. In fact, one could argue that the first player should make the minimum bid and the other player must stay out.

O'Neill (1986) shows that the optimal strategy for an actor who is given the first move is to bid an amount of money that is a function of the stakes of the game (in our case the stakes are a dollar—or twenty nickels) and on the player's bankroll. All other players should simply stay out of this auction. Without going into technical details, O'Neill's solution is based on the notion that actors are able to look ahead and think of all possible responses to any given first bid. The limit of a player's bid is his or her bankroll. Reasoning backward from the end of the large tree of possible responses to a given first bid, one can calculate an optimal strategy. For example, if the bankroll of the first player is $2.50 (50 nickels), and bids are set to a minimum of 5 cents per bid, he or she should bid 60 cents and the other player should stay out. Thus, in theory, this is a simple game with a seemingly simple solution.[5]

However, experimental evidence from the game suggests that what players do differs markedly from what they should do.[6] First, players err in entering the game. Once they do, the pattern of play is one of infinite escalation. The typical process is one wherein players start out with low bids, which escalate rapidly until they reach the vicinity of a dollar (around 90 cents). There, players hesitate a little bit, but before long bidding continues and goes well above a dollar. The game ends not in some reasonable last bid, but at a point where the player with the second-largest bankroll has exhausted his or her money. Of course, this game has no winner: the players differ only in that one of them loses a dollar less than the other. But both lose because the final bids are way over a dollar.

The process of unintended escalation in this game is a direct consequence of a very simple and quite reasonable process of reasoning. Each party enters the auction with the perception that the auction has a clear termination point that no one will be stupid enough to cross. Given that knowledge, the issue is who will be the first to back down, not whether one is going to cross the dollar threshold. Thus the bidding continues until it reaches a dollar. At this point we have the front-runner who bid a dollar and a sucker who bid 95 cents. The net gain of the front-runner is zero: he or she pays a dollar to get a dollar. The problem is that the sucker is about to lose 95 cents. This player's problem is how to cut down on his or her losses. The obvious solution is to outbid the front-runner: by bidding $1.05, the sucker becomes the front-runner and loses only 5 cents instead of 95 cents. However, the former winner becomes the potential loser, with a choice between losing a dollar (by dropping out) or losing 10 cents (by bidding $1.10). Obviously, bidding further at this point is seemingly rational because a loss of 10 cents is preferred to a loss of a dollar. So the process continues. At each point a player who becomes the second-highest bidder reasons as follows: if I drop out of the auction now I lose $x$ nickels. However, if I continue to bid I lose $x + 1 - 20$ nickels. Since the second alternative (to continue bidding) is immediately more attractive than the first alternative (dropping out), the escalation process continues well beyond the seemingly obvious termination point.

But why is this an illustration of a paradox of unintended escalation, given the fact that the game does have a rational solution? In fact, it could be argued that what we have here is a clear illustration of why rational models of choice behavior are not adequate explanations of how people actually behave. If people only knew what kind of mess they could get into simply by beginning to play this game, they would surely have stayed out. The problem is that the average player—in political or any of the other arenas of life—is not capable of reasoning into the distant future. In order to be able to see that the clear termination point is an extremely misleading concept, people must be able to envision what will happen when they get to the neighborhood of a dollar and are designated suckers. But this is too far ahead to think for people who have just entered the auction with a 10 cent bid and who have hopes that their opponent will drop out well before that happens.

O'Neill's (1985) solution requires very restrictive assumptions about the ability of people to reason ahead and to solve problems. O'Neill states that, in a dollar auction in which bids are in increments of a nickel and each of the two players' bankrolls is $2.50, the game tree one needs to develop in order to reach this solution consists of about 2,500 different branches (or possible positions) (p. 223). It is clearly unreasonable to expect from people even to approach this computational ability in real life. If people cannot look far ahead and make complicated calculations about thousands of possibilities afforded by the rules of the game, then it is not very clear that the game has any stable solution that does not involve unintended escalation. O'Neill realizes that when he discusses some other solutions offered by game theorists:

> Constanza states that the "only truly rational thing to do is not to enter the game in the first place. Once the game is entered by at least two bidders, their fate is sealed if they behave rationally from that point on." Those who played the game and lost might agree, but this strategy is not an equilibrium: if you know your opponent would not bid you should clearly make some small bid. Thus, if the rational strategy for both is not to play and if you know your opponent is rational, then you can deduce that the rational strategy for you is to play, which is a contradiction.

> Another suggested ploy is to bid 95 cents. Your opponent will not bid a dollar since there will be nothing to gain, so you are sure to win 5 cents. This strategy may be better than doing nothing but it

is not necessarily the best strategy: perhaps bidding less than 95 cents would also induce a rational opponent to drop out. Shubik suggested that bidding one dollar at the outset is part of an equilibrium strategy, but I disagree that it is part of a perfect (or sensible) equilibrium for reasons just given. (p. 221)

The fact that the only strategy that seems to offer a solution that is both stable[7] and sensible (in the sense that a dollar is sold for less than a dollar) is one that can be discovered only by computerized human beings makes this paradox a real one. Average, but still rational, people cannot find anything in game theory that can offer them a clue as to how to behave in this game: if they know or have reason to believe that everyone will stay out, they should definitely enter the bidding; if they are already in the process of bidding, the only way to cut their losses is to continue escalating.[8]

The lesson of the Dollar Auction game is what the paradox of crisis escalation is all about: recklessness is the consequence of perfectly reasonable calculations involving the notion that escalation is controllable because war is something that nobody wants. Each side believes that it can frighten the opponent by manipulating the risks of war. But when the parties reach the threshold of war they cannot back down because nobody can afford to become the loser.

## Prudent Escalation

The notion that crises are competitions in risk-taking implies that management problems are best understood in terms of choice under uncertainty. Decision makers attempt to decide what to do without being sure how their opponents are going to react to their actions. Part of this uncertainty stems from the fact that actors are not really sure what kind of opponents they are dealing with. And even if they have a good sense of who their opponent is, this is not enough to allow precise behavioral predictions.

Uncertainty about the type of opponent one is dealing with may mean one of several things. First, it may mean simply that one does not know how the opponent rank orders the various outcomes formed by the intersection of choices. Another part of this uncertainty is that one does not know how likely the opponent is to take risks, even if one knows what its preferences are. Part of the action and reaction pattern in crises is devoted to attempts to uncover the opponent's preference structure or its propensity toward risks through its revealed behavior. One hopes that what one's opponent does will provide clues about what it wants, how it evaluates the situation, and how far it is willing to go. Incomplete knowledge of the opponent's preferences suggests a number of possibly interesting analyses. However, it is not something with which we will concern ourselves at this point. Rather, our focus is on how actors might entrap themselves by trying to use revealed behavior as an indicator of risk propensity.

But there is another aspect to crisis-induced uncertainty. This aspect stems from incomplete knowledge of how much time actors have before the crisis escalates to war. The notion of crisis entailing short-of-war interaction implies that the parties do not view war as the most preferred outcome, at least at the outset. If they did, it would be stupid for them to bargain through the demonstrative use of force or through the limited use of force. For one thing, they would lose the advantage of a first strike without warning: surprise, determination of the scope and location of the first strike, and so forth. Moreover, bargaining may prevent the crisis from going to war, thereby depriving an actor of whatever benefits are associated with war.

For example, following the 1938 Munich crisis, which gave Hitler complete control over the formerly Czech Sudetenland region, Hitler complained that Chamberlain deprived him (Hitler) of the pleasure of entering Prague at the head of his victorious army. If this complaint represented Hitler's true preferences, then it was stupid for Hitler to agree to negotiate over the Sudetenland: he should have attacked Czechoslovakia. Uncertainty about the time available to the parties before the "point of no return" is typically a function of the conditions of interdependence under which crisis management takes place. Because the amount of time before war depends itself on the choices of the parties, that is, on the kind of actions they take, it is impossible to predict with any degree of reliability what it would be.

The amount of time available to parties in the course of the crisis can be defined operationally as the number of actions (verbal or physical) they have before the crisis escalates to war or terminates short of it. Morrow (1987) has developed a model of crisis bargaining that allows for only two steps of offers and counteroffers before a war breaks out. Effectively, this means that one actor challenges the opponent and the opponent can either accept the offer or submit a counteroffer. The challenger faces, at this point, a choice between a prewar settlement on the basis of the counteroffer of the defender or the initiation of a war. This model is somewhat limited in that its outcomes are too dependent on its structure. For example, if the defender has reason to believe that its counteroffer will be rejected by the challenger, it might wish to break the rules by initiating a war before the opponent does. Thus, instead of making a counteroffer and providing the challenger with the opportunity to start the war, the defender might start the war itself. If the challenger expects that to be the case, it might present the challenge in the form of an all-out attack.

Alternatively, an actor might really be in no mood to play Persian bazaar with national security, yet, for a variety of reasons, it does not want to be the first to start a war. If a war is bound to occur, the actor may want it to be clear that the opponent started it. Therefore an actor might have a strong incentive to respond to each offer made by the opponent with a counteroffer, even though the actor knows that there is no chance that the opponent would accept it. The purpose of such a strategy is to give the opponent the last clear chance of avoiding war or to bear responsibility for starting it. Setting the number of moves in the crisis as fixed and known to the actors leads one to ignore some important mechanisms of crisis bargaining.

To model the second version of the escalation process, I use a variation on a game that I believe was first introduced by Schelling (1963) as an example of a game of tacit cooperation. My interpretation of this game will be somewhat more pessimistic than the one suggested by Schelling. This is due partly to the changes in the rule of play introduced herein.

Suppose that two players are requested to divide a dollar between themselves. The game is played by each player writing down on a card a certain amount he or she wants for him- or herself. (The amount can range anywhere between 0 and 100 cents.) The game-master then collects the two cards and adds up the players' offers. If the total exceeds a dollar, the players get nothing and the game ends. If the total is precisely a dollar, the dollar is divided between the players such that each player gets what he or she had written on the card, and the game ends. Finally, if the sum of the offers is less than a dollar, each player gets what he or she had written on the card, and the game resumes. Players can make additional bids on the remainder of the dollar according to the same rules. However, once players' demands are in excess of the amount to be divided, all their previous gains are taken away. In principle, the length of this game ranges from one iteration to an infinite number.[9]

This is a cooperative game in terms of the incentive structure of the actors involved: players win together or lose together; the game contains no outcome that represents a gain to one actor and a loss to another. Moreover, losses are identical to both players. (Both end up empty-handed whenever the sum of offers exceeds the dollar.) Thus, there are seemingly no conflictive incentives. However, a closer inspection reveals a significant degree of incompatibility in the interests of the players. While both wish to avoid the disaster outcome, each wants to get the most of the dollar at the expense of the opponent.

Schelling's version of the game allows for a single iteration. In such cases, the notion of a "prominent solution" becomes a reasonable prediction about the way the game is solved. Each actor should write 50 cents on the card because this amount represents the fairest and clearest division that both maximizes joint gains and minimizes the prospect of losses. Indeed, this is what experimental plays of this game show. The problem is that the 50 cent outcome, although stable, is not the only stable solution of the game. There are a large number of stable outcomes for this game.[10] What makes this solution attractive is that it is seemingly "prominent." Actors have only one chance of playing the game. They cannot correct their mistake if they have written amounts that exceed the dollar, nor can they pick up the slack if they were overly cautious and have written down amounts that sum to less than the whole dollar. Faced with one and only one choice, the 50 cent outcome is both stable and reasonable.

However, the rules of the game described above allow actors an opportunity to correct at least some of their mistakes. If one of the actors is reckless and/or believes that his or her opponent is overly cautious, then that actor may make an excessive demand that would harm both actors despite the reasonableness of the other player. The temptation to guess what the opponent is going to bid is great when one is not given an opportunity to correct for excessive prudence. However, the repeated play version awards prudence by giving players a second, third, or fourth chance. In fact, actors are given ample opportunities to learn something about each other without paying a high price for this learning experience. Presumably, the repeated-play version of this game should reduce the chances of disaster compared to the single-play version.

However, this is not so. It may well turn out that it is precisely this chance to learn and the prize for prudence that make for a fatal combination. Because players know they will be given another chance, they will tend to play prudently the first time the game is played. Consequently, the sum of their bids will be less than a dollar. In the second iteration they have additional information: they know how much of the dollar is left for division in the second round and they also know how their opponent behaved in the first round. Since each actor knows that his or her opponent behaved in a way suggesting risk aversion, the temptation to exploit this increases, because now the actors know more about their opponents than they knew before the first iteration. Each player uses the proportion of the dollar that had been offered by the opponent in the first round as an indicator of the proportion of the remainder of the dollar that will be offered by the opponent at the present round. Consequently, one would offer the remainder of this proportion. If everyone behaves according to this logic, the sum of the requests will exceed the remainder of the dollar to be divided in the second round. Both actors who had behaved prudently in the first round and attempted to exploit each other's prudence in the second round wind up with disaster.

An example is in order here. Suppose that in the first round the two bids were 30 cents and 40 cents by players *a* and *b*, respectively. This leaves 30 cents to be divided in the second round. Since *a* knows that *b*'s first request was for two-fifths of the amount to be divided in the first round, he might reason that *b* will repeat this pattern, requesting 12 cents of the remaining 30 cents. It will therefore not be unreasonable for *a* to request 18 cents. On the other hand, *b* sees that *a* had requested only three-tenths of the dollar in the first round, so if she expects *a* to continue to play in a risk-averse manner, she predicts that *a*'s request will amount to 9 cents, so *b* can ask for 21 cents. If each player attempts to exploit the opponent's prudence, the result is that both end up with nothing.

Seen from this perspective, the chances of mutual disaster increase with the number of iterations. Each player believes that his or her estimates of the other player's prudence become increasingly reliable with each additional iteration, so the temptation to exploit the opponent's prudence increases as play continues. In the third or fourth iteration, players become very confident in their predictions, as these are based on trend data rather than on single observations. Gambles under such circumstances seem safer than they had been at the outset. Paradoxically, when disaster strikes at subsequent iterations it is over stakes that are much smaller than those at the start of the confrontation.

In what way do the Dollar Auction and the Divide the Dollar games represent paradoxes of unwanted escalation? Both games exhibit prominent solutions and common interests. The expectations of the parties stemming from these factors lead the parties to believe that they can exploit the opponent's awareness of these and get away with it. However, precisely because such expectations lead the parties to overcommit themselves, when they reach the point where it is necessary to back down, they are unable to do that. In the Dollar Auction, the expectation that the other will back down when the bidding nears a dollar renders the entry into this game seemingly rational, even if one is not the first to enter. In the Divide the Dollar game, increased expectations about the opponent's prudence cause the focal actor to try to exploit it. Because such expectations are sometimes mutual, disaster follows.[11]

## Explanations of the Paradox

### *The Rational Explanation*

The structure of the games representing the paradox of crisis escalation is such that they offer no clear rational prescription as to optimal choices. In the Dollar Auction, if no player enters the bidding, then each player has an incentive to enter because a small investment can yield large returns when no one else is willing to take the risks. But the would-be second bidder can reason that there is a certain investment that the first bidder cannot or will not go above. (If I can top this, then I might make some profit, even though I am not the only bidder and hence the risk of losing my investment—if I am the second-highest bidder—does exist.) The Dollar Auction offers no equilibrium that is easily recognizable if calculations are rational but myopic. If you can envision the game only a few steps forward, it is still reasonable to enter as long as you believe that there is a maximum point beyond which neither you nor the opponent will go.

The problem is that your calculations change once you reach this point, although—in principle—they should not. When the bidding is still below the dollar level, players think in terms of how to maximize gains. Once they near a dollar, they think in terms of how to minimize losses. Expected utility theory suggests that there should be no difference between the choice outcomes in these two settings, but experimental evidence suggests just the opposite: people are risk-averse with respect to gains and risk-acceptant with respect to losses (Kahneman and Tversky, 1979; Quattrone and Tversky, 1988).

In the Divide the Dollar game, the fear of the joint disaster outcome and mistrust of the opponent leads to prudent behavior. This kind of prudent behavior is eminently rational. One would rather lose a portion of a dollar due to prudence than lose the whole dollar due to excessive trust in the opponent's rationality. Moreover, the loss of the remainder between one's initial offer and 50 cents is recoverable in the iterative version, hence, the adverse results of excessive prudence are not terminal. But excessive prudence is justified only if one has a basis for believing that one's opponent is imprudent. If evidence suggests that one's opponent is overly prudent, being prudent oneself is suboptimal. The more confident one is in the opponent's prudence, the less prudent one should be in this game.

## The Cognitive Explanation

Brockner and Rubin (1985) suggest that the factors that determine the extent of entrapment in social conflicts are numerous and varied. There is no "single most important" cause of entrapment. However, the factor that may be most directly relevant to political processes of entrapment is what they call "processes of justification and rationalization."

Processes of rationalization and justification are attempts to explain and rationalize apparently stupid choices made in the past (e.g., entry into the Dollar Auction game) by getting something out of them anyway. However, to make such a justification good, one needs to show results. Such results cannot be obtained unless one deepens one's commitment, thereby further entrapping oneself. Obviously, the need for rationalization and justification of past choices arises when one is held accountable for one's choices. That is why the rationalization explanation is particularly relevant as an explanation of political entrapment. Because political settings are those in which decision makers are constantly being judged and evaluated by constituencies and competing elites, leaders who make stupid choices feel compelled to come up with such rationalizations in order to survive criticism or avoid being overthrown. The need for showing results is stronger when one's accountability is public in nature. Indeed, Brockner and Rubin (1985: 58–144) present persistent experimental evidence suggesting that social settings, high levels of accountability, and need for positive self-presentation are important factors affecting the magnitude of entrapment.

How does the process of rationalization and justification affect entrapment in the Dollar Auction game? From the cognitive perspective, what requires explanation is not so much the entry into the game, for one cannot be expected to see what the end result of the process is going to be. The key problem is to understand why one would want to deepen one's entrapment even though one is aware that further participation in this game is going to produce precisely this result. The justification process suggests that one can best justify past and present behavior by coming out on top. That this means losing everything one has except the dollar is immaterial—at least the dollar was won. The entry into the auction is explained as rational goal-attaining behavior. The dollar is the prize. Retrospective justification of past behavior must therefore be related to the prospect of attainment of that goal. The actor becomes obsessed with the prize and views his or her whole political future as dependent on this prize, while the costs entailed in obtaining the prize are discounted, ignored, or explained away.

In the Divide the Dollar game, players who are evaluated by their peers or by a constituency feel a need to explain their "overly" prudent behavior given revealed information about the prudence of the opponent. Because they feel that they were expected to get the maximum, the tendency to entrap themselves will increase with the number of iterations played. It will also vary with the extent to which their gains compare with those of their opponents. According to the cognitive explanation of behavior in the Divide the Dollar game, players are engaged in constant comparisons of payoffs: they believe that their performance is judged not only in terms of the payoffs they obtain but also in terms of how much they get relative to their opponent. The lower the relative gains of actors in previous iterations, the more likely they are to entrap themselves in subsequent iterations, because of their efforts to "catch up" with their opponents.

The need to justify and rationalize past decisions is interpreted in this context somewhat differently than it was in the Dollar Auction.

The current interpretation is that future behavior is designed to correct (rather than to rationalize) stupid past behavior. Players become obsessed with the feeling that they have lost in at least one way, and, in many cases, in two ways. They lost in their effort to obtain for themselves as much as possible, and, if they got less than their opponent, they lost in the sense of becoming the major "sucker." Their subsequent behavior is guided by the need to correct those mistakes. Gains are interpreted as losses if they are less than what could have been obtained given the opponent's prudence, let alone if these gains are lower than those of the opponent. When one feels a need to justify unwarranted prudence, the tendency is then to justify past stupidity through future cleverness: I may have been overly cautious the first time around, but this caution paid off because I learned that my opponent is a sucker. Once I realized that, I exploited him.

## Comparing the Two Models of Unwanted Escalation

Both types of games seem to satisfy the definition of paradoxes. In both cases we have varied only actors' expectations about each other while leaving everything else constant. Nonetheless, the logics that drive these processes differ in some important ways. Before discussing these differences, let us look at the principal commonalities of these two models of entrapment.

First, common to the models is the belief that there exists a clear termination point. Each actor thinks that he or she knows exactly where to stop. Yet, precisely because they think they know when to quit, they fall readily into the trap. Second, actors are aware of the rules of the game and of each other's preferences. In the experimental play of the Dollar Auction game players were allowed to communicate, to threaten and to make coalitions. Indeed, a substantial proportion of these games terminated in one iteration where a coalition of players had one of the members bid 5 cents and then divided the spoils among the lot. However, there was a substantial proportion of cases where players failed to form coalitions or used communication to threaten each other without any significant results (Teger, 1980). Experiments using the game of Chicken (Rapoport et al., 1976) show a similar pattern.

But there are fundamental differences between these models. The Dollar Auction model is a case of initial opportunism that is converted into an extended effort to recover some of the sunk costs. The Divide the Dollar game is a case of mutual prudence that causes opportunism. Entrapment in the Dollar Auction is a continuous affair that starts with the first bid and extends well over the stakes of the game. In

Divide the Dollar, entrapment is singular: one error ends the game. The Dollar Auction game is driven by the desire of the actors not to be the second-highest bidder. The Divide the Dollar game is driven to some extent by a similar desire. However, it is an exploitative urge that drives the actors into the trap.

These differences suggest that the historical analogues of entrapment will exhibit some variation in terms of the process of entrapment. Unwanted escalation can be seen as a continuous affair that extends over a long period, or it can be illustrated by one moment of imprudence that breeds disaster. The kind of primary considerations that drive actors' behavior may also differ markedly from one case of mutual entrapment to another. These differences notwithstanding, the fundamental implication of this behavior is identical. It is the same process of unwanted escalation that occurs not only because each wants to avoid escalation, but also because each player thinks he or she knows where to stop.

## Entrapment in War

It is ironic that a book titled *The War Trap* (Bueno de Mesquita, 1981) conveys just the opposite message. Namely, it argues that wars are the result of carefully calculated choices of national policymakers and that, because they are well thought of, the initiators of wars tend to emerge as victors. The empirical evidence for this argument is impressive and, in many ways, indisputable. Yet, critics of this point of view typically use World War I as a major counterexample. The argument being advanced by critics of Bueno de Mesquita's argument is that this war displays a case study in loss of control either due to malfunctions in the decision process or to the overtaking of political discretion by organizational routines and narrow military considerations. I am going to discuss World War I, but not as a case of unwanted escalation, because I have some problems with the extent to which the Austrians did not want to escalate against the Serbs. Instead, my cases in this chapter are taken from more recent history: the Chinese intervention in the Korean War, and the chain of events leading to the Six Day War.

Several things must be shown in the historical cases in order for them to qualify as instances of wars that nobody wanted. First and foremost, it must be shown—as much as is possible with recent historical events—that none of the participants in the episode really wanted war. Second, it must be shown that each party made some honest attempts to avoid war. Moreover, since the abstract illustrations of the paradox emphasize two different mechanisms of entrapment, it must be shown that escalation involved either the attempt to recover sunk costs, as suggested by the Dollar Auction, or an attempt to capitalize on the perceived prudence of the opponent, as suggested by the Divide the Dollar game.

## One Step Too Far:
## The Chinese Intervention in the Korean War[12]

When President Truman ordered the direct intervention of the United States in Korea, he thought he was doing it to prevent World War III (Truman, 1964: 333). Seen in this light, the American decision to intervene in the war was a case of a deliberate and calculated effort of deterrence by example. Restoration of the status quo in Korea was seen as important not only because the United States believed in the right of the South Koreans to noncommunist self-determination, but because the U.S. decision makers felt that they "had to draw the line." The assessment of the administration was that the invasion was a Soviet ploy designed to test American resolve—sort of a trial balloon. "Russia [General Bradley] thought, was not yet ready for war, but in Korea they were obviously testing us, and the line ought to be drawn now. I [Truman] said that most emphatically I thought the line would have to be drawn" (Truman, 1964: 335). Because Mao Tse-tung, the Chinese leader, had spent nearly three months in Moscow at the beginning of that year, the assessment in Washington was that China was involved. Yet the American decision to intervene in the war was based on a premise that the two instigators of the North Korean invasion would not actively intervene to bail out their stooge.

The original war aim in Korea as defined by the United Nations was to restore the status quo ante bellum, that is, to repel the North Korean army and reestablish the 38th parallel as the border between the two Koreas. A major concern of American decision makers at the time was that the North Korean attack on the South was only a diversionary move in a Soviet strategy aimed at Europe or the Middle East, or in a Chinese strategy aimed at the Nationalist Chinese forces under Chiang Kai-shek in Formosa. Accordingly, the decision to send troops to Korea was implemented in relatively small doses in order to maintain a high state of readiness in those sensitive areas that were seen as vulnerable to a Soviet attack. To defend Formosa, the Seventh Fleet was ordered to move to the Strait of Formosa, not only as a show of commitment, but as a means to deter against a Chinese attack and to defend Formosa if such an attack came. On July 31, MacArthur flew to Formosa and as a result of the visit the president approved a program of far-reaching military aid.

Thus, the American strategy at the start of the war had been to intervene directly in order to show both the Soviets and the Chinese that America intended "to draw the line." Whether or not the Soviets and the Chinese had any concrete aggressive designs is unclear. What is known is that they refrained from giving North Korea significant military aid in the period between June and October. It is also known that the Soviet Union did not make an effort to veto the U.N. resolution to send an international force to Korea. Finally, neither the Soviets nor communist China made any effort to initiate or even indirectly instigate conflict during those months. It seems that if these two states had had aggressive designs against other states, the U.S. decisive action must have deterred them from carrying out these plans. Thus, by August 6, Averell Harriman, President Truman's roving ambassador, could report of MacArthur's assessment of Soviet and Chinese intentions: "He [MacArthur] did not believe that the Russians had any present intention of intervening directly or becoming involved in a general war. He believed that the same was true of the Chinese Communists" (quoted in Truman, 1964: 350).

The high point of the American military intervention was the daring landing of U.S. forces in Inchon on September 15, 1950. This attack was planned almost from the beginning of the American intervention in the war and was designed to encircle the bulk of the North Korean army. The successful landing marked a major turning point in the war. Seoul, the South Korean capital, was occupied by U.S. forces on September 28, and the North Korean army was in general disarray. On October 1, South Korean forces crossed the 38th parallel north and General MacArthur issued a statement demanding that North Korea surrender and accept the U.N. terms of peace. On October 7, the U.N. Security Council endorsed a resolution that fundamentally altered the war aims in Korea, from return of the status quo ante to unification of the two Koreas. American units crossed the 38th parallel the same day.

The turning of the tide of battle in Korea and the apparent intention of the United States to expand the war to the north put the Chinese communists on the spot. Since the United States had fundamentally altered its war aims with the change in its military fortune, what guarantee was there that it would not do so again when its forces reached the Yalu River separating North Korea from China? The Chinese were aware of the massive economic and military aid the United States had given Chiang Kai-shek during the 1945–49 civil war. The increased U.S. naval presence in the Formosa Strait area and the aggressive policy of aid to Chiang were supplemented by a number of official and semiofficial statements about the importance of Formosa as a U.S. naval and air base.[13] Whiting (1960) reports Chinese allegations regarding the intrusion of U.S. planes into Chinese airspace during September and early October. All these events made alarm a natural reaction in Peking. Chinese decision makers must have misinterpreted warnings issued by President Truman (in his broadcast speech of September 1) regarding a possible expansion of the war due to "Communist imperialism." The MacArthur demand for unconditional North Korean surrender and the U.N. resolution of October 7 reaffirming the new war aim as the unification of Korea did not leave much room for interpretation: if North Korea surrendered, China would be encircled from the east by a mass of hostile forces. Even if the United States did stop at the Yalu at that point, the prospect of a future invasion of China was too serious to dismiss.

Throughout the period of September 15 to October 15, Chinese authorities issued a number of fairly explicit threats that China would not and could not tolerate the overthrow of the communist government in North Korea and the unification of Korea under U.S. auspices.[14] After the entry of U.S. forces into North Korea on October 7 and the U.N. resolution of the same day, the Chinese realized that action was required when the verbal threats and diplomatic warnings failed to produce an apparent result. On October 14, the first Chinese units, given the unofficial status of "volunteers," entered Korea. Although their entry was done secretly, reports on the entry of Chinese forces reached American intelligence almost immediately.[15] The first Chinese prisoner was taken by a South Korean force on October 25, and three others were taken the following day. All prisoners reported, upon their arrival at Pyongyang, that they were part of a large Chinese contingent. By October 26, the first massive encounter between the First Division of the South Korean army and a large Chinese force resulted in the encirclement of the former (Alexander, 1986: 262–265). An additional ROK division (the Sixth) was virtually destroyed by Chinese forces by October 29. The first massive encounter between the U.S. 8th Cavalry regiment and Chinese forces took place on the night of November 1–2 in the Unsan area. It ended with a rapid withdrawal of U.S. and ROK forces from Unsan (Alexander, 1986: 269–277).

The Chinese were, however, still politically reserved about their intervention. The first semiofficial report regarding Chinese participation came on November 7 through a North Korean radio broadcast, followed by a November 11 response by a Chinese spokesman to MacArthur's statement (Whiting, 1960: 137). Chinese forces, however, broke all contact with the ROK and American units by November 7. Whiting (1960: 160–161) suggests that a plausible interpretation of the lull in the fighting is that one of the principal Chinese objectives was to allow time for diplomacy, in the hope that some compromise solution would be reached. This interpretation is also supported by Alexander (1986: 287). However, this was not quite the military and political assessment in MacArthur's headquarters or in Washington. The view was that "the Chinese intervention was only a parting jab" (Goulden, 1982: 311). The broader political interpretation was that the Chinese volunteer action was just a token show of solidarity with North Korea and that it ended when it exhausted itself. The withdrawal of the Chinese forces was thus taken as a signal of fundamental Chinese prudence rather than as a warning of the shape of things to come. Amid this background, the "back by Christmas" offensive started on November 24, designed to end the final resistance by the PRK army. On November 26, the Chinese formally intervened, and by the end of November, all U.N. and ROK forces were in the process of a rapid retreat.

The chain of events described above serves as a good illustration of the Divide the Dollar game. The primary theme of virtually all analyses of this unfortunate war is aptly summarized by George and Smoke (1974: 184).

> Historical perspective serves only to deepen the tragic feeling, held by many at the time, that this "new war" with China was unnecessary and avoidable. The conflict of interests . . . led to war only because of misperception, miscalculation, and inept action . . . the Chinese-American military confrontation in Korea was one which neither side wanted and both tried to avoid.

This near consensus in historical and analytical interpretations of the Chinese intervention in the Korean War suggests that cognitive factors had a lot to do with the escalation. Indeed, there is ample evidence that the Chinese interpretation of the expansion of the war north of the 38th parallel to be a prelude to an invasion of China had nothing to do with actual American intentions. Likewise, there is an overwhelming amount of evidence that American military and political decision makers made fatal errors of judgment and of decision because they failed to see that their actions constituted a direct threat to China. Despite the information at their disposal, they chose to see what they liked and ignored unpleasant realities. It is clear that something has gone terribly wrong when politicians admit that they made mistakes.[16]

Yet, not everything is explained as a comedy (or tragedy) of errors. What happened was that—at least on the American side—the cautious Chinese withdrawal of November 7 was interpreted as a sign of terminal prudence. The dominant thinking was that this withdrawal marked the end of China's participation in the war. The Chinese got used to the idea of a unified Korea under Western influence, and—although they did not like it—realized that they had to live with it. Thus, this cautious behavior was seen as something to capitalize on, which led to MacArthur's famous comment on the November 24 offensive, calling it the last major act in the war. Throughout the preceding months, optimistic estimates of the opponent's intentions and capabilities drove American decision-making process in both Korea and Washington. The expansion of the war aim is the chief exemplar of a logic that wished to take advantage of what was seen as the opponents' (both China's and the Soviet Union's) prudence. This logic pushed American units into North Korea.

It is impossible to dismiss the political support that MacArthur received throughout the period from Washington as a result of misinformation orchestrated by the theater commander. U.S. reaction in Korea was not only a move of deterrence by example. It turned into a real boost to the administration internally. Not only did MacArthur's popularity grow in the United States, but that of the president grew as well, despite the minor clashes between the two men. The logic of rationalization and justification helps explain the expansion of the war aims to unification of Korea. Since things had been working out well in terms of the military aspects of the war (since Inchon), and the political ground for expansion (that is, Soviet and Chinese prudence on the one hand, and U.N. participation on the other) seemed clear, it would have been stupid not to go all the way.

But is not the Chinese behavior an actual counterexample of the logic that drives the paradox of unwanted escalation in the Divide the Dollar game? Not if we accept the hypothesis regarding a Soviet-China joint sponsorship of the North Korean attack. If, indeed, one of the things discussed by Stalin and Mao was the plan to have the North Koreans attack the South, it must have been a reaction to what was seen as a prolonged display of American prudence in the Far East. During 1949 and the early months of 1950, various military and political officials excluded Korea and Taiwan from the American "defense perimeter" in the Far East.[17] This might have increased the Soviet-Chinese estimate of success when they evaluated the prospects of a North Korean attack on the South. The notion that they could capitalize on the opponent's seeming reluctance to get involved in two areas that were known to have been politically shaky seems to suggest that there was a sense of adventurism in the calculus leading to the North Korean invasion.[18]

Seen in this light, it is not implausible that the Chinese intervention in the Korean War was motivated by a number of things. One of them may well have been some sense of threat invoked by the advance of American troops toward the Yalu. However, another factor might have been a wish to recover a sunk cost. If there was indeed Chinese instigation of the North Korean attack, the imminent North Korean defeat could have markedly harmed the Chinese image of credibility. Whatever designs China had with regard to other revolutionary movements in Southeast Asia, they would have gone down the drain if China failed to make a sincere effort to prevent a North Korean collapse. The same can be said about the Soviet Union, but in the Soviet case, the revolutionary zeal and rhetoric subsided quite a bit under Stalin.

## Long Escalation and a Short War: The Making of the Six Day War[19]

The title of this section suggests the essence of the whole story. The chain of events leading to the outbreak of the Six Day War in

June 1967 resembles a long series of rehearsals for a play that is to be put on stage only once. The origins of the Six Day War are not to be found in Nasser's decisions to move Egyptian troops into the Sinai on May 15, 1967. Rather, as some political scientists and most historians argue, the Six Day War originated somewhere in summer-fall 1966 with the intensification of the limited border skirmishes on the Israeli-Syrian border.[20]

The Israeli-Syrian rivalry was not, as most Israelis would like to believe, over Syria's fundamental hostility to the idea of an independent Jewish state. Nor was this rivalry, as most Syrians would like to believe, over the Palestinian right of self-determination. Rather, it was over water and several very narrow strips of territory. In the late 1950s, the Israeli government decided to initiate a large-scale project that would allow irrigation of the southern portion of Israel, the Negev. This project, called the National Carrier, was a plan to transfer water through a system of canals and pipes, from Lake Kinneret in the north to the Negev in the south. The Arab states, concerned about the political and economic implications of such a project, searched for ways to subvert it. Syrian initial attempts to damage the project consisted of shelling and use of small-scale firearms on the working teams and other Israeli settlements. Israeli responses came first through diplomatic channels (complaints to the U.N. Security Council) and, when these failed, through major raids on Syrian outposts along the Golan Heights (Yaniv, 1985; Maoz and Yaniv, 1989).

In 1964, the Arab Summit, failing to halt the Israeli National Carrier project, decided on a policy of economic pressure via the diversion of the Jordan River away from Israel. Syria was permitted to start diversion of the river. Israeli decision makers were extremely disturbed by this development, for such action would not only damage the National Carrier project, but it would cut Israel's most important source of water. The problem was that since the sources of the Jordan River were within Syrian territory, the diversion project did not violate any international law.

Schemes to bypass international law are not too difficult to find: all one needs to do is find some good pretext to shoot. And it did not take the Israelis too long to figure out a way to destroy the diversion project without appearing overly aggressive. In the border between Israel and Syria, there were a number of territories that had been actual no-man's land. Both Israel and Syria had claimed sovereignty over these territories (which amounted to a few dozens of acres), but up to that point no one had done anything to materialize the claim. Israel decided to use these disputed territories as bait for the Syrians, and started sending in tractors to cultivate them. Syria reacted by firing on the tractors. Israel responded by shelling the diversion equipment. Syria responded by shelling Israeli settlements along the border. Israel used its air force to destroy the equipment and canals used by the Syrians for the diversion project. This series of small-scale skirmishes extended from 1964 to 1966.

In 1964, with the formation of the Palestinian Liberation Organization (PLO), Arab states started competing over sponsorship of this organization, with the competition between Syria and Egypt being especially strong.[21] As part of this competition, Syria allowed free operations of PLO guerrillas from within its territories. As Yaniv (1985: 162–163) observes, the first PLO raids into Israel were designed to damage the National Carrier. Over time, however, these infiltrations from Syrian territory intensified and Israel expressed increasing concern over the sponsorship of the PLO by the Syrians. Thus, toward mid-1966, Israel intensified its retaliation hits on Syrian targets, relying increasingly on air attacks (Yaniv, 1986). The Israeli chief of staff, Yitzhak Rabin, said in an interview in September 1966 that if Syria did not stop its sponsorship of PLO operations, Israel would have to hit directly at the Syrian regime. Two types of escalation occurred during the 1964–66 period. First, limited artillery battles both intensified and were supplemented by active guerrilla infiltrations into Israel and by air attacks. Second, Israeli threats of retaliation began to sound increasingly as if Israel was seriously considering a major blow to the Syrian army. Israeli decision makers also began to hint that they viewed PLO activities as part of a coordinated Syrian policy that was intimately connected with the Ba'ath ideology. Hence, reprisals would have the political objective of "amputating the hand that feeds the PLO." This kind of threat was aimed directly at the Syrian regime.

Fears of a large-scale Israeli operation prompted the Syrians to request Egypt to display some form of commitment to Syria that would deter the Israelis. Indeed, on November 4, 1966, an Egyptian-Syrian defense pact was signed in Damascus. Its principal aim was to signal the Israelis that the Arab states were not going to sit idly by while Israeli troops marched to Damascus. Yet the Israeli government was under increased domestic pressure resulting from the skirmishes along the Syrian border and the continued PLO raids. As a result, Israeli retaliation raids intensified throughout the winter and spring of 1967. The Syrians became increasingly alarmed and started spreading rumors of large-scale Israeli troop concentrations along the border, which Israel categorically denied. On April 7, 1967, a massive dogfight took place in which six Syrian Mig-21 jets were shot down by Israeli Mirages. The Syrian leadership thought that this incident was a prelude to a large-scale Israeli attack. In addition, statements by the Israeli chief of staff and other government ministers before the Israeli independence day (May 14, 1967) again hinted that something really big was brewing and that this was directed at the Syrian regime.

Throughout this period, a lot of political pressure was put on Egypt to do something that would get Syria (and Jordan) off the hook. The Arab press continuously hammered the Egyptian leader Nasser for "hiding behind the UNEF skirt."[22] Nasser, however, was not eager to enter into a direct confrontation with Israel. His assessment was that the Arab world lacked both the material capabilities and the political unity needed to defeat Israel (Moore, 1989; Stephens, 1971: 453–454). Yet, faced by persistent criticism from the Arab states, and by information on Israeli troop concentrations along the Syrian border, he felt compelled to move in order to deter the Israelis. On May 15, 1967, he ordered two Egyptian divisions into the Sinai. On May 16, Nasser requested the withdrawal of UNEF along the Sinai.[23] The Israelis declared a partial mobilization on May 18 following reports that Egyptian troops were being pulled back from Yemen, where they had been fighting a losing war since 1963. The next step was the Egyptian decision of May 23 to close the Strait of Tiran, denying Israel access to the Red Sea. Israel began a frantic diplomatic campaign designed to bring about the opening of the straits. It attempted to invoke a tacit U.S. promise made in 1957 to assure it free passage in the straits. Indeed, the United States made an effort to organize an international flotilla that would open the Strait of Tiran, but this proved futile, as no other state wished to get involved. The Americans were also not very eager to make their promise good.

While the Israelis were working on the diplomatic front, the Egyptians and Jordanians signed a defense agreement on May 30 putting the Jordanian army under Egyptian command and allowing Egyptian troops to enter Jordan. As far as the Israelis were concerned, this was the last straw. Between May 14 and May 30, Egypt's moves had violated three Israeli *casi belli*. Israeli decision makers realized that their deterrence policy, which had worked reasonably well since 1957, had failed miserably in this crisis. The major problem was not the risk of an Egyptian attack, for the Egyptian army was in a strictly defensive posture and changing into an offensive position required time. Rather, the chief Israeli objective at this point was to reestablish deterrence by example. This is what prompted the Israelis to start the war. Nasser's actions, starting with the violation of the de facto demilitarization of the Sinai, suggested that unless Israel acted, the strategic status quo would be altered largely to Israel's disadvantage.

The signature of the Egyptian-Jordanian defense treaty led to a government change in Israel, with the joining of Moshe Dayan, Shimon Peres, Menachem Begin, and Elimelech Rimalt, all of them on the more (or most) hawkish side of the Israeli political spectrum. Nasser, although viewing at this point the chances of war as high (in fact, he thought that they had approached certainty), did not order the Egyptian troops to move to offensive positions, nor was the state of alert in the army increased significantly. As far as Egypt was concerned, every move on its part would bring about an Israeli attack. However, Egypt need not have moved. As far as Israel was concerned, the issue had been decided. Israel attacked in full force on June 5.

This chain of events consists of two fundamental steps of escalatory activities. The first dates from mid-1966 to mid-May 1967. The second step was what most researchers refer to as the May-June crisis. In the first step the key actors were Israel and Syria. In the second, the key actors were Israel and Egypt. In order to make the case for a Dollar Auction-like process, we must establish three things. First, none of the three actors involved in the process was at all interested in escalating the conflict to the war level. Second, the actors perceived a clear termination point at the outset but could not stop when they reached it due to a change in the way the stakes were defined. Finally, the wish to avoid the status of second-highest bidder describes the motivations behind the actors' behavior.

That Syria did not want war is very clear from the way it had managed limited confrontations with Israel since 1948 (Maoz and Yaniv, 1989). It is also very clear from two aspects of the way Syria handled the conflict during the 1966–67 period. First, Syria was willing to accept the fact that the diversion project was doomed. By the end of 1966, work on this project all but stopped. The fact that Syrian responses to the Israeli air strikes was fundamentally limited to shelling of selected targets also suggests that the Syrians did not have any illusions about their ability to win a war. Second, this impression is strengthened by the considerable Syrian alarm as a result of the increased escalation in April 1967. It is by now clear that the rumors spread by the Syrians and Soviets regarding Israeli troop concentrations were—if not completely false—vastly exaggerated. Nonetheless, it is also clear that Syrian alarm had been genuine in light of both the threatening Israeli statements and the escalation of the border skirmishes following the April 7 dogfight.

But if the Syrians were genuinely alarmed by the intensification of the warfare along the border, why did they not initiate deescalatory moves? Due to its precarious domestic situation, the Syrian leadership felt that it could not afford to appear to be trailing the Israelis in managing the border dispute. The Syrian leadership had been hard-pressed by both domestic considerations and inter-Arab political factors to instigate low-level conflict against Israel (Bar-Simantov, 1983). Moreover, the initial Syrian belief had been that such low-level activity would be sufficient to quell domestic opposition to the regime and would loom large in inter-Arab politics. This belief had guided Syria's willingness to take responsibility for the diversion project. Once this project had failed, Syria virtually stopped initiating hostile actions with its own troops. There is also evidence that PLO activities assumed a fairly independent pattern by 1967 and the Syrian control over the PLO was not as complete as the Israelis had suspected. By that time, the Israelis had stepped up their military activities, and what Syria viewed as manageable conflict management strategy turned into a grave fear of an all-out Israeli attack.

A similar logic describes the Israeli management of the conflict with Syria.[24] The Israelis faced a severe problem with the inception of the Syrian diversion project, and the strategy of limited provocations was perceived as a means of dealing with this problem in a manner that provided an adequate solution with minimal escalatory potential. The perception of the Israeli general staff was that the Syrians would have to yield to Israeli compellence eventually and quit the project, and that this strategy would not be misinterpreted as an offensive strategy whose ultimate aim was to attack Syria. But the policy of controlled confrontation had some unforeseen domestic side effects. The constant shelling and countershelling along the border proved a heavy burden on the population of the settlements along the Israeli-Syrian border and, on a larger scale, a source of domestic criticism of the "indecisive" handling of the Syrians. The escalation in verbal warfare toward the fall of 1966 should be seen partly in this light.[25] Like the Syrian government, the Israeli government found it increasingly difficult to accept the role of the second-highest bidder, and, like the Syrian government, it believed that this strategy was not going to lead to war as long as both parties played by the unwritten rules of limited confrontation. Indeed, the year of 1967 was seen by Israeli military planners as one of relative tranquility, allowing them to reduce the length of service in the regular army from 2.5 years to 2 years and 2 months for men and to 18 months for women.[26]

The Egyptian entry into this crisis represents the entry of another bidder into the Dollar Auction.[27] Nasser's decision to enter the crisis was triggered by three factors: (1) increasingly vocal criticism by both Jordanian and Syrian presses of his failure to come to Syria's help, (2) Soviet and Syrian intelligence reports indicating considerable Israeli troop concentrations along the Syrian border, and (3) statements by Israeli Prime Minister Eshkol and Chief of Staff Rabin suggesting that a large-scale military operation against Syria was imminent. Again, from Nasser's point of view the gamble was manageable up to a point. Although the risk of war increased with every move he made, he sincerely believed that he could stop the process one step short of war and win diplomatically (Moore, 1989). Indeed, the steps Nasser took suggest this belief. While launching a massive diplomatic and propaganda attack on Israel, strategically, the positioning of the Eyptian forces in defensive positions made it evident that the Egyptians had no offensive designs. Indeed, it was clear to the Israeli military planners that the Egyptian forces in the Sinai were digging in rather than preparing for an offensive.

Moore (1989) argues that Nasser thought that he could escalate and get away with it as long as he did not go too far. And given the Israeli responses to his moves, he thought that he was not pushing them overboard.

From the Israeli perspective, the mere continuation of the crisis was what made an attack necessary. For Israel to accept the changes in the status quo in the Sinai was unthinkable, because it would mean that the policy of deterrence that had been the cornerstone of Israeli-Egyptian relations collapsed overnight. Even if Egypt had no intention of attacking at the moment, one could not assure that the Egyptians would not attempt to convert their diplomatic victory into a military one in the future. Moreover, as long as the crisis was not resolved (the key was the opening of the Strait of Tiran and the withdrawal of Egyptian troops from the Sinai), Israel could not afford to cancel the general mobilization. However, as long as general mobilization was in effect, the Israeli society and economy came to a standstill. Thus, what was seen by Nasser as a constraint on Israel's ability to escalate was seen by the Israeli leadership as a major incentive for escalation (Yaniv, 1986: 121-123; Stein and Tanter, 1980; Brecher, 1980).[28]

The result of this was that precisely when Nasser realized that he could not continue to escalate without risking war, and therefore stopped the escalation process just one step short of an attack, the Israelis realized that they could not afford to play the role of second-highest bidder and decided to strike. Nobody wanted the war to break out, and all three principal parties (as well as other parties, such as the United States and—to a lesser extent—the Soviet Union) made efforts to avert it. Yet war broke out. Moore (1989) argues that one of the major problems with the way the crisis was managed by Nasser was that at no stage during the crisis was he given clear and unequivocal signals by the Israelis that they could not continue for long under that situation. This made further escalation rational for him, and the Israeli attack rational for them (Stein and Tanter, 1980; Brecher, 1980).

The cognitive interpretation of rationalization and justification raised in the Dollar Auction context helps shed additional light on the process. The investment of each party in the game was such that, at each point, justifying previous moves could be done only by escalation. Syria could justify its investment in the futile diversion project only by showing that, after all, the past struggle had paid in that Israel was bothered by the new type of problem introduced by the PLO. Israel could justify the escalation of the warfare along the northeast border, which started as an effort to thwart the diversion project, only by escalating the warfare against Syria when the latter increased its support of the PLO.

Moore (1989) argues that while the rationalization and justification argument might shed light on why Nasser kept escalating despite the increasing danger of war, it does not explain why Nasser did not continue to escalate beyond May 30. Most important, this explanation does not tell us why Nasser failed to alert the Egyptian troops in the Sinai or to move them to offensive positions, despite the fact that he was nearly certain of an imminent Israeli attack. Moore's analysis of Nasser's decision-making process suggests that Nasser's actions could be made consistent with both a myopic version of rational behavior and a nonmyopic version. Nasser escalated the conflict as long as he thought he could get away with it. The Egyptian-Jordanian defense pact was the last escalatory move that Nasser could afford: afterward, any move would have led to a certainty of an Israeli attack. Where he apparently erred was in thinking that the Israelis had not yet cast the die in favor of war, and that ending the escalatory process at that point might have resulted in a new status quo representing a major diplomatic victory for Egypt. The mistake was only in the assessment of the number of moves available before the game terminates. And such a mistake was largely a result of the relatively moderate Israeli reaction to Nasser's previous moves. The fact that the Israelis failed to make their intention clear gave Nasser the wrong clues during the evolution of the crisis.

## Avoiding Wars That Nobody Wants

This chapter argues that not wanting a conflict to escalate to war is not sufficient for preventing actual escalation. Statespersons have to work hard at avoiding such unfortunate clashes. One of the problems in crisis management is how to strike an optimal balance between assurances that signal the opponent that we do not want war and threats designed to persuade the opponent that we do not mean these assurances to be seen as a sign of weakness. Not only is it difficult to prescribe just the right dose of resolve and prudence, there is a distinct possibility that any prescription of this sort would be self-defeating. What the Dollar Auction game suggests is that, once there are two of you in the bidding game, the best thing to do is to forget about the sunk cost and get out of the bidding as soon as your turn comes. If you are trying to recover the sunk cost, you are doomed to lose your whole bankroll. But if you realize that staying in the game would indeed lead to such results, and you get out, you might be in more trouble in the future. If bidders in the Dollar Auction know that the reputation they establish will affect the behavior of other actors in future games, they might continue bidding until their opponents drop out. Because they attempt to maximize both present gains and long-term ones, dropping out early in one Dollar Auction may be taken as a sign that they would drop out in another.

There is a way out of a Dollar Auction, just as there is a unique optimal strategy in the Divide the Dollar game. This strategy requires just one thing: communication. Once in the game, the best actors can do is to strike a deal. No matter how far they have gone in the escalatory sequence, dividing spoils or sharing costs (Raiffa, 1982: 187–204) may provide for a way out. Collusion could lead to deescalation, to finding new twists to the game that would not be possible in the absence of negotiation.[29]

## Notes

1   The data in Maoz (1982a) is based only on wars covering the 1816–1976 period. However, all international wars that have broken out since then (Somali-Ethiopia, 1977; Tanzania-Uganda, 1978; Sino-Vietnamese, 1979; Afghanistan, 1979–89; Iran-Iraq, 1980-88; Falkland, 1982; Lebanon, 1982) have also been preceded by crises.

2   For a review of definitions of crisis, see Maoz (1982b).

3   However, see my earlier argument for the inclusion of a variable of perceived opportunity in the definition of decisional stress (Maoz, 1982b, 1989).

4   For a summary of research on crisis decision making, see Tanter (1978) and Maoz (1985c).

5   This solution is simple, even though the precise details of O'Neill's analysis are fairly complicated and technical.

6   For experimental evidence on the Dollar Auction game, see Teger (1980). A fascinating psychological analysis of these and other instances of entrapment is Brockner and Rubin (1985).

7   In a game-theoretic sense, stability means simply that once an outcome is reached it will persist. This is due to the fact that no player has an incentive to change his or her behavior unilaterally because he or she cannot benefit and might be damaged by doing so.

8   Leininger (1987) shows that O'Neill's solution holds only if offers are restricted to certain discrete minima (e.g., 5 cents). If an offer can be made continuous, the stability induced by O'Neill's solution disappears.

9   A similar game was analyzed experimentally by Kelley et al. (1967). In this game (called the Game of 9), subjects were asked to divide a certain figure through communication, and they were allowed to leave negotiation at any time if they so pleased. The difference between the Divide the Dollar game and the Game of 9 is that in the latter game players drew reservation prices from decks of cards, each player knowing what his or her reservation price was but not the reservation price of the opponent. Another difference is that the sum of maximum gain at each iteration was fixed.

10   The game presented by Schelling is, in fact, a unit-square (or continuous) version of Chicken (see Brams and Kilgour, 1988). The version presented here is, therefore, an iterated version of Chicken with decreased cooperative payoffs but identical noncooperative payoffs. As in the 2 × 2 version of Chicken, the Divide the Dollar game has many equilibria. In fact, any outcome of the game that has a sum of offers that is exactly a dollar is stable. Thus, to the extent that the dollar is infinitely divisible, the game has an infinite number of stable solutions.

11   The problem of unwanted escalation in iterated Chicken is this. Suppose that the game is played simultaneously. Both players start by cooperating (where cooperation means that each makes an offer of less than half the

amount to be divided). The outcome of the game is unstable: each can improve his or her situation by defecting (offering an amount in excess of half of the remainder to be divided). If each attempts to move to the equilibrium favoring him or her, the outcome is disaster.

12  This case study is based on Truman (1964), Goulden (1982), Alexander (1986), George and Smoke (1974), Lebow (1981), and De Rivera (1968).

13  Whiting (1960: 95–96) details the statements made by the U.S. secretary of the navy, Matthews, and the famous (and controversial) statement of MacArthur to the convention of U.S. Veterans of Foreign Wars, and their possibly threatening interpretation by China. On the commotion caused by MacArthur's statement, see Goulden (1982: 160–163).

14  Chou En-lai's warning to the United States on October 1, through the Indian ambassador to China, Panikkar, is the most explicit statement of intent issued by China throughout the crisis. Chou stated that China would join the war if U.S. forces crossed the 38th parallel, but it would not join the war if only South Korean forces crossed the parallel. This statement was dismissed in the United States because, as Truman (1964: 362) notes, "Mr. Panikkar had in the past played the game of Chinese Communism quite regularly, so that his statement could not be taken as that of an impartial observer."

15  Truman (1964: 372) mentions a CIA report dated October 20 that discusses Chinese troop activity along the Suiho power plant (on the Korean side of the Yalu). On the same day, navy intelligence analysts reviewing raw intelligence data concluded that there was Chinese military presence in North Korea (Goulden, 1982: 284)

16  This is reflected in Acheson's memoirs: "This government missed its last chance to halt the march to disaster in Korea. All the President's advisors in this matter, civilian and military, knew that something was badly wrong, though what it was, how to find out, and what to do about it they muffed" (cited in Alexander, 1986: 288–289).

17  MacArthur's March 11, 1949, statement and Acheson's January 12, 1950, statement are the most clear expression of this view. See Whiting (1960: 39) and George and Smoke (1974: 185–190).

18  Both Whiting (1960: 34–46) and George and Smoke (1974) provide detailed discussion of the Chinese and Soviet calculations.

19  Sources for this analysis include Brecher (1974, 1980), Geist (1974), Wagner (1974), Stein and Tanter (1980), and Yaniv (1986) for the Israeli side; Maoz (1982b), Yaniv (1985), Maoz and Yaniv (1988), Bar-Simantov (1983), and Van Dam (1979) for the Syrian side; and Lacoture (1971), Nutting (1972), Stephens (1971), Sadat (1978), and Moore (1989) for the Egyptian side.

20  Most analysts of decision-making processes during the prewar crisis use May 15 as the starting point of the crisis. This is, for example, the case in the studies of the Israeli decision-making process (Brecher, 1974, 1980; Stein and Tanter, 1980; Geist, 1974; Wagner, 1974), and the single analytical case study of the Egyptian decision-making process (Moore, 1989). However, students looking at the multilateral interaction process in the Middle East identify 1966 as the key starting point of the crisis (Maoz, 1982b; Burrowes and Muzzio, 1972; Maoz and Yaniv, 1989). Both historical studies of Syria (e.g., Bar-Simantov, 1983; Van Dam, 1979) and biographies of Nasser (Lacoture, 1971; Nutting, 1972) look at the whole pattern of Israeli-Syrian escalation as a cause of the Egyptian embroilment in the conflict.

21 Kerr (1967) argues that the formation of the PLO was an Egyptian ploy to create a puppet organization that would provide for those states that did not wish to confront Israel directly—a political decoy. Unfortunately, the PLO turned out to be more active than expected, in many cases becoming a real thorn in the side of the Arab states that had established it. See also Stephens (1971: 450–453).

22 The UNEF was an international force under U.N. auspices placed in various places in the Sinai peninsula (in the Gaza Strip and in the Sharm-a-Sheikh area) following the 1956 Sinai war. The purpose of this force was to separate Egyptian and Israeli forces and to avoid clashes along the border between the two states. In effect, the Sinai had been a demilitarized zone, with only a symbolic Egyptian presence consisting of few troops and police forces in the desert.

23 Incidentally, the request was only for the withdrawal of the U.N. forces along the northern portion of the Egyptian-Israeli border, not in the Sharm-a-Sheikh area. However, U Thant, the U.N. secretary general, chose to withdraw the entire force (Stephens, 1971: 471–472).

24 The information available on the Israeli management of the conflict, especially in terms of the calculations and politics that affected the process, is much more detailed and accurate than in the Syrian case. Yaniv (1986: 104–115) provides a detailed analysis of these aspects.

25 The November 13, 1966, Israeli raid on the village of Sammua, south of Hebron, was criticized in the Israeli press and in the Knesset as a sign of weakness and impotence. Instead of attacking the Syrian aggressors who were chiefly responsible for the PLO operations, the Israeli government chose to attack poor Jordan.

26 Gilboa (1968) points out that Israeli military intelligence estimated the probability of war in 1967 as extremely low. This analysis was based on factors that were extremely similar to those that characterized the Israeli "conception" of 1973: Syria wanted to attack Israel but could not do it without the Egyptians; the Egyptians felt that they lacked sufficient capability to win a war and hence would not attack. In 1967 the intelligence estimate had been based on the deep Egyptian involvement in the Yemeni civil war.

27 Precisely as the Dollar Auction game unfolds in theory and in experimental settings, one of the previous bidders drops out, leaving the process a two-person game. In this case the party that dropped out was Syria. I will elaborate on this phenomenon in the chapter on the ally's paradox.

28 In order to highlight the extent that this sequence of events marked a loss of control for Israel, it is interesting to mention a historical footnote. On May 26, following the announcement of the Tiran blockade, David Ben-Gurion, the first prime minister of Israel, who was then in partial retirement in Kibbutz Sdeh-Boker in the Negev, called the chief of staff, Rabin, to a talk. According to unconfirmed reports, Ben-Gurion berated Rabin for escalating the conflict with the Syrians to a point that brought about Egyptian intervention. Following that discussion, Rabin had a nervous breakdown and was confined to his bed for two days. Ezer Weizman, then the chief of operations in the Israeli general staff, claims that Rabin called him over and asked him to take command. According to Weizman (1975), he had to use all his powers of persuasion to prevent Rabin from resigning.

29 Raiffa (1982: 88) suggests that an interesting aspect of a conflict process is the opportunity to deescalate. In the Dollar Auction, that amounts to changing

the rules of play to permit bidding downward. Players are allowed to reduce bids. Thus, if a player finds him- or herself to be the second-highest bidder, he or she is allowed to deescalate. This would still make the player a sucker, but it would allow him or her to reduce loss. The highest bidder has the opportunity to bid again, and he or she can bid upward or downward. The rational thing to do, of course, is to bid downward in a manner that will still preserve one's position as the highest bidder but will close the gap to the opponent's bid. The opponent will then have the incentive to bid further downward. This allows for a seemingly rational process of deescalation. However, as players approach the dollar amount on their way downward, the situation might again begin to look complicated and, as Raiffa puts it, "life would become especially precarious."

# PART II
## Paradoxes of War Management

# 5
# *The Paradox of Attrition*

Enemy advances, we retreat.
Enemy halts, we harass.
Enemy tires, we attack.
Enemy retreats, we pursue. (Mao Tse-tung)

Once decision makers decide to go to a forceful arbitration of a conflict of interests, they want the war to be as swift and decisive as possible. The chief question for the manager of military operations is how to accomplish military objectives with the minimum amount of cost and time. That there are political constraints on the military planning of war operation is obvious. Generals who do not do well on the battlefield often resort to arguments about how their hands were tied by the politicians. And in many cases that is true. The paradox of attrition is not concerned with such borderline cases, where politics constrained military operations in time of war. These cases make it difficult to discern how much of the blame for failure is due to political restrictions and how much must be attributed to the incompetence of generals.

The paradox of attrition describes cases where the most well-planned military operations run aground not because of defective planning, but because they are well planned. We deal here with carefully planned and initiated wars designed to bring about a quick military fait accompli. The swift military victory is designed to give the political leadership something to bargain with. Hence, the military is given a clear objective (typically in terms of territory to occupy and perhaps a time frame to accomplish it) and complete freedom as to the selection of strategy. Military operations typically start with a swift and massive offensive, one that catches the opponent by surprise and goes smoothly for the attacker. However, in some cases, the swift military operations intended to bring war to a quick end result in extended and messy wars of attrition that last a long time without resolution. Precisely because of the swiftness of the initial military offensive and its initial success, what was designed to be a quick and decisive victory is converted into a prolonged war of attrition, often ending with the defeat of the initiator.

Some of the terms used thus far require clarification. In addition, the relationship between the purely military nature of this paradox and the political conduct of war merits discussion. I will try to show that the freedom of action one side accords to its military planners may be a source of disaster. I will also show that it is political wisdom and determination on the part of the opponent that converts the war into a static disaster for the attacker.

## Managing the Use of Force

George et al. (1972) distinguish among four strategies of the use of force in international politics. The first strategy is the fait accompli approach. This is a swift military act designed to establish control that cannot be altered by the opponent unless the latter can acquire the occupied territory by force. The second strategy, *coercive diplomacy,* reflects a combination of military moves with diplomatic maneuvers in order to compel the opponent to do something it would not otherwise have done.

The third strategy, *attrition,* is one wherein an actor attempts to wear out an opponent through a static warfare that avoids direct confrontation between mass military forces but entails many minor skirmishes and artillery exchanges, guerrilla warfare, and so forth. The emphasis here is not on accomplishing a direct military victory. Rather, actors relying on this strategy hope that the opponent's will to continue fighting will gradually erode through the irritation that the attrition strategy causes. This is a military strategy whose prime aim is psychological: it is designed to disarm the opponent of its resolve and determination through constant harassment at low levels of warfare.

The fourth strategy is *acceptance of the opponent's ground rules.* The essence of the strategy is replication. An actor essentially emulates the opponent's strategy, whatever it is. In a way, it is an attempt to beat the opponent at its own game rather than to devise a game wherein one has relative advantage over the opponent. When actor $A$ selects a strategy of attrition and the opponent $B$ uses a similar strategy, we must be able to distinguish between cases in which $B$'s participation in the war of attrition is a matter of choice—in which case $B$ uses the acceptance of the ground rules strategy—and when it is a matter of necessity—in which case $B$ uses a strategy of attrition. The difference lies in the factors that affect a selection of an attrition strategy by an actor confronted with an opponent who uses a strategy of attrition. When one views a strategy of attrition as a best strategy for one's own sake, that is, as the strategy that maximizes the chances of accomplishing the military (and thus the political) objectives, then one is said to use a "strategy of attrition." However, when one uses attrition because one is compelled to abide by the strategy adopted by the opponent and cannot change strategy for a variety of military and political reasons, one is said to accept the opponent's ground rules.

For example, in 1969, the Egyptian leadership decided to adopt a policy of attrition in order to harass the Israelis along the Suez Canal. The decision was made because the Egyptians felt they could not initiate a conventional mobile attack due to their military inferiority, yet they wanted to put pressure on Israel that would eventually lead the Israelis to conclude an agreement with Egypt or to withdraw unilaterally from the Suez Canal (Stein, 1985). The Israelis were not very pleased with the way the war was progressing, but could not find a political pretext for attacking Egypt. They did escalate the scope of fighting through deep-penetration bombing raids (Shlaim and Tanter, 1978), but they could not afford to start a mobile ground offensive that would accomplish a swift military victory. In this case, political constraints forced the Israelis to accept the opponent's ground rules (Bar-Simantov, 1980).

A typical example of the combination of attrition and acceptance of ground rules is that of guerrilla warfare. The inferior side in a war, *A,* which has already been overrun by the opponent, *B,* resorts to a warfare that avoids any sort of frontal military confrontation with the opponent. Instead, it uses low-level infiltrations and attacks that harass and demoralize the superior opponent. The opponent obviously wants to convert the war into a conventional one, because that would allow it to express the things that make it superior—size, technology, organizational structure, command and control, firepower, and so forth. The problem is that *B* cannot do so because *A*'s forces are dispersed and elusive. Although the army may have a free hand in the management of military operations, it must play the game dictated by the guerrilla forces.[1]

Rational use of military strategy in war is supposed to give an actor an edge due to the fundamental attributes of the opposing sides. If one is given the opportunity to devise military plans without political constraints, those plans—provided that the people who develop them are competent and bright—seek to capitalize on one's own relative advantages and on the opponent's weaknesses. In addition, good plans are those that deny the opponent any opportunity of expressing those features of its army that are superior to one's own. Strategy seeks to manipulate the strengths and weaknesses of the opposing parties in a manner that maximizes the chances of victory. But because the opponent has plans of its own, devising an optimal strategy that is independent of the one devised by the opponent is not easy. Another problem is that strategy is based on the types of military objectives pursued. One type of strategy might be best for accomplishing one objective, such as the occupation of an enemy fort. However, to maintain the fort once occupied, quite another strategy might be required, involving different skills, different types of forces, and different logistical and organizational setups.

There is a trade-off between versatility and expertise in the conduct of war. Versatile forces that are trained and equipped for the execution of different types of military operations are less effective in carrying out any single type of operation than forces that are specifically trained and equipped to carry out that type of operation. On a macro level of military planning, general staffs make hard choices on grand strategies that impose constraints on versatility. For example, the Israeli reliance on an offensive military strategy designed to carry the war onto the opponent's territory led to logistical and tactical structures emphasizing offensive mobility, rapid troop concentration, the conversion of an overall numerical inferiority to local numerical superiority, and flexibility in command and control procedures. As a result, defensive tactics and logistical structures were relatively neglected (Luttwak and Horowitz, 1975). Resource scarcity, political constraints, and other bureaucratic factors often lead to preference of expertise and professionalization over military diversification. When the political objective and the military variables seem fairly constant and clear, versatility is sacrificed almost completely for the sake of a force structure equipped and trained to accomplish a very specific set of objectives. Professionalization may be an asset if the army prepares for the kind of war it will actually be fighting. It may, however, turn into disaster if the war it actually fights develops differently from what had been envisioned. The difficulty of adapting to the changing structure of the battlefield, to different political goals that might impose constraints on the conduct of military operations, significantly impairs the army's ability to adjust to the changing circumstances and thus gives the advantage to an opponent that is now playing the game by its own set of rules.

The idea of a first strike is strategically compelling in that it allows the army to choose the timing, location, and form of the attack. Strategists seek to capitalize on the strength of their army. If the army is trained and equipped for a mobile armored attack, with a second infantry wave following it, this is how the initial attack is executed. Rational planning of the first strike must also take into account whatever countermeasures the opponent may have in store that can deny the initiator success. These factors may include specific weapon systems that one wishes to destroy, specific defensive fortifications that one wishes to bypass, specific tactical patterns employed by the opponent that one wishes to subvert, and so forth. An opportunity to plan a first strike and a plan that pays attention to all those details can make a first strike the key to final victory.

First strikes may run into a lot of problems, not the least of which is that of friction, which can lead to unintended consequences for reasons that have nothing to do with the plan itself. Unanticipated bad weather, garbled messages—which occur in even the most sophisticated communication networks—mechanical breakdowns, and similar misfortunes can destroy even the most detailed and sophisticated military plan. First strikes that run aground due to friction in their execution are interesting in that they can and usually do teach military planners lessons that are typically utilized the next time. The idea of friction suggests that military planning should make provisions for unanticipated mishaps. But even the best plan that takes account of all possible friction contains a substantial element of gamble. What distinguishes a well-planned and well-executed first strike from a poorly planned and executed one is that the risks of friction and of strategy are well calculated in the first but not in the second (Luttwak, 1987: 10-15).

Failure of well-planned first strikes due to friction is not to be taken as paradoxical, because friction is random. It is not a systematically generalizable factor and therefore cannot be predicted precisely. You can have a reserve of $x$ parts for your tanks, an amount that is more than enough under any reasonable circumstances, but if in the course of battle the unexpected happens and $x + 1$ parts are required, this should be seen as a regrettable event rather than as a paradoxical consequence of a first strike. Hence, friction is important to mention as a factor that adversely effects the outcome of first strikes, but it is not part of the explanation of the paradox of attrition.

Another factor that must be discussed prior to an explanation of the paradox of attrition is that of military adjustment in the course of war. I call this the "Plan B" syndrome. The question here is how an army adjusts to the fact that a given plan does not seem to be working. Part of good strategy planning is the conception of an alternate set of programs that are seen as fallback strategies if the primary strategy seems to be going nowhere. By nature, fallback strategies are more modest than initial plans in terms of their goals, but they too require a lot of planning and consideration and careful investment in terms of training forces and equipping them. But, conceptually, they are a diversion, because they divert resources from the main strategy. By now, the notion of reserve forces that are kept out of the battle zone is well established in tactical sciences. Commanders in the field always have a strong urge to commit reserves to the combat zone, either when they confront the first sign of trouble or when they want to capitalize on success. However, premature commitment of reserve units might turn out to be a disaster, because if reserves are committed to one area of the battle prematurely, they will not be available to help in other areas of the battle where they may be needed.

On October 8, 1973, the Israelis launched their counteroffensive in the canal zone. The plan was to have two armies attack simultaneously along the canal in order to push the Egyptian forces to the east side. The third army, under the command of General (res.) Ariel Sharon, was supposed to stay back, in the middle region between the two armies, so that it could be rushed to help one of the two primary armies once the dust of battle cleared. When the initial attack of the northern army seemed to be going well, Sharon moved his army to the south in order to provide assistance to the southern army. Unfortunately, this movement was premature. The northern army, under the command of General "Bren," Abraham Adan, got into heavy trouble, and suffered considerable losses. The reserve army was by then too far south to be of any real help (Van Creveld, 1985: 203–226).

Because alternate plans are a distraction, the likelihood of their being less carefully developed than primary plans is high; Plan A is typically given more consideration than Plan B. Thus, if Plan A—a very carefully developed plan—fails, chances are that Plan B, to which less time and mental effort have been devoted, is even less likely to work. Likewise with reserve units. Main efforts require the best units in order to maximize success. When the primary effort does not work, the reserve troops that are brought in as part of Plan B are even less likely to prove effective. Why then do we need reserves? The role of reserves is not to alter the qualitative balance of factors, but rather to alter the quantitative balance. The hope is that quantitative superiority will help when the qualitative balance (either the planning aspects of the balance or the quality of the forces) seems to have failed. But if the enemy has outwitted us in terms of tactical planning, is it not absurd to commit our reserve troops? After all, if the enemy is sufficiently smart to subvert Plan A, is it not sufficiently smart to assume that we have a Plan B that rests on reserve forces and thus to have some reserves of its own? And if our best units were stopped by the opponent, is it not even more likely that our reserve units will meet the same fate?

## The Economy of Force in War

War is not only a duel of forces, nor is it only a duel of wills; it is most of all a duel of wits. This implies that opponents compete in applying their plans. However, the implementation of military plans is not symmetrical. The initiator is given an opportunity to carry out its plan of war first (Posen, 1984). To the extent that such a plan entails a concentrated effort to disrupt the opponent's plans, the latter is at a major disadvantage. The initiator has a strong incentive to launch a swift and decisive initial attack in order to maximize the chances of success. The initiator of a swift military operation fights not only against a political and military opponent but also against an abstraction called time. Time is not an element of friction, because it is a permanent enemy of strategists, and because it is foreseeable, whereas friction is incidental and—in many cases—unforeseeable. Time means cost for the planners of military operations. Because so much depends on the speed with which a military operation is conducted, if the war extends beyond the limits set by the initiator, it becomes more expensive than had originally been intended. Leites (1981: 187) quotes a Soviet military analysis of the logic of modern warfare ("modern" warfare is defined 1927 style):

> The concentration of *all* means on one . . . operation may yield a big economy of force. An enemy front capable of enduring dozens of small strikes may be broken by one big strike. In certain conditions, a certain mass of operation is necessary in order to obtain even minimal results.

The analysis of war management provided by Maoz (1985b) illustrates this issue. An actor expects to gain some political benefits from war. These benefits are represented by the expected utility of war alternative. At the time the war starts—we shall call this point $t_0$—this expected utility term contains no cost component. As costs begin to accumulate over time—people are killed, equipment is lost and needs replacement—the expected utility of war goes down. The planners of the war are aware of this, and thus when they calculate the expected utility of war, they take into account the expected costs associated with it. But expected costs accumulate over time; hence, to calculate before the war what its expected utility might be, military planners must set an expected time frame for the accomplishment of the war aims.

The notion of swiftness can thus be made more precise: it is simply the ratio of military objectives to be accomplished to time. The higher the ratio (that is, the more objectives, or the more important objectives per unit time), the swifter the attack. A swift first strike means that one plans to occupy a lot of territory in a short time or to destroy many enemy forces in a short time. To do that, one needs to throw all one has into the initial attack. One also needs to commit reserve forces rather early in the war to capitalize on the initial success. In other words, a *blitzkrieg* requires the initiator to place all its eggs in one basket. It is extremely difficult to plan a swift military operation that is both effective and flexible in the sense that there would be enough forces for the implementation of a Plan B.

It is also in the interest of the planners of a swift attack to lure the opponent into an early all-out confrontation. Because the initiation of the first strike is presumed to give the initiator the edge, it is important to have the key battle of the war as long as the edge is still on the initiator's side and before the target has had a chance to recuperate from the first blow. This would maximize the chances of victory and minimize the costs. This also requires total investment of resources in the execution of the first strike and little flexibility. Just as in professional basketball, much of the outcome of the game depends on momentum.

By the same token, it is in the interest of the disadvantaged party to slow down the pace of battle. In order to minimize its costs and maximize its chances of victory, the target is interested in moving the game into an arena in which it possesses the advantage. Its ability to turn the tide of battle depends on self-discipline and willingness to make temporary sacrifices in order to restore rules of war with which it is familiar. This logic is illustrated graphically in Figure 5.1.

In this figure, actors $i$ and $j$ make assessments regarding the evolution of an armed conflict between themselves. At the start of the war (time $t_0$), each places a certain value on the war (this is denoted by $EU_0^i$ and by $EU_0^j$ for $i$ and $j$, respectively). This valuation reflects only the political stakes each actor has in the war and the probabilities of victory and defeat; it does not include estimates of the costs in men and equipment entailed in war. The valuation of war that includes war costs is denoted by $EU_w^i$ and $EU_w^j$. Actors also make estimates about the expected duration of the war. This is given by $t_e^i$ for $i$'s estimate, and by $t_e^j$ for $j$'s. The distribution of the costs of war over the expected time of war defines what we shall call the *decay function*. The decay function reflects the assessment of each side about how intense the war is likely to be; it reflects the belief of the actors regarding how the war's costs are to be distributed per unit time. The steeper the decay function, the more casualties are expected per unit time, and thus the shorter the war one can afford. The fact that the decay functions in this figure are linear reflects a belief that the distribution of costs over time is likely to be uniform (for example, the number of people killed on day ten is expected to be roughly equal to the number of people killed on day seven). But the linear shape of the decay function is only a presentational convenience; there is no good reason this should be the general case.[2]

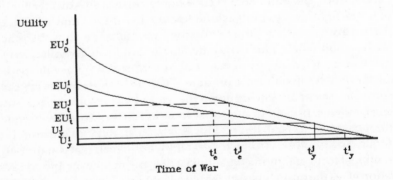

**Figure 5.1**  Utility, Cost, Time, and Expected Outcomes of War

The idea that the expected utility of war declines over time reflects a belief that costs increase over time while political objectives do not change. Thus, the longer the war, the less attractive it is. But declining attractiveness does not mean that it is irrational to fight. On the contrary—the figure shows that even if the actual duration of the war exceeds that expected, it still makes sense to fight. Fighting is rational as long as the expected utility of war exceeds the utility of yielding ($U_y^i$ and $U_y^j$, for $i$ and $j$, respectively). The utility of yielding reflects the valuation of defeat by an actor. The more one values defeat, the less inclined one is to fight. The less one values defeat, the more costs one is prepared to incur and thus the longer one is willing to fight.

The initial valuation of the war, the decay function, and the valuation of defeat all determine the maximum rational time of war for each of the actors. The points $t_y^i$ and $t_y^j$ denote the breakpoints of actors $i$ and $j$, respectively. The figure suggests that the longer one can hold, the more likely one is to emerge a winner.[3] It is important to note that the calculations of decay functions, and thus the maximum rational time of fighting, assume that actors throw all they have into the battle and that the war is sustained and involves continuous large-scale military confrontations. Under these conditions, the first actor who finds it rational to give in is the loser and the other actor is the winner. Herein lies a problem. If actors have complete information about the parameters of this figure—that is, each knows the opponent's decay function, the initial valuation of war, and the valuation of defeat—then war becomes an irrational instrument of policy. Rational actors could predict the outcome of the war before it started. The would-be winner would know it would win and the would-be loser would know it would be defeated. The actors would also know how much they would get at the end of the war. Thus, they could reach a better deal without having to assume any of the costs associated with war. Even if actors do not have complete information about the opponent's expectations, but can make even roughly correct guesses, there is no point in fighting. As long as one knows that it is bound to win and the other knows it is bound to lose, an exchange short of war is possible and rational for each individually and for both collectively.[4]

The principal object of the would-be loser is to reduce the pace of decline in its utility for war over time. This can be done by cutting costs. Costs can be cut by slowing down the pace of war, avoiding large-scale engagements, using a strategy that lets the first strike of the opponent run out of steam, and so on. This is what a strategy of attrition is all about. An actor resorts to such a strategy when it feels that a mobile conventional form of fighting entailing large-scale maneuver and confrontation gives the opponent substantial advantage. The purpose is to wear down the opponent and slow its momentum, or, better yet, to let the opponent feel that it can advance rapidly into the enemy territory, where it will suddenly find itself trapped. Luttwak (1987: 19) describes this paradoxical logic very aptly:

> Consider what happens to an army advancing victoriously in a typical setting of continental warfare. One battle or many have been fought, and one army prevails over the other, forcing it to retreat. Perhaps the defeated are scattering in panic or are about to be cornered and destroyed; the war may therefore be coming to an end by negotiation or capitulation. . . . If, however, the defeated army fights on, even in retreat, a pattern of reversal will begin to appear.

> The victorious army is advancing away from its homeland and forward bases, whose training camps, industry, storage depots, and workshops sustained its recent success—and must now obtain what it needs by routes of reinforcement and supply that are becoming progressively longer. The defeated army by contrast is presumably falling back toward its bases, so that its own routes of reinforcement and supply are becoming shorter. The victorious army must make an increasing effort to sustain itself and may have to take men and equipment away from frontline combat to expand its supply units, or at least divert reinforcements for the purpose. The defeated army by contrast can now reduce its own transport effort and may skin combat-worthy manpower and equipment from supply units to strengthen the frontline forces.

> The victorious army is entering territory until then in its enemy keeping, which may contain an unfriendly population with armed partisans, perhaps, or regular troops deliberately left behind to fight as guerrillas. At best, the military government of the newly occupied population will demand some manpower and resources. . . . If there is armed resistance, with raids and sabotage against rail lines, road convoys, supply dumps, service units, and rear headquarters, the victorious army will have to take away combat units from frontline duties to provide guards, security patrols, and quick-reaction forces in rear areas judged unsafe. Or, if the victorious army is liberating friendly civilians who will offer no resistance or shelter to stay-behind parties, there is still a relative disadvantage in the advance; it is the defeated army that will have been the occupier, and it can now return guards, patrol units, and reaction forces to frontline duty.

There are two accounts of the conversion of a swift military attack into a double-edged weapon that can be used against its initiator. The first is the one that is discussed by Luttwak: the defeated party retreats and lets the attacker overextend its supply and logistics and weaken itself by transforming combat units into counterguerrilla forces and guards of supply lines and rear installations. The other entails a quick initial retreat to areas that are geographically defensible (such as a high mountain range or some other kind of natural obstacle), and establishing a line of defense, letting the opponent waste considerable forces on an attempt to break through, thus halting its momentum and wearing it down in the process. In either case, the purposes of the defeated army are to cut down its costs and, while avoiding a major confrontation that would determine the outcome of the war, to try to recover from the initial defeat until it is strong enough to strike back in full force. In fact, the more successful the initial blow, the stronger the incentive to resort to this kind of attrition strategy. In terms of the formal analysis of war described above, this process can be illustrated by Figure 5.2.

When states throw their entire capabilities into the battle, the initiator $i$ has the clear advantage, and if both parties were rational and endowed with complete information there would be no rational reason to fight. But if war broke out and the initiator were able to control the rules of combat, it would clearly be in its interest to have an all-out confrontation in which it has the advantage. Indeed, if the target puts all its forces into battle, it is bound to be badly defeated. Converting the war into one of attrition means that the defeated party wants to cut down costs, thereby slowing the decline in its expected utility. Instead of confronting the opponent directly and in full force, the target retreats while constantly jabbing the initiator on a small and local scale, or converts the dynamic war into a static one.

Paradoxically, the greater the advantage an actor has in swift military operations, the more likely it is to fall into the trap of attrition. The wish to capitalize on one's advantage is enhanced when this advantage is of a major magnitude rather than a marginal one. When the initial attack goes well, the initiator wishes to capitalize on success by committing its reserves early in the war. On the other side of the battlefield, the target

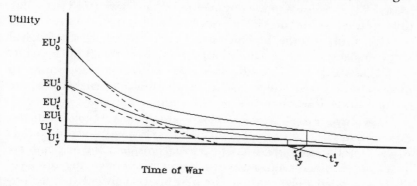

**Figure 5.2**  War Management Effects on Cost, Time, and War Outcomes

is more likely to resort to an attrition strategy when it recognizes that the opponent has the edge in mobile warfare.

There is, however, a significant price that a state pays when choosing a strategy of attrition. Such an actor must be willing to prolong the war, to surrender territory and population to the opponent. It is this cost that prevents actors from resorting to a strategy of attrition every time they are confronted by a swift attack. The kinds of resources necessary for a prolonged struggle—which for a long period may seem hopeless—are in short supply. For example, one must have enough territory to hand to the opponent so that the latter can overextend itself. One must be sure that the occupied population will indeed collaborate in guerrilla warfare against the powerful opponent. Finally, since the opponent can adapt to the new kind of warfare it is facing, it must be forced into accepting the ground rules of the war of attrition. A war of attrition will do no good if the opponent does not feel limited to the rules such a war implies. Because strategy does not lay dormant during a war of attrition, the opponent may find ways of restoring momentum and may achieve a decisive victory from which the target cannot recover.

In earlier work, I examined this process in terms of a search for optimal strategies that entail less than a full-fledged commitment of forces to battle (Maoz, 1985b). The defeated actor wishes to cut its costs to a minimum (that is, to make the decline in expected utility over time as small as possible), but it also wants to minimize the duration of the war. The initiator, who has the advantage when both sides deploy all their forces in an all-out confrontation, must react to the new strategy of the target with a new strategy of its own; the previous strategy of swift advance is no longer suitable, because, if it were continued, it would run way ahead of its supply lines and become extremely vulnerable to a major attack. The new strategy requires less than total commitment of forces to battle, slowing down the advance. The initiator also attempts to cut its costs by prolonging the war. But this is precisely what the target wants. The slowdown in the opponent's advance gives the target time to reorganize and rebuild its forces while forcing the opponent to get used to a form of battle for which it had not prepared, for which it had no good plans, and under conditions that might be totally unfavorable. While the initiator of the swift attack is in the process of adjustment to the new type of war, the target strikes; the strategy marshaled by the initiator of the war is now used by the target to defeat the initiator.

The slowdown in the pace of battle also has psychological effects. *Strategy* refers not only to a plan for troop deployment and the conduct of war; it is also a state of mind. The gradual erosion of the swift military attack of the initiator into a war of attrition breaks down the morale of the commanders and the troops who were brought up with the ideology of the offensive. On the other hand, a strategy of disengagement on the part of the target allows it to build up the initially low morale of the troops because it is not confronted by major military defeats. On the contrary, it can use minor guerrilla attacks, which cause very little physical damage to the opponent, as morale-boosting devices.

Finally, friction becomes an ever-important factor in the management of war. Changing weather conditions, lack of planning for a prolonged war, and the distance between the forward units of the initiator and the supply bases all cause unintended breakdowns that were unanticipated because the initiator was not prepared for a long war. Good plans for the management of short wars full of sustained and decisive battles are bad plans for the management of long, static wars with many small skirmishes and few, widely spaced major engagements. The initiator begins to pay the price of putting all its eggs in one basket.

## Explanations of the Paradox of Attrition

There are two key issues that the explanations of the paradox must address. The first concerns the role of politics in this paradox. The description of the paradox in the previous section seems to be focused on the strategic level rather than on the political one. I have stated that the paradox of attrition arises when military planners are given a free hand by politicians. Does this fact serve as a cause of the paradox, and, if so, can it be helped? The second issue concerns the question of planning: Why is it that military planners who are smart enough to mastermind a major military attack (and, as we shall see in the next section, those plans are quite elaborate) are so stupid as to miss the fact that the opponent can mess it up simply by not playing the game as the planners expect?

### Rational Attrition

The resort to a strategy of attrition by the target of a swift military attack is a matter more of necessity than of choice. If the target could resist the opponent via conventional means it would do so, for the attrition strategy—in and of itself—is incapable of deciding the war. Attrition is the only rational method of resistance for a state that finds itself alone against a more powerful opponent. While attrition can be applied by a conventional army, guerrilla warfare is the most typical form of this strategy. This suggests that attrition is the best, if not the only, weapon of the weak, determined, and patient party. The resort to this strategy occurs whenever a target actor acknowledges that the choice is between a long, devastating war in which a lot of sacrifices must be made, with no relief for a very long time, and giving in to the opponent now. Actors who have employed this strategy stop using it when they feel that they are strong enough for conventional warfare. The search for a strategy that will slow down one's decay function, independent of what the opponent does, suggests that under these circumstances attrition is seen as the optimal management strategy of the weak target of a swift military attack by a powerful opponent.

The resort to a strategy of attrition by the weak is not really a problem in need of explanation from a rational perspective. What does require explanation is why the superior initiator of a swift military attack (1) does not see before the attack is launched that this will indeed be the opponent's strategy and take appropriate strategic measures against it, and (2) once faced by a strategy of attrition, accepts the ground rules of warfare that are clearly to its disadvantage.

Let us start from the second question, because its answer helps clarify the answer to the first. We need to consider two cases wherein a swift military campaign is converted into a war of attrition: the case of guerrilla warfare (examples are Yugoslavia and China in World War II, and Vietnam, Algeria, and Afghanistan afterward), and the case of conventional wars of attrition (examples are the trench warfare during World War I, the Korean War between June 1951 and June 1953, the Israeli-Egyptian war of 1969–70, and the cases discussed in more detail in the next section). A guerrilla war is one that can be converted into a conventional one only if and when the guerrillas are ready. The conventional army cannot do a thing about this form of fighting, because the whole logic of this warfare is of a hit-and-run type; the guerrillas deliberately avoid any direct confrontation with the conventional army. The guerrillas, almost solely, determine the type, timing, location, intensity, and aims of whatever limited confrontations take place.

The options available to the conventional army concern the treatment of the occupied population, such as the form of punishment for sheltering and aiding the guerrillas, search-and-destroy raids of the type used by the Americans in Vietnam and by the Soviets in Afghanistan, and so forth. But this means precisely acceptance of the opponent's ground rules: the conventional army operates in small units, disperses itself according to the types of hits by the guerrillas, does not use its most massive weapon systems, and cannot make its numerical superiority felt in the battlefield. It loses all of the attributes that had given it the military edge, and there is nothing it can do about it as long as it cannot cause the opponent to concentrate its forces in one place.

In the case of conventional warfare, there are some reasons that compel the initiator to abide by the ground rules of the opponent. If the opponent retreats to a line of defense that is geographically impenetrable, the initiator must occupy this line before it can advance. High mountains or wide rivers create natural obstacles that prevent a superior actor from bringing to bear those elements that make it superior, such as armor and mobile artillery. The other factor is the inability of the initiator to establish a sufficiently strong line of defense to hold off the target's counterattack when it comes. The only way it can terminate the war is by continuing the offensive advance in the hope of compelling the opponent to confront it in a decisive battle. Yet, the point where the initiator finds it tactically necessary to stop (because of logistical problems, political constraints, or the opponent's resistance) is one in which it possesses no strategic or tactical advantage over the opponent in the best case, or one in which it finds itself logistically, topographically, and psychologically inferior to the opponent.

The key problem in a conventional war in which one army overextends itself is the problem of external versus internal lines. As the target withdraws, its lines—even if they have been external before the war started—become shorter and internal. It is better able to concentrate its forces and control them than it had been at the beginning of the war, before it had started to retreat. The initiator, on the other hand, moves from internal to external lines, but it is unprepared to deal with this kind of warfare in terms of doctrine. Luttwak (1987) discusses the German thrust through the Ardens (in summer 1940), where the armored force had to rely almost exclusively on local sources of food and gasoline. In contrast, the German invasion of Moscow had to contend with both long lines of supply and bad weather conditions, factors that made for a fatal combination.

Can one slow down the pace of advance in a conventional war and wait for its supply units and logistics to catch up? In principle this might be possible. In practice, however, time is important for political or other reasons. In terms of politics, a swift attack is seen as important in order to establish fait accomplis so that allies of the enemy will have no chance to intervene. Concomitantly, weather conditions might be a major element in the military plan. The Germans knew that they must break the Soviet army before the winter, and counted on that. Slowing down for reorganization would have defeated this purpose.

Now, is it not possible to prepare for a war of attrition when one is planning a swift military attack? The answer is, again, probably yes in principle and probably no in practice. One can know in advance, given the state of relations between oneself and the adversary, that if one occupies large portions of the opponent's territory, one will have to deal with widespread guerrilla warfare. But knowing this is not enough for developing a strategy of fighting guerrillas that is based on massive use of force and swift military operations. Other drastic measures for dealing with guerrilla warfare, including vicious suppression of the occupied population so as to deny the guerrillas local support and shelters, may be politically inadmissible or may require so many resources that might hamper the major military effort.

It is also possible to know in advance that the best strategy the opponent can pursue is that of conventional attrition, but the optimal strategy against it is to find some optimal mixture of adherence to the ground rules of the opponent and controlled escalation. This is shown in the model discussed in Maoz (1985b). The target of the swift military attack chooses a strategy of force economy that is optimal in the sense that it is seen as the most appropriate response independent of the strategy chosen by the initiator. This strategy of limited confrontation happens to be the best response to the strategy of swift military attack. The best counterstrategy to such a strategy of attrition happens to be acceptance of the opponent's ground rules. But this implies abandonment of the swift military attack. I have argued that the first stage of war is a test of strengths and weaknesses, in terms not only of the opponents' capabilities but also of their strategies, just as two boxers spend the first couple of rounds trying to figure each other out (Maoz, 1985b). If the swift military attack decides the war in the first round, the game is over. If, on the other hand, one resorts to a strategy of attrition, the best the other can do is beat the first at its own game. Here develops a long and tedious duel of wills, which ends only when both decide it is time to push ahead in full force. No prior planning, no matter how good it is, is capable of avoiding this process.

## The Psychology of the Offensive

J. S. Snyder's (1984) work on the strategy of the offensive that dominated strategic thinking prior to World War I treats the belief in the effectiveness of this strategy as an "ideology." This implies a total devotion to the idea that there is a single best way of doing things and that alternative approaches to the problem are at best wasteful and inefficient, and at worst disastrous. Two principles explain the strong motivational attachment to a strategy of swift single-minded attack and the tendency to dismiss its disadvantages, to prepare or invest in Plan B, and thus to fall into the attrition trap. The first is a tendency to deduce strategy from technology. The other is a tendency to attribute to others the logic that one attributes to oneself. Both principles may lead to valid inferences in most cases, but in some situations they may be highly misleading.

Obviously, there is a close linkage between technology and optimal strategy. What is best to do is determined to a large extent by what one *can* do. The availability of means affects the ability of actors to pursue their goals and, in many ways, influences how these goals are best pursued. Because modern strategy is heavily influenced by technology, the linkages are even more apparent in this area of human activity than in others, and more in modern times than in ancient ones. The relations between the major powers offer perhaps the clearest example of this linkage. The Strategic Defense Initiative (SDI) is an attempt to open strategic opportunities for oneself through new technologies of missile detection and destruction in space, while at the same time foreclosing the ability of an opponent to carry out what is seen as one of its key strategies—a disarming first strike. Whether this technology makes offense strategically superior to defense is debatable. The point is that both sides of the argument make claims about the relationship between SDI and the optimal strategies of the two superpowers.[5]

The impact of technology on policy in general and on military strategy in particular can be positive or negative depending on whether learning is biased or not. Posen (1984) argues that organizational learning is largely biased and thus generals often fail to see the implications of technological innovations on strategy. Two aspects of biased strategic learning can be associated with the paradox of attrition. One is what we often call the tendency of generals to "fight the last war all over again." The other is the tendency to focus on a single technology while failing to see that other technologies have strategic implications that are opposite to those of the technology one is focusing on.

Lessons about future strategy are drawn from the last war. Strategic planners examine what seemed to have affected the outcome of the last war. If there is evidence that a certain technology was instrumental in deciding the military outcome of war, strategists will attempt to build future plans on the exploitation of this technology. A technology that seemed to have had no significant effect on the outcome of war is typically abandoned as a major element in military doctrines. There are some problems with this thinking. One is that the time that elapses between wars is accompanied by new technologies that render the previous technology of limited relevance. What caused victory in one war might cause defeat or stagnation in another. For example, the Israelis won the Six Day War largely due to the innovative use of air power and mobile armored units. This caused them to build their strategy on these two elements, believing that one does not abandon a winning combination. However, they failed to realize between 1967 and 1973 (although they had ample information) that the Soviets introduced major innovations in weapon systems that were designed to counter just these advantages—specifically, fairly accurate antiaircraft missiles and mobile antitank missiles. In 1973, the Israelis were astonished not only by the timing of the Egyptian-Syrian attack, but also by the effective use of antiaircraft and antitank missiles. The Syrians, who learned the lessons of success in 1973, were surprised again in 1982 when the Israelis destroyed all their missile batteries in Lebanon using new devices.

Paradoxically, if these examples have anything to teach us it is that the loser of the last war typically makes better use of technological innovations in the next war because it learns from disaster, whereas the winner learns from success. Thus, while World War I was a source for a lot of strategic lessons, those that were learned by British strategists such as Liddell-Hart and Fuller were heeded by the German military planners rather than by the British (Geyer, 1986: 586; Bond and Alexander, 1986: 600–603). The French, who, as we shall soon see, were able to beat the German offensive strategy through patient—if costly—trench warfare in World War I, decided that defensive technologies (trenches, fortifications, machine guns) give a clear advantage to the defense and thus put all their eggs in the Maginot line, which the Germans simply bypassed in their 1940 invasion of France.

If technology is said to give advantage to the offensive, and if there is evidence for this assertion from the last war, there is emerging strategic investment in offensive deployment. This investment creates commitments that lead to further investments in what is thought to be a winning strategy. These commitments and investment cause the strategic planners to ignore or discount technologies that are developed by opponents in response to the offensive technologies. But the chief problem of the linkage between technology and the selection of optimal strategy is that it ignores the fact that technology is only an intervening variable in the strategic equation, not an independent one. Technology enables one to do what one could not have done without it. However, it also has a lot of side effects that may render its use superfluous or overly costly. For example, reliance on air power and mobile forces requires more and more sophisticated logistics than defensive strategies because the forward forces are separated from their bases once they start moving. They also create dependence on communication and fuel, which are less important when the military forces are dug in permanent trenches served by internal lines.

Because wars are political instruments, they should be (and usually are) guided by political calculations. However, when politicians become impressed by technological arguments and are blinded to the political implications of strategies, they are likely to err miserably in the choice of strategy. During the 1969–70 war of attrition in the Middle East, the Israelis obtained F-4 fighter bomber planes from the United States. The long flight range and high performance of those planes created possibilities for deep-penetration bombing in Egypt that had not existed before. The Israelis decided that it might be a good idea to compel the Egyptians to end the war by hitting them where it really hurts: deep in central Egypt. The Israelis launched the deep-penetration bombing policy (Shlaim and Tanter, 1978; Bar-Simantov, 1980), which caused the Egyptians a lot of casualties. But this also led to direct Soviet involvement in the war, which caused a great deal of concern in Israel (Brecher, 1974).

Reasonable people are well aware of the interactive nature of military doctrines. Good strategists are also aware that a given technology rarely can be monopolized. It is this awareness that leads them to believe that a strict reliance on an offensive strategy is optimal. An offensive strategy requires an opponent to "cooperate" in the sense that it must commit its forces to large-scale confrontations in which the attacker has the edge. The opponent will play by these rules if it shares this belief in the superiority of the offensive, but will play by a different set of rules if it believes otherwise. The tendency to attribute to the opponent a belief system similar to one's own in terms of the relations between technology and strategy means that one will expect the opponent to play by the same rules. This makes an attachment to an offensive strategy even more pronounced. The strategy of the offensive becomes a dominant strategy: if we don't use it the opponent will, so we had better use it first. And once it is used and shows initial signs of success, our attachment becomes even greater, and our ability to see that it has its limits declines.

## Wars of Attrition in History

Wars of attrition have many faces; not all of them are paradoxical. Some wars start out in a fairly static fashion and therefore are deliberate and calculated attempts at war limitation due to the weakness of the initiator and the political constraints of the target. The 1969–70 war of attrition between Israel and Egypt is a case in point. Other wars of attrition start only after the conventional war is over. This applies to guerrilla wars that take place after the occupation of the state by an external power. In some of these cases, the victory of one state opens for it a Pandora's box that might lead to sacrifices even greater than those made during the conventional war. This case might be another paradox, wherein the victor's problems are a result of the victory. The Japanese occupation of China, the German occupation of Yugoslavia, both prior to or during World War II, and the Israeli occupation of Lebanon might be good examples of this case.

However interesting, these cases are beyond the scope of this study. Here I want to limit myself to cases of conventional wars that started with trumpets and drums and soon changed into prolonged tragedies accompanied by much suffering: World War I and the Iran-Iraq war. What we are looking for in these cases is whether the initial success of the offensive strategy was followed by a tactical retreat of the target that was soon converted into a static war of attrition. We are also looking for the reasons the initiator chose to abide by the new rules of war, which were clearly to its disadvantage.

## The Short-War Illusion:
## The Collapse of the Schlieffen Plan[6]

The Schlieffen plan is a classic case of long-range planning of a grand strategy. Its execution in 1914 is an excellent example of a process wherein not only was the army given a free hand in the conduct of war, but the military considerations may have been a key factor leading to the outbreak of the war. The plan itself was a culmination of long years of planning, war gaming, and strategic debates in the German general staff. These debates focused not only on narrow military notions about the best military setup that would assure victory, but also on what combination of enemies Germany would be fighting in the next war and what it would take to score a decisive military victory. The Schlieffen plan was a retirement present that the former chief of staff left to his successors. It assumed that Germany would have to face a two-front war, with the Russians in the east and the French in the west. An attempt to fight both parties simultaneously and split the military effort equally across the two fronts was seen as a sure prescription for defeat.[7]

The plan was to hold off the Russian army with three German corps (and relying—but not too much—on an Austro-Hungarian offensive in Galicia), while concentrating the bulk of the German army in the west in a major envelopment of the French army through Belgium. The plan called for luring the French into an offensive in the Rhine area with the deliberately weak left wing of the German army (five corps only) while taking the remainder of the army westward in a sweeping circle through Belgium that would end in the occupation of Paris and a French surrender. Because of the weakness of the German army in the east, the whole war with the French had to end within two months of the start of the offensive. Time constraints were determined also by political factors. The key element of the Schlieffen plan was the quick occupation of Belgium, a state whose neutrality was to be guaranteed by all major powers. The German generals, who were working under worst-case assumptions, believed that the violation of Belgian neutrality would most likely bring about British intervention. It was thus necessary to have the battle in the east decided before the British made up their minds about intervening.[8]

The final version of the plan, written by Schlieffen himself,[9] called for a wide sweep of Belgium that would prevent an early deployment of British troops on friendly Belgian soil. Thus, Schlieffen stated: "Let the last man on the right brush the channel with his sleeve" (Tuchman, 1962: 25). The fact that the plan required a blatant violation of a pact of which both Germany and Great Britain had been guarantors, and therefore entailed a nonnegligible possibility of British intervention, suggested that in order to be implemented, it could not have been constrained by customary diplomatic caution. It also required that the entire German army be mobilized and in place when the first shot was fired.

After his death in 1913, Schlieffen's plan underwent some noticeable changes. The left wing of the German army in the west was strengthened considerably. Schlieffen's successor, General Helmuth von Moltke, the great field marshal's nephew, feared that while the strong right wing struck in the west, the French might break the weak right wing in the Alsace-Lorraine area. In addition, he chose to strengthen the center of the German army at the expense of a shorter radius of the right-wing envelopment. These changes were modifications of the Schlieffen plan rendered necessary by what Moltke viewed as logistical problems with the original plan (Rothenberg, 1986: 322). They did not constitute, however, major modification in the logic, the boldness of the attack, or the political and diplomatic risks associated with it.

The military requirements for full mobilization and rapid deployment of the army no doubt played a major role in the German decisions leading to the outbreak of the war. The kaiser and his political advisers knew that a full-scale mobilization would provoke a similar mobilization by the French and thus would make a war more likely. The belief of political leaders that it was still possible to keep Great Britain out of the war if Germany restricted its campaign to the eastern front prompted them to advocate a partial mobilization that would demonstrate resolve but would not provoke. Indeed, a telegram sent by Linchowski, the German ambassador to England, raised the possibility that the French would remain neutral and that the British would guarantee that neutrality. This prompted the kaiser to suggest that the German army be redeployed in the east and that the German attack be directed at the Russians. However, Moltke's response to both issues was: "This was impossible. The deployment of an army a million strong was not a thing to be improvised, it was the product of a whole year's hard work and once planned could not be changed. If His Majesty were to insist on directing the whole army to the east, he would not have an army prepared for the attack but a barren heap of armed men disorganized and without supplies" (quoted in Barnett, 1963: 7).[10] On August 1, 1914, the whole of the German army was in the process of full mobilization and deployment as planned. And following a letter from King George V of England that clarified that it would aid the French in the war no matter whether or not the French decided to attack Germany, Moltke was given by the kaiser what amounted to a blank check. A modified version of the Schlieffen plan went into effect. Between August 6 and 17, the Germans carried 3,120,000 men in more than 11,000 trains to the western front. By

August 20, the German army entered Brussels and appeared before Namur, the last Belgian fortress before France. On the western part of the front, the left wing of the German army held off the French attempts to occupy Alsace and Lorraine, handing the latter a devastating defeat. By August 25, the French armies in the east and the combined French and British armies in the west were in the process of retreat. The German army was in the process of rapid advance, outrunning its supplies and changing its plans as a result of the unexpected ease of its advance.

The swiftness of the German attack in the west and the thinning of the right wing of the German army (which was a sharp deviation from the Schlieffen plan) exposed the German army to a counterattack at its weak spot. The battle of the Marne, fought on September 6–9, 1914, handed the German army its first defeat in the war, and stopped its advance. The line stabilized in French and Belgian territory, with its most forward post being some 60 miles northeast of Paris. This line remained, for the most part, stable until the end of 1917. Thus, between October 1914 and November 1917, the quick and decisive offensive turned into a long, static, and devastating war of attrition that lasted—for all practical purposes—nearly four years.

The sequence of events seems to illustrate rather well the workings of the paradox of attrition. The swiftness of the initial attack and the relief of the army of political constraints can be a major disaster for a state. In the German case it led political leaders to choose policy strictly on the basis of military considerations, and it led strategists to fall into the trap of their own plans.

There are many explanations for the failure of the German offensive. One is that the Schlieffen plan was never fully carried out. What Moltke did was to alter not only the margins of the plan but its whole logic. The plan would have worked had it been carried out as its originator had seen it. But whereas Schlieffen placed greater and greater emphasis on the right wing of the envelopment, Helmuth von Moltke strengthened the center, reduced the radius of the sweep, and, when the war was in progress, oscillated between different plans of attack depending on momentary opportunities. Another explanation asserts that this plan was unrealistic from the start, and that it could never have been successful because it required logistical and technological capabilities that Germany (or anyone else) simply did not have.

Be that as it may, some of the underlying assumptions of the Schlieffen plan indeed proved correct at the beginning of the war. First and foremost, the estimates regarding the ability of the small detachment of the German army to hold off the Russians in the east and the French in the eastern sector of the western front were accurate. Whether or not this was due to correct assessment by Schlieffen in 1906 or to the strengthening of the German army in these fronts by Moltke is of secondary importance. Second, the ability of the German army to pull off the complex maneuver of envelopment through Belgium was shown to be feasible logistically. Logistics was definitely not a factor in the conversion of the rapid offensive to a war of attrition. Third, the invasion of Belgium came as a real surprise to the French, who had expected the Germans to attack from the east (the Meuse River area). The time it took the French to realize the nature of the German main effort helped the latter considerably in their initial advance. Fifth, the German expectations that the French would play the role assigned to them in the Schlieffen plan—that is, attempt to compete with the German army on seizing the initiative—was supported. Farrar (1973: 11) states that the French commander Joffre was driven by the "conviction that the German strategy served his purpose by weakening the German center. Although the initial French attacks were repulsed with heavy losses, Joffre ordered his major attack in the expectation that the German center had been depleted. In fact, the German center was superior because it had been reinforced in anticipation of the French attack."

Despite these correct assumptions and the initial German successes, the tide of the war was turned in the battle of the Marne. The initial defeats in the eastern sector of the western front and the rapid German advance through Belgium served as a bitter learning experience for the allied forces. But these events also told the allies that the best they could do was to retreat in an orderly fashion and concentrate their forces where the stakes were the highest rather than to confront the German advance where it was still gaining strength. The significance of the battle of the Marne was that, while the German forces were dispersed along a wide front in a massive envelopment, the allied forces, fighting in internal lines, were able to accomplish local numerical superiority, and were fighting over the defense of Paris. Although these things were not sufficient to drive the Germans back, they were enough to halt the German advance. The mutual realization that this is as far as anyone could go for the time being required some time to set in. Both parties attempted to attack each other in the ensuing two years, but neither was dramatically successful.

Could the Germans have acted otherwise? The first issue to consider in response to this question is political: Was it possible to prevent the British intervention if Belgium was not invaded? Available evidence suggests that, although the official pretext of the British intervention in the war was the violation of Belgian neutrality, the British would have entered the war anyway.

The second element in this answer is a strategic one. Namely, the issue here is whether the Germans could have anticipated that the massive invasion would gradually turn into a war of attrition, and that once this happened, Germany would be in real trouble. Of course, it should have been anticipated from the point of view of anybody with 20-20 hindsight, but the evidence available to the German staff at the time suggested quite the opposite. Would the French attempt to seize the initiative through a bold offensive strategy in a war with Germany? Consider the following statement of Marshal Foch, a leading French strategist, in a lecture given at the Ecole de Guerre in 1900:

> The laurels of victory hang on the enemy's bayonets, and have to be plucked from them, by man to man struggle if need be. . . . To flee or charge is all that remains. To charge, but to charge in numbers, as one mass, therein lies safety. For numbers, if we know how to employ them, allow us, by the superiority of material placed at our disposal, to overcome the enemy's fire. With more guns we can reduce his to silence, and the same is true of rifles and bayonets, if we know how to use them at all. (cited by Howard, 1986: 514)[11]

Thus the Germans had every reason to believe that the French would play the game by the rules of the offensive. Just as the commander of the French army, General Joffre, believed that the German strategy served the French purpose, Moltke believed that the French strategy served his. But why did the Germans miss the implications of the new fire technology for the offensive/defensive balance? How could they have ignored the lessons of previous wars (e.g., the 1900 Boer War, and the 1904–05 Russo-Japanese War) in which all the technologies available to them in 1914 had been tried in the field? Howard (1986: 519) argues that the main lesson that had been deduced from the Russo-Japanese War was that

> in spite of all the advantages which the new weapons gave the defense, the offensive was still entirely possible. The Japanese successfully took the initiative from the very beginning of the war and in a series of set-piece attacks drove Russian forces slightly larger than their own out of southern Manchuria. The cost had been high, but as a result Japan had Graduated as a Great Power; and any nation that wished to remain a Great Power . . . must be prepared to face comparable costs. . . . The real lesson of the Russo-Japanese War was widely seen as being that the truly important element in modern warfare was not technology but *morale;* and the morale, not of the army alone, but of the nation from which it was drawn.

The German assumption had been that morale is dynamic and that it is fueled by success. Success was defined in terms of rapid movement, occupation of territory, and defeat of enemy forces. Because morale is also highly fluid, and masses cannot long endure a costly war without tangible achievements, an all-out offensive was seen as the logical solution on political, military, and psychological grounds.

There was a clear emphasis in Germany on the effects of technology on the nature of warfare, but the emphasis was on the fact that modern technology offered a great degree of mobility and greatly facilitated the ability of the logistical branches of the army to provide good supplies to the front units and the flexibility of troop movement that allowed transferring great numbers of men and equipment from one place to another through a highly developed railroad system. The German general staff also considered the destructive power of modern artillery and the newly developed magazine rifles and machine guns. However, it was not at all clear that these weapons offered any kind of advantage to the defense. As we have seen from the Foch speech, artillery could be used as an umbrella to advancing troops that softens the defender's positions as much as it could be used by the defender to stop advancing troops. Machine guns could be used by mobile troops to cover exposed troops as well as they could be used by static troops in trenches.

Because new technologies did not have a clear-cut implication for the type of strategy that was considered best, it was not easy to discern the ideology of the offensive. In fact, the seeming advantage that the weapons gave to the defensive was a lesson that was learned only during the war, but no leading strategist before the war was sure about that.[12] It must be noted that, despite what many writers on the war degrade as a single-minded German devotion to a strategy of quick and decisive offensive, and their tendency to ignore the kind of impact that technology had on the battlefield of the future, the notion of a decisive offensive strategy was based on some solid politicostrategic foundations. The assumption of a two-front war was not that farfetched given the alliance structure the Germans faced. Given the need to fight a two-front war, the German general staff developed a plan that was a reasonable answer to the strategic problems posed by such a war. That this strategy did not work in the final analysis cannot be taken as an indication that it was not the best chance Germany had.

## Ripe for a Quick Victory: The Iran-Iraq War[13]

Lack of primary sources prevents a clear assessment of the calculations underlying the Iraqi offensive of September 22, 1980. Increased tensions, fairly stiff propaganda warfare, and border clashes characterized the relations between Iraq and Iran since the rise of Khomeini to power in Iran. Not that relations between the two states had been friendly beforehand—they were far from that. Three factors seem to have influenced the Iraqi decision to launch an all-out campaign on Iran. The motivation for attack was twofold. First, there was an acute fear of the spread of the fundamentalist Islamic revolution to Iraq. This fear was prompted by two facts: the ethnic composition of the Iraqi population, of which Shi'ite Arabs constitute about 55 percent (Pipes, 1983: 9), and the inflammatory rhetoric of Khomeini and other Iranian clergy, who called for the overthrow of reactionary and secular regimes in the Arab world, with repeated references to Iraq.[14] The fear of the spread of the revolution was also exacerbated by the resignation of the more moderate government of Bazargan in Iran and its replacement with more radical elements. The repeated claims the Khomeini regime put on Iraq's Shi'ite leaders—for example, the requirement to move the Shi'i seminary from al-Najaf (in Iraq) to Qum (in Iran)—suggested that the loyalty of the Shi'ite population of Iraq was constantly being put to test by the Iranian regime (Helms, 1984: 159–162; Marr, 1985: 292–293).

The second motivation was the unresolved border dispute between the two states. The two states shared a long and disputed border that had been a source of a lot of clashes, the most severe of which had taken place in 1975. Probably the chief area of dispute along this border was the gateway of the Shatt Al-Arab to the Persian Gulf. The 1975 clashes ended with an agreement (signed March 6) that granted control over half the river to each party. Saddam Hussein, the chief Iraqi negotiator at the 1975 talks, is reputed to have signed the agreement against his better judgment. Grummon (1982: 10) claims that Hussein considered the terms of the treaty "a personal humiliation" and negotiated under duress. In 1979 he became the president of Iraq. From a broader Iraqi perspective, the treaty had clearly been a strategic compromise. The main policy problem the Iraqis had been facing at the time was the civil war against the Kurds in the north and the constant support the Kurds had been receiving from Iran. The concessions that had been made on the border issues had been given in return for an Iranian promise to stop aid to the Kurds. Thus, the immediate result of the treaty was that the Iraqis were able to crush the Kurdish rebellion. But once the rebellion was no longer a problem, it was time to return to the border business.

The fear of the spread of the Iranian revolution to Iraq and the outstanding border grievances account for the incentives for escalation. They do not, however, explain why Iraq chose to launch an all-out offensive at the time that it did. This aspect of the attack is explained by what the Iraqi leadership saw as an occasion of great opportunity, that—if passed up—would never return. The Iranian army had been one of the chief victims of the Khomeini revolution. Most of the high commanders of the army had been either executed or imprisoned by the revolutionary guard. Those who had not been caught fled Iran or were in hiding. During the revolution, there were mass desertions from the army, and it was unclear to what extent the army had returned to the size it was during the Shah's regime. The reconstruction of the Iranian army was progressing slowly for two main reasons. First, it was supervised by revolutionary guards who were far from being professional soldiers. Second, the modern equipment that the Shah's army had possessed was in terrible shape and—given the embargo imposed on Iran during the U.S. hostage crisis—it was unlikely that spare parts and new weapons would flow in (Staudenmaier, 1983: 31).

There were also rumors and actual indications of widespread opposition to the regime inside and outside Iran. Iranian opposition groups were organizing resistance to the regime outside the country. The rift between Khomeini and Ayatollah Shariat-Madari indicated that even in the mosque things were far from smooth. Helms (1984: 165) suggests that the Iraqi leadership was operating under the assumption that "there is a government on every street corner in Iran." Given the state of unrest and instability inside Iran, a military defeat of the Iranian army would considerably deflate the Khomeini regime, leading to its overthrow by groups that might be more amenable to Iraq. Grummon (1982: 11) points out that the preoccupation of the superpowers with their own domestic international problems (the hostage crisis and the upcoming presidential election in the United States, and the Afghanistan war of the Soviet Union) suggested that the Iranians could expect little international help. Moreover, the inflammatory rhetoric of the Khomeini regime managed to alienate the moderate gulf states, thereby assuring their tacit support of Iraq's efforts (Helms, 1984: 164–166).

All these factors served to convince Saddam Hussein that an all-out attack on key targets in Iran would lead to a chain reaction resulting in the downfall of the regime. Thus, the political strategy employed by Hussein during the summer and early fall of 1980 was designed to prepare the ground for the swift attack. The war of accusations became highly intense. Iraq repeatedly charged Iran with infringements on Iraqi territory. On September 10, Iraq abrogated the 1975 treaty. And on September 22, the attack started. Because of the conviction that the Khomeini regime hung by a thread, Saddam Hussein felt that a small military push would be enough to topple the regime (Helms, 1984: 168–171). The military balance between the two states favored the Iranians in terms of quantities, but the Iraqi army had the edge in dynamic warfare, tank and mobile forces. This advantage in mobile warfare dictated the nature of the fighting (Staudenmaier, 1983: 32). The major objective of the Iraqi attack was to capture the disputed Shatt Al-Arab gateway, in particular the cities of Abadan and Khorramshar. While Abadan was never really captured by the Iraqis (although it had been besieged for an entire year), Khorramshar was captured on October 24. This marked the culmination point of the Iraqi attack. At that point, Iraq was in possession of a strip of Iranian territory some 600 kilometers long and ranging in width from 5 to 60 kilometers.

The first phase of the war was seen largely as a major Iraqi success. The Iranian army had to withdraw eastward, and was incapable of launching a counteroffensive. The Iraqi success was not complete, however. Because of either self-imposed constraints or gross military miscalculations, the Iraqis failed to take Abadan and refrained from attacking major strategic Iranian roads and supply lines. On the other hand, the Iranian strategy had been to stall the Iraqi advance as much as possible while avoiding major confrontations. From December 1980 to May 1981, the situation was pretty much stalled; the Iranians used the winter to lick their wounds and regroup, and the Iraqis used the winter to dig into their new positions. In May 1981, the Iranian counteroffensive began with a number of futile attacks on the Iraqi fortifications in the south and center of the new front line. The real Iranian effort began in September 1981. By September 28, the Iraqi siege of Abadan was broken, and other major posts at Bustan were recaptured.

Once the Iraqi advantage in mobile movement was converted into static firepower along defensive lines, the Iranians devised an "original" strategy of their own. The "human wave" strategy utilized by the Iranians was based on the notion that quantities make for quality if they are large enough. The Iranian army (which was actually run by revolutionary guards) counterbalanced the Iraqi firepower with an unbelievable ability to invoke a readiness for martyrdom among hundreds of thousands of newly mobilized soldiers. By April 1982, most of the Iraqi forces were driven back to the old border. On May 24, 1984, Iranian forces recaptured Khorramshar. The Ramadan campaign of December 1982 moved the Iranian forces into Iraq. The tide of battle had clearly turned against the Iraqis. Iraq started suing for peace.

But once Khomeini declared that the aim of war was the overthrow of the Ba'ath regime in Iraq and the Iranian forces advanced into Iraqi territory, directly threatening the city of Basra, the Iraqis were fighting for their lives. They resorted to the same attrition tactic that the Iranians had used some two years earlier. Repeated Iranian attacks were repelled by the Iraqis. The Iraqi strategy since 1983 has been to take the pressure off in the south by attacking Iranian cities by missiles and by naval and aerial raids on Iranian oil refineries and ships in the Persian Gulf. Much of the warfare that took place during the period of 1983 to 1988 centered around the gulf area and over the main population centers of both parties. Yet, with only a few exceptions, the lines of combat in the border between the two states have stabilized. Now Iraq was trying to exhaust the Iranians through a war of attrition tactic, and the Iranians were forced to accept the ground rules of the opponent.

The (tentative) end of the story is, of course, that the Iranian strategy of human wave offensives has also exhausted itself. Once that happened, the Iraqis, using their superior firepower, started their own offensive along the northern part of the border, recapturing not only what the Iranians had held of formerly Iraqi territory, but at places some formerly Iranian territories. The Iranians sued for a cease-fire. The war ended pretty much along the territorial lines where it started. If over a million people were not killed in eight years of war, one would not have noticed that any-thing had changed in the political geography of the Middle East.

## Conclusion

The changing fortunes of the Iran-Iraq War demonstrate two important aspects of the paradox of attrition. First, the attrition tactic is typically invoked by the party that finds itself with its back against the wall. When the identity of that party changes, so does the tendency toward attrition. It is typically the strong party that has the momentum and wants to reach a swift decision through the use of conventional mobile warfare, and it is this party that finds itself forced to accept the ground rules set by the opponent. Second, although one can plan the beginning of a war, one cannot plan its termination, no matter how meticulous one is, for the end of the war is determined by the opponent as much as by the initiator.[15] The Iraqis considered the war over and done with about a month after it had started. From a military point of view most (if not all) of their objectives had been accomplished. It was up to the political leadership to have the Iranians accept the new status quo. Unfortunately, the Iranians were not willing to play the game by the Iraqi rules. But neither were the Iraqis willing to play by the Iranian rules once Iran started staging its offensive.

Because wars are duels of wills and wits, even the most master-ful plan, carried out well, might run aground because it forces the opponent to resort to strategies that render the initial plan useless. In the initial months of the war, the Khomeini regime was fighting for its life. A defeat in the war would have meant the end of the Islamic republic. The Khomeini regime's interest in the continu-ation of the war is clearly affected by what Coser (1957) calls "the social functions" of conflict; that is, the war was used to suppress any sign of opposition to the regime. On the other side of the coin, the Iraqi regime was fighting for its life, hence, despite the momentum on Iran's side, it could not reach a military decision.

How can one avoid conversion of a swift initial attack into an end-less war of attrition? Modest military objectives might help, but they are not a guarantee, as was shown by the Iran-Iraq War. Probably the most important factor is the recognition that nations use military strategy much like professional chess players: when one player recognizes the opponent's strategy, he or she adopts the best counterstrategy; when the opponent becomes aware of this fact, he or she must have a good Plan B in stock—if not he or she might end up losing the game.

## Notes

1   See Luttwak (1987: 131–140), Laqueur (1976), and Harkabi's (1978) discussions on this type of warfare.

2   For example, recall the Japanese assessment (discussed in Chapter 3) that if the war with the United States lasted more than a year, costs were apt to increase sharply. This implies that if the Japanese generals were required to present the decline in the expected utility for war over time, they would have probably presented a linear decay for the first year and an increased marginal decay thereafter.

3   This is precisely what Rosen (1972) calls "the will to suffer" and I have called the "breath ratio" (Maoz, 1982a), namely, the relative ability of the actors to hold their breath and suffer the costs of war without giving in.

4   A similar point is made by Blainey (1988). He argues that war is a contest between two states that cannot decide which is more powerful. If each knew which is the more powerful, the weaker would not have a reason to challenge the stronger and the stronger could get what it wants without war.

5   Some recent literature in international politics has examined the relations between technology and strategy. The key issue is whether technology gives the advantage to offense or defense, and whether presumed advantages to one type of strategic posture or another affect stability at the systemic level (Jervis, 1978) or bilateral level (Maersheimer, 1983; Jervis, 1984). See also the game-theoretic treatment of this issue relating to SDI by Brams and Kilgour (1988).

6   This analysis is based on Rothenberg (1986), Liddell-Hart (1930, 1967), Farrar (1973), Howard (1986), J. S. Snyder (1984), Barnett (1963), Tuchman (1962), Van Creveld (1983), and Levy (1988b).

7   The assumption of a two-front war was not new. It had been inherited from a former chief of staff, Moltke. However, Schlieffen was dissatisfied with Moltke's contingency plans, which called for an attempt to absorb a French attack and to counterattack (Rothenberg, 1986: 316).

8   It must be noted that the assumption of British intervention in a continental war was made by the German general staff but was not shared by the civilian politicians. In fact, Levy (1988b: 19–22) shows quite clearly that, as late as July 30, 1914, the German kaiser and his chief advisers still entertained the illusion of British neutrality. However, the general staff never shared this belief, or was not willing to base its plans on such a notion.

9   There were several different versions of the plan that were revised by Schlieffen repeatedly between the years 1906 and 1913. They differed from one another essentially in that each subsequent version placed more emphasis in terms of forces on the German right wing, which was assigned to the occupation of Belgium. So obsessed was Schlieffen with this plan that he is reported to have muttered before his death: "It must come to a fight. Only make the right wing strong" (cited in Tuchman 1962: 25).

10   Both J. S. Snyder (1984) and Levy (1986) conclude that while military considerations and organizational routines were important, they could not explain the whole sequence in and of themselves.

11   Howard is quick to add that "too much emphasis has been placed on the importance and influence of Foch as a military theorist. He did no more than echo views generally held, not only in the French army, but in others as well." Regardless, this was the French theory of war that the Germans faced since the beginning of the century, and the Germans did not need good spies to know how prevalent Foch's ideas were in France.

12   Van Creveld's (1983: 84–116) analysis of the role played by supplies and logistics on the German attack is particularly telling about the ambivalent impact of technology on mobile warfare. He shows that the complex and elaborate network of railroads constructed by the Germans prior to the war inside German territory was instrumental in enabling the Germans to survive militarily against the whole world while on the defensive. Yet, the same system of railroads was of little use in the mobile warfare the Germans initiated, and in fact adversely affected the effectiveness of the German plans.

13   This analysis is based on Abdulghani (1984), Levy and Forelich (1985), Ismael (1982), Helms (1984: 135-208), Litwak (1987), Tahir-Kheli and Ayubi (1983), Grummon (1982), Marr (1985: 291–312), Nonneman (1986), Baram (1980), and Raz (1985).

14   Radio Teheran repeatedly called for a Shi'ah uprising in Iraq. For example, on April 9, 1980, Khomeini urged the Iraqis to "wake up and topple this corrupt regime in your Islamic country before it is too late," and the next day he expressed the hope that the Iraqi regime would be "dispatched in the refuse bin of history" (from the *New York Times*, cited by Pipes, 1983: 11).

15   Ikle (1971) provides a good discussion of the problems involved in planning for war termination.

# 6

# *The Paradox of Surprise*

The paradox of surprise is actually one of the few paradoxes that is not empirically rare. The observation driving this chapter is that the vast majority of the surprise attacks in the twentieth century have ended in the defeat of the initiator. A surprise attack is one wherein the military and political establishment of the target state failed to assess correctly the intention of the attacker, its actual plan of attack, or its timing. Consequently, the unanticipated attack handed the victim an initial military blow. The wars falling into the category of surprise attacks, along with their outcomes, are given in Table 6.1. The paradox of surprise is this. A state mounts a successful surprise attack, handing the opponent an initial military defeat. Yet, it may turn out that precisely because of the successful accomplishment of surprise, the war ends in a—sometimes disastrous—defeat for the attacker. In many cases, the success of the surprise attack is not the chief reason for the attacker's defeat, but it is a contributing reason. In other cases, the surprise factor is a key cause of the attacker's failure.

## Surprise in War

Why do states planning an attack place such a premium on surprise? The element of surprise is seen as a key determinant of success in military strategy. As Levite (1987: ix) puts it:

To catch one's rival(s) by surprise is commonly considered a desirable feat. Surprise . . . is seen as a factor that could significantly diminish costs and risks and enhance chances for success of whatever initiative one is contemplating. On occasion, surprise assumes even greater importance being (or at least perceived to be) the *sine qua non* for success. This happens when one attempts action that is a long shot with the odds very much against him. . . . The overall importance of the surprise phenomenon is further enhanced by the traumatic experience associated with it, the public perception of its consequences, the widespread belief in the frequency of its

**Table 6.1**   Surprise attacks in the twentieth century and their consequences

| Date of attack | Name of war | Initiator | Target | Winner |
|---|---|---|---|---|
| 6–30–1913 | Second Balkan War | Bulgaria | Serbia, Greece | Serbia, Greece[a] |
| 5–5–1919 | Greko-Turkish War | Greece | Turkey | Turkey |
| 12–19–1931 | Manchurian War | Japan | China | Japan |
| 6–22–1941 | Operation Barbarossa | Germany | USSR | USSR |
| 12–7–1941 | Pearl Harbor | Japan | U.S. | U.S. |
| 6–24–1950 | Korean War I | North Korea | South Korea | tie |
| 11–26–1950 | Korean War II[b] | China | U.S. | tie |
| 10–29–1956 | Sinai War | Israel | Egypt | Israel |
| 10–31–1956 | Suez War | England, France | Egypt | Egypt |
| 10–20–1962 | Sino-Indian War | China | India | China |
| 6–5–1967 | Six Day War | Israel | Egypt | Israel |
| 10–6–1973 | Yom Kippur War | Egypt, Syria | Israel | Israel |
| 10–30–1978 | Ugandan War | Tanzania | Uganda, Libya | Tanzania |
| 9–22–1980 | Iran-Iraq War | Iraq | Iran | tie |
| 4–2–1982 | Falkland-Malvinas War | Argentina | England | England |

[a] Romania and Turkey also rank among the winners, but they were not a target of the Bulgarian attack.
[b] This is the second stage of the Korean War discussed in Chapter 4.

occurrence, and the extensive (and costly) measures commonly taken to guard against it.[1]

Some of the more notorious features attributed to surprise can be summed up by the following points.

- Surprise attacks catch the victim unprepared and undeployed for war: the victim's forces are not mobilized, the standing army is not under alert, many of the troops are away from the border regions, and the logistics are not in a state of combat readiness.
- Surprise enables the initiator to optimize the timing of the attack, its location, its scope, and its method. It allows the initiator to have almost free choice in defining the opening stage of war. The initiator can maximize the factors in which it has relative advantage while offsetting the factors in which the victim has relative advantage.
- Surprise attacks disrupt the victim's command, control, communication, mobilization, and logistical systems. They cause chaos and disarray in the victim's military and political command.
- A surprise first strike enables the initiator to wipe out at least a portion of the victim's retaliatory force.
- Surprise puts the victim's political, military, and social institutions in a state of psychological disorientation and panic.
- Surprise imposes on the victim unfavorable opening conditions.

It may force a state into a defensive when the military doctrine of the state is offensive in nature; it may force it to fight in its own populated territory (bogging down its military effectiveness due to the need to evacuate civilians from the arena of fighting) when its doctrine calls for transferring the battle into the enemy's territory.

- Surprise is considered to be—for the above reasons—a force multiplier. It may provide the weak side with the marginal advantage that transforms the balance of forces in its favor.

Surprise plays a key role in the planning of an offensive strategy because the opponent's unpreparedness greatly reduces its ability to resist. It usually takes the opponent some time to mobilize troops, to move them to the battlefield, and to stage a real resistance to the attack. By that time, the attacker will have advanced considerably, creating chaos and confusion in the opponent's ranks. Mobilization and troop movements to the battle zone are done under stress and acute time pressure, factors contributing to the ineffectiveness of the defensive efforts. The rapid advance of the attacker is further facilitated by the fact that the opponent feels pressed to rush units to the front without adequate preparation and proper equipment just to slow down the attacker's advance. Hence, the element of surprise is a chief ally of military planners.

Another advantage of surprise attack is that the initial success of the attack defines to a large extent the rules of combat, although this is due more to the initiation act than to surprise. What the initial attack does is to enable an attacker to capitalize on factors that give it an advantage over the opponent. If one's strategy relies heavily on air superiority, and if an initial attack allows one to wipe out the opponent's air force, a major step toward victory in the war has been taken. The opponent's responses, at least initially, are defined by the ground rules laid out by the attack. This is of special importance if the opponent is notorious for having put all of its military eggs in one basket. Examples are not too difficult to recount. The German attack on France through the Ardens, which caught the French totally unprepared, is one. Note that there the surprise was not that of the timing of the attack, but of its direction. The French blind reliance on the Maginot line was a first-rate blunder. The Japanese attack on Pearl Harbor had major military implications because of the senseless concentration of the American fleet in the Hawaiian port.

Why then have most surprise attacks ended in the defeat of their initiators? One factor that explains not only why most surprise attacks have ended in disaster but also why most modern strategists have failed to realize a genuine paradox in this context is that most surprise attacks have been staged by states that were militarily inferior to their opponents. The superior opponent was able to absorb the devastating first strike, regroup its forces, and launch an effective counteroffensive. Given its numerical, technological, and tactical superiority, the victim overcame its initial problems and emerged victorious.

What can one do to surprise one's opponent in war? First, one must have a good idea of what the opponent expects and has prepared for. Sometimes one can aid in the process of establishing a set of expectations among the enemy's military and political elites by creating a consistent behavioral pattern that makes one's future behavior seemingly predictable. This predictability may serve as a basis for the opponent's expectations. If one can make the opponent certain that it can predict one's behavior, one can accomplish surprise by behaving unexpectedly. Hence, surprise and deception usually go hand in hand.

Second, one must make the preparations for the surprise, excluding those that are deliberately designed to deceive, as unobtrusive as possible. Every move that might give the enemy a clue about what is about to happen must be either camouflaged or presented as part of some routine behavior. When the Egyptians planned the surprise attack in 1973, they scheduled their annual maneuvers along the canal at the time the attack was about to begin and informed the Israelis, through third parties, that they were holding a major exercise. A fundamental principle of deception is that every move that is instrumental to the launching of a surprise attack (such as troop concentrations, higher levels of alert, consultations among allies if the attack is to be a joint one) should have a logical explanation that is consistent with a routine nonviolent form of behavior (Handel, 1987).

Surprise attacks require secrecy. Thus, the planning for surprise attack is usually a highly centralized process; very few people know about what is being planned. This is necessary in order to minimize the chances of leaks. Often not only is the opponent kept in the dark, but most people in the planner's state and its allies are ignorant of what is going to happen. Assumptions about allies' reaction to the surprise attack must be made, and it sometimes turns out that such assumptions are quite inaccurate. For example, when the French and British planned the takeover of the Suez Canal in 1956, they assumed that the United States would support its allies, or—at worst—would not take sides due to the presidential election. This prediction turned out to be far off the mark. Not only was the Eisenhower administration not paralyzed by the presidential election, it expressed its opposition to the attack very strongly by putting pressure on England, France, and Israel to withdraw promptly from Egyptian territory.

Finally, a key element of surprise attack is timing. Because surprise is a scarce resource, it can be used only once, and therefore should be used at the time that it is most crucial in determining an outcome that the initiator cares about a great deal (Axelrod, 1979). Scheduling of the attack is significant in two respects. First, it allows the initiator to determine when the opponent will be least prepared for an attack and most vulnerable to it. The scheduling of the 1973 surprise attack for Yom Kippur, the holiest day for Jews, was not incidental. The Egyptians and Syrians knew that the Israeli society would be completely paralyzed—no radio and newspapers in operation, with most people being in synagogues and no traffic in the streets. This was an optimal date for an attack because it would take the Israelis longer than usual to mobilize reserves given the starting point.

Second, a surprise attack must have a maximal effect in terms of the damage it inflicts upon the target. When a weak party wishes to overcome its weakness through a bold and surprising first strike, it wants to put into this first strike as much weight as it can possibly muster, so that the opponent will not be able to recover from it. Hence, the problem is that of finding a point in time when the opponent forces are most vulnerable and the yield of the first strike can be maximized. The Japanese could not have been more content than to have the whole Pacific navy of the United States in one place. If the American assessment of Soviet intentions during the Cuban missile crisis was correct, then the Soviet Union intended to reveal the nuclear missiles it had placed in Cuba during the session of the U.N. General Assembly in October 1962, in order to maximize the diplomatic fallout.

Planners of surprise attacks are usually aware that surprise—in and of itself—cannot decide the war. It is at best a contributing factor, but it is neither a precondition for initiation nor a substitute for a plan for a longer war, of which the first strike is but one element. In virtually all the cases mentioned in Table 6.1, the initiator would have attacked whether it thought it could surprise the target or not. The ability to accomplish as many military objectives as possible while the opponent is busy reorganizing and recovering from the initial shock is a key to successful completion of the war. To do this, the initiator must have a clear plan of what it wants to accomplish, both before the opponent has recovered and afterward. When this is not entirely clear, the initiator might find itself in trouble. For example, the Japanese spent a lot of time and effort planning the first stage of the war against the United States and its allies, but had only a vague notion of how to end the war (Toland, 1970; Butow, 1962). If the Russians or the Chinese were indeed behind the North Korean invasion of South Korea in 1950, then some grave diplomatic errors were committed that suggest that the operation was not very well thought through. It is difficult to explain the Soviet absence from the U.N. Security Council meeting that decided on the dispatch of an international force to fight the North Koreans.

As with any other military planning, the planning of a surprise attack requires some sort of Plan B. The accomplishment of surprise is due as much to the initiator's ability to deceive the opponent as to the opponent's susceptibility to deception and other factors that may prevent it from seeing the coming disaster. Some of the moves that the initiator must make prior to the attack are highly suspicious. It is, therefore, impossible to stage a fool-proof camouflage of the imminent attack. When the general diplomatic climate is tense, military moves, even disguised as routine maneuvers, are bound to raise some suspicion in the military intelligence of the target. In 1973, intelligence analysts noticed that the communication networks the Egyptians had set up during the "routine maneuvers" were too complex for a routine maneuver. It is as Thomas Schelling observed regarding the surprise at Pearl Harbor: no matter how good the deception staged by the initiator, there is always enough information around to be picked up by the target. Surprise attacks, therefore, are the result of both good planning by the initiator and intelligence errors by the target.[2]

Whether or not the opponent will be deceived by the initiator's deception or by the former's own errors of judgment is beyond the initiator's control. Therefore, the planner of a surprise attack must have two plans: one for the case in which the planned attack surprises and one for the case in which it does not. Nobody really speaks of what would have happened had the Japanese failed to surprise the United States at Pearl Harbor, or had the Germans failed to surprise the Soviets in 1941, or had the Egyptians and Syrians failed to surprise the Israelis in 1973. Available evidence suggests that each attack would have been carried out anyway, and pretty much according to the plan that was indeed carried out. This suggests that the planners of the attack viewed surprise as the icing on the cake. However, this is not a general rule. It is conceivable that a state might prefer to attack if it thinks the opponent would be surprised, but will not attack if it has reason to believe that the opponent is ready. It is difficult to find empirical examples of such cases, because they represent a problem of the "dog that didn't bark." However, one example might be the 1960 minor crisis between Israel and Egypt, in which the latter moved a couple of divisions into the de facto demilitarized Sinai peninsula. The Israelis responded with a secret partial mobilization and the Egyptians, realizing Israel's readiness, did a round tour of the desert and returned west of the Suez Canal (Yaniv, 1986).

# The Paradoxical Story of Surprise Attacks

There are two facets to the paradox of surprise; one is that it works better than expected and hence catches the initiator unprepared. The ease with which the initiator accomplishes its objectives finds it unprepared to deal with the second stage of the battle. The other facet is that the success of the surprise attack increases the target's resolve and willingness to suffer, which cause the initiator's failure.

## *The Surprise That Surprises the Surpriser*

Suppose that a state *i* is fed up with the status quo to such an extent that it decides to attack an opponent *j* whether or not *j* expects an attack. Of course, *i* prefers to attack an unmobilized and unprepared opponent, but would rather attack if the opponent is mobilized than not attack. Hence, *i* has a dominant attack strategy. Nonetheless, the attacker thinks that it pays to invest in some deception in order to achieve surprise. The would-be attacker knows that *j* prefers not to mobilize if it thinks that *i* would not attack, but clearly prefers mobilization if it thinks that *i* plans to attack. Therefore, *i* might be skeptical about the possibility of achieving surprise, expecting a mobilized and prepared opponent. This is illustrated in Figure 6.1.

But what happens if *i* is wrong about either *j*'s preferences or its ability to see the coming attack? Since *i*'s preparations assume no surprise, the actual attack might have unexpected positive results. The resistance that the attacking forces meet in reality is meager, the enemy forces are unprepared and shocked, fleeing from *i*'s troops, and the attacking army is advancing faster than expected. It is this ease with

The Target

|  |  | *j* | |
|---|---|---|---|
|  |  | Mobilize | Don't Mobilize |
| The Attacker   *i* | Attack | 2     *     2 | 1     4 |
|  | Don't Attack | 3     1 | 4     3 |

**Figure 6.1**   The Mobilization Dilemma

*Note:* Initiator's (*i*'s) preferences are given in the lower-left corner of each cell; target's (*j*'s) preferences are given in the upper-right corner of each cell. Outcomes are ranked from best = 4 to worst = 1.

which the attacking force moves forward that can be a cause of trouble. Because the attacker expects fierce resistance, its force deployments and especially its logistics are set up under conservative assumptions of rather static warfare. For example, it assumes that the distance between the forward units and the supply and logistics will be short, hence, there is no need to provide the forward units with independent supply of food, fuel, repair facilities, and so on. All these are to be supplied by static units located in the rear. Yet, the rapid advance of the attacking force causes the forward units to disengage themselves from the supply and logistics. Before long, the forward units find themselves out of fuel and food in hostile territory, which may not even have such supplies that can be extracted locally.

Worse, because of the rapid retreat of the stunned opponent, the advancing forces might find themselves suddenly in areas they had not expected to reach, with no adequate plans for advance or for the treatment of occupied territories and their population, and no adequate means to deal with their new possessions. The rapid advance stretches the lines of combat to points that might be beyond the capacity of the advancing force to deal with.

At the same time, the opponent is withdrawing inward, increasing its ability to concentrate forces; it is capable of turning overall numerical inferiority to local superiority. The inward withdrawal facilitates the target's recovery from the initial shock because of the shortening of the lines of supply and communications. As in the case of attrition, swift surprise attacks are converted into frustrating long and static wars. Finally—when the target recovers from the shock and reorganizes its forces on better terms than the initiator—the initiator is gradually pushed back and rolled over.

The unexpected success of the surprise attack does something to the initiator's ego, evoking perceptions of omnipotence. This is especially typical of decision makers in states that had a self-perception of inferiority—military or otherwise—vis-à-vis the opponent. The success of the attack and the ease with which it penetrates the victim's defenses invoke beliefs that the latter's power had been vastly overestimated. This often gives birth to ideas that the initiator can—indeed, must—capitalize on the initial success and depart from the seemingly conservative original plans of attack. The successful first strike causes a radical and uncontrolled transformation of the initiator's perceptions of itself and of its opponents, thereby leading it to overlook the fact that all the attack did was temporarily alter the balance of forces.

Most important, the success of the surprise attack causes the initiator to overlook the fact that this very success increases the intangible elements of the opponent's power, most notably, its resolve and willpower. This radical alteration of the initiator's perceptions results in a hasty and often unrealistic expansion of the political and military objectives of the war, and this expansion is what prevents the initiator from implementing what might have been an optimal plan of war. It is also this alteration of plans that leads eventually to the initiator's demise.

## Shock Treatment and National Resolve

Even if the attack is well planned, including provisions for unexpected possessions of new territories, flexible logistics, and so forth, it might lead to unintended outcomes because of the political and psychological consequences of surprise on the target. I call it "shock treatment" because the sudden, often unprovoked, attack evokes rage, feelings of hate, wishes for revenge, and all sorts of emotional reactions that had not existed before. Under such conditions, domestic conflicts are easily forgotten or set aside for a later time. Mobilization is complete and national resolve and determination are converted into a resistance to surrender and also a greater will to suffer for the sake of final victory and punishment of the aggressor. A hitherto weak or controversial government becomes a united representative of all people, and its capacity to mobilize national resources increases sharply. To the extent that popular will to sacrifice and take active part in the war is an element of national power, paradoxically, national power following the absorption of a surprise attack might be greater than prior to the attack.

A government might be in the midst of purges and suppression of opposition groups in the army or in other sectors of the society that make up national power, but the initial success of the surprise attack imposes on the government a need to declare a truce in its domestic struggles. It is now willing (or forced) to bring back to the scene sectors that previously had been excluded from national politics. The net effect is that the ability and willingness of a surprised government to mobilize national resources increases. In the final analysis, a surprise attack may put a domestically troubled nation in better shape to fight and win a war than if a war were initiated by such a government. It is easier to generate a "rally around the flag" effect when one is attacked by surprise than when one initiates an attack.

The added emotional aspects, as well as the increased cohesion that is invoked by the surprise attack, serve to increase national resolve. And it has been shown that resolve is a crucial factor in the conflict equation: it can help tip the balance to the side with higher doses of national will and determination even if the balance of capabilities might suggest a different result (Maoz, 1982a, 1983). While the initial defeats of the target indeed cause panic and demoralization, not to mention many tangible costs, the rage at the surprise attack increases national resolve and strengthens national determination to suffer and defeat the "aggressor." It may enable a government to rally the population even if—objectively speaking—the stakes of the war seem rather stupid, thereby counterbalancing whatever damages the initial attack may have caused.[3]

## The Surpriser's Dilemma

If there is indeed a problem in terms of the unintended consequences of surprise, then why not wage war in the old, gentlemanly style, whereby a state makes a public demand of the opponent, and, if the latter refuses, the state declares war and gets the troops moving afterward? A formal declaration of war might at least prevent rage at the unprovoked attack. The population of the target might still view the attack as an act of aggression, but the process leading to war might be used by the initiator's diplomats to make a public case that would soften the blow.

The initiator's dilemma is obvious. If it could afford such a style of war, it would have gone step by step. In addition to softening the blow on the target, a gradual escalation of hostilities has several other advantages. For one thing, it allows the initiator to put the blame for the war on the opponent. Even in a world composed of self-centered, power-driven states, an image of morality seems important. One does not want to be blamed for starting a war by third parties, and such calculations are especially important when one is dependent on important allies. The gradual escalation of tensions allows for internal opposition in the target state to challenge the government's tough stance. When a war breaks out, the opposition to the war in the target state might weaken its resolve; the debate over the necessity of war might become a part of a more general domestic struggle within the target's state. The ability of the initiator to place at least some of the blame for the war on the target may be instrumental in preventing a truce in the internal struggle within the target's state.

But the temptations of a surprise attack are also very strong. The aim of war is to break the opponent's will to fight; this can be done slowly or quickly. The slow way entails a combination of political and military pressure through gradual escalation of hostilities. The quick way is to take away the opponent's ability to resist by breaking it militarily. Surprise attacks may bring about not only disorientation and chaos within the opponent's ranks, but also a decisive battle that may disarm the opponent. No matter how strong the national will and resolve of the defeated target, it cannot fight back without an army. And the objective of the surprise attack is just that: to accomplish some military goals that cannot be accomplished (or can be accomplished only at an unacceptable cost) if the target is ready and waiting for the initiator. This is why the Argentinean government risked international condemnation and the loss of U.S. support in its fight with Great Britain. Had it escalated the conflict gradually, the British government would have almost surely fortified the islands and added extra forces. Under such circumstances it would have been impossible to take the islands without loss of British life (and possibly Argentinean life as well). The loss of British life would have increased substantially Britain's determination to resist the fait accompli.

An important aspect of the staging of a surprise attack is that military considerations and arguments clash with political and psychological ones. The military considerations usually have the advantage: they are more concrete, more precise, and more deterministic than the political and psychological ones. Generals who advocate the staging of a surprise attack can discuss how much territory can be occupied, which weapon systems of the opponent can be destroyed, how many of their soldiers' lives can be spared given an unprepared opponent, how much more likely military victory is, and so forth. Because surprise attacks involve detailed plans, this kind of argumentation can sound extremely convincing, especially to those politicians who are unaware of the uncertainties of battle, the impact of friction, and so forth.

On the other hand, politicians making an argument for a gradual escalation of conflict, and for giving the target a fair warning of what might be coming, have a lot of ifs, maybes, and other expressions that involve intangibles. Will surprise weaken internal conflict within the target state? Maybe, if the leaders can forget their old enmities, and the opposition views the external enemy as worse than the internal one. Will the target be able to gather its remains before it is forced into a decisive battle that disarms it? Maybe, if it is able to mobilize its resources and withdraw in an orderly fashion; if it can maintain communications; if it can change its strategy in a manner that would allow it to deal with an unexpected form of warfare. Will our allies side with us despite the surprise attack? They may or may not, depending on whether they can afford not to. The same can be said about the opponent's allies. Even in the worst case, where the opponent's allies decide to join in, it would take them a lot of time to intervene actively, given that they too are caught unprepared. By that time, the war might be over.

The arguments for gradualism are not easy to make; they are even less easy to make convincingly. During the Cuban missile crisis, when the Executive Committee discussed options for dealing with the Soviet missiles, supporters of destruction of the missile sites via a surgical air strike were dissuaded eventually only because the air force could not guarantee destruction of all missile sites. There was a severe danger that these missiles would be used to retaliate against the American heartland. In a way, supporters of a blockade on Cuba got their way by default; it was not clear how a blockade, in and of itself, would bring about the removal of the Soviet missiles (Allison, 1971).

The asymmetry of persuasiveness and concreteness that characterizes debates between supporters of political gradualism and supporters of surprise attack often leads to oversimplification of the latter option. The focus of the discussion is on the first stage of the attack and its immediate implications: How likely is the opponent to be surprised? How would third parties react to the surprise attack? What would be the major accomplishments of the attack as opposed to an attack following a fair warning? And so forth. The long-term implications of surprise are often swept under the rug. When the Japanese cabinet discussed Pearl Harbor, they focused their attention on the advantages of a surprise attack but discussed only vaguely how, when, and under what conditions the war would be terminated (Butow, 1962). Likewise, the Egyptians and Syrians had detailed plans for starting the war against Israel in 1973, but only vague notions about how to end it (Shazli, 1980; Stein, 1985).

The surpriser's dilemma is composed of two factors: a rational one and a cognitive one. The rational factor is the trade-off between the military benefits of a surprise attack and the diplomatic and political benefits of a fair warning following a gradual escalation process. Quite often it may be a now-or-never case: a surprise attack versus no war at all. The gradualist approach may be militarily infeasible. Had Hitler given the French a fair warning that he was planning to reoccupy the Rhineland in 1936, they would have moved in and rendered the remilitarization a dream. In such cases, both the short-term and long-term disadvantages of surprise might be seen as acceptable risks because the alternative may be giving up whatever can be accomplished through war.

The cognitive factor is a heuristic that is often applied by decision makers in prediction tasks. It is called the *availability* heuristic, and it suggests that things that are more available in one's memory will be seen as more probable than things that are difficult to remember, imagine, and so forth. Since the tangible immediate benefits of surprise are simple—easily described and easily imagined—surprise is given high probability of success. As a result, people tend to ignore or downgrade the long-term implications of surprise, fail to plan for the next stage of the war, and thus get caught unprepared by the success of the surprise attack they had initiated.

## Historical Paradoxes of Surprise

There is very little in the theoretical and empirical literature on surprise attacks that directs us to the issues discussed above. Most of the literature examines why states were surprised, and some work examines how attackers have managed to stage successful deception campaigns. Surprise is seen as one of the immediate background conditions leading to war, not as an element in the management of violent hostilities. Explanations of the impact of war upon the political and social conditions within the participating states (e.g., Coser, 1957; Wilkenfeld, 1973; Stein, 1979) did not attempt to draw connections between the conditions under which the war broke out and the effects it had on the participating societies.

The implication of all this is that we do not know what the modal case looks like in terms of the effects of surprise attack on the process and outcome of war. Consequently, we are not in a position to state—and the following case studies do not attempt to redress this deficiency—whether this chapter discusses a general phenomenon or an exceptional set of cases wherein successful surprise causes the defeat of the initiator. The cases discussed in the following pages document the two facets of the paradox of surprise. The first case describes the effects that a successful surprise attack has on the target. The second case describes the effects that a successful surprise attack has on the initiator who had planned for surprise but was surprised by the extent to which this strategy was successful.

### Surprise and National Will: The German Invasion of Russia, 1941–43[4]

The surprise that the Germans managed to stage on June 22, 1941, could not have been more devastating to the Soviets. It could also not have come at a worse time. The Soviet Union was still licking the wounds left by the great purges of 1937–39, in which the Soviet army was hit especially hard. The army was going through a dramatic period of transition. The whole supreme command of the Soviet army was made up of second-echelon officers with minimum experience in commanding large-scale military operations. Some commanders, such as Zhukov, had successful command experience in the Mongolian war with Japan in 1939. Many other senior officers were new additions to the staff, following another miniseries of purges following the humiliating victory over Finland in the winter war of 1939–40. This war had also led to purges among divisional commanders of the Leningrad military district (Seaton, 1976: 90). Following the Finnish war, both the doctrines and the military organization were subject to revision and major changes.

Opinions vary regarding the extent to which the surprise of the German attack accounted for the initial German successes across the front. It is clear that the unpreparedness of the Soviet army was more general than its failure to foresee the impending attack and to deploy forces in a manner that would minimize the initial blow. The surprise simply worsened a bad state of affairs. But it also caused a major shift in the Stalinist style of dealing with "mistakes." The first and last political victims of the surprise attack were the highest-ranking officers of the western front. On June 28, Stalin issued an order relieving General Pavlov from his duty as the commander of the western front. Pavlov, his chief of staff, Klimovshikh, and the heads of the artillery and signals were arrested, publicly denounced, imprisoned, and shot. This practice then ceased completely during the entire war, though the Soviet defeats accumulated throughout 1942. Stalin realized that public denunciation of senior officers caused demoralization of the army and aggravated matters.[5]

The German invasion found a state torn apart by conflict, terror, and divisions within the party and the government. The shock and outrage caused by the swift attack enabled Stalin to mobilize unparalleled support and public enthusiasm for national values in comparison to other periods in Russian history. Conflicts within the ruling political and military elite did not disappear, but they were not allowed to distract the national effort from the main objective: fighting the Nazis.[6]

As in other cases of swift military attacks that were converted into prolonged wars of attrition, the initial stage of the war was characterized by complete confusion and chaos within the Soviet ranks. This confusion was not due strictly to the surprise attack; it may have been an outgrowth of fundamental failure to adjust to the nature of the German attack and to the notion that the Soviet territory must be defended. This notion led to devastating blows to the Soviet army at Minsk and later on in Smolensk. In both cases, the Soviets threw into the battle large numbers of poorly equipped and poorly trained troops in a series of desperate counterattacks that served only to increase the chaos and demoralization in the Soviet army; they had little effect on the German advance.[7]

Gradually, however, the Soviet supreme command came to the realization that the only way the German advance could be halted was through gradual attrition. Stalin took somewhat longer to realize that direct confrontation with the Germans would be futile at that in point time. It took the collapse of the entire southwest front and the capture of some 650,000 Soviet prisoners in the Kiev area to convince him to follow the advice of Zhukov and other local commanders. At the same time, long imprisoned or otherwise outcast officers were brought back to active duty, and the most intense process of national mobilization in history started.

While the Soviet army began to prepare for the defense of the Moscow and Stalingrad areas and to mobilize for a long and desperate struggle, the non-Russian people in the west easily switched sides. The Ukrainians, Lithuanians, and Latvians became the main allies of the Germans in the administration of the occupied areas and the systematic imprisonment (and later execution) of Jews, Gypsies, and other minorities. On the other hand, the Russian people, who had been terrorized for years by the Stalin regime, stood as one in their resistance to the Germans. The ability of a people to stage such a long and desperate resistance to an enemy, and to suffer so many casualties in the process, cannot be explained simply in terms of their fear of immediate sanctions imposed by the indigenous regime. Nor can it be explained strictly as a result of a fundamental enmity or national character.[8]

Clearly, the evidence regarding the effect of national resolve and the will to suffer displayed by the Russians is based on *modus operandi;* we do not have direct evidence as to the motivational sources of the mobilization efforts. Also, it is unclear to what extent the total mobilization of Russia was due to the fact that the German attack caught the Soviets by surprise, nor is it clear what the effect was of the initial German successes on the resistance efforts staged by the Russians. However, an assessment of the effectiveness of the Russian war effort is based on two factors: the ability of the regime to mobilize resources, both human and material, to the war effort, and the extent of resistance of the population in occupied territories to the foreign forces.

Reliable data regarding the changes in the size of the Red Army are unavailable. Zhukov (1982: 172), who hailed Stalin's efforts to prepare the army for war during the 1939–41 lull years, points out that on January 1, 1941, the size of the Red Army was 4.2 million soldiers. Estimates of direct battle deaths during the war, which include only military personnel killed, generally stand at 15 million soldiers, the largest figure of human losses in history. At the end of the war, the Red Army numbered over 12 million soldiers. This figure does not include irregular civil defense forces and partisan forces whose size is unknown.[9] Rice (1986: 671) assesses the factors contributing to the Soviet victory in World War II:

Russia's victory in World War II was in many ways a victory for the concept of the whole country mobilized for war. Effective resistance by the population . . . buttressed the effort of the Soviet Union's forces at the front. Partisan warfare, which had been little understood by the makers of Soviet strategy, triumphed in urban and rural areas. An underestimated contribution to the Soviet effort was made through massive industrial relocations. . . . Remarkably, during the German advance, large portions of Soviet industry were moved, sometimes brick by brick, out of reach of the Germans. In seeking the support of the population, Stalin dropped distinctions between proletarian and peasant, communist and nationalist. Stirred by the heroic music of the finest Soviet composers that was written expressly for the war effort, the battle against the Germans became a struggle for mother Russia, a struggle that had been waged many times in Russian history.

The ability of the Soviet army to adjust to the new requirements imposed by the German successes was also significant. According to Rice (1986: 672):

The most important alteration occurred in the area of defensive strategy and tactics. In the early stages of the war, Soviet soldiers did not know how to maneuver defensively and, according to German observers, stubbornly held their positions well beyond the point at which retreat would have been advisable. When they did retreat, they found it difficult to maintain order. The need for strategic withdrawals had been recognized, but little effort had been devoted to train commanders and troops. The most successful part of the Soviet retreat, the scorched-earth policy, was learned through experience, often out of frustration and anger, rather than by central direction, facilities were denied to the Germans.

The lack of attention to defense was reversed with the Field Regulations of 1942. Defense was finally discussed explicitly as a "normal form of combat," although offense was hailed as the "fundamental aspect of combat action for the Red Army." The Soviets went to great lengths to encourage their forces to defend in depth and to use active, flexible tactics. Defense did not have to be static. In fact, those who had fought according to static, "linear" principles of defense in the early days were assailed by Stalin himself, who said, "Tens of thousands of Red Army commanders have become expert military leaders . . . they have thrown out the stupid and pernicious linear tactics and have finally adopted the tactic of mobile warfare."

The role of partisan warfare inside the occupied territories by the Germans has been estimated by Soviet military leaders and strategists as a major factor in the critical stages of the war. Zhukov (1982: 322) argues that in 1942 the Germans were forced to activate almost 10 percent of their forces in the eastern front in combating the partisans. In 1943, the Germans allocated to this task police units of the S.S., S.D., and auxiliary troops, in addition to regular Wehrmacht troops totaling 25 divisions.[10] This resistance was without precedent in Russian history and extensive compared to other states that were occupied by the Germans during the war, even those states in which the prewar regime rested on a far broader base of legitimacy. Russian propaganda that focused on the war in nationalistic rather than communist terms seems to have been very effective in mobilizing popular support for the struggle. This support was reflected by resistance to the Germans within both the territories they occupied and those they did not. Clark's (1970) conclusion is that this ability to mobilize the whole nation to the war effort and to extract from the population a total devotion to it suggests that the Soviets could have defeated Germany even without the aid they received from the West.

Be that as it may, virtually all writers on the war, Soviet military and political leaders included, agree that Germany was on the verge of a total victory over the Soviet Union in the summer and fall of 1942. The occupation of Moscow, Stalingrad, and Leningrad—though it would not have ended the war—would have dealt the Soviet Union a blow from which it probably could not have recovered. It is impossible to determine with any degree of precision what the combination of reasons was that denied the Germans their victory when they were so close to it. However, the determination and stubbornness of the Red Army in those critical battles, as well as the activity of the partisans in the occupied territories, had at least something to do with the Soviet victory. My argument is that this kind of resistance and devotion to a cause, given the political and military background of the German attack, cannot be explained without reference to the context in which the attack broke out and to the initial success of the attack, which no doubt was due to the successful surprise.

A similar effect can be seen in the case of the Japanese attack on Pearl Harbor. Prior to the attack there had been an intense political debate in the United States regarding the intervention of the United States in the war in Europe. Public opinion polls made during 1941 showed that a majority of Americans favored an isolationist, hands-off policy toward the war. The Roosevelt administration, on the other hand, was intensely in favor of joining the war, and acted to provoke the Germans into naval warfare, WWI style, in the Atlantic in order to find a proper political pretext for entry into the war (Beard, 1948; Friedlander 1967; Russett, 1972). However, the Germans refused to cooperate with this scheme and displayed extreme caution and tolerance. They knew very well that for them American military intervention spelled disaster. Whether or not the "back door to war theory" (see Chapter 3) has any validity, it is clear that the nature of the Japanese attack had an immediate impact on American attitudes toward the war. The rage toward the Pearl Harbor attack in the United States was so intense that nobody even questioned the decision to tie the war against Japan with the war against Germany and Italy. It seemed obvious and natural that these confrontations were two sides of the same coin, though in historical perspective it is far less clear.

## Discovering Paper Tigers: The 1973 War in the Middle East

We know quite well why nations are sometimes surprised. And, if we accept the argument of some scholars (e.g., Betts, 1978; Handel, 1976), we know that surprise attacks are inevitable because there is no ultimate cure for the illness of national intelligence. However, the favorite cases of the studies of surprise attack suggest that the role of surprise is secondary in nature. That is, it is quite clear that surprise was a desirable feature of the attack, not a condition for it. Given this bias, it is quite clear that the effects of the surprise on the surpriser are not well understood, and it is not implausible that the significance of the surprise factor in initiation decisions has been vastly exaggerated.

While I do not intend to amend this state of affairs fully here, the case study of the 1973 attack from the perspective of the surprisers should suggest some counterintuitive ideas about this side of the coin of surprise. Elsewhere, I have analyzed Sadat's calculations prior to the 1973 attack (Maoz, 1989: ch. 8). Given Sadat's preference structure, I argue that Sadat hoped that a surprise attack would improve Egypt's chances in the war, but it is likely that he would have attacked in October even if he had failed in achieving surprise. This argument is corroborated by post hoc statements of Egyptian leaders, including Sadat himself (Sadat, 1978; Shazli, 1980; Heikal, 1975). The fact of the matter was that Sadat, though hoping for surprise, did not even expect it. And even if he did expect that the attack would surprise the Israelis, he vastly overestimated the capacity of the Israeli army to withstand the Egyptian attempt to cross the Suez Canal. Sadat estimated that the canal crossing would result in some 50,000 Egyptian casualties. In fact, less than 2 percent of the estimated Egyptian casualties were incurred during the canal crossing (Israeli, 1985: 130).

Though we have considerably less information about the Syrian expectations prior to the attack, the Syrian *modus operandi* during the war is quite telling. The initial Syrian attack was conducted along three fronts: the southern front, the central front, and the northern front, where commando units attacked and occupied an important Israeli outpost on Mount Hermon. The major Syrian effort was in the central front, where they also made the most significant advances. The Syrian attack caused heavy casualties to the Israelis on October 6 and 7, and the major fighting developed along a narrow strip of road known as the Tapline Route. A Syrian brigade, commanded by Col. Shafiq Fiyad, bypassed the main Israeli command post on the Golan Heights in Nafekh, and reached the Old Customs House some 4.5 miles east and overlooking the Bnot-Ya'akov bridge over the Jordan River, which separates the Golan Heights from Israel proper (Herzog, 1975: 122). At that point in time (Sunday, October 7), these tanks did not encounter any Israeli resistance. It seemed that the road to Israel was open before the Syrian armor. What was puzzling about this incident was that the Syrian tanks stopped and waited for further orders. Apparently, they realized that they had accomplished far more than was expected, and their operational plans did not include going down into the Jordan valley and crossing over to Israel.

The anecdote about this small forward Syrian force is indicative of the confusion in the Syrian command, which was surprised by the ease with which their forces were able to penetrate the Israeli defenses. Because the speed of the advance far exceeded the attacker's expectations, the Syrian command did not have clear plans as to what to do in order to take advantage of the situation. Worse, the quick advance of the Syrian tanks led them far from their bases of supply; the logistical units had to be rushed much farther than anticipated. This would not have been so bad if the Syrian antiaircraft missiles had covered the range of operations, but they had not. The antiaircraft missile batteries had been deployed in the rear for two reasons. First, the major Syrian concern had been of deep-penetration Israeli aerial strikes, as in the 1969–70 war of attrition. Second, the Syrian plan had been limited to occupying a narrow strip of land along the Golan Heights, because they had thought that was all they could get away with. The range of the SAM-6 antiaircraft missiles had thus been designed to cover only the eastern part of the Golan heights. When logistical units were rushed forward on the second day of fighting, the Israeli air force struck and destroyed most of the convoys coming from the Syrian rear with logistics and supplies of food, gasoline, and munitions.

Once the Israelis were able to stop the Syrian advance all along the front, they started their counteroffensive in the central and northern parts of the front. This counteroffensive (contrary to the disastrous counteroffensive of October 8 in the Suez Canal area) proved quite effective, pushing the Syrian forces back well beyond the October 6 border. The Syrians began to feel the heat and called on the Egyptians for help. By October 10 it was obvious that the Israelis were in the process of handing the Syrian army a severe blow. This was Sadat's chance to sue for cease-fire while Egypt was in possession of a strip of land five miles wide all along the Suez Canal area and the Israelis had been devastated following the futile counteroffensive of October 8. It would not only have left Egypt with a major victory but would have made Syria more humble than it had been in the past. However, the ease with which the Egyptian army had crossed the canal and the victory in the armored battle of October 8, coupled with the Syrian cries for help, prompted Sadat to order an armored attack on the Israelis in order to relieve the pressure from the Syrians and to capture some additional land.

The armored battle of October 14 is considered to be one of the largest in the history of armored warfare (with an estimated total of 2,000 tanks participating). It also was a devastating Egyptian defeat. The Israelis no longer entertained any thought of freeing the *Ma'ozim* (the strongholds along the Suez Canal). They reverted to their original tactic of allowing the Egyptian armor to enter a kill zone and be destroyed there. In one day, Egypt lost nearly 300 tanks and an estimated 1,000 soldiers, with Israeli losses being about one-tenth those of Egypt in tanks and one-fiftieth in personnel (Herzog, 1975: 205–206; O'Ballance, 1978: 155–167; Dupuy, 1978: 485–491).

If this were not enough, Sadat kept waiting, in apparent departure from his original plan, for an opportunity to gain more territories. Thus, on October 15, an army commanded by General Ariel Sharon crossed the canal in the area between the Egyptian second and third armies, followed immediately afterward by the army of General Abraham Adan. A large maneuver of envelopment began to develop on the west bank of the Suez Canal. The Israeli forces started encircling the Egyptian third army in the southern half of the canal. Another Israeli force prepared for a similar maneuver on the Egyptian second army. This move was initially discredited by the Egyptian commanders, who were overcome with their initial successes. Yet, the Soviet satellites overseeing the combat operations revealed the full extent of the Israeli attack and the dangers it posed for the Egyptians. By October 17 the Syrians were in even worse shape, as the Israeli forces in the northern part of the front began occupying formerly Syrian territories in the Mazra'at-Beyt-Ja'an area and threatening Damascus. Kosygin, the Soviet premier, was rushed to Cairo, pledging Sadat to accept a cease-fire before the Israelis finished the encirclement. It took no less than three days to convince Sadat that the Suez-Cairo road was in imminent danger of being cut off, putting the Egyptian third army at the mercy of the Israelis. Sadat sued for cease-fire at the United Nations, but by that time it was far too late for both the Egyptians and the Syrians. Even if the first cease-fire (which was signed and went into effect on the night of October 22) had not been violated by the Israelis, the fruits of victory would have been taken away from the surprisers.[11]

The Israeli victory was no doubt due to both the ability of the IDF to adapt to and recover from the surprise and superior combat capabilities and doctrine. It was no doubt also due to the fact that the Israeli society rose as one (as it had done in each of the previous four wars) to the challenge, eliminating all internal political and social debates. There is no question that American military aid was crucial in enabling the Israelis to turn the tide of battle, even though someone in Washington made an effort to delay it nearly to the point that it would be useless. Yet, all these things considered, the Israeli victory was accomplished with the generous aid of the Egyptians and Syrians, who were blinded by the ease with which they had been able to penetrate Israeli defenses. This initial success, because it was unexpected, evoked perceptions that more could be accomplished and that—at least on the Egyptian side of the alliance—the initial success could be expanded because the Israeli army was in disarray.

A funny thing happened on the way to an Arab victory. In the Syrian case, too much was accomplished in the initial stage of the battle. The Syrian planners did not anticipate such an extensive penetration. Hence, they had to improvise in terms of supplies and planning, to their eventual detriment. In the Egyptian case, the same surprise with the magnitude of penetration and the ease with which the canal crossing was accomplished convinced the political and military leadership of Egypt to take bites that turned out to be more than they could chew. Moreover, the initial success apparently blinded Sadat to the fact that the Israelis were in the process of taking the victory out of his hands.

What should the Egyptians and Syrians have done to convert the surprise attack into a major military victory? The answer is simple: they should have followed their initial plan, which was to occupy a narrow strip of land held by the Israelis and sue for cease-fire. An Egyptian-Syrian plea for cease-fire backed by the Soviets would have had a high chance of success. The United States would have been unable to veto it in the U.N. Security Council, and might even have supported it to prevent escalation to superpower confrontation. Given a U.N.-imposed cease-fire, Israel would have had little choice but to accept. The cease-fire would have left both Egypt and Syria in control of territories east of the Suez Canal and west of the Kuneitra line in the Golan Heights, a minor but remarkable military achievement for armies that had been defeated so badly only six years before. As we have seen from Chapter 3, the political aims of the Egyptians did not require a major Egyptian victory; a small attack would have been enough to alert the superpowers to the explosive potential of the

Middle East conflict. An occupation of a narrow strip of land along the Suez Canal would have done the trick; at least that had been the prewar definition of the situation.

So what do we have here? We have a story of superb execution of an innovative military plan, not only of those aspects that had been based on pessimistic assumptions but also of those aspects that had been based on a long-shot hope of surprise. The success of the initial surprise left the surpriser without adequate plans for the next stage of the war (Syria) and caused overconfidence and additional appetite (Egypt). The improvised alterations in the original plans enabled the surprised opponent to seize the initiative and turn the tables on the attackers.

## Conclusion

Surprise is one of the chief tools of a weak party that wishes to overcome its weakness in a confrontation against a superior adversary. The actor who resorts to surprise must be willing to take the political responsibility for starting the war. It cannot try to share responsibility with the adversary. Such sharing can be done only through a process of gradual escalation, and only at the expense of surprise. Because the more powerful adversary is usually confident it can win even without surprise, it typically pays more attention to the diplomatic justification of a war, tries to share some of the blame for the war or transfer all of it to the enemy by pursuing a policy that attempts to give the other a last clear chance to avoid confrontation. This state of affairs makes strong adversaries justly worried about being surprised. It also tempts weak ones justly to opt for surprise attack whenever they think the time is ripe for war.

The purpose of the present chapter was to highlight some hitherto unknown dangers associated with surprise attacks. These are dangers to which successful surprisers (rather than successful surprisees) are exposed. Thus, the moral of this story, like that of other stories in this book, is that war, no matter how carefully planned and executed, can be a trap from which there can be no escape precisely because it is well planned and well executed. The paradox of surprise is a true paradox because it allows no escape. If the surprise works it can cause a transition in the balance of forces; but precisely because it works it causes the victim of surprise to mobilize resources it could not have mobilized otherwise. The victim of surprise attack becomes stronger, paradoxically, *because* it was weakened by the successful first blow of the surpriser. From the other side of the battlefield, the surpriser is likely to be surprised by its own success to such an extent that it might fail completely to carry out its initial plans.

Can we conclude that one should abandon surprise attacks? Definitely not. The only lesson I wish to convey here is that when planning a surprise attack, one must consider what kind of effects it could have on the opponent, not only in terms of what the first blow can accomplish in terms of military goals, but also in terms of long-range societal and psychological reaction. Once one is aware that the former effects can be more than offset by the latter, the whole calculus of surprise, as well as the calculus of war initiation, may be altered, usually in the direction of prudence. Another point that is suggested by the paradox of surprise runs parallel to the lesson derived from the paradox of attrition: when planning a war, one must plan both for its initial phase and for its termination. Knowing when to stop a war is perhaps more important than knowing when and how to start it. This lesson is of particular importance when one trusts one's fate to a surprise attack. What this suggests is that surprise attacks have their limits, beyond which the returns might be more than marginally diminishing. Crossing the limit of what can be accomplished due to surprise might cause a general collapse of the whole operation.

This suggests that when basing war plans on the achievement of surprise in the first stage, initiators must be aware that surprise does not necessarily alter the balance of forces or the balance of resolve between the opponents; what it might do is shift it marginally in favor of the initiator. And this too is true only for the first phase of the war. As I have pointed out in earlier work, the effects of surprise on the probability of victory in war are marginal, and they are most pronounced when the opponents are about equal in capability (Maoz, 1984a). When the would-be initiator is slightly inferior to the opponent, surprise attack might give it the edge, but this too is only at the margin. It follows that surprise, like any other military strategy, must be optimized; its timing is crucial, as Axelrod (1979) suggests, but so is the mileage that can be extracted from it. Just as one cannot base a whole military operation on the certainty of surprise, one should not be misled by the accomplishment of surprise into believing that one can gain more than one had planned.

## Notes

1  See also Hybel (1986) for a discussion of the conditions under which actors resort to strategies of surprise.
2  See Wohlstetter (1962), Handel (1976), Shlaim (1976), Ben-Zvi (1976), Lanir (1983), George and Smoke (1974), Herbig and Herbig (1982), and Offer and Kober (1987).
3  The case that immediately comes to mind in this context is the surprise takeover of the Falkland Islands by Argentina on April 2, 1982. The islands'

population consisted of 70 British soldiers, a couple of hundred civilian residents, and a couple of thousand sheep. Despite the distance of the islands from England and despite their political and strategic insignificance, the "Iron Lady"—Prime Minister Margaret Thatcher—was able to mobilize unconditional public support for a fairly costly small war (a total of 255 soldiers killed and about 1,000 wounded). The number of British soldiers killed in the effort to reoccupy the islands was larger than the islands' human population. On this war, see the articles in Brown and Snyder (1985: 9-75).

4   This analysis is based on Ulam (1974), Zhukov (1982), Grey (1979), Bialer (1984), Sokolovsky (1975), Seaton (1976), Clark (1970), and Leites (1981).

5   Zhukov (1982: 217–218) reports that following the encirclement and capture of over 300,000 Soviet troops in the Smolensk area, he and Marshal Timoshenko, the commander of the western front, were ordered to Stalin's dacha, where Stalin relieved Timoshenko of his post. Zhukov argued before Stalin that such a move would not only demoralize the army but would also hamper military operations because frequent changes of command prevent experienced commanders from making use of their knowledge. Stalin allowed himself to be persuaded into changing his mind about Timoshenko.

6   Both Zhukov and Khrushchev detail numerous incidents of conflict between Stalin and his military commanders. Bialer (1984: 15–44) and Seaton (1976) provide good discussions of the politics of war.

7   On July 29, 1941, Zhukov suggested to Stalin the transfer of large numbers of Soviet troops from the Far East to the west, and the evacuation of the city of Kiev. Stalin was angered by the latter recommendation, calling it "nonsense." Zhukov was promptly relieved of his duty and transferred to the command of the reserve front (Zhukov, 1982: 225–227).

8   The same people, fighting against the same enemy 27 years before, displayed much less enthusiasm and will to suffer. This is indicated by the mass desertions and lack of resistance to the Germans in occupied territories during World War I.

9   See Small and Singer (1982) for casualties, and Garthoff (1953) and COW (1986) for data on military personnel.

10   This estimate is echoed by Marshal Sokolovsky (1975: 162). It apparently does not include large German and Italian forces that were held down in the Balkans (especially Yugoslavia) due to partisan activity in those areas. (On this issue, see Chapter 7.)

11   The Egyptian writers (e.g., Sadat, 1978; Shazli, 1980; Heikal, 1975) all attempt to minimize the extent of confusion and miscalculation that characterized the Egyptian decisions during October 16–19. The fact was that Kosygin spent three whole days in Cairo trying to persuade Sadat to agree to a cease-fire. It was not until October 18, when Kosygin showed Sadat aerial photographs that depicted the magnitude of the Israeli breakthrough, that Sadat realized the gravity of the situation and agreed to a cease-fire. Even then, he gave only halfhearted consent (Heikal, 1975: 235–236; Israeli, 1985: 120–130).

# 7

# The Ally's Paradox

With friends like these, who needs enemies?

Sometimes allies can be a lot of trouble. An alliance is an agreement between or among states to act in a specified manner (typically this involves some measure of coordinated action) under a given set of circumstances. Formation of alliances involves some calculation on the part of the would-be friends, because the alliance causes a trade-off between autonomy and power. A state that joins an alliance gives up some degree of autonomy in order to gain some degree of power that it cannot obtain on its own. The autonomy lost is the ability of a state to be a master of its own decisions if and when the conditions of joint action arise. For example, a typical defense pact is an agreement among states to react to an attack on one of them as if it were an attack on all of them. By joining a defense pact a state agrees to relinquish its right to neutrality if a member of the alliance is attacked. In return, it receives assurance that other alliance members will do the same if the focal state becomes the victim of an attack.

That alliances can be a burden is obvious, for the trade-off between autonomy and power renders the management of alliances a rather complicated matter. The test of the alliance is when one of its members is actually attacked. However, that is also when the temptation to defect is the greatest. Another problem is to ensure that members fulfill their obligations in times of peace. For example, sometimes the actor with the least need to preserve an alliance pays the most for maintaining it; this is the problem of the United States in financing NATO.

The ally's paradox as described here is one of war management: it deals with situations in which alliances work in the sense that an ally does what is expected of it. The story of the paradox is as follows. Two states form an alliance in which each of them is committed to come to the other's help when it is in trouble. Now, suppose that one of the allies, *a*, gets into war against *c*. The other ally, *b*, realizing the situation, gets involved in an effort to relieve *a* of its burden. Yet, once *b* gets into the conflict, *a* gracefully withdraws. Thus, what started as a conflict between *a* and *c* ends in a conflict between *b* and *c*, where poor *b* carries the entire burden and the state that got *b* into trouble does little to help.

The irony is more pronounced if one considers the fact that the war started because *a*, confident that it could rely on *b*'s help, behaved in an arrogant manner that caused the conflict with *c* to escalate. If *a* suspected that *b* might not fulfill its treaty obligations, it would probably have behaved more prudently, thereby avoiding the whole mess. Thus, the paradox is that an ally suffers because it is reliable; if it were less reliable, both allies would have benefited.

An introduction of the ally's paradox requires some discussion of the logic and processes that go into alliance formation. These issues, in turn, can be seen in the context of the role of alliances in world politics.

## Alliances in World Politics

As noted, an alliance is an agreement among states to behave in a coordinated manner under certain circumstances. This manner may differ markedly depending on the type of alliance entered into. There are alliances in which states agree to coordinate policies or to resolve differences of opinion in a peaceful way once these arise, and those in which each state pledges neutrality when the other gets involved in war. Finally, there are alliances that are designed to ensure that their members would be on the same side if war breaks out. These are the focus of the present chapter. In some of these alliances, called defense pacts, each state pledges to view an attack on one of the members as if it were an attack on oneself, and therefore each member is, presumably, guaranteed the support of other members in case of an attack. This is the most binding kind of alliance in the sense that it involves the greatest loss of autonomy (Altfeld, 1984).

Alliances—even if they are called defense pacts—can be of a defensive or offensive nature. Whether an alliance is defensive or offensive depends not so much on its label, but rather on the objectives of its members. The alliance is of a defensive nature if it is committed to the preservation of the prevailing order. Such alliances may be formed not only to guarantee a better ability to defend the status quo in an event of an attack. One of their primary functions may be to deter such an attack in the first place. By joining forces, members of an alliance attempt to convince a would-be attacker that the costs of an attack on one of them far outweigh its benefits, because the attacker will find itself in war with all the members of an alliance.

The credibility of such deterrence depends on the ability of the members of an alliance to convince an opponent that they would indeed fulfill their treaty obligations. All this immediately brings to mind the situation in Europe. There, the problem of the United States is in persuading the Soviets that Americans would actually view an attack on West Berlin as if it were an attack on downtown Manhattan, and that they would be willing to lose New York and a couple of other major cities to defend West Berlin.

Of course, some alliances are strictly offensive: they represent an effort to join forces in order to overcome a superior adversary. The alliance enables members to do what they are unable to do on their own: attack. The Balkan alliance of Bulgaria, Greece, Montenegro, and Serbia, signed in 1912, was precisely of this sort. It was designed to allow for a joint attack on Turkey. Later, after the first Balkan war ended in a victory for the allies, this alliance disintegrated and another alliance was formed. This was the alliance between Greece and Serbia designed to gain disputed territories from Bulgaria. This type of alliance is one wherein members are out to change some aspect of the status quo that they view as unsatisfactory or otherwise damaging. Between these two types of alliances we occasionally observe so-called non-aggression pacts. These are agreements wherein each member allows other members to engage in aggressive acts against other states, as long as this aggression is not directed toward other alliance members. The most infamous nonaggression pact was the Ribbentrop-Molotov Agreement between Nazi Germany and Communist Russia, signed on August 22, 1939. The idea of this pact was, in addition to a secret part in which the two signatories agreed on how to divide Poland, to allow the Germans a free hand in Western Europe and the Soviets a free hand in Eastern Europe (i.e., Finland and the Baltic states).

System theorists view alliances as one of the key ingredients of international stability under anarchy (Bull, 1977; Kaplan, 1957). The making and unmaking of alliances is a process that changes the structure of the international system, because alliance changes cause shifts in the distribution of capabilities in the system. The pattern of alliance formation is seen to follow some fundamental logic of balancing. Alliances are formed in order to prevent one state from becoming preponderant; they dissolve when the threat of preponderance disappears. Unfortunately, there is little agreement as to whether alliances contribute to the stability of the international system. Empirical examinations suggest that the number of alliances are related to the amount of war in the interstate system. Yet, this relationship is not stable over time. In the nineteenth century, it appears that the more alliances, the less war. But in the twentieth century, the opposite has happened—the more alliances, the more war (Singer and Small, 1968).[1]

However important these issues, they are not of main interest here, for our aim is to examine how alliances relate to war management. On this topic, the main finding of the quantitative literature on international war is that alliances are a key factor affecting the expansion of wars. Empirical evidence (e.g., Siverson and King, 1980, 1979) suggests that wars among aligned states are likely to be larger and more extensive than wars among nonaligned states. A key question that relates alliances to war management is that of reliability, that is, how frequently alliance commitments are honored and under what conditions.[2] But the literature offers little theoretical basis for the examination of the relationship between how alliances serve to constrain or otherwise determine the behavior of the various parties once war is already under way.

History, however, is rich with examples about how alliances affect decisions about the management of war. For example, the alliance that was formed among Great Britain, the United States, and the Soviet Union during World War II suggests many anecdotes about war management. Stalin's pressure for a second front forced the Western Allies to postpone the invasion of France and to show that they made a token effort to distract the Germans in Italy. Likewise, the race between the Allies to occupy Germany is also an interesting story about how politics never lays dormant, even in the heat of battle. The following section might suggest some ideas about a theory that relates alliances to war management and attempts to uncover the typical pattern of association rather than the residual one.

## With Friends Like This . . .

One of the uncertainties confronting states in crises is the question of how allies would react in the case of a war between themselves and their opponent.[3] If one can count on the aid of allies, one might view the chances of winning in a war as higher than if allies are seen as unreliable. Aid, in this respect, does not necessarily mean that allies are expected actually to commit troops to the battle zone. It might simply mean that one expects allies to block or otherwise deter the opponent's allies from coming to the latter's help. For example, when planning their attack on the Suez canal zone in 1956, Great Britain and France did not expect the United States actually to get involved in the war operations. They did hope, however, that the United States would deter the Soviets and prevent them from aiding the Egyptians. It turned out that this hope was premature, but this suggests some of the calculations states make about allies and how these calculations affect their assessment of the outcomes of war.

Another example is the 1911 Agadir crisis. The Germans challenged the French attempt to establish a protectorate in Morocco. However, Germany's willingness to take risks in the crisis depended as much on its assessment of French behavior as on the behavior of the allies of the disputants, Great Britain and Austria-Hungary. Once it became evident that Great Britain stood fully behind France while the Austro-Hungarians explicitly denied their support from Germany, the tough German stance softened considerably. The Germans were given only a token of their demands as a face-saving measure.[4]

Consider the following situation. A state, *a*, allied with another state, *b*, contemplates a war against state *c*. The opponent, *c*, is more powerful than either *a* or *b* but is weaker than the combined military strength of *a* and *b*. Thus, if *b* does not join the war, *a* stands to lose, and hence it prefers a war in which it can win over no war and no war over a war in which it is about to lose. This implies that *a* prefers fighting if *b* joins, but it prefers not fighting if *b* does not join.

What about the opponent? Assume that *c* is a fundamentally peaceful state that has no aggressive designs toward either *a* or *b*. In this case, *c* prefers no war over any kind of war. However, if it is destined to defend itself given an attack, it would rather defend itself against *a* alone than against both *a* and *b*. Finally, the ally, *b*, is also a fundamentally peaceful state, having no aggressive designs against *c*. It would rather not fight at all than fight. Yet, for a variety of reasons, it cannot afford to be seen as an unreliable ally. For example, *b* may have other more important allies that constantly watch its behavior. If *b* fails to meet its treaty obligations with *a*, those other allies are likely to regard *b* as unreliable and may be reluctant to join forces with it against opponents about which *b* really cares. The alliance between *b* and *a* is seen as a test case of the general credibility of *b*. It follows, then, that *b* prefers to side with *a* over letting its ally be defeated by its adversary.

The three actors in our little game consider three possible situations: no war (labeled hereafter as the NW outcome), a war in which the two allies *a* and *b* fight *c* (labeled hereafter WWA outcome, for war with the ally), and a war fought by *a* against *c* without the participation of *b* (labeled the WNA outcome, for war with no ally). The alternatives of the actors are the following: *a* and *c* can either attack (F) or not attack (NF) each other. If either of them attacks the other (or if both attack simultaneously), a war breaks out. However, the type of war—and presumably its outcome—depends upon *b*'s decision to join or not to join the war. Given the preferences of the three actors, we have the three-person game shown in Table 7.1.

Note that the NW outcome is the best collective outcome. It is the most preferred one for both *b* and *c*, and even for *a* it is not so bad (certainly better than the WNA outcome). However, this is not the actual

**Table 7.1** A three-person game of allies' choices and war initiation

| State (preferred order) | Strategy | | | | | | | | Dominant (ultimately admissible) strategy |
|---|---|---|---|---|---|---|---|---|---|
| | 1 | 2 | 3 | 4 | 5 | 6 | 7 | 8 | |
| a (WWA > NW > WNA) | F | F | F | F | NF | NF | NF | NF | F in second reduction |
| b (NW > WWA > WNA) | J | J | NJ | NJ | J | J | NJ | NJ | J in first reduction |
| c (NW > WNA > WWA) | F | NF | F | NF | F | NF | F | NF | NF in first reduction |
| Outcome | WWA | WWA | WNA | WNA | WWA | NW | WNA | NW | WWA |

*Notes:* F = attack; NF = do not attack; J = join your ally; NJ = do not join your ally. NW = no war; WWA = war between c and the ab coalition; WNA = war between a and c with b remaining neutral. The solution of the game is due to Farquharson (1969). For the solution procedure of games of this sort, see the appendix in Maoz and Felsenthal (1987).

outcome of the game. What happens is that the ally $b$ has a dominant strategy: whatever $a$ or $c$ does, the outcomes $b$ gets when it supports $a$ are at least as good and sometimes better than the outcomes it gets by withholding its support from $a$. Hence, it would support $a$ for better or worse. On the other hand, $c$ has a dominant no attack strategy: no matter what its opponent or the ally does, $c$ is better off not attacking $a$ than attacking it. Knowing that it can rely on its ally's support, and that $c$ will not attack no matter what happens, $a$ can now safely turn to an attack on $c$. It turns out, and this is the big surprise, that because it has a dominant support strategy, $b$, the poor ally, is done in, getting involved in a war that was not of its own doing. If $b$ had made clear to $a$ that it would not support it no matter what happened, it would have been able to obtain its most preferred outcome NW. The outcome of this game is not only a trap for the poor reliable ally; it is normatively inferior to the NW outcome from a collective point of view.

But this is only half the story, for what we are after is the choices of the various parties once war is under way. The little game represented by Table 7.1 was designed merely to set the stage for the major aspect of the ally's paradox. This aspect concerns a war that is already under way. This is, of course, the war that $a$ had started against $c$ and that $b$ reluctantly joined. Here the three players have two choices each. A player can continue fighting or it can quit. If one of the two allies quits, the war continues as a bilateral war between the remaining ally and the opponent $c$. If $c$ calls it quits, the remaining ally wins the war. If the war goes well for the two allies, there is really no problem. However, problems start when the war is not going well, and the allies face the prospect of a prolonged war. In addition, a prolonged war may suggest that, contrary to initial expectations, the chances of victory are smaller than the allies originally thought. Let us review the various outcomes that are formed by the combination of strategies available to the actors. Table 7.2 displays these outcomes.

The key to the solution of this game is whether $a$ prefers outcome 1 over outcome 5. If all goes well in the war, and the combined capabilities suggest that the allies can see the light at the end of the tunnel, it is reasonable to suggest that $a$ would prefer to continue fighting because the eventual victory would allow it exploitation of the spoils of war. If, however, $a$'s leaders realize that the war is being prolonged and quick and easy victory is no longer at hand, they might prefer to have $b$ finish the work while cutting their own costs. This is precisely the idea behind the ranking of outcome 5 ahead of outcome 1. If these preference orders are representative of such a situation, then the ally's paradox is revealed in full force. From $b$'s perspective, whatever the other players do, $b$ is strictly better off by continuing the war than by leaving it. Thus, $b$ is said to have a dominant fighting strategy. The same applies to $c$:

**Table 7.2** A three–person game of allies' choices and war management

| Outcome | a's strategy | b's strategy | c's strategy | Meaning of outcome | a's preferred | b's preferred | c's preferred |
|---|---|---|---|---|---|---|---|
| 1 | CF | CF | CF | Long war, heavy costs to all parties involved, uncertain outcome. | 4 | 4 | 4 |
| 2 | CF | CF | SF | Both allies remain in the war, c yields; a and b share the spoils. | 7 | 6 | 3 |
| 3 | CF | SF | CF | a is deserted by b and loses the war eventually; b is humiliated diplomatically but does not incur high tangible costs. | 1 | 3 | 7 |
| 4 | CF | SF | SF | a is deserted by b but c yields anyway; great victory for a, which gets all the spoils; grave humiliation for b, which is seen as an unreliable and ineffective ally. | 8 | 5 | 1 |
| 5[a] | SF | CF | CF | a deserts b; b gets entangled in a long war with high propects of losing. | 5 | 2 | 6 |
| 6 | SF | CF | SF | a deserts b but c yields; b wins and gets all the spoils. | 3 | 8 | 2 |
| 7 | SF | SF | CF | The allies surrender; victory for c. | 2 | 1 | 8 |
| 8 | SF | SF | SF | Compromise—the war ends in a tie. | 6 | 7 | 5 |

*Notes*: CF = continue fighting; SF = stop fighting. Outcomes are ranked from best = 8 to worst = 1.
[a] Sophisticated outcome.

once the war is on, $c$ would rather fight than surrender, whether it fights one ally or both. (Of course, $c$ would rather fight one of the allies than both, but it has no control over this outcome.)

Our first ally, $a$, however, does not have a straightforward choice. It generally prefers to stay in the war if the chances of winning are good, but it prefers to get out if it is bound to lose. Now, given that both $b$ and $c$ are determined to continue fighting, it faces a choice between outcome 1 (in which it continues fighting) and outcome 5 (in which it leaves $b$ to carry the burden of war). Once it decides that the latter outcome is preferred to the former, it gets out of the war. Consequently, $b$—the poor ally that did not want this war in the first place—is left to carry the entire burden of the war. Not only is $b$ deserted by the ally that had drawn it into the mess, but $a$'s departure increases substantially the probability of $b$'s defeat.

## Explanations of the Ally's Paradox

The ally's paradox shows that being a credible ally gets one into trouble, whereas being unreliable affords an actor superior outcomes. If that is the case, why would decision makers work hard at demonstrating reliability and credibility of alliances? Why are they making all kinds of commitments that are designed to show that they would support their allies, for better or worse? Why is their support unconditional on the ally's behavior? Finally, why would states want to make alliances with allies that are both treacherous and incompetent?[5]

### The Rational Explanation

Even if the poor ally $b$ knows that unconditional support of the minor partner $a$ would result in its demise, there is little $b$ can do about it. The rationalization of this process is simply that what is at stake is an issue larger than the relations between the two partners or the relations between the minor partner and the opponent. Reliability is part of what major actors are concerned about because it is something that establishes reputation in world politics. And reputation is not only a status symbol, it is an important asset when a state wants to deter opponents or bargain with noncommitted states. It is also an attribute of major significance if a state is interested in maintaining other alliances that it values highly. Conditional support of a minor ally is risky for two reasons. First, other minor states are likely to be deterred from aligning with a state involved in such an alliance for fear that this alliance might tie their hands. These states might look for less constraining allies, and the alternative alliance partner may turn out to be one's chief opponent. Second, conditional support of an ally can easily be interpreted by both friends and foes as a device for gracefully backing out of a commitment. Thus, such support might constrain one's ally's behavior in a favorable manner, but it might also erode one's image of reliability.

For these reasons, major allies might find it hard to convince their minor partners that support is conditional on nonaggressive behavior on the latters' part. In Table 7.1 it can be easily verified that if *b* commits itself for supporting *a* only if *a* is attacked (i.e., columns 1 and 5) but not if *a* unilaterally attacks *c* (which amounts to convincing *a* that *b* prefers column 4 over column 2), then *a* would refrain from attacking *c* and the second part of the ally's paradox is averted. The problem is that *a* must be made to believe that *b* can afford not to support it in one type of war and yet convince other allies that it would have supported *a* had the latter been attacked. If *a* behaves as if it did not believe that *b*'s commitment is conditional, *b* will find itself supporting its ally in spite of itself. The historical examples discussed in the next section will accentuate this no-win trade-off between eroding reliability and the costs of an unwanted war.

But given that the ally was drawn into a war it did not want by the scheming minor partner, is there a way it can prevent the latter's defection? One way of doing that is to convince the minor partner that a prolonged multilateral war is preferable to a war without the minor partner. This can be done by making the chances of victory sufficiently high so that *a* will want to stay in order to share the spoils. The problem, of course, is that the chances of victory depend as much on the opponent's behavior and its military effectiveness as they do on the allies' behavior and their military effectiveness. When the chances of the allies' victory are high, *b* need not convince *a* to stay in the war. However, when the chances of victory go down, *b* might find it difficult—if not impossible—to persuade *a* to stay in the war.

## The Cognitive Interpretation

In Chapter 2, I noted that actors are apt to dismiss adverse behavior of allies as incidental. This is done to preserve prior expectations about the friendly nature of their allies. Relations among allies are characterized by norms of reciprocity. Thus, an ally's paradox arises—according to the cognitive interpretation—because of the tendency to interpret adverse behavior of the minor partner as incidental and unmotivated. This leads the ally to believe that one can convert an initially bad outcome into an ultimately good one. In the first stage of the paradox, the aggressive behavior of the minor party is likely to be dismissed as somehow inconsistent with its national interest. Explanations such as the leadership yielding to domestic pressures are typically invoked. This causes one to miss the fact that getting the ally into the war was part of a general and calculated ploy. On the other hand, the expectation of reciprocity leads one to dismiss the possibility that the minor partner would back out of the war when things do not work out as expected.

In both parts of the paradox, the minor partner behaves according to a rational calculation. In the first part, it brings the major partner in so that it can start the war with the opponent. In the second part, it can afford to withdraw without losing precisely because it knows that the major partner has no choice but to continue. However, in both cases, the major partner expects the minor partner to subscribe to norms that are generalized from the realm of interpersonal relations to the realm of international politics but that have little empirical foundation in the latter realm. Of particular importance is the notion that since the major ally honored its commitment and stepped into the war to bail out the minor partner, the latter will reciprocate by fulfilling its part in the fighting.

The rational explanation of the ally's paradox ignores the fact that—underlying national interests—alliances involve personal relations between leaders. The personal dimension in alliance politics cannot be ignored because, in some cases, it might account for perceptions of commitments in interpersonal terms. A feeling of commitment, or a need to maintain an image of reliability, may develop on a personal level, and that personal sense of loyalty and commitment may intervene in the process where actions are supposed to be guided by national interests.

## The Ally's Paradox in International Politics

To show empirical parallels to the abstract examples presented above, it is necessary to point out what it is that the ally's paradox requires us to look for. First, we are looking for cases where one of the allies clearly started a war or a severe conflict with a high escalatory potential and the other ally joined in when the process was well under way. Preferably, historical evidence should indicate that the latter ally stepped in because it was "invited" by the former who was not doing well in the conflict. Second, we are looking for evidence that, had the first ally not started the war or the conflict with the opponent, the major ally would not have started such a conflict. Although evidence of this sort is very difficult to establish in historical research, its existence would lend credence to the notion of logical exclusiveness by suggesting that the ally's paradox was—at least in part—a consequence of the belief that the major ally is drawn into war against its better judgment. Third, there should be clear evidence that the first ally stopped fighting while the second ally was left with the whole burden of continuing the war. To make this paradox really provocative, it might be of interest to show that the major ally suffered a severe defeat. At a very minimum, it must be established that the costs incurred by the major ally were disproportionately larger than the costs incurred by the minor one.

The clearest and most recurring example of the ally's paradox in international politics concerns what one might typically characterize as internationalized civil wars (Small and Singer, 1982). These are cases where a faction engaged in a civil war within a state invites a foreign state to join in, with the latter tending to carry the entire burden of the war. The United States in Vietnam, the Soviet Union in Afghanistan, and the Syrians and Israelis in Lebanon are only three recent examples of such episodes. However, these cases are weak examples, for the political group had no choice but to continue fighting alongside the ally in the civil war. The seemingly paradoxical burden-sharing pattern is due to the fact that the foreign state is typically more potent and militarily better equipped than its minor ally. What follows, therefore, is an attempt to describe what I would characterize as genuine cases of the ally's paradox: The Italo-German wars in Greece and North Africa during World War II, and the inter-Arab origins of the 1967 war.

### The Spaghetti Wars:
### Greece, North Africa, and Italy 1940–1943.[6]

Mussolini had grand designs for Italy all along. However, when World War II broke out he remained de facto neutral despite his alliance with Germany. The Germans were not all that displeased with the Italian position, for they had fears that Italian excessive adventurism was in spirit only. The Italians were not well equipped to fight a serious war, and having the Italian army fight alongside the German forces was not something to which the German general staff looked forward. More important, the political implications of an Italian involvement in the war were not all that positive. Germany knew that Italy had designs for North Africa and Greece, and during the first half of 1940, Hitler was concerned more with Norway and France (and by implication with Holland and Belgium) than with the Balkans. In fact, Germany made it clear to the Italians that it strongly preferred that the latter not make waves in North Africa, the Balkans, or anywhere else.

The first half of 1940 was the most victorious part of the war for Germany. On April 9, Germany launched its attack on Norway and Denmark. On May 10, the attack on France started, with German troops pouring into Holland and Belgium. Within two weeks it became evident that France was on the verge of collapse. Mussolini could hardly control himself. As Kirkpatrick (1964: 461) notes, "he was now itching for action." He firmly rejected last-minute appeals by France, Great Britain, and the United States to remain neutral, but refrained from actual declaration of war and commitment of Italian troops until June 10, after the French had pleaded for a cease-fire. The little skirmish between Italian and French troops was a major disaster for the former. They had all but failed to move into French territory.

The swiftness of the German victory in France and the failure of the Italian troops prevented Mussolini from getting anything significant in the west, but this served only to increase his appetite. His ambitions in the east and the south were evident all along. But they ran contrary to the German plans, which—at that point in time—were directed toward Great Britain. Indeed, Germany put strong pressure on its ally to restrain itself. On August 7, 1940, the Italian foreign minister, Ciano, wrote in his diary summarizing a discussion he had with Ribbentrop, the German foreign minister, earlier that day that the German position amounted to "a complete order [to Italy] to halt all along the line [of the Balkans]" (Shirer, 1960: 815; Kirkpatrick, 1964: 473).

But Mussolini could not restrain himself for long. On October 28, 1940, emulating a German tactic of informing its allies of its military moves only after they had already begun, Mussolini informed Hitler triumphantly: "Victorious Italian troops crossed the Greco-Albanian frontier at dawn today" (Kirkpatrick, 1964: 478). It soon became clear that the adjective that opened the statement was a bit premature. The Italian troops in the east encountered fierce resistance from the vastly outnumbered Greek forces. Before long, it became clear that the Italian troops were stuck in grave trouble in the mountains. By mid-November, a hasty retreat of the Italian troops into Albania was begun. Simultaneously, the Italian forces in North Africa were driven back by a small British force.[7] To add salt to the German wounds, the British dispatched a force of about 50,000 soldiers to Greece and established air bases there and in Crete.

This put the Germans in a precarious position. The bungled Italian campaign was more than a major embarrassment. It allowed the British to add strategic positions in the Mediterranean and Aegean seas, which presented a potential threat to the German plans for invading Russia. The Italian campaign in North Africa may have been in line with German wishes in that it was supposed to threaten British possessions in North Africa, chiefly Egypt. But the attack on Greece was totally unnecessary from a German point of view, and its failure created strategic problems. The German aid to Italy was not given due to the friendship between the two dictators; it was done out of strategic considerations. The forces sent by Germany to North Africa and the occupation of Yugoslavia, Greece, and Crete by Germany clearly amounted to bailing the Italians out.

For Germany, however, the distractions caused by these campaigns turned out to have disastrous consequences. First, Rommel's African campaign, which had been very successful initially, turned out to be a disaster. The German–Italo attack at El-Alamein that started on August 31, 1942 turned into a devastating defeat. By November 5, Rommel's forces withdrew some 700 miles westward, losing 59,000 soldiers (out of which 34,000 were German). The North African Campaign was, for all practical purposes, over. The Yugoslav–Greek campaign had two adverse consequences. First, it delayed the attack on the Soviet Union by over a month.[8] This was a crucial delay because it meant that a month of clear weather was lost. Second, Yugoslavia proved a tough nut even after it had been occupied. The fierce resistance of the Yugoslav partisans forced Germany to place a significant number of troops in that country.[9]

When the tide of battle turned against the Italians, and especially when they began suffering directly from the British and American air attacks, the Italians started having second thoughts. As long as Mussolini tagged along on the successful German campaigns in Russia and North Africa, no one in the Italian political system dared resist him. When one disaster after another struck, the Italian politicians and the king started contemplating a separate peace with the Allies. Indeed, on July 25, 1943, Mussolini was forced to resign and was put under arrest. On September 3, a secret armistice was signed between the Badoglio government and the Allies. Simultaneously, Allied forces landed in southern Italy. The Italians expressed their will to get out of the war. The German situation was critical. The German forces in the vicinity of Rome were outnumbered by the Italian divisions, and so were the German forces in Yugoslavia. Facing the risk of an Allied landing in the Rome area, Italy could have been lost to the Germans and the Allies would have accomplished a major bridgehead to Germany in Southern Europe (Shirer, 1960: 1000–1002).

Germany, of course, could not afford for this to take place. Fortunately for the Germans, Italian military incompetence struck again. The five Italian divisions near Rome surrendered to the German forces without firing a single shot. Moreover, the Allied landing took place south of Naples, leaving most of Italy under German control. The Italian betrayal was characterized by Hitler as "a gigantic example of swinishness." But its consequences were more far-reaching than simply raising questions of morality and loyalty with a leader such as Hitler: it forced Germany to carry the entire burden of fighting the Allies in Italy.

What this case suggests is not that Germany's fate would have been different had it been better able to control its Italian ally. Rather, the point is that Italy's adventures were an added burden for an already overextended Germany. In fact, it is clear that Germany could have easily done without the Italian involvement in the war. This point is not based on "what if" speculation—it was the view of key figures in the German general staff. Those voices that urged the German politicians to restrain the overzealous Mussolini in the fall of 1940 had not done so out of bad sentiment; they did not have much faith in the prowess of the Italian army, nor did they view the proposed Balkan campaign as crucial to the German war aims. The Germans knew all along that the Italian army was badly equipped, and it had revealed its general incompetence over and over in Ethiopia, in Spain, and in the brief intervention in France. Hitler was also not surprised by the changing of the political winds in Italy in 1943. In fact, on July 19, 1943, six days before the overthrow of Mussolini, the two dictators met in Venice. The purpose of the meeting was to dissuade the Italians from defecting.[10]

Why did the Germans not invest more effort in restraining the Italians? Why did they, on the other hand, invest so much effort in bailing the Italians out once the latter found themselves in deep trouble? What was the role of strategic considerations as opposed to nonrational factors?

The chief problem from a rational perspective is explaining why Hitler failed to exert more pressure on Mussolini before the invasion of Greece. There were two basic reasons for that. The first was that Hitler had hoped to draft both Mussolini and Franco into the main effort of fighting the British. Franco's role was to be crucial: the capture of the Gibraltar Straits, which was designed to close the Mediterranean to the British fleet. This would have enabled a major German-Italo drive in North Africa and the Middle East, the final aim of which was to encircle Russia from the south. This was the main theme of a memo sent by Admiral Raeder to Hitler in September 1940 (Shirer, 1960: 813). Accordingly, Hitler met Franco on October 23. This was a frustrating meeting from Hitler's point of view because Franco requested an impractically high price for his entry into the war. He was unwilling to lift a finger for less than all of French Africa and some territories in French Catalonia. Hitler hoped that Mussolini would attempt to persuade Franco, thus, he could not have risked a rift with the Italian dictator at that point.[11] Another reason for Hitler's reluctance to restrain Italy was that the newly reaffirmed Axis alliance (with Italy and Japan, signed September 27, 1940) was important from the point of view of the planned attack on Russia. Hitler needed the Japanese to distract the Russians with troop concentrations in Korea. Pressure on Italy would have had a negative effect on the relations with Japan.

Most important, however, Hitler must have overestimated the ability of Italy to overcome Greek resistance. Although the German military command was hardly impressed by the Italian military might, the

Italian army was ten times the size of the Greek army and had behind it extensive combat experience from Ethiopia and Spain. The primary reason for wishing the Italians to stay out of Greece was not the fear that the latter would be defeated. Rather, it was the fear that the invasion would cause political complications in the Balkans that would interfere with the plan to invade Russia.

Once the Italians got into trouble in Greece and North Africa, Germany had little choice but to come to their aid; Italy's problems could not be separated from those of Germany because they involved the British. As we have seen, the British advance in North Africa and the air bases in Crete and Greece directly threatened German oil supply from Rumania. The British had acquired a foothold in the Balkans and their movement westward in North Africa threatened to put an end to the planned occupation of Gibraltar. Instead of closing the Mediterranean to the British fleet, Germany faced the prospect of complete control by the British navy and air force on the southern flank of the planned attack on Russia. Precisely as the abstract analysis of the ally's paradox suggests, the major partner could not restrain the minor one, nor could it refrain from aiding the minor partner once it got into trouble.

From the point of view of the cognitive explanation, these questions have a simple yet persuasive answer, especially in light of the personalities involved. The key to understanding what happened was the concept of wishful thinking. Initially, the Italian forces started advancing in the North African desert eastward, meeting little British resistance. Since it was in the interest of Hitler to see the British driven into Egypt, he did not put much pressure on Mussolini, hoping that the Italians might indeed push the British forces back. The same applied to the Italian invasion of Greece. Hitler wanted to believe that the Italians could pull off the invasion because that would have put increased pressure on the British in the Mediterranean. Once the Italian offensives were halted, Hitler started thinking that he could convert a bad and potentially dangerous situation into a profitable venture. For one thing, through 1941 and 1942, the advance of Rommel in Africa put the British on the spot, forcing them to retreat and to focus their efforts on their African battle. Second, the invasion of Greece provided Hitler an opportunity to enter Yugoslavia, clearing the way for the invasion of Russia. The month delay in the invasion seemed at this point to have been worth the effort. The fact that the British were driven out of Greece was also of major military significance and not a minor boost to the German morale.

Finally, military considerations were only part of the factors that affected Hitler's behavior toward Mussolini. The personal ties between the two leaders were long and strong. Hitler could not forget Mussolini's supportive position during the 1938 *anschluss* of Austria. Nor could he forget his partial mediation during the Munich crisis. Moreover, the alliance between Germany and Italy had a major ideological significance for the German dictator. All these things made Hitler reluctant to exert strong pressure on Italy or to reprimand Mussolini for his behavior. They were also important factors in affecting Hitler's support of his ally when the latter got his country into a seemingly disastrous situation. The dramatic release of Mussolini in 1943 from his house arrest also provides credence to this interpretation.

## Is There a War Going On?
## The Making of the Six Day War[12]

Nasser's initial involvement in the crisis started on November 4, 1966, with the signing of the Egyptian-Syrian defense pact. This pact was signed in light of repeated clashes between Israel and Syria along their common border. The Syrian elite were caught between two primary enemies: the external enemy and the internal foes of the Ba'ath regime. The year of 1966 was filled with both military clashes in the southwest border and violent riots and demonstrations by religious and other opposition groups against the regime (Bar-Simantov, 1983). The Syrian leadership was in a no-win situation: it could not afford to stop its support of the PLO and its harassment of Israeli settlements due to the domestic situation. On the other hand, it became increasingly threatened by the escalation of the Israeli artillery and aerial warfare along the border, which—as of September 1966—was supplemented by more or less explicit threats of a large-scale Israeli action aimed directly at the Syrian regime.

Amid this background, Nureddin Atassi, the Syrian leader, called on Nasser for a diplomatic gesture designed to deter Israel. Nasser was far from enthusiastic about this defense pact. His past experience with the Syrians had been less than pleasant.[13] Indeed, he was extremely reserved about the provisions of this treaty. Hassnin Heikal, his confidant and editor of the major Egyptian newspaper *Al-Ahram*, wrote shortly after the signature of the treaty that the Syrian leaders should not assume that Egyptian troops would intervene against any Israeli attack on Syria (Nutting, 1972: 392). This was a clear signal to the Syrians that the defense pact should not be construed to allow Syria reckless behavior vis-à-vis Israel. However, the problems started not from the Syrian capital, but rather from Amman. On November 13, the Israelis raided the Jordanian village of Sammua. This was immediately followed by massive demonstrations in the major West Bank cities against the king. The response of the Hashemite regime was to point out Egypt's lack of response to the Israeli aggression. For the first time, the expression "Nasser hides behind the UNEF skirt" was raised by the

Jordanian press. This expression was to be repeated over and over in the following months.

The period between November 1966 and March 1967 was marked by repeated artillery clashes along the Israeli-Syrian border. The Israeli raid of April 7, 1967, was a major blow to the Syrian regime. Six of its top-of-the-line jet planes were shot down in a well-planned Israeli aerial ambush. One of these dogfights was seen over the skies of Damascus. By that time, both the Syrians and the Soviets were sufficiently alarmed by the escalation of the warfare to start spreading rumors of major Israeli troop concentration along the Syrian borders. Now the "UNEF skirt" expression became a favorite all over the Arab world. Nasser felt he had little choice but to move his troops into the Sinai in an attempt to deter the Israelis. The rest of the story was covered earlier in Chapter 4.

What was not told, however, was the story of the war itself. Here is where the ally's paradox comes in. On June 30, 1967, Egypt and Jordan signed a defense treaty putting Jordanian forces under Egyptian command. Two Egyptian paratroop battalions were sent to Jordan. What prompted the generally prudent Hussein to enter into this bind is not entirely clear. The point is that, by June 1, the Syrians dragged not one ally into the confrontation, but two. When the war broke out on June 5, all three allies (plus Iraq, whose forces were also stationed in Jordan) became a target of a massive Israeli air raid that virtually destroyed their air forces. The first and major Israeli concern was with the Egyptian forces in the Sinai. There is no evidence that Israel had immediate operational plans to invade the West Bank. However, Hussein, apparently fooled by the Cairo Radio announcements of major Egyptian victories, ordered a general shelling of West Jerusalem and the various settlements along the Israeli-Jordanian border. He also sent a token Jordanian force to occupy the U.N. Alenbi camp on the border between East and West Jerusalem. The Syrians also joined with a shelling campaign and a token raid on the Israeli Kibbutz Dan, which was easily repulsed.

By the end of the first day of war it became evident that Israeli forces were in control of the situation along both the Syrian and Jordanian fronts, that the Israeli air force was free to operate anywhere it wanted, as there was nothing to challenge it. Most important, the Israeli attack on Egypt was devastating. The city of Gaza was about to be encircled. Israeli armored forces advanced deep into central Sinai. And the Egyptian army showed signs of collapse and disintegration. On the second day of the war, a major Israeli offensive started in the West Bank of the Jordan river. One armored column started an advance from the west, another column started a major advance from the north toward the cities of Jenin and Nablus, and a third force, composed primarily of paratroopers and infantry, started an attack on the eastern sector of Jerusalem. Toward the end of the second day of the war, it was clear that both Egypt and Jordan were about to be handed a massive military blow.

Where were the Syrians? Nobody is really sure. What was clear at this point was that the Syrians were not doing any fighting. In fact, the shelling of Israeli settlements turned into a trickle, and toward the third day of war it stopped completely. Not a single Syrian unit had moved an inch since the end of the attack on Dan.[14] As Stephens (1971: 499) points out: "Apart from these small-scale forays, the Syrian army, with a force of nine brigades, two of them armoured, in the frontier area, sat tight in its Maginot Line-type defences on the Golan Heights." Yaniv (1985: 168) describes the Syrian dilemma:

> Having dragged Egypt into the war, should Syria come to Egypt's rescue? Had Egypt started the war, or at least succeeded in checking Israel's initial strike, Syria would have been likely to enter the war in order to be able to claim her fair share in the political spoils. But the Syrians were informed by the Soviets on the first day of the war of the full scope of Egypt's disastrous defeat. Hence, while joining the conflict made no sense, Syria could not afford the risk of being blamed by Egypt, Jordan, and the others of causing the war but shrinking from actively participating in it. The Syrian decision to put in merely a token military effort and, at the same time, make vastly exaggerated claims of great victories, must be seen in this light.

On June 9, Egypt, Jordan, and Syria filed for a cease-fire. The U.N. Security Council, which had debated a cease-fire from June 6 on, finally voted a resolution putting a cease-fire in place, leaving Israel in control of the entire Sinai peninsula and the West Bank of the Jordan river. Syria's losses in the four days of war were several dozen casualties, many planes, and not a single inch of territory. June 9 was marked by bitter debates in the Israeli cabinet regarding the Syrian border. Israeli Prime Minister Eshkol, and his newly appointed defense minister, Dayan, were under a lot of pressure from several cabinet ministers (headed by the education minister, Yigal Allon), the commander of the northern front, General David Elazar, and an ad hoc lobby composed of the residents of the settlements and kibbuzim along the Israeli border with Syria to occupy the Golan Heights. After a long and inconclusive debate in the cabinet, Dayan ordered in the early hours of June 10 an offensive on the Golan Heights in clear violation of the U.N.-imposed cease-fire.

Within two days, the Syrian "Maginot line-type" defenses in the Golan Heights collapsed and the Syrian army started a hasty retreat that left the Israeli forces in control of a strip of land some 25 miles wide in the Golan Heights, including Kuneitra, the major city in this area. The irony is that, had the Israeli cabinet decided against the occupation of the Golan

Heights, Syria—which dragged Egypt and Jordan into the war—would have emerged completely unharmed, while its two allies suffered the worst defeat in their history. Even so, compared to the 10,000 Egyptian soldiers and the 6,100 Jordanian soldiers killed in the war, Syria's 2,500 battle deaths were both relatively and absolutely minor.[15]

We need not elaborate on Nasser's dilemma in coming to Syria's aid, for this was explored at great length in Chapter 4. What we must discuss here is why it was rational for Syria to limit its involvement in the war to "sitting tight" along its defense lines. Yaniv's (1985: 168-170) discussion and Maoz and Yaniv's (1989) game theoretic analysis suggest precisely what the ally's paradox predicts: once the ally realizes that the tide of battle has turned against the ally and its partner, whatever happened before is a sunk cost, history. All that matters at that point is how to cut present costs, and the way to do this is to refrain from making things worse by joining a war that cannot be won.

This is precisely the kind of calculus the Syrian leadership was engaged in during the first day of the war. As long as there was some uncertainty about the outcome of the war, Syria attempted to put some military pressure on Israel through shelling and a minor armored attack. The size of the attacks was designed to make it clear to the Israelis that the Syrians did not intend to escalate as long as the fog of battle lay low on the Sinai desert. Syria was playing it safe. Once the fog cleared, there was no point in aggravating the Syrian losses by doing something crazy. The Syrian leadership knew that the Israelis were waiting for an appropriate pretext to hand Syria a major military blow. Provoking them further at this point in time would have amounted to committing suicide.

In fact, this analysis suggests that the Syrian leadership preferred facing tremendous criticism from Egypt, Jordan, Iraq, and the rest of the lot for not lifting a finger to help them. It was, ironically, the Israeli attack on the Golan Heights that saved Syria from a major political embarrassment. By losing territory, Syria was able to salvage some respect.

The Middle East offers another example of the ally's paradox. In March 1981, the Phalange militias in Lebanon engaged the Syrian forces in Zahle. This led to a crisis culminating in the Israelis shooting down two Syrian helicopters and Syria placing anti-aircraft missiles in Lebanon. This was one of the main causes of the Israeli decision to confront the Syrians a year later. The Israeli involvement in Lebanon was done in close coordination with the Phalanges. However, the latter not only failed to fulfill their part of the deal during the war itself, they also converted into Syrian puppets as soon as their leaders (first Bashir Gemayel and later his brother Amin) were elected to the presidency.[16]

## Conclusion

The ally's paradox raises a fundamental question about the value of loyalty in international politics. The supreme test of international allies is the ability and willingness to help each other in times of war. It is tough enough to get a public to agree that personal sacrifices of a magnitude that wars require are justified when national security is at stake. However, the decision makers of an ally must convince their public and their soldiers that helping an ally in trouble is a goal worth risking one's life for. Given what the ally's paradox suggests, one might question how much such sacrifices are indeed called for. Clearly, the ally's paradox raises questions about the value of unconditional commitments. Before a state makes such commitments, it is worthwhile to examine their long-range implications if it wishes to avoid the dishes that some allies may cook up.

What we are concerned here with is not with cases where alliances represent a true and equal partnership between states, where everybody contributes—if not equally, at least proportionally—to the collective good that the alliance provides. History suggests numerous examples of such arrangements. Yet, history also supplies abundant examples of allies—especially minor ones—slapping their major partners in the face while the latter do nothing to sanction such behavior. Olson and Zeckhauser's (1966) analysis of the collective-good aspects of alliances and the finding that large members tend to pay a disproportionately high cost for the maintenance of the alliance is only one aspect of it. Another aspect of this phenomenon is that lesser allies behave in a way that directly damages the interests of their major ally without the latter doing anything about it. The version of the ally's paradox demonstrated above represents a wartime manifestation of this problem.

Other kinds of problems with allies are those that arise after an alliance wins a war. Problems of division of spoils cause major rifts and damage postwar relations. The two Balkan wars that will be discussed in Chapter 8 are one example, and the two world wars represent another example. So, even when allies do not stab each other in the back during war, and even if the purpose of an alliance was served in the sense that all allies fulfilled their commitments and win the war, their troubles do not end when they lay down their arms.

Ultimately, however, some treacherous allies receive their punishment. Italy's punishment came in the form of German occupation. Syria's punishment came some fifteen years later, when no Arab state lifted a finger to help it during the Lebanon war.

How does an ally escape this paradox? I think that the first trick is to investigate very closely the motives of states that are candidates for alliances. A state must analyze not only why it needs an ally; it

214 *Paradoxes of War*

is equally important to ask what the ally needs. Because the motives of partners entering an alliance might be different, ignoring motives might sometimes render friends worse than enemies. If the cognitive explanation is correct, then the second lesson of the paradox is not to let feelings of personal commitments and promises be converted automatically into perceptions of national commitments. As much as personal commitments are important, they should not overshadow national interests. Another lesson stemming from the cognitive explanation is that entry into alliances should be based on considerations of a combination of capabilities and preferences. Because alliances invariably involve some degree of loss of national autonomy, a close inspection of what this loss entails must precede decisions to ally.

A key lesson of the rational explanation is that states must shun irrevocable commitments in alliance politics. Defense pacts should be defensive. Just as verification and sanctions are important in cases of violations in treaties between former enemies, states must design sanctions and securities against exploitation in the cases of cooperative alliances. The lesson is, if you do not take your enemies for granted, do not take your friends for granted.

## Notes

1  For reviews of the literature on these issues, see Zinnes (1980a) and Bueno de Mesquita (1980). Job (1979) and Ward (1982) provide relatively recent reviews on the literature on international alliances.

2  See Ward (1982: 27–53) for a review of the literature on this topic.

3  G. H. Snyder's (1984) work on the security dilemma in alliance politics is probably the closest account of allies paradoxes to that provided below.

4  See Snyder and Diesing (1977) and Maoz (1989: ch. 8) for different game-theoretic analyses of this crisis.

5  The last question seems somewhat outside the scope of the theoretical analysis of the ally's paradox. It is, however, of major importance in the analysis of the historical instances of the paradox.

6  This analysis is based on Deakin (1962), Shirer (1960), Bullock (1952), Kirkpatrick (1964), and Churchill (1948).

7  The British force that drove the Italians back into Libya was a third the size of the Italian force. During the British counteroffensive, the entire Italian army was virtually eliminated, with some 130,000 Italian prisoners and over 500 tanks captured (Shirer, 1960: 818).

8  The originally planned starting date of "Operation Barbarossa" was set for May 15, 1941. The actual starting date was June 21.

9  In a meeting between Ribbentrop and Mussolini on February 26, 1943, it was revealed that Italy had 25 divisions (about 100,000 troops) and the Germans had 6 divisions (about 24,000 troops). These were fighting against a combined partisan force that consisted of 15,000–20,000 Yugoslav rebels (Deakin, 1962: 195–196).

10  What is ironic about this episode is that the turning of Italy against Germany was not without precedent. In 1915, Italy abandoned its pledge of neutrality in exchange for promises of territorial concessions (among them were South Tyrol and Trieste) and declared war on the Central Powers.

11  The Franco case is also a good example of an ally's treason. Franco had received massive help from both Germany and Italy during the 1936–39 civil war with no strings attached, but he was unwilling to reciprocate in 1940. To Franco's "credit" it might be mentioned that he helped mobilize over 3,000 Spanish volunteers in the "Blue Brigade" that participated in the invasion of Russia.

12  The sources for this section are Bar-Simantov (1983), Nutting (1972), Sadat (1978), Stephens (1971), Yaniv (1985, 1986), and Maoz and Yaniv (1989).

13  The union between Egypt and Syria between 1958 and 1962 was a complete disaster, and Nasser was extremely upset with the Syrian depiction of his handling of the union in a dominating fashion. The years 1963–1966 were also not exactly a high point in inter-Arab relations; they were characterized by both diplomatic rivalries and military competition in Yemen. See Seale (1965) and Van Dam (1979) on the relations between Syrian power struggles and inter-Arab rivalries and Kerr (1967) on inter-Arab relations.

14  Incidentally, the Syrian losses in that attack were about ten soldiers and two tanks.

15  See Small and Singer (1982: 93) for data on battle deaths for the Six Day War.

16  Yaniv (1987, especially 85–90, 216–245) provides an excellent account of the whole process. He argues that the Phalange attack on the Syrian outpost was deliberately designed to draw the Israelis into the war (p. 86). He also claims that Bashir Gemayel needed the Israelis to put him on the throne in Lebanon, but had no intention of cooperating with them (pp. 149–153).

# PART III
## Paradoxical Consequences of War

# 8

# *The Paradox of Power and War Outcomes*[1]

He who accumulates possessions, accumulates solicitude.
(old Hebrew proverb)

Political leaders operate, plan, and implement policies the underlying logic of which is "more is better." So, they accumulate more
arms, more sophisticated weapons, and larger armies. But sometimes,
when the real test comes, it turns out that not only is more not
better, but it might actually be worse. The paradox of power and
war outcomes is, I think, more severe—and certainly much more
mind-boggling—than the observation that states with greater capabilities lose wars against militarily inferior adversaries. It is that such
states lose wars *because* they possess superior capabilities.

My purpose in this chapter is to show that excessive control over
resources may sometimes cause loss of control over outcomes. It is
not unreasonable to expect such a result either in theory or in practice.
Moreover, knowing that the paradox of power and war outcomes is
a distinct possibility is not a sufficient condition for resolving it. The
rational and cognitive models are invoked to shed light on this paradox
and on two empirical paradoxes of power in international politics. The
implications of these issues for the study of international conflicts are
also discussed.

## Capabilities, Power, and Paradoxes of Power

The centrality of power in the study of politics is second only
to the number of definitions assigned to this concept. In general,
three conceptualizations of power seem to be common to all the
various definitions and empirical measures: (1) power as control over
resources, (2) power as control over actors, and (3) power as control

over outcomes.[2] Each of these conceptualizations of the term has much going for it. Control over resources affords an actor a wide range of feasible alternatives in any given situation, and therefore considerable freedom of action. Obviously, not all resources afford the same level of freedom of action in a given situation. Yet, an actor who has more relevant resources in a given situation can do more than an actor who is stuck in the same situation but has fewer resources. In interactive settings with more than one acting organism, and in which no single actor can single-handedly determine the consequences of its behavior, control over actors is a crucial element of power. The ability of one actor to induce others to behave as this actor wants seems a straightforward way of determining the actor's power. Finally, the ability of actors to secure desired outcomes or to prevent the occurrence of undesired ones is obviously the most sensible and widely accepted conceptualization of the term. Unfortunately, it also happens to be the most difficult one in terms of its empirical referents. Measuring power in terms of the potential to control outcomes is a risky business because it is susceptible to tautologies, that is, to inferences of power based on actual observation of outcomes. In other words, since there are no straightforward ways of determining a priori the potential to control outcomes in an interdependent setting, it is very difficult to tell which actor had more control over outcomes in a given situation unless one knows what outcomes obtained. This danger also applies to the conceptualization of power in terms of control over actors, albeit to a lesser extent.

Perhaps this difficulty of transforming the most sensible conceptualizations of power into empirically observable indicators gave birth to the widespread intuition that the three approaches to power are logically and empirically associated. It is generally believed that this relationship—if not perfectly linear—is of at least a monotonically increasing functional form: the more resources an actor controls, the more likely it is to control the behavior of other actors, and—consequently—the more likely it is to determine the nature of outcomes in its environment. This intuition is shared by both scholars and practitioners of international politics. Most of the attempts to measure national power by students of quantitative international politics have focused almost exclusively on various combinations of national capabilities.[3] The logic of nuclear and conventional arms races, as well as the recurrent subscription *realpolitik* by foreign policy elites provides a clear substantiation of the influence of this intuition on political leaders.

Let us now try to understand what the paradox of power is all about. First, it is instructive to examine what a paradox of power is not. A paradox of power is not merely a situation where an actor with considerable control over resources has little control over outcomes. For one thing, there are some outcomes that no amount of resources can change. Both the richest person and the poorest person on earth are going to wind up dead. Second, the possession of certain resources makes one more susceptible to certain undesirable outcomes than the lack thereof. Both a rich person and a poor one prefer living over dying, but the former is more likely to die in a plane crash than the latter because the former can afford to fly and the latter cannot. Third, the ability to control outcomes may require things other than the control over resources. For example, actors who possess relevant resources may fail to obtain favorable outcomes because they do not wish to spend these resources for a whole set of reasons. On a more general level, a discrepancy between control over resources and control over outcomes is, in itself, not sufficient for establishing the existence of a paradox of power. To prove a paradox of power it is necessary to demonstrate that an increased control over resources (or over actors) *produces* a reduced control over outcomes.

Basically, a paradox of power is one wherein a change in an actor's control over resources or over the behavior of other actors causes an inverse change in the actor's control over outcomes. This can mean two things: (1) an increase in the actor's ability to control resources or actors causes a decrease in the actor's ability to control outcomes, or (2) a decrease in control over resources or actors causes an increase in control over outcomes. A paradox of power can also include situations where increased control over outcomes causes a decreased control over resources, but this aspect of power paradoxes will not be discussed here.

## Extra Power Can Hurt

Sometimes, people who are already doing well in whatever they are doing want to go an extra step just to make sure that they get what they want. Yet, it is this extra step that sets in motion processes that eventually lead to their demise. Such cases do not apply to actors who are initially weak and are in a process of increasing their capabilities. Obviously, such actors may harm themselves as they are drawn into conflict by stronger actors who feel threatened (Levy, 1987). The case where focal actors are already more powerful than others in the sense that they have the potential of controlling outcomes is interesting because, if a paradox of power can be shown in such cases, it is reasonable to expect similar paradoxes to arise for more typical ones. The paradox of power can be best illustrated in the well-structured setting of voting in committees, wherein members know one another's preferences and are capable of acting sophisticatedly. I will use two examples to illustrate this paradox. One concerns the accumulation of supporters for a certain candidate. The other concerns the acquisition of prerogatives designed to ensure a more favorable outcome. Let me start by specifying the assumptions that underlie these analyses.[4]

First, I assume that all actors involved are rational expected utility maximizers, who are out to get the best they can under the circumstances. Second, I assume that the setting is characterized by full information. Actors know one another's preferences (though not their cardinal utilities). Third, I assume that all actors possessing identical preferences behave (vote) the same way. I will call this the "bloc voting" assumption. Fourth, I assume that cooperation among actors with different preference orders is disallowed. In other words, actors with different policy preferences cannot form coalitions or reach binding agreements. This does not rule out tacit cooperation; only formal collusion among distinct blocs of actors is considered foul play. (I will show that, at least in one of the cases, this assumption can be dropped without loss.) Fifth, I assume that ties between or among candidates with the same number of votes are broken by a random mechanism that assigns to each of the tied candidates the same probability of eventually being elected. Finally, the assumption that actors are rational implies that they would use only admissible strategies, that is, strategies that are not initially dominated.

The problem under consideration is one in which a committee of $m$ members must elect one of three candidates—$a$, $b$, or $c$—to fill a certain position. Each committee member has one vote and the candidate with the most votes is elected. These assumptions form an $n$-person noncooperative game (with $n \geq 2$ being the number of blocs of voters with different preference orderings of the three candidates). Suppose that in our case there are four blocs of voters, with sizes and preferences as given in the two left-hand columns of Table 8.1.

It is easy to see that in this voting body only the four voters with the *cba* preference have a dominant strategy. The outcomes they obtain by voting for their top choice are at least as good and sometimes better than those they obtain by voting for their second-best candidate, regardless of what other voters do. Given the dominant strategy of the *cba* bloc, the 14 *acb* voters and the 16 *cab* voters can now safely assume that the *cba* voters would not cast their votes for candidate $b$. Thus, they can eliminate the outcomes associated with *cba*'s strategy $b$ (the even-numbered columns in Table 8.1). Now, these two blocs can determine unique admissible strategies $a$ and $c$, respectively. The remaining *bac* voters, knowing how all other blocs intend to vote, are faced with a choice between two outcomes (columns 1 and 5). Since a vote for their top-ranked candidate would result in the selection of their worst candidate, they prefer voting for their second-ranked candidate $a$,

**Table 8.1** Sophisticated voting with three candidates and four voting blocs

| Number of voters | Preference order | 1 | 2 | 3 | 4 | 5 | 6 | 7 | 8 | 9 | 10 | 11 | 12 | 13 | 14 | 15 | 16 | Sophisticated strategy |
|---|---|---|---|---|---|---|---|---|---|---|---|---|---|---|---|---|---|---|
| | | | | | | | | | | *Admissible voting strategies* | | | | | | | | |
| 14 | *acb* | a | a | a | a | a | a | a | a | c | c | c | c | c | c | c | c | *a* second reduction |
| 18 | *bac* | b | b | b | b | a | a | a | a | b | b | b | b | a | a | a | a | *a* third reduction |
| 16 | *cab* | c | c | a | a | c | c | a | a | c | c | a | a | c | c | a | a | *c* second reduction |
| 4 | *cba* | c | b | c | b | c | b | c | b | c | b | c | b | c | b | c | b | *c* first reduction |
| Outcomes | | c | b | a | a | a | a | a | a | c | c | c/b | b | c | c | a | a | Winner is *a* |

| Pairwise contests | | | Social preference order |
|---|---|---|---|
| *a–b* | *a–c* | *b–c* | *a* > *c* > *b* |
| 30–22 | 32–20 | 18–34 | |

*Source*: Felsenthal and Maoz (1988). The solution of sophisticated voting games is due to Farquharson (1969); Felsenthal and Maoz (1988) and Maoz and Felsenthal (1987) provide examples of how such games are solved in a more detailed manner.

*Notes*: Read preference order as follows: for *abc*, *a* is preferred to *c*, and *c* is preferred to *b*. Transitivity implies that *a* is preferred to *b*. Slashed outcomes indicate ties between or among candidates.

leading to *a*'s election. This is a reasonable outcome since *a* is the Condorcet winner, beating all other candidates in pairwise contests. Note, however, that *a* has the smallest number of devoted supporters (those who view *a* as the best candidate).

Now suppose that *a* wishes to increase her power by rounding up some really devoted supporters, voters who think *a* is a great candidate and that *b* and *c* stink. Suppose that *a* wishes to make sure that such supporters would not vote for *b* and *c* out of strategic calculations; so the type of voters *a* is looking for are those who strictly prefer *a* over both *b* and *c*, but are indifferent between the latter two candidates. Let us denote this type of voter by a preference order *a*[*bc*]. Suppose, further, that this is *a*'s lucky day; she has been able to round up seven *a*[*bc*] voters. Since none of the other voters has changed preferences, intuition would have it that not only is *a* expected to win, but her margin of victory will be substantially higher than had been originally the case. However, intuition turns out to be a poor guide to prediction. The increased support for *a* leads to her demise. This is seen in Table 8.2.

This table offers a major surprise. Candidate *a* has increased her control over actors in two important ways. First, we noted that *a* had initially the smallest number of first-place votes; now she has the largest number of first-place votes. Second, *a*'s margin of victory in the pairwise contests against *b* and *c* has increased sharply. (Compare the bottom parts of Tables 8.1 and 8.2.) Yet, not only does candidate *c* win the election, *a* actually comes out last. How is such a perverse result possible? The answer emerges clearly from the strategic calculus shown in Table 8.2. The addition of the seven *a*[*bc*] voters has changed the nature of the possible outcomes of the game: in Table 8.1, *a* is the winner in 8 of the possible 16 outcomes; in Table 8.2, *a* is the winner in 11 of the 16 outcomes. This determines dominant strategies of *a*, *b*, and *c* for blocs *a*[*bc*] (by definition), *bac*, and *cba*, respectively. Now, the *acb* voters, fearing that if they vote for *a* they would allow the election of *b*, their worst candidate (column 2 in Table 8.2), decide to vote for their second-best candidate *c*. Finally, the *cba* voters, facing a choice between their top preference and their second preference (columns 10 and 12) have no hard time deciding to vote for *c*, rendering *c* the winner and *a* the loser of this election.

The fact that *a* has increased her control over actors sets into motion a process of strategic voting by the other blocs; it also leads some of *a*'s devoted supporters to vote for their second preference out of fear that, if they don't, they will get their worst outcome. All in all, this is a process where actors with inferior capabilities attempt to compensate for their inferiority by sophisticated behavior and tacit cooperation against the more powerful ones. From this example, the first lesson readily follows: more control over actors (after all, *a* got the seven

**Table 8.2** Sophisticated voting with three candidates and increased support for candidate $a$

| Number of voters | Preference order | Admissible voting strategies | | | | | | | | | | | | | | | | Sophisticated strategy |
|---|---|---|---|---|---|---|---|---|---|---|---|---|---|---|---|---|---|---|
| | | 1 | 2 | 3 | 4 | 5 | 6 | 7 | 8 | 9 | 10 | 11 | 12 | 13 | 14 | 15 | 16 | |
| 7 | a(bc) | a | a | a | a | a | a | a | a | a | a | a | a | a | a | a | a | a first reduction |
| 14 | acb | a | a | a | a | a | a | a | a | c | c | c | c | c | c | c | c | c second reduction |
| 18 | bac | b | b | b | b | a | a | a | a | b | b | b | b | a | a | a | a | b first reduction |
| 16 | cab | c | c | a | b | c | c | a | a | c | c | a | a | c | c | a | a | c third reduction |
| 4 | cba | c | b | c | b | c | b | c | b | c | b | c | b | c | b | c | b | b first reduction |
| Outcomes | | a | b | a | a | a | a | a | a | c | c | a | a | c | c | a | a | Winner is c |

| | Pairwise contests | | | Social preference order |
|---|---|---|---|---|
| | a–b | a–c | b–c | $a > c > b$ |
| | 37–22 | 39–20 | 18–34 | |

*Source:* Felsenthal and Maoz (1988).
*Notes:* Read preference order as follows: for *acb*, *a* is preferred to *c*, and *c* is preferred to *b*. Transitivity implies that *a* is preferred to *b*. Slashed outcomes indicate ties between or among candidates. Alternatives in parentheses indicate indifference.

extra voters to show up) can sometimes cause reduced control over outcomes.

Now, what about controlling more resources? Does an actor who increases his or her control over resources invariably benefit from doing so? Consider a similar problem wherein a committee of rational voters must elect one of three candidates to fill a position. Suppose that, before the voters cast their ballots, we allow one of the committee members to choose among prerogatives, each entailing a different amount of voting-related resources. Let us call this committee member *cba* (these are his preferences for the three candidates). This member may select any one of the three following prerogatives:

(1)   To have no voting resources (in our voting context, this means that *cba* is not allowed to vote).
(2)   To have the same amount of voting resources as those of any other committee member, that is, one vote.
(3)   To become a chairman, and to have the same amount of voting resources as in 2 above, plus an extra prerogative that no other committee member has, that is, to have both a regular vote and a tie-breaking vote that is to be cast if and only if a tie between or among candidates occurs.

Again, intuition would suggest that the choice problem is ridiculously easy: our focal actor should grab the chairmanship. It would allow him influence equal to that of any other committee member on the outcome of the election in the absence of ties, and a decisive influence on the election outcome if a tie occurs. However, intuition is wrong again. The focal voter obtains his most favorable outcome if he relinquishes all voting resources, and the worst outcome if he becomes chairman with a regular and a tie-breaking vote. Let us examine what happens when *cba* selects each of the three options.

The assumptions of the following analysis are the same as those underlying the previous one, namely, rationality, full information, bloc voting, and noncooperation. However, in this case we have two versions of the tie-breaking rule. If *cba* has no vote or if he has only a regular vote, ties between or among candidates are broken randomly. If *cba* becomes chairman, he can break ties any way he wants by casting his tie-breaking vote. Since *cba* is rational, and since his tie-breaking vote is decisive, he will cast the tie-breaking vote in accordance with his preferences. Thus, in case of a three-way tie (denoted as *a/b/c*) or in a case of a two-way tie between his most preferred candidate and any of the other candidates (denoted by *c/a* or *c/b*) he will cast his tie-breaking vote for *c*. In case of a tie between his two least preferred candidates (denoted by *b/a*) he will cast the tie-breaking vote for *b*. This time the committee consists of nine members plus our focal actor *cba*. The preferences of the various members are given in Table 8.3.

Table 8.3.1 analyzes what would happen if *cba* decided to choose the first option and not show up for the committee meeting. Table 8.3.2 performs the same analysis, this time assuming that *cba* selected the alternative giving him only a regular vote. Table 8.3.3 examines the consequences of *cba* becoming a chairman, with a regular and a tie-breaking vote.

The three parts of the table tell a simple yet surprising story: the more voting resources our focal actor has, the worse the outcome he obtains. Since, other than changing the amount of voting resources available to the focal actor, nothing else changed in the electoral setup, we can safely conclude that the loss of control over outcome was exclusively due to the increase in the voting resources of actor *cba*. Two lessons follow. One is that increased control over resources can cause loss of control over outcomes. The other lesson is that sometimes one's interests are better served by others than by oneself. When *cba* does not show up for the committee meeting, the other members get his top choice elected. When *cba* shows up and has the same voting resources as any other member (a regular vote), the outcome is indeterminate. This means that, from a game-theoretic perspective, anything is possible. Obviously, an indeterminate outcome (which means that any of the three candidates may be elected) is worse from *cba*'s perspective than the certainty of his best outcome. Yet an indeterminate outcome involving some nonzero probability of *cba*'s best outcome and some nonzero probability of obtaining his second-best outcome is definitely better than a certainty of *cba*'s worst outcome, which is what happens when he becomes a chairman with both a regular vote and a tie-breaking vote.

The explanation of the chairman paradox is that acquisition of extra resources by an actor sets into motion a process whereby actors with fewer resources tacitly "gang up" to offset the extra preroga-tive of the chairman. Since everyone knows how the chairman is expected to break ties if they occur, and since ties serve the inter-ests of the chairman, the tacit collusion among voters is designed to prevent the occurrence of ties. It is important to note that the collusion among members is not, and need not be, a formal one. For one thing, formal coalitions are disallowed. Even if they were permitted, cooperative game theory would be of little help here. Since the social preference in any of the parts of Table 8.3 is cycli-cal, the game has an empty core. In other words, every possible coalition that might form is vulnerable to the defection of at least one of its members as a result of an offer made to him or her by another member or another coalition. Thus, no coalition is sta-ble.

### 8.3.1. cba does not show up for the meeting

| Number of voters | Preference order | Admissible voting strategies | | | | | | | | Sophisticated strategy |
|---|---|---|---|---|---|---|---|---|---|---|
| | | 1 | 2 | 3 | 4 | 5 | 6 | 7 | 8 | |
| 4 | abc | a | a | a | a | b | b | b | b | a first reduction |
| 3 | bca | b | b | c | c | b | b | c | c | c second reduction |
| 2 | cab | c | a | c | a | c | a | c | a | c first reduction |
| | Outcomes | a | a | c | a | b | b | c | b | Winner is c |

### 8.3.2. cba has a regular vote (random tie-breaking)

| Number of voters | Preference order | Admissible voting strategies | | | | | | | | | | | | | | | | Sophisticated strategy |
|---|---|---|---|---|---|---|---|---|---|---|---|---|---|---|---|---|---|---|
| | | 1 | 2 | 3 | 4 | 5 | 6 | 7 | 8 | 9 | 10 | 11 | 12 | 13 | 14 | 15 | 16 | |
| 4 | abc | a | a | a | a | a | a | a | a | b | b | b | b | b | b | b | b | a or b |
| 3 | bca | b | b | b | b | c | c | c | c | b | b | b | b | c | c | c | c | b or c |
| 2 | cab | c | c | a | a | c | c | a | a | c | c | a | a | c | c | a | a | c or a |
| 1 | cba | c | b | c | b | c | b | c | b | c | b | c | b | c | b | c | b | c or b |
| | Outcomes | a | a/b | a | a | c | c | a | a | b | b | b | b | c | b/c | b/c | a | Outcome indeterminate |

### 8.3.3. cba has a regular vote plus a tie-breaking vote

| Number of voters | Preference order | Admissible voting strategies | | | | | | | | | | | | | | | | Sophisticated strategy |
|---|---|---|---|---|---|---|---|---|---|---|---|---|---|---|---|---|---|---|
| | | 1 | 2 | 3 | 4 | 5 | 6 | 7 | 8 | 9 | 10 | 11 | 12 | 13 | 14 | 15 | 16 | |
| 4 | abc | a | a | a | a | a | a | a | a | b | b | b | b | b | b | b | b | b first reduction |
| 3 | bca | b | b | b | b | c | c | c | c | b | b | b | b | c | c | c | c | b third reduction |
| 2 | cab | c | c | a | a | c | c | a | a | c | c | a | a | c | c | a | a | a fourth reduction |
| 1 | cba | c | b | c | b | c | b | c | b | c | b | c | b | c | b | c | b | b second reduction |
| | Outcomes | a | b | a | a | c | c | a | a | b | b | b | b | c | c | c | a | Winner is a |

*Source:* Brams et al. (1986). For another example of this paradox with applications to international politics, see Maoz and Felsenthal (1987). The original discussion of the chairman paradox is to be found in Farquharson (1969).

## Explanations of Power Paradoxes

Why would sensible people who are capable of making sophisticated decisions—consciously or unconsciously—harm themselves by increasing their capabilities regardless of the consequences of such policies? I invoke the rational and cognitive explanations to shed light on the power paradoxes just described.

### The Rational Explanation

In the paradoxes of power discussed above, as well as in other paradoxes of rationality, the rational model argues that actors simply do not have much choice. The rules of the games are defined exogenously (by the interdependent nature of the system, by the structure of actors' preferences, or by external actors that are not an integral part of the paradoxical game). Since actors act under a predetermined set of rules, they cannot resolve the paradox if they do not have control over the rules of play.

The abstract examples were presented as if focal actors had free choices among alternatives, with varying degrees of control over resources or other actors. The outcomes were seen as paradoxical or nonparadoxical depending on which alternative of resources an actor selected. If that were the case in reality, a rational actor who realizes that he or she is playing a game wherein extra control over resources can hurt should willingly give up any resources or other prerogatives that would harm him or her. However, in many cases actors do not have a free choice of resources. Even if such a choice were available, it might be rationally inadmissible, given that the paradoxical power game is only a part of a larger strategic context. In the sophisticated voting game, the election of candidates $a$, $b$, and $c$ might be only one part of a larger multi-issue agenda. On other parts of the agenda, the vote of the seven devoted supporters, $a[bc]$, might be pivotal in securing desirable outcomes for $a$. However, since the order of issues on the agenda is not known in advance and cannot be controlled by the focal actor, $a$, it would be irrational to tell the $a[bc]$ voters not to show up for the committee meeting. Even if these $a[bc]$ members declare in advance that they will not vote in the election among the three candidates, there is no a priori reason they would be believed. Other committee members would still behave as if the $a[bc]$ voters intend to vote, inducing $a$'s worst outcome.

In the chairman paradox, even if the poor chairman realizes what the extra prerogative would accomplish, he cannot always relinquish it. For example, suppose that this is a political science department meeting, discussing recruitment of candidates to a vacant slot. The dean will abide by the department's choice of a candidate, whatever it is, but will take the slot away and cut the department's budget if the department is deadlocked between or among candidates. While members might disagree on the ranking of candidates, all agree that a tie is disastrous and far inferior to the selection of any candidate. In such a case it would be irrational for the chairman to relinquish his tie-breaking vote, because by doing so the election might result in a tie and the loss of the slot and money. Likewise, knowing that his absence from the committee meeting would provide the chairman with his best outcome provides a possible solution of the power paradox, but may not be sufficient for actually resolving the chairman's problem. If the chairman's responsibilities include the organization and management of the meeting, it might be impossible for him to absent himself. Thus, the chairman may have little choice but to maintain his prerogatives and hurt himself in the process.

## The Cognitive Explanation

The cognitive explanation of power paradoxes is based on a familiar misperception involving relations between premises and conclusions. This misperception concerns an assumption that agreement over facts should yield agreement over the conclusions derived from these facts. The misperception is that agreement on facts does not imply agreement on conclusions derived from them because the relation between facts and conclusion is mediated by rules of inference on which people may differ. Even if everybody agrees on facts and draws the same logical conclusions from them, these conclusions are not equivalent to actual behavior. Logical conclusions form the basis for calculations prior to behavior, not the equivalent of behavior. A related problem concerns a tendency of decision makers to assume that observable data that are consistent with one interpretation must invariably be inconsistent with another interpretation (Jervis, 1976).

The problem is not, however, that actors disagree on the interpretation of the distribution of resources; it is that they draw different conclusions from this distribution of resources in terms of what must be done to convert control over resources to control over outcomes. There is some fundamental bias at work here. The notion that one can reduce motivations of states to a simple-minded pursuit of resources leads to an unrealistic disregard of the fact that resources are merely means that can be used to accomplish desirable outcomes or to prevent undesirable ones from occurring; they are not ends in and of themselves.[5] Actors have preferences for outcomes, hence, their choice of resources should really be seen in the context of which outcomes can be secured by certain resources. Thus, the distribution of capabilities in a system is only a starting point for strategy planning, not the end result. Weak actors do not willingly submit to strong ones simply because they know they are weak, and strong actors do not simply swallow up weak ones simply because they are strong. Simplistic extrapolation from capabilities to outcomes is not only unrealistic; it might be erroneous and very costly if relied upon. States with superior capabilities must examine the options that are available to the weak ones, because strategy can compensate for inferiority in capabilities.

The essence of the cognitive explanation of the paradox of power is that states with superior capabilities that ignore the options and strategies available to their inferior opponents are likely to get into deep trouble, not because their perception of the balance of capabilities is off the mark, but because they derive the wrong conclusions from the shared and agreed-upon knowledge of the distribution of capabilities. If inferior actors do not like the outcomes induced by the actor with most resources, they will try to figure out a way of changing them. This is accomplished via strategy, not via submission to the conclusion.

Another aspect of this explanation concerns a different interpretation of the first abstract example of the power paradox. Why would candidate *a* seek extra support for her candidacy in the first place? A possible answer is that the number of voters putting *a* on top of their list is smaller than the number of voters who have either *b* or *c* as the most preferred candidate. Since *a* fears that people will vote sincerely, that is, each voter will cast a vote for his or her most preferred candidate—she can expect that *c* will be elected. The assumption of sincere voting (and the disregard of the possibility of strategic behavior) causes *a* to seek additional support. It also causes her to ignore the outcomes associated with the sophisticated strategies in each of the two cases (i.e., the one without the seven *a[bc]* voters and the one with those voters). Candidate *a* gets herself into trouble by thinking that the additional support of the seven *a[bc]* voters will give her a relative majority in a sincere vote.

What happens here is one of two things. First, candidate *a* might base her prediction of outcomes on only part of the information available to her, the first preference of each voter. Disregarding the second and third preferences of the voters renders assumptions of sincere (as opposed to strategic) behavior perfectly reasonable. Second, candidate *a* might take into account the entire preference scale of the voters but assume that they would vote sincerely. Assuming sincere voting seems quite reasonable when there is reason to believe that other voters are incapable of making complex strategic calculations. In either case, seeking more devoted supporters seems like the sensible thing to do under the circumstances. It might be argued that this explanation violates to some extent the assumptions of rationality and strategic behavior. But this is—after all—a cognitive explanation suggesting that people are fallible and not always capable of complex calculations, as a rational model would have us believe.

It might reasonably be argued that this little analysis has nothing to do with international politics. The tightly structured setting of committee voting has little in common with the chaotic and anarchic international arena. Many of the assumptions that seem reasonable in the context of committee decision making are quite farfetched—if not totally irrelevant—in an international context. To dispel such accusations, I would now like to discuss possible analogues of paradoxes of power in international politics.

## Paradoxes of Power in International Conflicts

Many nations that become involved in wars are extremely optimistic about the war's outcome. In many cases, both sides in a war believe that they will come out victorious (Blainey, 1988). Obviously, it is quite impossible for both sides to be objectively correct. In international conflicts, control over resources is measured in terms of some combination of military, economic, demographic, and political capabilities. The widely shared intuition of the monotonically increasing association between control over resources and control over outcomes implies that actors with superior capabilities should emerge victorious when these capabilities are put to the test in international conflict. That this is not always the case should not surprise anyone familiar with the scientific study of international conflicts. By now there is a considerable body of evidence suggesting that the relationship between control over resources and control over conflict outcomes is either weak or nonexistent.[6] Those who are not satisfied with rigorous evidence emerging from quantitative analyses need only look at the performance of the nuclear powers in the post-World War II era. The United States, with near monopoly over nuclear weapons, was barely able to get a draw in the Korean War, and was badly beaten in Vietnam. The French and British forces took a bad beating in Suez. France got burned in Vietnam and Algeria. The Soviet Union has only recently extricated itself from a deep mess in Afghanistan. China's adventure in Vietnam in 1979 was far from a stroll in the park. Even if these examples do not constitute a majority of cases in terms of frequency counts, they are begging for an explanation (Mack, 1975).

Yet, this evidence does not constitute an empirical validation of paradoxes of power, for no clear causal structure accompanies it. It merely suggests that a more thorough examination of the widely shared intuition is in order. However, any attempt to establish the causal elements entailed in the paradox of power in a historical context runs into serious methodological problems. What was done in the abstract examples to satisfy the logical exclusiveness condition was to show which outcomes obtain under a given level of control over resources. Reality does not afford such flexibility. We know what has actually happened, but it is impossible to tell with any degree of confidence what would have happened if the superior actor had had less control over resources or actors. So we need to take an indirect route to the empirical demonstration of these paradoxes. In order to suggest that the paradox of power might provide a potential explanation of a given historical episode, we must show that events in that case followed a certain sequence that is similar or identical to what one would expect according to the substantive interpretation of the process that gave rise to the power paradox in the abstract examples. If such a sequence is consistent with the facts in the historical case, then we cannot rule out the abstract process outlined by the power paradox as a plausible explanation.

Thus, several things must be established in an empirical analysis of the power paradox. (1) An actor increased its control over resources relative to other actors. (2) The actor had resources superior to those of any of the other actors, but these resources were not necessarily superior to those of all other relevant actors combined. (3) Other actors were not in a coalition—formal or informal—directed at the focal actor prior to the latter's acquisition of extra control over actors or resources. (4) There should be some evidence of formal or tacit collusion of the inferior actors against the superior actor, as a result of that actor's increased control over resrources. (5) The result of this collusion is that the focal actor lost control over outcomes. (6) Once this has happened, the formal or informal collusion among the inferior actors ceased.

Granted, the correspondence between the sequence of events in the abstract cases and the sequence of events in the historical cases does not render the paradoxical explanation an exclusive one. Nor does it make it the best possible explanation of the histori-cal facts. But since my objective is to suggest some new ways of thinking on the relationships between resources and outcomes in world politics, showing that the power paradox provides a plausible interpretation of seemingly puzzling events in history seems sufficient in this context. This will be done by a brief analysis of the two Balkan wars of 1912–1913 and of Israel's invasion of Lebanon in 1982–1985.

## On the Art of Dividing Spoils: The Balkan Wars, 1912–1913[7]

The story of the Balkan wars should be one of great interest to stu-dents of international politics for several reasons. First, both wars are cases wherein weaker actors prevailed over stronger ones. Second, it is an extremely interesting case of alliance politics, and how these politics relate to war.[8] Third, the entire period before, during, and following the wars was characterized by intense multilateral negotiations, both among the various Balkan states and between the Balkan states and the Great Powers. Yet, it is surprising that very few analytical efforts have been made to analyze these wars, especially in terms of how they relate to the outbreak of World War I.[9] I do not wish to correct this deficiency in the present discussion of the wars. Rather, I intend to show how these wars can be understood in terms of a paradox of power.

The first Balkan war broke out after a period of intense bargaining among the three Balkan states—Bulgaria, Serbia, and Greece—and Turkey. This process was closely monitored by the Great Powers, Austria-Hungary, Russia, Germany, and—to a lesser extent—Great Britain and France. Formally, negotiations focused on the rights of the Christian population in the area controlled by Turkey in Europe. The real issue, however, was the Turkish territories in Europe, populated by Slavic people of very diverse origins and with affiliation to various Balkan governments. All three Balkan governments felt that the time was ripe to acquire those territories from Turkey, which was weakened by corruption and domestic turmoil since the 1908 Young Turk revolution. Throughout the spring of 1912, intense negotiations took place between Bulgaria and Serbia, on the one hand, and between Bulgaria and Greece, on the other, to establish a joint front against the still overwhelmingly large Turkish army. On March 13, 1912, an alliance treaty was signed between Bulgaria and Serbia, and on May 17, 1912, a similar treaty was signed between Bulgaria and Greece.[10] The central element in the Balkan alliance was Bulgaria; Serbia and Greece had no alliance with each other.

Once these alliances were announced, the Great Powers realized immediately their offensive nature and began a series of mediation efforts designed to reduce the risks of war in the Balkans. These efforts were halfhearted, however, because the Great Powers were themselves split in terms of their views of the appropriate solution to the problems. Russia was interested in reduction of the Turkish rule in Europe and wanted to maintain good relations with the Balkan states. Austria-Hungary was concerned about the risk of a "greater Serbia" and the implications this entailed for an old and ethnically divided empire. Nonetheless, the Great Powers issued a joint proposal designed to bring about a peaceful settlement of the dispute. This proposal, submitted to the parties on October 8, 1912, contained an explicit Great Power commitment to the preservation of the territorial status quo in the Balkans (Helmreich, 1969: 130). Hence, there was a chance that the Balkan allies might face a strong opposition of the Great Powers, if not to the war

**Table 8.4** The balance of forces in the Balkans, 1908–1913

| Year | Turkey | | | Bulgaria | | | Greece | | | Serbia | | | Romania | | |
|------|--------------|-------------|------------|--------------|-------------|------------|--------------|-------------|------------|--------------|-------------|------------|--------------|-------------|------------|
| | Mil. pers. | Mil. exp. | Total cap. | Mil. pers. | Mil. exp. | Total cap. | Mil. pers. | Mil. exp. | Total cap. | Mil. pers. | Mil. exp. | Total cap. | Mil. pers. | Mil. exp. | Total cap. |
| 1908 | 319 | 12908 | 0.55 | 59 | 1203 | 0.08 | 25 | 1148 | 0.05 | 29 | 8620 | 0.19 | 94 | 2148 | 0.13 |
| 1909 | 312 | 13728 | 0.64 | 60 | 1456 | 0.10 | 25 | 1106 | 0.05 | 36 | 1070 | 0.06 | 104 | 220 | 0.15 |
| 1910 | 324 | 9436 | 0.60 | 61 | 1586 | 0.10 | 30 | 1373 | 0.07 | 35 | 1031 | 0.07 | 89 | 2425 | 0.16 |
| 1911 | 336 | 10637 | 0.61 | 61 | 1586 | 0.10 | 35 | 1182 | 0.07 | 30 | 1071 | 0.06 | 97 | 2746 | 0.17 |
| 1912 | 341 | 9203 | 0.59 | 58 | 1620 | 0.10 | 29 | 1202 | 0.06 | 31 | 1184 | 0.06 | 100 | 2951 | 0.18 |
| 1913 | 341 | 9203 | 0.57 | 55 | 1620 | 0.10 | 27 | 1920 | 0.08 | 32 | 1194 | 0.06 | 109 | 3236 | 0.19 |

*Source:* Correlates of War Project (1986).

*Notes:* Mil. pers. = number of soldiers in active army (in thousands). These numbers refer only to the regular armies, not to the size of the mobilized forces of the combatants during the wars. Mil. exp. = military expenditures in thousand pounds (sterling). Mil. cap. = average proportion of military capabilities (personnel and expenditures) expressed as percentage of the total of the states in the table. This method of computation was used by various authors, for example, Singer et al. (1972), Bueno de Mesquita (1981), Maoz (1982a).

itself, then to any shrinkage in Turkey's European possessions. Even without this opposition the combined forces of the Balkan states were not even close, numerically speaking, to the Turkish army. The balance of forces in the Balkans from 1908 to 1913 is given in Table 8.4.

Turkey was not only numerically superior to each and every member of the Balkan coalition; it was superior to all three Balkan states combined. Notwithstanding the Great Power commitment to the status quo, or Turkish numerical superiority, the Balkan states declared war on Turkey (with the Montenegro declaration on October 13, and the Greek, Serbian, and Bulgarian declarations five days later). The war had two essential phases. The first, lasting to late November 1912, was marked by a rapid and decisive advance of the three Balkan armies and a hasty retreat of the Turkish army after a series of defeats. With the siege of Adrianople by the Bulgarian army and the way to Constantinople virtually open, it was clear that the war was over for Turkey. Indeed, the Turkish government appealed to the Great Powers for an armistice, which was granted. After futile attempts to resolve the territorial disputes through negotiation in London, battles resumed on January 28. While the military objectives of the war were accomplished from the Serbian and Greek perspective, Bulgaria still had unfinished business with Turkey in Adrianople. The occupation of Adrianople was completed on March 30, 1913, and the London conference was resumed in early April.

The weak prevailed in the first Balkan war, but this is hardly an illustration of the power paradox discussed above. Turkey did not lose because it was more powerful. It lost because its army was technologically and organizationally weak; because political chaos inflicted the army's command and the quality of the troops and weapons was poor. Diplomatist (1915: 192) quotes another anonymous authority of military affairs of the time, explaining Bulgarian success in the war: "Superior numbers are an undoubted advantage; but skill, better organization and training, and above all, a firmer determination in all ranks to conquer at any cost, are the chief factors of success." But the territorial gains of the first Balkan war were unequal in terms of the goals the allies set for themselves and what they eventually accomplished. Bulgaria was clearly the biggest winner of the war, though the price it paid was obviously the highest. In fact, Bulgaria emerged from the war as, arguably, the most powerful state in the Balkans, excluding Romania. Thus, if territory and population are elements of national resources, then all the allies gained in the war. But Bulgaria gained the most, and therefore increased its resources the most.

This, indeed, was Bulgaria's problem. During the negotiations in London, the former allies began to debate the division of spoils. Serbia and Greece felt that the territorial gains awarded to Bulgaria by the

Great Powers were excessive, especially in light of denial by the Great Powers of gains to the other two allies. Serbia felt that it should be compensated for not getting territorial access to the Adriatic Sea. Greece, too, felt deprived, in that it was forced to give up territory acquired in Thrace and Macedonia. If this were not enough, Romania joined the list by requiring revisions in its border with Bulgaria. The Bulgarians rejected all the claims by its former allies and, while agreeing to some modifications of its border with Romania, refused to make sufficient concessions to pacify the Romanian government. The Great Powers showed, in general, sympathy to the Bulgarian position. In particular, both Austria-Hungary and Germany were willing to support Bulgaria in order to frustrate the Serbians. They urged the Bulgarians, however, to make concessions to the Romanians, a policy that Bulgaria did not want to consider at that point.

Even before the postwar negotiations ended in the Treaty of London (May 30, 1913), Serbia and Greece started negotiations on an anti-Bulgarian alliance. At the same time, they sought Romanian support in the war. On June 1, the Serbo-Greek alliance was signed. A tacit understanding was established with Romania that it would join in the event of a war. With Romania included, the new coalition was clearly superior to Bulgaria; without Romania, it would have been militarily inferior. While the Greek and Serbian army had started a process of demobilization (as they had concluded their part in the first Balkan war by November 1912), the Bulgarian army was still fully mobilized. In fact, in June of 1913 it was slightly larger than it had been before the start of the first round.[11]

Facing a hostile alliance directed at itself, and feeling a momentary advantage (or perhaps a necessity to preempt), the Bulgarian army launched a simultaneous attack on the Greek and Serbian armies on June 30, 1913. This was the signal for a general collusion process against Bulgaria: Romania jumped into the battle and so did Turkey, which, only a month earlier, had signed the Treaty of London, including an agreement to give Adrianople to Bulgaria. Within two weeks, Bulgarian forces were defeated on all fronts; the most embarrassing defeat being the recapture of Adrianople by Turkey. The treaties of Bucharest (August 10, 1913) and Constantinople (September 29, 1913) granted the victorious parties almost everything they had been able to gain during the second Balkan war. By refusing to give in to Serbia's and Greece's demands, Bulgaria lost—in effect—not only those territories, but also most of what it had gained in the first Balkan war (including a sizable piece of real estate to Romania).[12]

Let us examine whether this case corresponds to our power paradox. First, it is evident that the temporal sequence matches that described in the abstract example. Bulgaria gained resources following the first Balkan war that, both relatively and absolutely, were considerable. Moreover, the Treaty of London legitimized Bulgaria's gains and Austria-Hungary gave it strong support vis-à-vis Serbia and Greece. On May 29, 1913, the Austrian and German ambassadors to Romania issued a strong warning designed to deter the Romanians from entering a war between Bulgaria and its former allies. This suggested that Bulgaria had some indication that it had secured some additional control over actors. This increase in control over resources and actors was followed by a both formal and tacit collusion among actors that (except for the indirect alliance between the Greek and Serbs through Bulgaria) had not been allied with one another in the past.[13] This collusion resulted in the demise of the previously superior actor. In fact, it is clear that Bulgaria would have been better off (even if we do not count some 25,000 Bulgarian fatalities in the second Balkan war), had it ceded the territories required by Romania, Serbia, and Greece, than it actually was following the war.

Second, it seems quite evident that this collusion was a direct result of the first Balkan war, and that it was aimed at the biggest winner. It is also apparent that this gang-up operation did not last long. Indeed, two years following the Treaty of Constantinople, Bulgaria and Turkey found themselves fighting side by side against Serbia, with Romania and Greece cheering on the sidelines. Thus the substantive interpretation of the power paradox seems to hold up.

Third, the increased control over actors (the securing of Austro-Hungarian and German support by Bulgaria) was less than reliable. All it did was generate misperception of the extent to which the Great Powers' statements would be effective in keeping the Romanians out of the war.

But why did the Bulgarians fail to respond moderately to their former allies' claims? Why did they plunge, head first, into disaster? The rational model suggests that the Bulgarian government was locked into a no-win situation: it had dragged the nation into a costly war and the only justification for the substantial sacrifices of the war were the territorial gains it was able to secure in London. To give these up was seen as tantamount to treason. By late June the Bulgarian government, faced with a proposal of Russian arbitration that it considered equivalent to a decision in favor of its former allies, perceived the choice to be between giving up Thrace and Macedonia as a result of arbitration or a war in which, given their superior capabilities, they had at least a fighting chance. The army could not justify continued mobilization following the Treaty of London. The prospect of prolonged arbitration, suggested that war was inevitable and remobilization would probably be required. War now was seen as better than war later (Helmreich, 1969: 359–362). While the Bulgarians were definitely surprised by the

Turkish attack, they were not surprised by the Romanian intervention. However, they did hope to launch a decisive attack on the Serbs and Greeks that would take these two opponents out of the game. They calculated that Romania would remain on the sidelines until the dust of battle cleared and would refrain from action if Bulgaria's offensive was successful. Indeed, Romania did not enter the war until July 15. By then Bulgaria had suffered major defeats in the south and west.

The cognitive explanation suggests that the Bulgarian leaders, especially King Ferdinand and Savov, the commander in chief of the army, were carried away by military considerations. Although the Bulgarian prime minister, Danev, supported an attack on the Serbs, there exists some ambiguity about whether he was aware of the details of the planned attack. What is obvious, however, is that the Bulgarian cabinet was not told of the planned attack. The conflict between the cabinet and the king resulted in the forced resignation of Savov on July 3. There is also evidence of wishful thinking on two issues: the first was Romanian attitudes and actions; the second was overconfidence in the ability of the Bulgarian army to defeat the Serbs and Greeks before the Romanians could mobilize (Crampton, 1983: 424; Helmreich, 1969: 363–367). The Bulgarian king and Savov viewed the attack as part of a strategy designed to strengthen Bulgaria's position in an ensuing arbitration. They hoped for a Russian intervention designed to stop the war and enforce a far more favorable settlement, taking into account Bulgarian accomplishments during the brief war. This was a clear case of wishful thinking, for the Russian foreign minister, Sazonov, had informed Bulgaria that as a result of its position regarding arbitration, Russia had no intention of getting involved in the conflict.[14]

## Israel's Lebanon Adventure: Anatomy of a Minor Disaster[15]

Israel had planned the invasion of Lebanon for a long time. The Israeli war aims were as follows: (1) expulsion of the PLO from Lebanon, (2) expulsion of the Syrian forces from Lebanon, and (3) helping the Christian militia to occupy Beirut for the purpose of establishing a central, Christian-controlled government, which would (4) stabilize the country and sign a peace treaty with Israel (Schiff and Ya'ari, 1984: 49–51; Yaniv, 1987: 100–103).

Nobody doubted that Israel had the military capabilities to carry out a strategy of all-out confrontation with the Syrians and the PLO. The Syrians knew it, the Palestinians knew it, and the Christians knew it: they would not have agreed to cooperate with Israel otherwise.[16] Israeli Defense Minister Ariel Sharon estimated that neither the Soviet Union nor any of the Arab states would actively support the Syrians and the Palestinians, and this assessment turned out to be correct (Yaniv, 1987: 102–107). The ability to secure secret U.S. support for a limited operation suggests that Israel had nearly everything working for it. Initially, everything went extremely well for the Israelis. Despite heavy fighting with the PLO and the Syrian forces, the Israeli army was able to advance rapidly into Lebanon, pursuing the Palestinian guerrillas into West Beirut, destroying the Syrian antiaircraft missile batteries, and pushing the Syrian ground forces into northeastern Lebanon. Within a week, the Israeli forces were in control of the southern part of Lebanon and of East Beirut and were putting the remaining Palestinian forces under siege. Following a period of prolonged negotiations, under the auspices of Phillip Habib, the special U.S. envoy, the Israelis were able to secure the evacuation of the Palestinian forces from West Beirut. The Lebanese parliament elected Bashir Gemayel to the presidency, and the Israeli government was elated. It had every reason to believe, that, as Menachem Begin put it "the country shall be peaceful for forty years."

When it seemed that Israel was in a position to dictate the political future of Lebanon through its Christian proxies, things began to fall apart. It all started with the assassination of Bashir Gemayel and the ensuing Sabra and Shatilla massacre. The Christian grip on Lebanese politics began to weaken, and the Syrian involvement in the internal struggle became more evident. The Israeli army became entangled in the local fights among various ethnic militias (initially in the Shouf mountains, between Druzes and Christians, and later on in Southern Lebanon between Shi'ites and Christians). The strong, Christian-controlled central government never emerged. Palestinian guerrillas began to infiltrate southern Lebanon in ever-growing numbers, launching an effective guerrilla campaign against the Israeli troops in the area in close collaboration with the Shi'ite militia. The initially "quick and efficient" military operation turned gradually into a military and political mess lasting nearly three years. When Israel pulled out from southern Lebanon in June 1985 it was no better off than when it had first started the invasion. None of the far-reaching war aims had been accomplished. When the economic costs of the war and the concomitant social turmoil in Israel are considered, it seems that Israel was worse off in 1985 than it had been in 1982. How can this collapse of the Israeli grand strategy be explained?

Once it seemed that the Israelis were in a position to establish a strong, Christian-controlled government in Lebanon, and that such a government would have to rely on a continued alliance with Israel, the other ethnic groups in the country, which had been previously engaged in a fight of all against all, found the common threat of Christian-Israeli domination far more severe than that of either the Syrian involvement or an unstable state. Hence, a tacit collusion occurred aimed at getting the Israelis out of Lebanon and thereby weakening the Christian domination of the Lebanese government. The Syrians were obviously happy to participate in the struggle against the Israeli presence as long as they could find someone else to do the job for them. The PLO was happy to supply both the logistics and the manpower to get back into the game of Lebanese politics. Amin Gemayel's policy shifted against his previous ally and toward increased cooperation and appeasement vis-à-vis the Syrians. These hit-and-run operations by local guerrillas did not do any significant strategic damage to the Israeli army, but they were effective in causing numerous casualties and considerable demoralization of the army and Israeli society in general. When the Israelis withdrew from Beirut and the Shuff area, leaving the latter under Druze domination, the Druzes calmed down. But, at the same time, the participation of the Shi'ite population in the guerrilla warfare in southern Lebanon escalated sharply. Not only did the Shi'ites actively participate in the struggle, they provided shelter and logistical support for Palestinian guerrillas who infiltrated to southern Lebanon from the Syrian-controlled Bekka valley and from northern Lebanon.

Although this does not clearly prove that the Israeli capabilities had a direct negative effect on their ability to accomplish favorable outcomes, the tacit collusion between factions who had been bitter enemies prior to the Israeli invasion suggests that this effect could not be ruled out. The fact that this collusion seems to have begun at precisely the time that Israel removed all the barriers for a Christian-dominated government in Lebanon strengthens this impression. Even more suggestive is the fact that the moment the Israeli forces withdrew from a certain portion of Lebanon, hostilities among rival factions resumed.[17] Let us now examine how Israel's misfortune in Lebanon is seen from the perspective of the two abstract explanations of power paradoxes.

If one is willing to take seriously the claims of the Israeli government during the Lebanon War, all that Israel wanted was some peace and quiet along its northern border, something that could not be accomplished unless the PLO and the Syrians were driven out of the country. But there had to be a strong central government to make sure they stayed out. Whether or not Israel wanted it, the Christians were the only faction with a strong interest in keeping the PLO and the Syrians out. The Israeli government may have had little choice in selection of allies in the Lebanese mess. Even if it had not planned to impose a Christian-controlled government in Lebanon, other factions would have behaved as if it intended to. Israel did not have other alternatives in terms of controlling actors or resources.

There is another, more subtle, aspect to the rational explanation of the power paradox in the Lebanese case. The PLO in Lebanon, although far from a military threat of strategic significance, posed a major political threat to the right-wing Israeli government of Menachem Begin. In July 1981, Israel had to sign—pretty much against Begin and Sharon's better judgment—an indirect cease-fire agreement with the PLO that the latter did its utmost to preserve despite repeated Israeli provocations. The Israeli government had every reason to expect strong political pressure for concessions coming from the United States. The self-imposed restraint of the PLO in southern Lebanon indicated that the Reagan administration which had been instrumental in arranging the cease-fire, might attempt to get the PLO into the negotiations on the future of the West Bank. Seen in these terms, a military blow to the PLO must have become a politically attractive option even though a possible entanglement in Lebanese politics was anticipated. The paradox of power that the Israelis have experienced in Lebanon can be seen as part of a larger strategic context in which not attempting to increase Israeli ability to control the behavior of other actors (in this case, the Christian Phalanges) was rationally inadmissible.

But what has been said so far does not adequately address the question of why the Israeli government made it its business to drive the Syrians out of Lebanon. The problem with the Israeli invasion of Lebanon was that it tried to accomplish too much, not that its goals were vague. But at least some of the goals the Israelis set for themselves (especially that of driving the Syrians out) were not necessary for the accomplishment of the main war aim of driving the PLO out of Lebanon. It is quite plausible that precisely the tendency to try to accomplish everything caused Israel to accomplish nothing. But, as some analysts have argued, Israel might have had little choice but to confront the Syrians (Yaniv and Lieber, 1983). The reason for this was that the Syrians had placed antiaircraft missile batteries in the Bekka valley that would have endangered Israeli aerial operations in Lebanon.

The cognitive interpretation of the Israeli self-made trap focuses on the nature of the predictions the Israelis made about the other actors' strategy choices given the shared knowledge of Israeli military superiority. Since the Israeli government correctly perceived the situation as one wherein everybody in the Lebanese game knew that it had the capacity to invade Lebanon and drive the PLO and the Syrians out, they assumed that the game would be over before it started. It was assumed that once the Syrian control over Lebanon was broken, other actors in the game would continue their old all-against-all struggle. This would allow the Israelis to impose a Christian-controlled government, with which everybody else would have little choice but to cooperate. This was a simple extrapolation from a commonly shared knowledge of the distribution of capabilities in the system to a belief that a divide-and-rule policy would accomplish peace and stability in Lebanon. But the Israeli government ignored the threat such a policy imposed on the other weak actors in Lebanon (e.g., the Druzes and the Shi'ite Muslims). Obviously, the other political factions in Lebanon did not particularly like the prospect of an Israeli-Christian condominium, so they started working at disrupting it.

## Conclusion

Expectations of a monotonically increasing functional relationship between control over resources or actors, on the one hand, and control over outcomes, on the other, are in most cases quite reasonable, and quite in accord with reality. However, this relationship is not as straight-forward as one might expect. The main theme of this chapter has been that extra control over resources or over the behavior of other actors can *cause* a deterioration in an actor's ability to accomplish desired outcomes or to prevent the occurrence of undesired ones. States initiate or get involved in violent international confrontations because they think that such strategies will improve their ability to control outcomes. Even when they are not involved in actual confrontations, the logic of military growth and the resources allocated to defense are predicated on this logic. Yet, this logic might, in some cases, be a crucial factor in causing the state to lose control over outcomes. Previous research on the determinants of success in interstate disputes demonstrates that when control over resources does not match actors' willingness to incur the costs associated with the management of international conflicts or the risks associated with their potential escalation, strong actors tend to perform very poorly in those violent competitions.[18]

My argument is that it is not the acquisition of extra resources that, in itself, invokes tacit collusion among inferior actors. *Rather, it is the mix of extra resources and the known preferences of the superior actor that make for a fatal combination. Inferior actors act to offset extra resources not because they feel directly threatened by the resources, but because they do not like the way these resources are going to be used given the preferences of the superior actor.* When the Israeli forces marched into the Shi'ite villages in the southern Lebanon area and into the Druze villages in the Shuff mountains, they were greeted with rice by the local population. What harmed the Israelis was that they sought a policy that threatened the other factions in Lebanon. The habit of throwing rice at the Israeli forces was replaced by the habit of throwing Molotov cocktails at them. When the Bulgarian army had difficulties with the Adrianople siege in the final phase of the first Balkan war, both Serbia and Greece dispatched forces to help them. What harmed the Bulgarians was not the extra resources that had been gained in the first war, but their unwillingness to share them with their former allies in a more equitable fashion.

The process of tacit or formal collusion of inferior actors against superior ones may suggest that what was presented above is nothing but a somewhat different formulation of the old balance-of-power argument. Indeed, this criticism is not without basis. Previous analyses of the chairman paradox have pointed out that balancing processes in the international system take a form similar to the tacit collusion process this paradox suggests.[19] However, despite these balancing aspects, the problem—as I see it—is primarily one of choice among different levels of resources. Three aspects of the paradox suggest that a balance-of-power interpretation might be less than satisfactory in this case. First, the paradoxes are driven by preferences and strategy, not by an automatic mechanism that prevents preponderance. The theoretical demonstrations of the paradox suggest that what determines the actual occurrence of an inverse association between control over resources and control over outcomes is not always how resources are distributed over the system of actors; it is how actors' preferences are distributed over a given array of outcomes. Acquisition of resources or prerogatives by an actor may or may not result in a paradoxical outcome, depending on the preferences of the actor and the strategies it pusrsues.[20] This suggests that a perspective focusing on the effects of structures—defined in terms of distributions of capability—on outcomes may provide only a partial account of the paradox.[21]

Second, from a unit-level perspective, the implication of power paradoxes is that—whether or not a balancing act is what accounts for the discrepancy between resources and outcomes—the focal actor gets hurt, sometimes badly so. This raises the question of whether a more judicious allocation of resources by one actor can prevent the balancing act of other actors. When one is aware of the possibly adverse consequences of extra resources, the motive to cut down is there. The rational explanation argues that in some cases, actors cannot afford to do that. In this sense, a systemic perspective is useful in that it highlights the constraints on optimal strategy selection by actors. Yet, even then, actors can sometimes manipulate the rules produced by systemic structures in a manner that allows them to have their cake and eat it too. Self-binding commitments on the part of superior actors may produce favorable outcomes that reestablish the positive relationship between resources and outcomes.[22] When actors make choices based on fundamental misperceptions about the implications of extra resources and about the relations between resources and outcomes, the balancing act, as well as other system-level explanations, has little to offer. The actors are done in by their rash selection of resources. A structure that cannot be destroyed by bad choices or manipulated by smart strategies has yet to be invented.

Finally, both the theoretical demonstration of the power paradoxes and the empirical cases suggest that a paradox of power may arise even in the absence of communication or coalition formation among inferior actors. Noncooperative game theory is a useful theoretical basis for this paradox because it shows that all it takes to defeat an actor with superior resources is strategic behavior on the part of all individual participants. The notion of tacit collusion has no operational meaning under the assumption of noncooperation employed in the theoretical demonstration of the paradox. It merely represents a process wherein acquisition of resources by one actor produces independent strategy change of other actors in a manner that directly harms the first and may or may not benefit the latter. In the Lebanon case there was no formal process of alliance formation among the various factions that fought Israel; each did it pretty much on its own.

Two questions remain. The first is a normative one: Should paradoxes of power be resolved? The nice thing about paradoxes of power from a normative viewpoint is that strategy provides for some justice in an international environment that has been extremely unfair to some actors in terms of the resources it has allocated to them. If those who have the dollar can hold those who don't by the collar, then all forms of injustice in international politics would be perpetuated: the era of Great Power imperialism would have been extended indefinitely, small states would have been gradually taken over by big ones, and so forth. Consider the empirical cases discussed in this study from a normative perspective. Why was it fairer to grant Bulgaria the territories it had occupied and deprive Serbia from access to the Adriatic sea, or not to compensate it for the denial of its demand? Why was it fairer to have Israel dictate the course of Lebanese politics through the Christians than to have the indigenous parties in Lebanon try to come up with their own structural solution to the problem, even if this required another ten years of civil war? The paradoxes of power suggest that the rules of the game in international politics may serve to correct structural injustices in the distribution of resources in the system. Hence, any attempt to resolve the paradoxes of power in a manner that reestablishes the monotonically increasing association between control over resources and control over outcomes is essentially reactionary, for it seeks to supplement one form of injustice with another.

This normative argument seems very appealing, but it is based on a misconception of the problem. Trying to resolve the paradoxes does not imply a wish to perpetuate injustice. Rather, the need to resolve such paradoxes might be due to a wish to correct some form of malfunctioning in the system that is harmful not only to the superior actor but to all the actors combined. For example, Maoz and Felsenthal (1987) show that the chairman paradox can be coupled with a social choice paradox wherein the chairman's worst outcome (which is realized when the chairman controls all the prerogatives) is also a bad choice for the voting body as a whole. By trying to offset the extra resources of the chairman, all other actors trap both the chairman and themselves in the process. In such a case, the resolution of the chairman paradox is not only in the chairman's egoistic interest; it is also a social imperative. Moreover, resolving the paradox of power does not imply the reestablishment of a monotonically increasing functional relation between control over resources and control over outcomes. Rather, it implies maintaining the complex relationship between the two, while showing actors how to avoid traps without a wasteful investment in additional resources. In international politics, investment of resources typically involves increased military capabilities at the expense of welfare expenditures. If it is possible to convince foreign policy decision makers that both their security interests and the welfare of their nations are better served by less, rather than more, military spending, then we have done an important service.

The second issue that must be discussed here is this: What do the paradoxes of power imply for the way we study, teach, and practice international politics? If the paradoxes of power discussed in this chapter have anything to offer in the context of the theory and practice of international politics, it is that some of the major premises of the realist paradigm must be reexamined. But the threat to the premises of this theory is not in its overly narrow assumptions or their empirical plausibility, as subscribers to complex interdependence paradigms would have us believe.[23] The key issue is not that power varies over issue areas. Rather, the rational explanation of power paradoxes suggests that a more thorough investigation of political realism in international relations must explore the dialectic relationship between capabilities and strategy. This requires incorporation into our models and empirical analyses components of actor preferences and the strategies such preferences imply. It also requires an examination of how the rules of play might affect the relationship between control over resources and control over outcomes.

For many students of international politics, paradoxes of power implied simply that "when the apparently weaker state wins . . . [international] conflicts [against stronger states], analysts of international politics who rely heavily on "power" as an explanatory concept face a paradox that creates doubts of the validity and utility of it" (Ray and Vural, 1986: 316). As a result, many of the "solutions" of these "paradoxes" were overly simplistic. For example, Organski and Kugler's (1980) analysis centers around the idea that the power disparity between the winner and loser is more apparent than real, and that if we measure national power correctly, we will discover that the winner of the "paradoxical" war was actually stronger than the loser. Therefore, the paradox of power seems illusionary.[24] The idea here is that measures of resources that do not reflect the political capacity of the regime and the aid the combatants receive from allies tend to distort actual evaluations of national power. Once these measures are incorporated, the discrepancy between control over resources and control over outcomes disappears.

Investigations that focus on factors other than control over resources (such as resolve, bargaining power, will to suffer, and expected utility) contribute to the confusion. (I am including my own studies of resolve in this category.)[25] The common denominator of all these studies is that, having defined the paradox of power in noncausal terms, they downgrade its theoretical significance and practical implications. Social paradoxes that have empirical referents are normally illustrated by puzzling empirical observations that seem to defy intuitive logic. But the converse is not necessarily true. Puzzling empirical observations do not necessarily constitute paradoxes. It is only that subset of puzzling observations that reflects a causally induced contradiction between premises of an otherwise logical system of theoretical premises that are true paradoxes. While each of the explanations of the David and Goliath phenomenon in international conflict may have some grain of truth, these are not explanations of paradoxical conflict outcomes. What they attempt to do is to downgrade or outright disregard the more severe penalties of resource accumulation in international politics. They attempt to restore linear logic to problems that defy such a form of reasoning. The power of an analysis of paradoxes in international conflicts is that it explores inherent weaknesses in popular theories of international politics, however refined these may be.

## Notes

1  This is an expanded version of my article, "Power, Capabilities, and Paradoxical Conflict Outcomes," *World Politics*, 41, No. 2 (January 1989). Copyright © 1989 by Princeton University Press. Reprinted by permission of Princeton University Press.
2  For a thoughtful discussion of these meanings of the term, see Hart (1976).
3  See, for example, Singer et al. (1972); Organski and Kugler (1980), Bueno de Mesquita (1981), and Maoz (1982a, 1983).
4  I am using voting-related examples for two reasons. First, voting resources and voting power (in terms of control over outcomes) are some of the most simple and straightforward concepts to measure. This is contrary to concepts such as military capabilites and national power, where no universally accepted definitions or measures exist. Second, the theory of

sophisticated voting developed by Farquharson (1969) provides the most convenient setting to show the paradox of power in a manner that satisfies the three criteria mentioned above.

5   On the tendency to interpret intentions from capabilities in the context of deterrence, see Jervis (1985) and Stein (1985; 1987).

6   See Maoz (1982a, 1983, 1984b), Wayman et al. (1983), and Mandel (1986).

7   This analysis is based on Petrovich (1976), Trotsky (1980), Crampton (1983), Helmreich (1969), Dakin (1972), Dedijer et al. (1974), Miller (1966), and Diplomatist (1915).

8   This case is an example of what Bruce Bueno de Mesquita (1981) considers a counterintuitive aspect of international politics: war among allies.

9   Works on international crises covering this period have generally ignored these two wars. For example, Snyder and Diesing (1977: 433) mention these wars only in passing in the context of Great Power diplomacy. Lebow (1981) ignores these wars completely. For an exception of a discussion of the series of crises leading to the First World War that deals explicitly with the Balkan wars, see Sabrosky (1975).

10   Although Montenegro was another participant in the alliance systems leading to the first Balkan war, I will not discuss it for two reasons. First, it was the weakest link in the chain, its capabilities having little effect on the total balance of forces. Second, it was heavily under Serbian influence, hence, its independence of choice was questionable.

11   The Bulgarian army numbered some 600,000 troops (as opposed to 592,000 during the first war), while the Greek army went down to 200,000 troops (from 215,000 during the war), and the Serbian army was reduced to 350,000 (from a total of over 400,000 during the war). These figures are given by Crampton (1983: 417–420). They generally agree with those given by Petrovich (1976: 603), who estimates the strength of the Romanian army at 437,000 troops and the Turkish army at 255,000 troops. Yet these figures differ markedly from the estimates of the combined strengths of the combatants in the first Balkan war given by other authors. Trotsky (1980: 139–140), relying on a noted German military commentator, put the size of the various armies at the start of the Balkan war as follows: Bulgaria, 200,000 (160,000 combatants); Serbia, 120,000 (95,000 combatants); Greece, 55,000 (45,000 combatants); Montenegro, 35,000; Turkey 450,000 (360,000 combatants). However, these figures are a gross underestimate. Later, Trotsky puts the total Bulgarian casualties in the war at 102,000 (p. 272), suggesting that the Bulgarian army should have been at least double the initial estimate. Diplomatist (1915: 176) cites an interview in the *Near East* with a leading Young Turk in the winter of 1911–1912 who estimated the mobilization capacity of the allies at 450,000, while the Turkish mobilization capacity was put at 800,000.

12   The Bulgarian balance sheet, following the two Balkan wars, showed some surplus. However, it was much smaller not only than what it had been at the end of the first Balkan war, it was also the smallest relative gain of all the allies in the two wars. Helmreich's (1969: 453) figures show that Bulgaria's territory was expanded by nearly 29 percent, and its population was expanded by 3 percent. This compares to a territorial expansion of 67 percent and a demographic expansion of 63 percent of Greece, a territorial expansion of 61 percent and a demographic

expansion of 100 percent of Montenegro, and a territorial expansion of 81 percent and a demographic expansion of 55 percent of Serbia.

13  In fact, Helmreich (1969: 350–351), reports that secret discussions between the two former enemies, Serbia and Turkey, took place throughout June 1913, in the best spirit of *realpolitik*.

14  "Now, after your declaration [requesting Russia to state its position within ten days] I communicate ours to you! Do not expect anything from us, and forget the existence of any of our engagements from 1902 until today" (quoted by Helmreich, 1969: 361).

15  This discussion is based on Schiff and Ya'ari (1984), Naor (1986), Yaniv (1987), Rabinovich (1985), and Sahliye (1986), who offer detailed interpretations of the war from the Israeli perspective and the perspective of the other participants in the war. Maoz and Felsenthal (1987) analyze the strategic process leading to Israel's decision to withdraw. Maoz and Yaniv (1989) discuss Israeli-Syrian interactions in the Lebanon war as part of a long-term protracted conflict from a game-theoretic perspective.

16  Yaniv (1986: 196–200) provides a telling estimate of the balance of power in the region. Israel's defense outlays have increased from $1.5 billion in 1980 to $8 billion in 1982. The combined military outlays of Egypt, Syria, and Iraq dropped from $6.4 billion in 1980 to $5.7 billion in 1982. (IISS, 1980–1985). In earlier work, I measured the relative capabilities of Israel and Syria using a modified version of the COW composite capabilities index, with GNP substituting for the traditional energy consumption and iron-steel production indicators of economic capabilities (Maoz 1985a: 78-80). I found that, in 1982, Israel's capabilities accounted for about 15 percent of the total capabilities of a reference group including Syria, Turkey, Egypt, Jordan, and Iraq. Syria, on the other hand, accounted for 7 percent of the combined capabilities of this reference group.

17  A discussion of the calculations made by the various parties in Lebanon is given by Maoz and Felsenthal (1987: 193–196).

18  See, especially Bueno de Mesquita (1981) on expected utility and conflict outcomes, Maoz (1983) on resolve, Rosen (1972) on willpower, and Baldwin (1979) on suitability of resources to political and military objectives.

19  See Brams et al. (1986: 253) and Maoz and Felsenthal (1987: 196–197).

20  Brams et al. (1987) show that chairman paradoxes are independent of the choice procedure or the distribution of resources. Felsenthal and Maoz (1988) show the same thing with regard to the monotonicity paradox.

21  The extent to which a structural perspective provides a solid context to an analysis of power paradoxes depends on which of Waltz's arguments is taken as the more characteristic of a systems theory of international politics. If it is the claim that "structures cause actions to have consequences they were not intended to have" (Waltz, 1979: 107), then I disagree that this claim is applicable to the power paradox. However, if it is the argument he makes that "structure is not independent of the parts, the states as actors, but constantly interacts with them" (Waltz, 1986: 338), then such a perspective seems a reasonable theoretical context within which the rational explanation can be cast.

22  Maoz and Felsenthal (1987) discuss how a chairman can resolve the paradox without relinquishing his prerogative. This is done by a credible

self-binding commitment to break ties strategically for less preferred alternatives rather than for more preferred ones.

23   For example, see Keohane and Nye (1977), Mansbach and Vasquez (1981), Vasquez (1983), and various authors in Keohane (1986).

24   See also Kugler and Domke (1986) for an analysis of the two world wars.

25   Ray and Vural (1986) and Ray (1987: 164–177) offer a comprehensive review of this literature.

# 9
# *Pyrrhic Victories, or Nothing Fails Like Success*

Another such victory and we are lost.
(Pyrrhus, king of Epirus, 279 B.C.)[1]

Sometimes people spend a lot of energy and other resources in order to gain something desirable. When they finally acquire what they had struggled for, they discover to their amazement that the effort required to maintain those possessions is even greater than that required to gain possession in the first place. They also realize that their situation prior to the new acquisition was far better than after the acquisition. Building a large and fancy house can make one susceptible to hazards that come with the new property (such as a greater likelihood of burglary, and hence substantially higher insurance costs, not to mention substantially higher property taxes). In the same vein, after a nation wins a war that was fought to solve some national problems, its leaders and people discover that they would rather not swallow what they fought to eat. The title "winner's paradox" covers three separate issues. The first concerns causally induced discrepancies between victory in war and failure on the negotiation table. The second paradox concerns victory in war that causes loss of much of a nation's colonial possessions. The third issue concerns a victory in which a nation acquires new possessions, which—in turn—cause domestic problems of a magnitude not known before the war.

Politicians find many interesting arguments to induce millions of people to go and get killed en masse, but two common themes run through the various justifications for mass suicide. One is the self-defense theme, which states essentially that there are values that are worth dying for, and that these values are being threatened by an enemy. Failure to risk one's life for these values would result in their loss. Such values may include national survival, the need to possess a specific piece of territory, or national honor. The other is the self-aggrandizement theme. It states that there exists a once-in-a-lifetime opportunity for the nation to acquire some desirable objective. Failure to be willing to sacrifice one's life for this objective would result in its nonacquisition. The desirable objective may be national survival, a specific piece of territory, or national honor.

Though these themes sound very similar, they are not the same. The self-defense theme depicts war as a reactive process, the purpose of which is to defend currently possessed assets. It suggests that war is a no-choice policy. And it does not envision life after war to be better than life before the war. When war is depicted as a self-defense situation, the sacrifices of war are compared to the (greater) sacrifices of surrender without a fight. The postbellum status quo is always worse than the antebellum one even in the event of victory: if we win we maintain our possessions, but we pay the price of war. This price is still worth the effort because the alternative is disastrous. The arguably popular notion "better dead than red" means that dying in the cause of (capitalist) freedom is desirable even if one knows that victory will not enhance freedom, but merely preserve it. According to the self-defense theme, war has always a negative expected utility; it always results in net losses. Yet, it is the least of all evils in that other alternatives imply far greater losses.

The self-aggrandizement theme depicts war as an act of net expected gains. Life after war will be far better than life before war, at least for those who survive it. Because the logic of a self-aggrandizement argument is that war yields extra assets, it is not the least of all evils. Rather, fighting is desirable because, considering the benefits of victory in war and the likelihood of victory, war will lead to the acquisition of currently unpossessed assets or to the expansion of currently possessed ones. Of course, there is a chance of loss in such a war, a loss that would not necessarily be realized if we choose not to fight. Yet, the notion of *expected* net gains suggests that the chance of loss or the magnitude of loss is relatively lower than the chance of gains or the magnitude of gains. Risking one's life in a self-aggrandizement war means that, even if one does not survive the war, those who do will benefit greatly. The sacrifice is justified on the grounds that it helped improve national life.

This dichotomy, like most other dichotomies, does some injustice to the ways political leaders justify war to their peoples. In most cases, argumentations are far more complex and cannot easily be put into one category or another. The typical justification of war will display elements of both self-defense and self-aggrandizement. Nonetheless, this distinction is useful in that it serves to warn that self-aggrandizement wars that lead to—expected or unexpected—extra possessions are a long-range disaster. Just as one must be cautious when confronted by a "no-choice" argument, one must be careful when confronted by a "quick and easy victory" argument. The paradoxes to be discussed in the following pages suggest that the problem with the "quick and easy victory" argument is not that victory in war is seldom quick and almost never "easy." Rather, it is that the seemingly intuitive association between the outcome of war and the quality of national life following it is sometimes extremely tenuous; sometimes this association is precisely the opposite of what most people think it is. Put differently, life after a victorious war can be far worse, from a variety of perspectives, than (1) life before the war, and (2) life after a devastating defeat and national humiliation in war. In the present chapter I try to establish the first aspect of the argument. The next chapter discusses the benefits that might accompany defeats in war.

The discussion in this and the following chapter departs from the standard format of the presentation of paradoxes of war in two ways. First, I present very briefly each of the paradoxes without going into a more rigorous formal analysis. Nor do I discuss the alternative explanations of the paradoxes that are deduced from the rational and cognitive model. Second, each of these paradoxes is very briefly illustrated by several cases. The historical discussion is brief and far more general than the style of the case studies established in previous chapters. There are two reasons for the departure from the standard presentation style. First, both this and the following chapter deal with multiple paradoxes. This requires a condensed discussion and illustration of each. Second, contrary to the other paradoxes discussed above, it is difficult to establish a direct relationship between expectations and behavior and between behavior and contradictory outcomes. Nevertheless, all of the issues discussed herein are true antinomies in the sense defined in Chapter 1, as I shall try to prove.

## Elusive Victory:
## Winning the War and Losing the Peace

The idea of war is that battlefield success in the service of politics should translate into political achievements. Sometimes, however, military victory causes a state to lose at the bargaining table. Sometimes military victory causes both the victor and the vanquished to act in a manner that prevents settlement. And sometimes it happens that this failure to translate military gains into diplomatic ones is more pronounced because the military victory is dramatic and extensive.

Not all wars end in decisive victories in which one state completely overruns the other and is able to dictate the terms of peace. In some cases, both sides lay down their arms, with the difference between winner and loser being that one is more exhausted than the other, and quits fighting just before the other is willing to call it quits, too. In other cases, one side wins decisively and the other simply surrenders what was at stake (territory or other forms of possessions) as an acknowledgment of the course of events on the battlefield. In Blainey's (1988) terms, the war is over because the parties agree on both the identity of the stronger and the magnitude of its advantage. But these are the only things the parties can agree on.

Victory secures for the winner possessions that the winner views as the prizes of war. It knows that to reach a political settlement it would have to make concessions at the bargaining table. Without going into negotiations, the winner can preserve what it had taken by force at the price of continued grievance and hostility by the vanquished. The winner may be well aware that the termination of the war without a diplomatic settlement makes for stability only due to the weakness of the vanquished. The vanquished, on the other hand, is aware that negotiation would be highly asymmetrical. Because the winner has already acquired most—if not all—of the values or assets at stake, the purpose of negotiation is to legitimize the new status quo at the price of some minor concessions by the winner. A settlement implies that the loser is willing (or forced) to legitimize a status quo that may be far worse than the status quo antebellum. Since the winner already possesses what the vanquished had wanted, negotiations imply de jure recognition of a de facto disaster. It stands to reason that sometimes the more dramatic the victory of one side and the larger the possessions it acquires, the less likely is an agreement that legitimizes the terms of peace and the less the subsequent stability in the relations between the protagonists.

In earlier work, I have shown that winners of past disputes are more likely to be the initiators of subsequent disputes with their past enemies (Maoz, 1984c: 239–240). I reasoned that the initiation of subsequent conflicts is done to preserve the fruits of victory. This is a direct by-product of winning the war and losing the peace. This analysis relied on two alternative perspectives: one was that of Aron (1966), labeled "peace by empire," and the other was that of Oren (1982), labeled "prudence in victory." The first perspective views peace as a state of affairs that continually rests on the points of bayonets. The more decisive the victory, the more the settlement—formal or informal—reflects the asymmetry of power between victor and vanquished. It follows that a settlement in which the winner imposes its terms on the vanquished tends to hold far longer than a settlement in which the winner makes concessions to the vanquished that are designed to pacify the latter. The second perspective claims that magnanimity in victory is the key to stability. The winner should be modest in terms of what it takes for itself as prizes of war. The settlement should minimize the grievance of the loser, otherwise the winner will face a frustrated opponent that is looking for the first opportunity to revenge the last war.

The empirical analysis of the two perspectives revealed support for the first perspective and lack of support for the second. Yet, since we are dealing with exceptions anyway, let us elaborate on the "prudence in victory" principle and see why it is difficult to implement. Oren (1982: 150) states this principle very lucidly:

> The essence of prudence in victory is the ability to skim off the cream of victory while causing the smallest possible increase in enmity on the part of the defeated. ... The imprudent victor, by being overly punitive, arouses in the vanquished a desire for revenge which threatens the new international habitat that the victor wants preserved. Prudence in victory is not to be confused with minimalism; rather, it is the optimization of victory in the immediate time-span after the war has ended. The design of the post-war setting must be based on a sober assessment of real national needs, not on a romantic notion of what the nation deserves.

There are several problems with this argument, empirical evidence aside. First, it requires relinquishing hard assets that were acquired at the price of many lives lost. These gains might sometimes be a result of a truly self-defensive war. These gains are tangible and the winner is required to exchange them for an intangible and uncertain pacification of an opponent. Even if a nation does not feel a strong emotional or strategic attachment to these assets, if they were acquired in a war of self-defense there is a strong urge to be tough with the opponent in order to punish it. Second, even if the winner wishes to express magnanimity, there still is the matter of the defeated actor, which must be persuaded to accept magnanimity not as an act of charity but as a settlement that is supposed to serve both parties' best interests, given the outcome of the war, rather than to legitimize and perpetuate an undesirable status quo.

Third, there are strong domestic pressures that operate on the leadership of the winner as well as that of the vanquished that make a mutually acceptable settlement less than desirable. For the winner, the public that has sacrificed a lot of valuable lives during the war demands to maximize the fruits of victory by punishing or otherwise exploiting the defeated opponent. These pressures are especially strong when the opponent is the party that started it all. Frustrated losers face charges of a knife in the back or other kinds of pressures for finding scapegoats for the defeat. These pressures create an atmosphere of a witch-hunt vis-à-vis the leadership. Often, political leaders find that the only way to mollify these charges is to adopt an uncompromising stand toward an opponent.

The upshot of these attitudes is that the war defines a new status quo that reflects a new territorial reality due to the outcomes of military operations. Yet, this status quo only worsens the relations between the actors, preventing the winner from converting military victory into a mutually agreed-upon status quo that reflects the new reality.

Consider two states, $i$ and $j$, with the latter being the winner of a war and the former the loser. The outcome of the war is military in nature. Nation $i$ sued for cease-fire and nation $j$ accepted it. The issue before them is whether or not to move forward toward a peace settlement. Each state has two options, broadly defined as *concede* and *stand firm*. For the winner, concession means withdrawal from some territories it had occupied during the war or some other concession that forces it to give back some of the fruits of victory. Standing firm implies failing to sign any settlement short of one that legitimizes the military and territorial status quo postbellum. For the loser, concession means granting formal recognition to the new status quo, whereas standing firm means refusing to recognize the new status quo. Figure 9.1 depicts the preferences of the players.

This game suggests quite clearly that a compromise settlement would have been the best collective outcome; the winner of the war pays some price in order to get a valued recognition of its rights to some of the new assets it has acquired. This is the best outcome for the winner because such a settlement adds a political stamp of approval to a military accomplishment and thus can lay the basis for a long-range settlement that would stabilize the relations between the two states for a long time to come. However, this outcome is unstable from a game-theoretic point of view. Once in it, the loser has a strong incentive to defect because it would provide it with a good diplomatic excuse to violate the new status quo once the military situation changes. In fact, the loser has an incentive to defect by not recognizing the post war status quo no matter what the winner does. If the winner is willing to make concessions, standing firm will enable the loser to recover some of its losses without making political concessions. If the winner is not willing to give up some of its newly acquired possessions, the loser is indifferent between conceding and defecting; each of these two cases is equally bad for it. Hence, the loser has a dominant nonsettlement policy. Knowing that, the winner can do no better than to adopt an uncompromising maximalist position. As is clear from Figure 9.1, the result is the DD outcome, which is, of course, both individually and collectively, inferior to the CC outcome. The war ended, but the peace seems even further away than before it had started. And, as pointed out above, when the winner's objective is to use its military advantage to bring

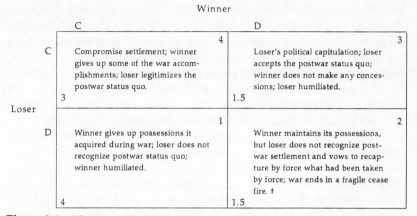

Winner

**Figure 9.1**   The Winner's Dilemma
*Note:* Loser's preferences are given in the lower-left corner of each cell; winner's preferences are given in the upper-right corner of each cell. Outcomes are ranked from best = 4 to worst = 1.                    † Nash equilibrium.

about a stable peace, its victory in the war provides it with just the opposite.[2]

## Territories That All Desire, But No One Wants

The circumstances under which the Six Day War broke out were discussed earlier, in demonstrating two different paradoxes: the paradox of crisis escalation and the ally's paradox. Now I want to return to this war again in order to discuss its consequences. Within six days, the Israelis smashed the armies of their three main adversaries; they occupied territories three times the size of Israel proper; they acquired a population that amounted to nearly a million people. This was quite an accomplishment for a state whose entire population at the time was slightly over two million. Not only did the outside world look unbelieving upon the extent of the Israeli victory; the Israelis themselves were astonished.

Even the Israeli government did not quite know what to do with those territories initially. Some of the newly occupied territories held a special religious and national value; this was particularly true about the eastern sector of Jerusalem as well as other places in the West Bank, such as the cities of Hebron, Bethlehem, and—to a lesser extent—Jericho and Nablus. In July 1967, the national unity government adopted a resolution that it would be willing to withdraw from all the occupied territories, excluding east Jerusalem, in return for a full peace treaty with its neighbors. However, they did set some conditions for such an exchange, the most important of which was that of direct negotiations (Eban, 1977: 436). The Israeli position was that the ball was in the

Arab court. As Dayan said in a TV interview when asked what Israel was going to do following the war: "We are waiting for a telephone call from the Arabs. We can wait, quite content with what we have accomplished" (Eban, 1977: 446). However, Dayan, as well as many other Israeli leaders, was under no illusion that such a phone call would come soon. As Dayan pointed out repeatedly following the war, the occupation of the territories was a bone in the Arab throat. They would try to reclaim the territories by force (Meir, 1975: 370).

Indeed, the Arab reaction to the Israeli offer of territories in exchange for peace was the famous Khartoum decision, which contained three "nays": nay to negotiation with Israel; nay to recognizing it; nay to peace with it. The Arab position was that what was taken by force shall be recaptured by force. The Arab states had no choice but to accept the military reality that emerged following the war, they could not alter that in the immediate future. However, the political elites in the defeated states could not afford to supplement a military defeat with a political humiliation. They were trapped by their own prewar rhetoric, wherein they had promised the destruction of the artificial Zionist entity. Having failed in the fulfillment of this promise, and having lost a good deal of real estate in the process, the Arab leadership (domestic or inter-Arab) could under no circumstances afford a political settlement. Their only escape from their own trap was to retreat further into their own rhetoric and accept the military reality until such time they believed they could do something about it. The result was that the Israelis failed to convert their military accomplishments to political achievements, and the Arab states had to adjust to life with frustration but without territories or apparent hope of recovering them in the near future.

The Israeli victory changed the stakes of the conflict for both sides. For the winner, the acquisition of territories provided Israel strategic depth and seemingly added some margin of security to a state that felt that it had been forced to live surrounded by wolves, with indefensible boundaries. The religious value of some of the territories made the Israeli leadership reluctant to return them. Paradoxically, this reluctance increased with time, fed by—among other things—what many Israelis felt was Arab intransigence in the face of Israeli generosity immediately following the Six Day War. The July 1967 decision to surrender all territories in exchange for peace may have been a genuine commitment. However, following the Khartoum declaration, the Israeli position hardened quite rapidly. In November 1967, Israel agreed to sign Resolution 242 only in accordance with its English version, which called for it to withdraw from "territories occupied in the war," but not according to the French version, which called for it to withdraw from "the territories occupied in the war." As time went by, Israeli officials changed their preferences with regard to the significance of certain territories. For example, Dayan was quoted as saying he preferred "Sharm-a-Sheikh without peace to peace without Sharm-a-Sheikh." The more time passed after the war, the higher were the domestic barriers to moderation imposed on the Israeli leadership.

For the Arabs, the burning issue was no longer the existence of Israel. This may still have been an idea many Arabs found hard to digest, but the immediate problem was one of redemption of the occupied territories and of their honor. Recognition of Israel would have been a major humiliation. It could simply not have taken place, not so soon after the defeat.

So the Israelis remained stuck with the territories, and the Arabs with the reality of defeat. What the Arabs wanted, the Israelis were not willing to give; what the Israelis wanted, the Arabs could not afford to provide. The status quo held on the points of bayonets; it took two more wars and numerous casualties to stabilize some of it through a formal agreement. Its other aspects have yet to be resolved. In some ways, the winner's paradox is more acute today, 22 years after the war, than it was when the war ended.

The war in the south Atlantic in 1982 offers another example of this paradox. This was a funny war to begin with, if "funny" is the right word to characterize an episode wherein numerous people lost their lives. The struggle was over a set of islands inhabited by far more sheep than people, islands of little economic, political, or strategic value. Even in retrospect this war looks kind of silly. Therefore, it is all the more surprising to see the same kind of winner's paradox that characterized the Arab-Israeli conflict.

The story of the war is familiar and need not be recounted here. The Argentinean military junta, faced with skyrocketing inflation and a multitude of other social and economic problems, tried out a little external diversion it thought it could get away with *because* the islands had little or no tangible value for Great Britain. Not so, thought Mrs. Thatcher, and along went the British public. After a period of intense bargaining during which each side dug in its own positions, the war was fought and won by Great Britain. Argentina suffered a humiliating defeat. And the Falkland islands remained an integral part of the realm. The junta in Argentina was replaced by a democratic government, but no settlement has been negotiated. There is a de facto Argentinean recognition of the British control over the islands, but no de jure recognition of the British sovereignty. Also, there has been no serious negotiation designed to reach a formal agreement over a mutually-acceptable status quo since the end of the war.

The lack of agreement forces Great Britain to hold on the islands a sizable military force. And as long as such an agreement is not reached, any attempt to violate the current status of the islands will be met by force, because the same factors that caused the British to resist the Argentine takeover of the islands in 1982 still operate at present. As Lebow (1985: 117) points out, the British felt that they had to retake the islands from the Argentineans not because of their national or strategic value, and certainly not to liberate the sheep from the oppressive regime, but rather because Britain could not afford to be seen as giving in to a blatant violation of British territory. On the Argentinean side, emotional attachment to the islands is still as present as it was during the height of the war. Frustration with the continued British occupation of the Malvinas prevents the government from reaching an agreement that would allow even some partial sign of British sovereignty. It is not implausible that the magnitude of the British victory makes an agreement over the future of the islands hard to accomplish.

## Defence of the Realm:
## Winning the Peace and Losing the Empire

Winning a war marks the end of a phase in a nation's life. It also marks the beginning of a new era in the history of nations because war is the great mechanism of change in human, certainly in political, affairs. Victory is supposed to mark the beginning of an era wherein the nation can sit back and enjoy the fruits of victory that had cost so much. Unfortunately, it is this cost, and sometimes the size of the fruits of victory, that creates the second aspect of the winner's paradox. When the war is long and extensive, and when the stakes are very high, the nation calls for total mobilization not only of the indigenous population, but also of auxiliary populations, the peoples who inhabit mandated or colonized territories. Big, long, and extensive wars also put a heavy economic strain on winners and losers alike. They stretch the resources at the nation's disposal to the limit.

The difference between winners and losers is simply that the former either maintain their old resources and their old responsibilities or acquire new resources and new responsibilities, while the latter sustain net losses of territory and the people residing in it. So, after the war, the winner's problem is to manage those vast resources. This requires a large army and extra expenditures of funds, which prohibit economic and social recovery of the homeland following the war and put an extra strain on an already devastated society. Most important, when some of the former colonies or the newly acquired ones are engaged in a violent struggle for national liberation, maintaining the realm requires the nation that thought it had finished one big war to engage in many new ones on a smaller scale. The physical and psychological strain of the war

makes the maintenance of colonial possessions difficult. The pressure for demobilization and for reinvestment of capital and human
resources in reconstruction projects reduces both the capability and
the will to resist demands for national liberation.

The victorious state that relied on the aid of its colonies during
the war accumulated both tangible debts and intangible IOUs that it
does not always wish to repay once the war is over. When it fought its
archenemy, the colonial power had to draft soldiers from the colonial
population. The natives joined the imperial army, and received a
great deal of combat experience in the big war. When the war was
over, the imperial power was forced to release the soldiers from the
colonized territories. The colonies then received cadres of well-trained
and combat-experienced men, who then became leading figures in the
struggle against their former employers. Large wars have some sort
of halo effect on colonized peoples, especially if the colonizers fight
for freedom and against oppression. Colonial demands for national
liberation following such wars are typically more persistent and more
determined than before. These demands are also backed up by acts
of violence and guerrilla warfare that require the exhausted colonial
state to send considerable reinforcements to trouble spots. When such
uprisings take place simultaneously at different parts of the empire, the
ability to handle all of them at once is usually more than the winner can
or is willing to handle. Soon it decides to grant independence to one
colony. Once this starts, the contagious process of national liberation
struggle reaches new heights. The troops that had been moved from
the former troubled colony are no longer sufficient to deal with the new
and more violent uprising elsewhere. The process of provision of independence accelerates, and, before long, there is no empire any more.

Is there a causally-induced contradiction in winning the war and
losing the empire? I believe the answer is yes. Winner or loser, following
a war a nation starts out of an economic pit. To emerge from the ruins
of war, a nation must reinvest more resources in its recovery than it had
done prior to the war. It cannot afford to maintain the kind of army it
had maintained during the war, and—in many cases—it cannot afford to
maintain even the kind of army it had prior to the war. So the war causes
greater pressure for demobilization than would have existed had there
been no war, because without the damage of war there would have been
no pressure for recovery. The war also causes local uprisings to become
more fierce, violent, and persistent than they had been before. The
rebels gain new recruits who are familiar with the colonial army inside
out, well trained, and highly experienced in modern warfare. In addition, the expectation of the colonized population is that the colonial
state will be more receptive to claims for self-determination because of
the help of the local population in the struggle against the common

enemy. When it turns out that the colonial state is unwilling to grant the colony formal independence, this frustration is soon converted into a struggle for independence of significant magnitude.

Struggles for national self-determination take place even without the involvement of the colonial power in a major war, and clearly some of them end in the acquisition of national independence and the loss of a colony. Still, the decline of states from the status of imperial powers with many colonies and protectorates to the status of a simple state with a clear and closed territorial domain seems to be fairly rapid—a process that, in some cases, started and ended within a 20-year period or less. The difference between the decline of empires following victorious wars and the emergence or stabilization of other empires following victories in the same wars seems to be not so much the ability of the old or newly founded empire to maintain its extraterritorial possessions, not even the magnitude of losses incurred by the various empires during the war. Rather, the rise or decline of imperial power following wars is a function of the willingness of the colonized population to stand up against the imperial power.

Exhaustion is the fate of all war combatants, but the local population determines for the colonial power if it needs to overextend itself following the victory against its arch-enemy. It is the local population that can put the necessary pressure on the victorious empire and force its decline. This is easier said than done, however. The struggle against the imperial power is extremely costly and requires considerable sacrifice. If the colony in question is deemed strategically or economically important, even declining empires can find the power to oppress such demands. The fact that the colonial power has disposed of an opponent that could have been a useful ally of local rebels does not bode well for the local resistance. Local rebels cannot rely on the external enemy to reduce the local capabilities of the imperial power. Nevertheless, when the will and determination of the local rebels is high, and when they are willing to persist in their struggle despite initially abysmal odds, the psychological, economic, and political pressure on the imperial power will do its part in the overall equation in the paradoxical way just described.

Two other factors work to weaken the colonial power's resolve in holding on to its possessions. First, the psychological attrition that the international war imposed on its society serves to reduce the will of its population for additional sacrifices. Although guerrilla struggles in colonized territories take an objectively small toll on the society in that few casualties are involved, they exact a heavy psychological toll. The army of the colonial state fights elusive targets and a hostile population. The colonial struggle is over stakes that are not primary: the colonial power's existence is not being threatened. Moreover, since persistence is one of the key determinants of the outcomes of colonial wars, the psychological exhaustion of the colonial power's population causes it to become impatient with what seems to be endless struggles in remote places over secondary stakes.

Second, the colonial power, fighting in concert with other powers, makes arrangements for the division of the globe—or parts of it—during or immediately following the termination of the international war. During these bargaining processes among the major powers, certain principles are adopted by the major powers, such as the principle of self-determination, which then serve indigenous populations in their struggle against the colonial power. These principles, which were used by the winners to impose limitations on the losers, are now used by the substate groups against the colonial power. The colonial power now comes under strong international pressure to grant independence to its colonies. Precisely those values that had been promoted by the imperial power during the war serve to weaken its resolve to hold on to its imperial possessions following the war.

## The Perils of Imperialism

World War I gave both Great Britain and France new territories in addition to those they had prior to the war. France got Syria and Lebanon. Great Britain was granted a mandate in Palestine. Its political influence in Iraq amounted to actual control over most political and economic decisions in that state. Both empires faced many problems in their old and new colonies prior to World War II. But both were able to handle those problems quite effectively, not because the resistance to their rule was weak, but because they did not have many problems in the heartland of Europe. Those problems they had in Europe were handled by diplomats; the armies were not put into action until the war broke out in 1939.

France is not a clean case in terms of the paradox discussed in this section because it is not clear whether it won the war. It might have won the war, but its empire had been taken from it during the war, and it was recaptured largely by the other allies. So one could argue that France got its empire back on a silver platter, and it is not obvious that its dubious victory in the war had anything to do with the decline of the empire.

But Great Britain is clearly a good case in point. It fought and won the war with its own troops, at a time being the single Western state resisting the Axis powers. It lost some territories that it had controlled prior to the war, but recaptured them largely on its own. And, with some exceptions in Southeast Asia, it ended the war with roughly the same empire with which it had begun. In some cases, it exerted considerable influence in states where previously it had little influence, such as Greece and Turkey.

During the war, some of the most important British colonies and protectorates were under direct threat of occupation by the enemy. Rommel's advance in North Africa put real pressure on the British forces in Egypt. The Iraqis, on their part, attempted a coup d'état in order to throw out the British and touch base with the Germans, who were advancing deep in Soviet territory. India, the most important British colony, was under direct pressure from the Japanese, who took Borneo, Sumatra, and Java and were making headway in Indo-China. The indigenous population in some of the territories mobilized in order to aid the British in their struggle against the Germans. In Palestine, the Jewish population sent volunteers to the British army, forming a Jewish brigade that fought in North Africa and Italy. Jewish volunteers from the underground organizations that had operated in Palestine aided in the British occupation of Syria and Lebanon in 1941. The Indians and Pakistanis also joined the British army, fighting the Japanese in Indo-China.

At the end of the war, there were no special arrangements among the major powers regarding the fate of their former colonies in Asia and Africa. It seemed that the status quo ante was to be preserved by default. The French were given back their colonies in Syria, Lebanon, Indo-China, and Algeria. And the British maintained their hold over India, Egypt, and Palestine, in addition to the British forces stationed in Greece. Soon it became evident that economic recovery from the war and the defence of the realm could not be pursued simultaneously. Some serious resistance to the colonial regime in some colonies required additional British troops to quell these revolts. It started with the struggles between the government and the communist resistance in Greece and the renewal of the revolt in Palestine and India. Within three years after the end of the war, Great Britain lost India, Pakistan, and Palestine. It called on the United States for help in Greece because it felt it could not hold its troops there any longer. It held a little longer in Egypt because of the strategic importance of the Suez Canal. However, with India becoming an independent state, the need to secure a safe passage to the Indian Ocean did not justify the expense of holding numerous troops in the face of mounting anti-British sentiments in Egypt.

Within a matter of five years, the British empire disappeared. Britain remained with some colonies in Africa (e.g., Kenya), and isolated—though not unimportant—bases in the Far East (Hong Kong) and the Middle East (Aden). Great Britain turned into a second-rate major power within five years of winning the greatest victory in its long and largely glorious history.

The causal effect of the victory in the war is seemingly tenuous. It may be rightly argued that the process of decolonization and "de-empire-ization" would have taken place anyway. It may have taken longer if it were not for World War II, but the outcome would have been the same. Moreover, even if the war had a truly causal effect on the decline of the British empire, it was the kind of war Britain fought, not the victory in the war, that explains this decline. These arguments notwithstanding, the winner's paradox is genuine. First, even if decolonization would have taken place anyway, the British exhaustion due to World War II clearly contributed to its pace. Had there not been the war that was, the process would have been much longer.

Second, decolonization in the British case was much faster and more general than in the French case. The French did not suffer as many tangible losses as the British. They had been overrun very early by the Germans and had been under German occupation through most of the war. Although the French forces under General de Gaulle fought bravely and the French resistance did a lot of damage to the German army, most of the French people were not under constant war-related pressure. The French army was split and only part of it participated in the fighting throughout the war. The population was not heavily and deliberately bombed by either side during the war. As a result, when the French were given back Indo-China, Tunisia, and Algeria, they hung in longer and were willing to invest much more resources and time in order to retain their colonies.

The decline of the empire was affected by the British decision to fight it all the way and by its decision to define victory in terms of total and unconditional surrender of the Axis powers. To accomplish such a victory, Britain had to give all it had, and it had to be prepared to suffer a great deal. This definition of victory required the kind of investment that drained Great Britain of its resources and reduced its will and ability to resist challenges to its control in the imperial territories. So the paradox is there; it is not an artifact.

## The Spoiled Fruits of Victory

If war is fought over a piece of real estate (with the population residing on it), then the winner gets to keep the prize. It turns out, in some cases, that only after the prize is acquired, does the winner find to its dismay that it was better off without it. Worse, the winner may be stuck with the prize *without* knowing that it would have been better off without it. The overall situation of the winner following the war is far worse than before the war, not only because of the suffering and cost of the war itself, but because it got what it wanted out of the war. The prize destabilizes political, social, and economic equilibria that had held the winning society together. It arouses new problems that are far more severe and dangerous than those that had been prevalent prior to the war. And the new problems make the solution of the issues on which the war was fought more difficult to accomplish.

The analysis of the Balkan wars in Chapter 8 reveals that victory in war can cause conflict due to disagreements over the division of spoils. The Balkan wars are, of course, not unique on this score, similar problems arose over the division of spoils following the two world wars. In such cases, the dispute is among states that joined forces to defeat a common enemy. Similar problems can take place within a single nation that fought and won a war against one or more adversaries. Before a state acquires a piece of real estate, there is nothing to fight about. Once new territories have been acquired, however, factions within the winning state start debating what should be done with the new possessions. This debate produces social conflict, increasing or creating political divisions over issues that never existed before. With the new possessions comes a population. Sometimes this population is sympathetic to the winning regime and is easily integrated into the new society, but sometimes the occupied population is hostile. If the winning nation had been ethnically homogeneous prior to the war, the war may cause it to become ethnically heterogeneous. It may force the winner to deal with the absorption of a large, ethnically distinct minority that is hostile to the new regime and works at changing the outcome of the war.

New territories cause both strategic and economic problems of a magnitude not experienced before. First, extra possessions require a larger army to defend them in times of peace. Given a hostile population, a nation has to cope with guerrilla warfare and civil resistance with which it has no experience and must devote a large part of its national security effort to the suppression of a new population and to the defense of larger boundaries. This, of course, has economic consequences. Human and material resources are diverted from productive enterprises to wasteful and nonproductive defense activities.

But the extra possessions have another economic effect. The local population starts penetrating the winner's traditional market, as a new and generally cheap labor force. Inexpensive products are brought into the existing economy without any protective barriers because the new territory and everything in it become part of the old economy. For the most part, this economic penetration goes both ways. There are also many mutual benefits associated with an added cheap labor force and tightened competition. But the main negative effect of this mutual penetration is that a new type of dependence is created. If this economic dependence deepens over time, it can be converted into a major weapon in the hands of the newly acquired population. It makes the winner vulnerable to a new kind of threat that it had not been forced to face as long as this territory belonged to its opponent. In the past, threats from the occupied population had been primarily military in nature. The dependence of the winner on the new population provides the latter with another weapon it can use against the winner.

The net result of this situation is that victory aggravates internal problems that had existed prior to the war and adds new ones of a magnitude not known before. Wars that are fought for extra possessions are justified in terms of the benefits associated with these extras. Yet, extra possessions can cause social polarization, strategic damage, and economic dependence of a magnitude not known before, and they may create so much sunk cost that resolution of this problem—once realized and once diagnosed as a problem—may be rendered virtually impossible.

## Problems of Territorial Multiplication: Israel and the Occupied Territories, 1967– . . .[3]

The Israeli victory in the 1967 war was the greatest victory in that nation's history; it was also a stunning military achievement compared to other international wars in history. Yet this victory was the worst thing that had happened to Israel, from strategic, social, and economic points of view. The war caused Israel to multiply itself in terms of territory and population. The result is that Israel is stuck with territories that it fought hard to acquire, and even harder to retain. Even if and when it withdraws from them, these problems are unlikely to disappear. So the territories, the argument goes, are a bone in Israel's throat; it can neither swallow them, nor throw them up.

Even as these words are being written, most Israelis do not realize the paradox, and most of them would dispute the two aspects of this theme. Those on the right wing of the political spectrum are likely to dispute the first part of the argument. They view the acquisition of the territories as the second-best thing to the coming of the messiah. They do agree, however, with the second part of the argument, that is, the notion that withdrawal from the territories would not solve the problems mentioned by the paradox. Those on the left side of the continuum agree that the acquisition of the territories represents a net loss. Yet, they challenge the notion that the damage is irreparable. To them, withdrawal from the territories, in return for peace and security arrangements, might repair most of the damage caused by the acquisition of the territories.

The first problem imposed by the occupied territories is demographic. They added over a million Palestinians to a state that, at the time, consisted of two and a half million Jews. The Arab growth rate is more than twice as high as that of the Jewish population in Israel. According to demographic predictions, in the absence of significant Jewish immigration to Israel, the number of Arabs and Jews in Israel will be equal by the year 2000. Given that the hostility of the indigenous population toward the Israelis has not changed over the 22 years of occupation, the size of the demographic problem will increase with the demographic changes. There exists an increasingly large population without political rights but with growing frustration and hatred toward their occupiers. And this growing frustration is unlikely to diminish over time, no matter what policies are pursued by the Israelis.

This population creates a dilemma that Israel will not be able to avoid in the future: the choice between staying a Jewish state, in which the Jews have a majority, and staying a democratic state. A Jewish state will have to find a way to define its sovereignty within boundaries that do not include such a large Palestinian population. In such a state, full democracy, including equal rights for ethnic and religious minorities, could be preserved. But this is possible only if Israel withdraws from the occupied and heavily populated territories. A Jewish and democratic state can be accomplished also if the Israeli government does what some extremist factions suggest: transfer the Palestinians from the occupied territories to Arab states. The latter option not only seems highly immoral, it also entails costs that render it unfeasible. The demographic trends that are not accompanied by political solution move Israel step-by-step to a South African model of government. A minority with full political rights will control a majority with no political rights.

This dilemma has caused an unprecedented polarization of the Jewish society in Israel. It has transformed a fundamental consensus on foreign and security affairs into a permanent debate that contains an explosive potential of a civil-war magnitude. It is unlikely that either withdrawal from the territories or their annexation would resolve this dilemma and hence lead to a fundamental change in the political split of the society. The split in this society is manifested in the fact that, for the first time in Israeli history, a significant number of people have refused to serve in the military in the occupied territories and have been willing to go to jail over the issue. It is manifested in violence of Jews against Jews. It is also manifested in the emergence of a vigilante Jewish organization committed to violent retaliation against the Palestinian population following acts of terrorism against Jews. This suggests a major legitimacy crisis. A growing number of Israelis are unwilling to trust the legal and political process and resort to taking the law into their own hands. The ability of the political system to cope with these problems has decreased due to this fundamental polarization. The government is forced to rely increasingly on the support of minor one-issue parties who extract concessions from the major parties sometimes at major costs to long-term national interests over which consensus does exist.

For example, there is a consensus that a strong army is the ultimate guarantee of the survival of Israel. In a state with a small population, the ability to mobilize all or almost all people of a relevant age-group to the army is a major determinant of the strength of the state. Yet, the required support of non-Zionist ultra-orthodox religious parties forced the Likud government in 1977 to make major concessions to those parties, including an agreement not to recruit to the army students of religious seminaries, and an agreement not to draft women who state they are religious. The running (conservative) estimate is that these agreements reduce the size of the army by 50,000 soldiers per year.

The territories and their maintenance are a cause of major strategic problems. The occupied territories do not contribute to Israel's security—in fact, they detract from it in virtually every respect. First, they increase the ability of the Arab states to surprise Israel because they force the main bodies of the armies to face each other without a buffer zone. Whereas the Israeli army is based on a major contingent of reserve forces, which take time to mobilize, the major contingent of the Syrian and Jordanian forces is made up of regular professional armies that are always ready and can be easily redeployed. When there are no demilitarized zones separating the Israeli and Arab forces, there are no clear indicators of when an attack is being planned by the opponent. Israel cannot afford to mobilize reserves whenever the bordering Arab states move troops in and out of the border zones. Indeed, the 1973 Egyptian-Syrian deception plan was based on repeated troop movements in and out of the border areas that were not accompanied by actual attack.

The Israeli claim that the territories provide it with strategic depth puts considerable constraints on the ability of Israel to launch a preemptive strike when it thinks that an Arab attack is imminent. Indeed, on October 6, 1973, the Israeli cabinet rejected a proposal by the chief of staff, Brigadier-General David Elazar, to launch a preemptive aerial strike on the Egyptian and Syrian armies. The reasoning was that Israel could not afford to be blamed for starting a war. Yaniv (1986) argues, correctly, that the acquisition of the territories in the Six Day War caused strategic confusion regarding deterrence postures up to the 1973 war. This confusion accounted for the lack of clear planning and execution of the war plans during the initial phases of the war. In this sense, the return of the Sinai to Egypt represents a net security gain even if the Egyptians decide to violate the peace treaty at some future point. It provides Israel with a clear indication of war preparations because the Egyptians must cross the entire Sinai desert with large forces before attacking, and this would give Israel sufficient time to mobilize reserves. It would also give Israel a legitimate justification for a first strike because, once the demilitarization of the Sinai had been violated, Israel lacks strategic depth.

But the West Bank and the Gaza Strip, being heavily populated territories, compound the strategic problems of lack of adequate warning and constraints on first-strike strategies. First, any war in those territories is conducted in external lines due to the hostile population. Israeli strategy must consider the possibility that its forces will be confronted by civil strife and guerrilla operations of the Palestinian population during a war. Moreover, the Jewish settlements in the territories are unable to defend themselves even from the local Palestinians, let alone from regular Arab forces. This implies that the IDF will have to engage in two activities that considerably diminish its power during war: the evacuation of the Jewish settlements and the maintenance of order or—more seriously—the suppression of revolts of the Palestinians. The occupied territories, being under the judicial responsibility of the Israeli army, cannot be considered as a kill zone during war in which every resistance to the army is seen as an act of war even if committed by civilian population. The constraints imposed on combat operations within the occupied territories do not apply to cases where these territories are under enemy jurisdiction before the war breaks out.

But numbers are more telling than any story about national security. The more secure you are, the less you need to invest in defending yourself against your enemy. If the territories, in and of themselves, provided Israel extra security that it did not have before the Six Day War, then the need to rely on a large army would diminish. Yet, paradoxically, since the end of the Six Day War the Israeli army has doubled in size. The length of the compulsory service period was increased from two years and two months to three years for males and from one and a half years to two years for women. The share of the defense budget in the GNP went up from an average of 10 percent in the 1957–67 period to an average of 25 percent in the 1968–1988 period. Table 9.1 shows some relevant before-after comparisons of Israel's military capabilities.

This table makes it clear that the territories added considerably to the burden of defense in that the amount of hardware and human resources required to protect them were without parallel to what had existed prior to the war. Of course, Israel's enemies did not spend the time relaxing under their grapevines; their armies grew at about the same rate as did the Israeli army. But if territory is a measure of extra security, they had a good reason for doing so; Israel did not. What is even more disturbing is that nine years of peace have passed between Israel and Egypt. The most powerful opponent of Israel seems to be out of the immediate conflict picture. Not only has this not changed the pattern of Israeli military spending, there seems to be no relief in sight.

But the Palestinians can cause more problems during peace than they can cause during times of war. The Israeli economy is so dependent on Arab labor that a prolonged general strike could devastate the Israeli

**Table 9.1** Israel's military capabilities before and after the 1967 war

| Indicator | Before 1967 | | After 1967 | |
|---|---|---|---|---|
| | 1956 | 1967 | 1974 | 1988 |
| Military personnel | 200,000 | 250,000 | 415,000 | 554,000 |
| Number of armored brigades | 4 | 7 | 10 | 33 |
| Number of tanks | 360 | 1,200 | 2,500 | 3,600 |
| Number of airplanes | 200 | 500 | 700 | 1,000 |
| Combat aircraft | 160 | 350 | 466 | 629 |
| Number of ships | 13 | 27 | 68 | 90 |
| Warships | 4 | 16 | 48 | 67 |
| Period | 1955–61 | 1962–66 | 1967–72 | 1974–80 |
| Defense expenditures/GNP | 0.083 | 0.101 | 0.217 | 0.278 |

*Sources:* SIPRI; U.S. Arms Control and Disarmament Agency (1978), Berglas (1986: 176).
*Note:* Defense expenditures as percentage of GNP averaged 0.25 over the period 1981–1987.

economy. It must be noted that it is not the sheer number of Arab laborers that accounts for the potential damage. Rather, it is the concentration of Arab labor in key economic areas that is important. Most of the menial construction force in Israel is Arab; the same applies to the menial workers in agriculture.[4] A general strike during the orange season or in the construction industry could cause tremendous losses. The cost of the first five months of civil unrest in the occupied territories, strictly in terms of military expenditures needed to maintain order and suppress the revolt, was $32.5 million, or about $215,000 a day.[5] The Arab revolt causes a major strategic damage to the army. It takes many army units away from their training schedule, forces the army to extend the mobilization period of reservists, and causes demoralization of the troops, which assume increasingly the role of police forces instead of combat units.

It is instructive to examine Israel's strategic history in comparative perspective. In 1956 Israel occupied the entire Sinai peninsula from Egypt. One of the key pretexts for the Sinai war had been the endless number of infiltrations from the Gaza Strip to Israel of Palestinian guerrillas. Due to combined Soviet-American pressure, Israel was forced to withdraw from the Sinai in 1957. Between 1957 and 1967, there were almost no border incidents involving Israel and Egypt, virtually no infiltrations to Israel. Even the outbreak of the Six Day War was a result of unintended escalation, rather than a culmination of some strategic design to destroy Israel. Following the Six Day War and the acquisition of territories, Israel fought three additional wars, none of them resulting in a clear and unequivocal victory. In fact, not only did the territories not improve Israeli performance, they actually reduced it. They increased the frustration, and thus the willingness to take risks, of Israel's main adversaries.

Probably the biggest damage caused by the Israeli insistence on holding on to the territories was in terms of Israel's international standing. The image of Israel as a weak state surrounded by powerful adversaries was over time gradually converted into an image of occupier and oppressor of the stateless Palestinian people. The Israelis were converted from Davids to Goliaths and the Palestinians gained the image of the Jews of the Middle East. This becomes especially clear in the kind of resolutions adopted by the U.N. General Assembly since 1974, among them the labeling of Zionism as racism. Even in the United States, where support for Israel among Jews and non-Jews has been very high historically, this support has started to erode significantly.[6]

The key issue in current Israeli political debates is whether there exist Arab leaders who want to make peace with it. The cost of the maintenance of the occupied territories has been, until recently, swept under the rug. But now it seems that the issue of the price of victory cannot be ignored. The future question facing Israel will not be whether there exists someone with whom to make peace. Rather, it might be how to get rid of the fruits of the biggest victory in that nation's history.

## Conclusion

The principal lesson of this chapter is that when leaders call upon their citizens to join forces in order to fight the enemy, people should ask not only "What happens if we lose?" but also, "What happens if we win?" This chapter suggests that the cost of victory should be analyzed as closely as the cost of defeat, because sometimes the former might be higher and more painful than the latter.

In analyzing what victory implies, attention should be given to the relations between military victory and political outcomes. Victory should be assessed not only in terms of the sacrifices required to accomplish it but also in terms of the cost of maintaining it once it is accomplished. The implications of territorial or other political acquisitions should be studied closely not only in terms of how much they add to our current possessions, but also in terms of how much damage they can cause. But it must be stressed forcefully that the issues discussed in this chapter are genuine paradoxes in that awareness of the perils of victory does not solve the problem. What is the alternative? Should nations fight to lose wars? Although the next chapter indicates that sometimes this might not be such a bad idea, I clearly do not want to suggest a general rule. Once one is in a war, victory is certainly more likely than defeat to accomplish one's goals. The point of the present chapter is that the victory is not the be all and end all of war. It pays to plan to live with victory because even if its fruits turn out to be spoiled, and even if there is little or nothing that can be done to prevent it, there might be ways of diminishing the bitter taste of victory—not by giving up the idea of winning, but perhaps by winning less to get more.

## Notes

1   This statement was made following the Epirian victory over the Roman army at Ausculum, which had been accomplished at tremendous losses to the Epirians.

2   It is important to note that this combination of preference structures is in no way general. For example, some winners, acting upon sentiments of revenge and out of deep hate for the loser, may prefer the outcome wherein the loser supplements its military defeat by political capitulation over the mutual compromise outcome. The result of that version of the game would still be the same, namely, mutual defection. And it would still be a collectively-inferior outcome to the mutual compromise one.

3   The principal source for this section is Sella and Yishai (1986). The first version of this section was written in May 1988, five months into the Palestinian uprising, known as the *intifada* (awakening). The final version was completed in December 1988, at the time of the U.S. decision to open negotiations with the PLO.

4   Sella and Yishai (1986: 182–184) show that the territories' labor force rose from 0.5 percent of the Israeli labor force in 1968 to 5.9 percent in 1979. They further show that Palestinian laborers accounted for an average of more than 50 percent of the total construction workers. They do point out, however, that over the years the economy of the occupied territories became highly dependent on the Israeli economy.

5   These figures are based on the defense ministry's request of a supplementary budget for the first five months of the intifada. This does not include economic costs caused by the absenteeism of Arab workers from their Israeli jobs, or the opportunity cost of training that is induced by the need to increase the army's presence in the occupied territories. If these figures are representative of the subsequent May–December 1988 period, then the intifada cost Israel over $78 million in additional defense spending over its already amazingly large defense budget.

6   A good analysis of the erosion of support for Israel in American public opinion is given in Gilboa (1987).

# 10
## Loser's Paradoxes:
## The View from the Pit

Out of the eater came something to eat
Out of the strong came something sweet. (Judges, 14:14).

This chapter focuses on the loser's (mis)fortune. It discusses two paradoxes. One is that awareness of defeat does not help the would-be loser cut down its costs; rather, it may actually contribute to them. This is the sunk-cost paradox. The second is the loser's fortune paradox: losing a war can do a nation a lot of good.

The sunk-cost paradox goes as follows. A nation enters a war hoping that it will win. Its assessment of the likelihood of victory is typically a function of the duration of the war and the costs incurred thus far. At some point, the duration and the costs of war lead the leaders of that nation to realize that it is going to lose the war. The time that has elapsed between the beginning of the war and the point where the realization of defeat has set in is the "optimistic" period. The period between the realization of defeat and the end of the war is the "pessimistic" period. The sunk-cost paradox is that it takes more time and more casualties to end a war once one knows it is lost than it takes to realize that one is going to lose. In some cases, realization of defeat prolongs the end of war and makes it more costly than what led up to the realization that victory is beyond reach.

The second paradox is the loser's fortune. It explores how the worst defeats in a nation's history can become the springboards of major economic and political development processes that supersede not only those that had characterized that nation's history, but also those of the winner. The causal element here is of special importance because it sheds light on both the benefit of defeat and the adverse consequences of victory. The importance of the loser's paradox is that it must lead us to a thorough reassessment of the utility of war as a political instrument. I am not dealing here with side effects, those implications of war that arise without the expressed will of any of the participants. Rather, what is at issue here is the whole ends-means logic that sees victory as the rationale for fighting; it is also the same logic that views defeat as the outcome one must spend a lot of resources and spill a lot of blood in order to avoid.

## The Paradox of Sunk Costs

This section shows how an actor can accumulate tremendous losses not because it mistakenly thinks it can win, but because it correctly expects to lose. In its efforts to minimize the costs of defeat, it actually acts to maximize them. One of the processes leading to this paradox has already been discussed in the analysis of unintended wars using the Dollar Auction game. Here I show that the same logic that got the players into a trap that neither desired keeps both of them in it against their will much after they realize there is nothing to gain.

To reiterate, the Dollar Auction is a game where two or more players are asked to bid for a dollar. The dollar is sold to the highest bidder for the price of the bid. The second-highest bidder, however, pays his or her bid and gets nothing in return. This game is typically used, as it was above, to model entrapment and unwanted escalation. Here I use the same game to model entrapment of a different sort. This entrapment shows why people stay in messes of their own doing despite the fact they know there is nothing to gain from continued bidding. This problem differs from the one posed by the classical Dollar Auction in two ways. First, the starting point is not the beginning of the auction but the middle of it. There are two people in the trap.[1] Second, contrary to the original formulation of the problem, this version allows for communication among players. At each point of the game the players can talk to each other; they can threaten each other or make promises, coordinate their moves, and so on. The only constraint is that when they are done talking, each must return to a corner and the player who has the next move must write his or her decision on a card. The decision is, as in the original version, to drop out of the game or to specify a new bid. This implies that there is no mechanism to enforce an agreement. A player can agree to divide the dollar that he or she gets with the other player, but there is no mechanism to guarantee it.

Suppose that the bidding goes way beyond the dollar, and the players already realize where this is leading. Let us also assume that the players have different bankrolls, and that both know what their bankrolls are. Once past the dollar, the parties know that the next and final barrier in that process is the bankroll of the least affluent. They also realize that the poor winner in the game is the richer actor who will remain with the difference between his or her bankroll and that of the opponent plus 95 cents (given that the bidding is done in 5-cent increments).

If communication is allowed, players can agree that whoever is given the next move will bid $1.55 and the other will quit. The dollar that is given back to the lucky winner will be split such that the highest bidder gets 52 cents and the lowest bidder gets the remaining 48 cents. In this case, each ends up losing only $1.02 instead of the whole bankroll of the would-be loser.[2] We can present the problem as a 2 × 2 game where each actor has two options: to quit or to continue the bidding. This game is given in Figure 10.1.

This is just a continuous version of the infamous Prisoner's Dilemma game.[3] Each defection at one point in time becomes the basis for subsequent agreement. And each agreement is worse for the parties than the previous one. Yet, no matter whose turn it is to move, one is always better off not agreeing than agreeing to terminate. Moreover, without a mechanism to enforce an agreement, the actor who gets the dollar has no incentive to give half of it to the opponent (not even a cent of it), hence, the opponent would be stupid to strike a deal when it is not his or her turn to make a bid.

To understand the kind of trap that is at work here, let us engage in what game theorists call *backward induction*, that is, reasoning back from the last point of the game to the first one. In the last iteration, the player with the $21.00 bids $20.05. The other player cannot counter this bid because he is out of money. So $j$ is the "winner," losing only $19.05 compared to the loss of $20.00 for the "loser." Of course, $j$ would be stupid to accept (or respect) an agreement offered to him by $i$ for anything that would entail a loss greater than $19.05. So an agreement whereby she loses $20.50 is unacceptable to her and $i$ knows that. The inescapable conclusion is that if they reach this stage, $j$'s bid of $20.05 is certain to be made. The last move is therefore known and can be dropped from further analysis. In the next to last move, $i$ has the option of stopping at $19.95 or bidding $20.00. No matter what $j$ will do in his turn, $i$ is better off bidding (and not keeping any agreement that was reached) than not bidding. If $j$ is expected to stop, $i$ is better off bidding (and not respecting the agreement) because he is going to lose only $18.95 without an agreement as opposed to $19.45 with an agreement. This process of backward induction goes on from the last move to the one we are in at present. The only thing to do is to continue bidding until you reach the tragic end.

Each agreement between the players seems a neat way out of a big problem. The trouble is that it is difficult to make it work. If the highest bidder gets the whole dollar, she would be stupid to give half of it to the second-highest bidder. The second-highest bidder cannot threaten

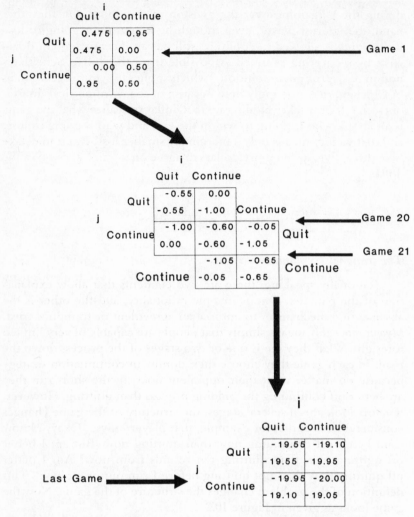

**Figure 10.1**  The Sunk-Cost Paradox—The Myopic Perspective

to continue bidding, because he has withdrawn already. Knowing that, the two players might spend a lot of time debating over who will be the last bidder, and even more on assurances that the highest bidder will transfer the required sum to the opponent. Unless such assurances can be given, it is difficult to make any agreement stick.

The unequal stakes make matters worse. The player with the higher bankroll knows that she is going to "win" if the game is allowed to continue because she can still afford to bid when the opponent runs out of money. Hence, she may wish to make use of that advantage during the bargaining over the division of the dollar. On the other hand, the inferior player, even though he knows he is going to lose if the game is allowed to continue, still has an incentive to cut down costs by recovering as much as possible from the dollar. Schelling's notion of a "prominent solution," which applies to symmetrical games of Chicken, may not apply here because of the asymmetrical disaster outcome. It only takes bidding up to a dollar to realize what the game is all about, who is going to win in the end and who is going to lose, and that victory means only a marginally smaller loss. But it may take two, three, five, or ten more dollars to agree on a "fair" division of the dollar.[4]

## Explanations of the Sunk-Cost Paradox

### The Rational Explanation

Rationally speaking, there are two elements that allow explanation of the paradox. One is myopic rationality, and the other is the absence of a mechanism to enforce an agreement or to induce trust. *Myopic rationality* means simply that people are capable of very limited foresight. What they see is one or two stages of the process down the road. In each game they choose their dominant continuation strategy because no matter what their opponent does, in the short run they are better off continuing the bidding process than quitting. However, if actors look ahead several stages, the structure of the game changes considerably. Assume, for example, that player $i$ says, "Okay, I know I am better off continuing now than quitting now. But am I better off quitting now than quitting ten rounds from now? Am I better off quitting now than not quitting before I run out of money?" This definition of the problem changes the structure of the game. Now the game looks as given in Figure 10.2.

This kind of reasoning suggests that if $i$ continues bidding now, the process will end in a huge loss at the end. The continuation alternative does not dominate the quitting alternative. In fact, if $i$ is the second bidder, with his turn to make a choice, he cannot improve the payoff he gets now unless he has good reason to believe that $j$ will quit too. So, as O'Neill (1986) has shown, if you can reason forward and see how the game ends, the sooner you quit, the better. If you fail to see the final outcome, you stay in and lose. Since the game upon which the paradox is predicated is sequential Chicken, it has a simple solution. No matter how much was spent thus far, once an actor realizes the game he is playing, he should quit the minute his turn arrives. If he

$$j$$

|  | QUIT | CONTINUE |
|---|---|---|
| QUIT | −1.025<br><br>−1.025 | −0.55<br><br>−1.5 |
| CONTINUE | −1.5<br><br>−0.55 | −19.05<br><br>−20.00 |

*i* appears to the left, between the QUIT and CONTINUE row labels.

**Figure 10.2**　The Sunk-Cost Paradox—A Long-Range Perspective

does not, the next time around he will reach the very same dilemma, only with substantially more sunk cost at each iteration. But here lies the catch. Unlike a simple case of sequential Chicken, bidding in the game means that an actor transfers the game from an inferior equilibrium, which does her in, to a superior one, which does the other in. The game is played by moving the imaginary pegs along the two off-diagonal (equilibrium) cells.

In plain English, each bid by an actor represents an attempt to impose a choice dilemma on the opponent. The same applies to an agreement about division of the dollar among the poor bidders. Unless there exists an external mechanism for forcing agreements, each actor wants to be the last to bid so that he will get the dollar, and let the opponent worry about whether the agreement will be carried out or not.

The key to the solution of the paradox of sunk costs lies in Maoz and Felsenthal's (1987) notion of self-binding commitment. The actor whose turn it is to move next should deposit the 48 cents to be transferred to the opponent to a third party before his move. Once the other player declares she is out, this money goes to her and the dollar goes to the former player. This way, an agreement can be made credible and both players are out of the mess. The difficulties of making such an agreement are many, and therefore its feasibility is not a simple matter, as these authors argue.

## The Cognitive Explanation

When one climbs a high tree and suddenly discovers that the branches are becoming dangerously thin, and that they begin to crack under one's feet, going down slowly by stepping on branches that are already weakened might be more dangerous than jumping off the tree.

Yet, for a variety of reasons, people may prefer risking a slow climb down over an immediate jump. Worse, once one discovers that the branch on which one stands begins to crack, the tendency is to freeze in place rather than to jump down.

Two reasons for the sunk-cost paradox are worth mentioning. The first one is that admission of total defeat arouses strong cognitive conflict because it suggests that entering the war was stupid to begin with. This conflict is especially acute for decision makers who had genuinely believed that they are going into the war in order to win. Jumping down from the tree is equivalent to acknowledging that starting the climb was a stupid move. In policy settings, getting out of a war is akin to admitting that there was no sense in entering it in the first place. The typical strategy of coping with such a cognitive conflict is a gradual modification of beliefs, or their substitution by notions that imminent defeat can be converted into less than a total disaster if at least some of the national investment can be salvaged. This can be done only by staying a little longer—but staying a little longer means extra costs.[5]

Related to this is the notion that national decision makers are conservative in terms of their choices. This conservatism stems from the commitment they have to their prior policies. It often takes a different government to take a nation out of a war it had started because the old government was too committed to its old policy to admit failure even when it saw it. This commitment prevents sharp departures from previous policies even when decision makers realize that previous policies were counterproductive. Whether politicians feel that they have personal stakes in the outcome of the war and hence suppress perceptions of failure, or whether they feel that the admission of failure would damage the national interest, the result is the same: a very gradual erosion in the war aims, typically starting from victory, going through honorable withdrawal, the maintenance of the status quo ante, and ending with a rushed exit at any cost.

The cognitive explanation suggests two related biases, both of which cause delayed and costly exits from bad wars. The first is delayed realization of defeat. Like a husband whose wife has cheated on him, the would-be loser is the last to know that it is going to lose. The second is that commitment to prior policies even in the face of much discrepant evidence causes delay in activity leading to an early exit. These biases serve to slow the realization of defeat, but they do not explain why actors fail to quit the game once the realization of defeat finally sets in. Commitment to prior policy is often seen as a valued political asset. Decision makers may wish to stay consistent because consistency seems to be a respected norm; one does not want to be perceived as a person who changes one's views every other day (Maoz, 1989: ch. 5).

The normative premium decision makers place on consistency suggests that what is important is not beliefs but rather public image. Decision makers might sometimes become trapped by their own rhetoric. Indeed, Brockner and Rubin (1985) and Teger (1980) suggest that commitment to an image of consistency is what renders players in the Dollar Auction reluctant to leave the game. Debriefed subjects in games of entrapment often pointed out that they could not just reverse their behavior out of the blue. They sought ways in which they could gracefully withdraw.

Changes of strategy on the margin (policies of gradualism) are thus seen as stemming not from some cognitive imperfections that cause systematic deficiencies in decision-making processes (Maoz, 1989: ch. 5), but rather from political factors. Because sharp departures from previous policies raise serious questions about the wisdom of the current move or about the wisdom of the previous policy that had been pursued for a long time, political entrapment puts decision makers into a no-win situation. They realize they are in a trap, but they cannot afford to quit it at once.

## The Art of Recovering Sunk Costs in Wars

By definition, long wars drag on because the parties cannot reach a military decision in a major battle. Without a decision on the battlefield, wars turn out to be a duel of wills, and victory is determined by who is capable of sustaining the costs associated with continued warfare for a longer time (Rosen, 1972; Maoz, 1982a). It is not implausible that actors at some point realize how the war is developing and wish to get out of it but for a variety of reasons cannot do so. However, actually showing the sunk-cost paradox in action is not a trivial task. First, actors usually do not admit that they are going to be defeated even if they know that they are. Such an admission implies also that a nation has grown used to the idea that it is willing to submit to the opponent's demands without arguing. Second, it is not easy to show that what prolongs the war and increases its cost is the fact that states are driven by the desire to recover sunk costs, despite the implicit admission of defeat. Finally, there are some near-miss cases of sunk-cost paradoxes, cases that would have been very interesting to analyze in terms of the variables suggested by the various versions of the paradox, but do not quite make it.

The Iran-Iraq war seems to be a case in point. The war lingered for years without any light at the end of the tunnel. At first, the Iraqis had the advantage, then the Iranians gained the upper hand. For several years the Iraqis seemed to have been on the defensive, fighting to keep the city of Basra out of Khomeini's hands. Saddam Hussein was not willing to relinquish power in Iraq as Khomeini demanded, nor did Khomeini want to give up his hope of toppling the Ba'ath regime in Iraq. In February 1988, the tide of battle changed yet another time. The Iraqis started a general offensive in the northeast region and reoccupied what they had lost in the past and then some. At that point the Iranians decided to accept the U.N.-sponsored cease-fire that they had turned down flatly a year before. While this looks like a strong candidate for a sunk-cost paradox, it does not quite make it. Beliefs about victory and defeat seem to have switched from one side to the other too many times in the course of the war to satisfy the logic of the paradox.[6]

The two cases discussed below, the Vietnam War and the 1982–1985 Lebanon war are interesting in more than the loser's paradox sense. In both cases it was the stronger nation that lost the war. These wars also happened to be the longest in the histories of the losers, dragging on partly because of the processes that are involved in the sunk-cost paradox.

To show a sunk-cost paradox in a historical context, several things must be established. First, one must demonstrate an awareness by the ruling elite of the would-be loser that the war cannot be won and might be lost. Second, this awareness must emerge at a point in the war that is less than halfway between the starting date of the war and its termination. Third, the number of casualties of the would-be loser up to that point must be smaller than half the total number of casualties it suffered throughout the war. Fourth, it must be shown that a gradual goal-modification process had been going on in the minds of the loser's leaders. Indeed, it must be shown that the whole effort of the war from the point that awareness of future defeat set in to the end of the war was on recovering sunk costs in terms of accomplishing some of the original goals of the war. Finally, to make this a really Machiavellian case, the outcome the loser got at the end of the war was feasible all along. It was the would-be loser who refused to accept it, and that is why the war lingered on and on.

## An Honorable Solution:
## America's Painful Exit from Vietnam[7]

January 1969 marked the entry of the Nixon administration into office, following an emotional election campaign in which the Vietnam War played a prominent role. The newly appointed national security adviser observed:

When we came into office over a half-million Americans were fighting a war ten thousand miles away. Their numbers were still increasing on a schedule established by our predecessors. We found no plans for withdrawals. Thirty-one thousand had already died. Whatever our original war aims, by 1969 our credibility abroad, the reliability of our commitments, and our domestic cohesion were alike jeopardized by a struggle in a country as far away from the North American continent as our globe permits. . . . by 1969 our country had been riven by protest and anguish, sometimes taking on a violent and ugly character. The comity by which a democratic society must live had broken down. No government can function without a minimum of trust. This was being dissipated under the harshness of our alternatives and the increasing rage of the domestic controversy. . . .

The Nixon administration entered office determined to end our involvement in Vietnam. But it soon came up against the reality that had also bedeviled its predecessor. For nearly a generation the security and progress of free peoples had depended on confidence in America. We could not simply walk away from an enterprise involving two administrations, five allied countries, and thirty-one thousand dead as if we were switching a television channel. Many urged us to "emulate de Gaulle"; but they overlooked that it took even de Gaulle four years to extricate his country from Algeria because he, too, thought it important for France to emerge from its travails with its domestic cohesion and international stature intact. He extricated France from Algeria as an act of policy, not as a collapse, in a manner reflecting a national decision and not a rout.

Such an ending of the war was even more important for the United States. As the leader of democratic alliances we had to remember that scores of countries and millions of people relied for their security on our willingness to stand by allies, indeed on our confidence in ourselves. No serious policymaker could allow himself to succumb to the fashionable debunking of "prestige" or "honor" or "credibility." . . . Clearly, the American people wanted to end the war, but every poll, and indeed Nixon's election (and the Wallace vote), made it equally evident that they saw their country's aims as honorable and did not relish America's humiliation. The new administration had to respect the concerns of the opponents of the war but also the anguish of the families whose sons had suffered and died for their country and who did not want it determined—after the fact—that their sacrifice had been in vain. (Kissinger, 1979: 226–228)

With this statement by the architect of the peace agreement and the termination of American involvement in Vietnam, and some few basic facts about the war, it seems that I could rest my case. The facts are the following. First, the realization of defeat in Vietnam has a very specific date: March 31, 1968. This was the date of Lyndon Johnson's address to the nation that called for a unilateral halt to the bombing of North Vietnam and for direct U.S.-North Vietnam talks. Almost in the same breath, Johnson announced that he would not run for a second term of office. One can hardly expect a more direct admission of defeat than this statement. Second, March 31, 1968, marked the 1,334th day of the undeclared U.S. war against Vietnam, a war that started on August 5, 1964, with the first American bombing of North Vietnam following the Gulf of Tonkin incident. The signing of the Paris agreement on January 27, 1973, marked the 3,141st day of U.S. involvement in the war. It took less time to realize that victory could not be accomplished in Vietnam than it actually took to end the war. The same applies to casualties. By March 31, 1968, 20,054 American soldiers had been killed in the war. By the end of the war, more than 54,000 Americans had lost their lives as a result of the conflict. At the date of the cease-fire, January 28, 1973, the last "official" American soldier, the 46,491st fatality, met his maker. By the time the last American troops left South Vietnam (March 29, 1973), this number mounted to 48,000 (Isaacs, 1983: 8).[8]

Hence, both the time it took the United States to realize that it is going to lose the war and the casualties on which this realization was based were less than the time and casualties it took to actually get out of Vietnam. The struggle for values of "honor" and "credibility" might have meant something if the agreement signed eventually with North Vietnam and the assurances the United States gave the Thieu regime in South Vietnam were worth more than the paper on which the states had signed. In that case, one could argue that the extra five years of fighting and the extra 34,000 American fatalities would not have been in vain. The way it turned out, with or without the benefit of hindsight, the argument that the Nixon administration could not ignore the concern of the families whose sons had died is extremely cynical. Was it necessary to sacrifice an additional 23,000 American soldiers between 1969 and 1973 so that the death of the 31,000 soldiers who had already been sacrificed when Nixon took office would not be in vain?

Of course, the answer to this question is that in 1969 no one could have known how long and how many more casualties it would take to end the war. Nixon and Kissinger's argument was that from the start of their tenure in office they sought a fair and rapid negotiated settlement. The problem was that the North Vietnamese were not willing to grant a settlement that would give a fighting chance to Thieu's regime. The United States could not afford to abandon Thieu. Worse, the United

States could not afford, for global reasons, to withdraw from Vietnam with its tail between its legs. The whole effort had been toward putting pressure on North Vietnam to make concessions that would allow the United States to show that it got something out of its involvement in the conflict.

For that reason, the administration stepped up military operations while maneuvering both in Paris and in Saigon, trying to extract concessions from both its opponent and its ally. On March 18, 1969, Nixon ordered a bombing mission of North Vietnamese bases in Cambodia, setting a new pattern in the war that peaked with the April 1971 invasion of Cambodia. On April 4, 1972, the United States resumed the massive bombing of North Vietnam (especially the Hanoi-Haiphong area) and on May 8, Nixon ordered the mining of North Vietnam's ports. The main objective of the escalation process was to induce the North Vietnamese to make substantial concessions in Paris. However, the negotiations had been stalled—for all practical purposes—since October 1968 due to the insistence of North Vietnam that any settlement would have to include the end of the Thieu regime in the south. This was viewed by the administration as amounting to American abandonment of an ally.

A major principle of the phased withdrawal of American troops was the so-called Vietnamization policy. This policy was designed to prepare the South Vietnamese army to carry the whole burden of the war if it continued, while phasing out American military participation in the war and gradually shifting it to financial and advisory assistance to the South Vietnamese army. Indeed, American involvement was reduced markedly, from the peak of 543,000 American soldiers in 1969 to 474,000 in December the same year, to 335,800 in December 1970, to 184,000 American soldiers in December 1971, and, finally, to a low of 29,000 in December 1972 (Kolko, 1985: 610–611).

This inducement process eventually bore some fruit. On September 11, 1972, North Vietnam made the first serious proposal that accepted Thieu's continuation in power, though it insisted on an immediate removal of all American personnel from South Vietnam. After some diplomatic and military maneuvering (including a vicious American bombardment of the Hanoi-Haiphong area, on December 18–30, 1972), the peace treaty was finally signed. The negotiation process is a story in itself, especially the latter part, but the bottom line is that the treaty that the United States got in January 1973 was almost the same as one it could have signed in October 1972, and very similar to one it could have accomplished a good couple of years before. What had happened in the interim was that the North Vietnamese had indeed modified their positions, but—more important—that the United States basically was willing to sign a treaty that provided no clear political guarantees to the Thieu regime. The United States almost literally shoved the treaty down Thieu's throat while providing him vague promises of aid in case of treaty violation. Tuchman's (1984: 373) assessment of the peace treaty is much harsher:

> In the final treaty, the two conditions for which North Vietnam and the United States had prolonged the war for four years—overthrow of Thieu's regime on the one hand and removal of North Vietnam's forces from the south on the other—were abandoned; political status of the old Viet-Cong, now metamorphosed onto the PRG, was acknowledged, though to spare Thieu's feelings not explicitly; the DMZ or partition line, whose elimination Hanoi had demanded, was retained but—going back to Geneva [1954]—as a "provisional not a political or territorial boundary." The Unity of Vietnam was implicitly recognized in an article providing that "The unification of Vietnam shall be carried out" by peaceful discussion among the parties, thereby relegating "external aggression" across an "international boundary"—America's casus belli for so many years—to the dustbin of history.

The irony of all this is that when the credibility issue was invoked by the joint North Vietnamese-Khmer Rouge invasion of Cambodia and by the North Vietnamese invasion of the south in 1975, the United States failed miserably to meet even its least costly promise to its ally, a commitment for which it had fought a wasteful and costly war for eight and a half years.

The characteristics of the war management process and the negotiation process during the Nixon administration superbly fit the logic of the sunk-cost paradox. There is a clear realization of imminent loss, a clear commitment to termination of the war, but a parallel pressure, stemming from both internal and external sources, to recover some of the sunk costs. This trade-off between the wish to quit and the wish to recover sunk costs is what the paradox is all about. It causes a gradual deescalation of the involvement in war in terms of numbers and a parallel effort at negotiation. However, to convince the opponent that one is not quite ready to quit at any cost, military operations continue whose primary function now is not to reach a military decision on the battlefield but to score points at the bargaining table. The aim of this strategy is both to demonstrate resolve and to increase the cost of continued intransigence for the opponent.

The catch is, of course, that such a strategy has also the strange side effect of causing substantial losses for its initiator. During the infamous "Christmas bombing" of December 1972, over 100 American soldiers died and about the same number were taken prisoner. In addition, at least fifteen B-52 bombers were destroyed. Since the would-be loser is already exhausted internally by casualties and its government faces strong moral opposition to the war in general, this strategy causes reduced resolve of the initiator more than it causes weakening of the opponent. Of course, it brings the would-be loser far closer to the maximum price it is willing to pay for remaining in the war. Indeed, Kissinger (1979: 1467) himself questions whether the Christmas bombing produced any significant changes in the agreement whose first draft had been discussed in October 1972:

> Was it [the January 23, 1973, draft agreement] worth it? Were the changes significant enough to justify the anguish and bitterness of those last months of the war? Probably not for us; almost surely for Saigon, about whose survival the war had, after all, been fought. Obviously, we thought the agreement of October adequate or we would not have proceeded with it. But the viability of any agreement depends on the willing cooperation of the parties. Once Thieu balked, we were doomed to what actually followed. We could not in all conscience end a war on behalf of the independence of South Vietnam by imposing an unacceptable peace on our ally. Had we attempted to do so in the last two weeks before the election, we would have been justly accused of playing politics with the destiny of millions. And the attempt would have failed. As it was, it required nearly three months, about twenty changes in the text of the agreement, and the threat of an American aid cutoff to obtain Thieu's acquiescence.

The problem was not North Vietnamese intransigence, nor was it a belief in the Nixon administration that only a massive show of resolve would bring about major concessions at the bargaining table. Rather, the problem all along, it seems, had been getting a reluctant ally to accept a treaty that it thought bad even when it was forced to sign it.

This is a typical form of entrapment behavior. The trade-off that produces this paradox is also a cause of erratic behavior on the part of the would-be loser. The two equally important goals pull it in different directions, intensifying escalatory tendencies at one time and deescalatory tendencies at other times. This kind of behavior only intensifies the entrapment process: it is neither consistently decisive to alter the military balance of power in the war (nor, for that matter, the balance of resolve, which is equally important for victory) nor sufficiently accommodative to make an agreement feasible at an early stage. The United States was trapped by its own commitments. These commitments produced further involvement. Continued involvement produced strong internal opposition to the war. Internal opposition to the war, as well as the psychological attrition of the decision-making elite, served to erode the initial commitments, while at the same time causing further losses. The upshot is that the exit from the war was under conditions that were either the same as or worse than those that could have been accomplished much before.

At least three separate schools of thought exist to explain the kind of behavior exhibited by the Nixon administration during the 1969–1973 period (which was fundamentally a continuation of the postreckoning period of the Johnson administration). The psychological school of thought focuses on the personalities of Nixon and Kissinger, the group dynamics that characterized the decision-making process, or the psychology of entrapment (Tuchman, 1984; Brockner and Rubin, 1985; Janis, 1982). The bureaucratic school of thought emphasizes organizational inertia, featuring gradualism and noncoordinated behavior as the primary characteristics of the process (Gelb and Betts, 1979; Allison and Halperin, 1972; Halperin, 1974). The rational approach looks at the dilemma from the perspective of an actor torn between its commitments and international image on the one hand and the domestic demands requiring it to put an end to the war on the other (Kissinger, 1979; Pillar, 1983).

It is difficult to assess which school of thought provides a better explanation of the kind of behavior exhibited by the United States during the 1969–1973 period. It seems that the value system of the Nixon administration did not allow immediate withdrawal from Vietnam, certainly not all-out abandonment of the Thieu regime. Yet, because these were the values that prevailed in Washington in 1969, the goal of an "honorable" end to the war that would guarantee the independence of South Vietnam was seen as necessary. Because of this goal, strategies had to be devised that were designed to compel the North Vietnamese to make significant concessions. This required escalation of the fighting, but domestic pressure required deescalation. This prompted the notion of Vietnamization and the gradual reduction of American troops in the area. The administration was in a no-win situation. All of its actions during the first term were compromises between conflicting and mutually exclusive tendencies.

Yet, the continuation of the war caused also considerable erosion in American commitment to its ally. This erosion first caused the United States to impose on the Thieu regime a treaty that it viewed as disastrous. It also caused the United States to fail to meet its military and economic commitments to the regime throughout the 1973–1975 period. Finally, when push came to shove, the Ford administration failed in convincing Congress of the need to reintervene in the war, or even of the need to provide emergency military assistance to South Vietnam. The fall of South Vietnam in 1975 signifies perhaps the greatest failure in American foreign policy in its two centuries of national independence. It took place precisely when the United States was the strongest nation on earth, and as such it is all the more astonishing. Yet, from our perspective, what is truly tragic is that if that were to be the end of the story, the American role in Vietnam could have ended at least five years earlier than it did and at least 26,000 American soldiers, not to mention hundreds of billion dollars, could have been saved.

## Coming to Sense:
### The Israeli Withdrawal from Lebanon, 1982–1985 [9]

In contrast to the Vietnam War, there was no specific point in time where one could pinpoint an Israeli reckoning of the defeat in the Lebanon war. In fact, most of the major players in the Israeli cabinet kept thinking (or at least made a public spectacle of the belief) that the war had been a great victory. Yet, the house of cards started its slow crash with the assassination of Bashir Gemayel on September 14, 1982, right after the evacuation of West Beirut by the Palestinians. The assassination forced the Israelis into West Beirut, immediately followed by the Sabra and Shatilla massacre, which started turning Israeli public opinion sharply against the war. This sequence of events also started the long entanglement of Israel in the Lebanese mess.

The irony of the whole thing is that it was precisely at the point where the Israeli administration was confident that the war had accomplished virtually all of its objectives that growing awareness of the magnitude of the mess started to infiltrate the minds of many people in Israel. The massive bombardment of West Beirut during the weeks of siege and the Sabra and Shatilla massacre began turning Israeli public opinion slowly away from the government. At that point (late September 1982), Israeli fatalities in the war stood below 200. By the time Israeli troops left Lebanon, nearly three years later, the body count was 666 dead and over 3,000 wounded. The realization that this war was slowly turning into defeat was one that came from below: from the Israeli public and from the parliamentary opposition. The Israeli government refused to admit failure. The first obvious sign of the magnitude of disaster was the resignation and retirement of Prime Minister Menachem Begin on August 27, 1983. But, as in the Vietnam case, it took a different government to get the country out of Lebanon; the government that put Israel in dragged its feet trying to salvage some of its investment, and—while doing it—sunk deeper into the mess.

Following the assassination of Gemayel, Israel started policing West Beirut and the Shouf area, which had been an arena of bitter conflict between Christians and Druzes. Israel soon found itself in a bind. The Christians were its allies, and in the Shouf area they were merely trying to preserve their possessions. The Druzes, who were threatened by the prospect of Christian domination under the Israeli umbrella, were trying to impose fait accomplis in the area. The Druze-Christian confrontation put the Israelis in the unpleasant position of a referee who is crushed by two fighters. To make matters worse, the Israeli Druzes, a minority with a long-standing loyalty to the state of Israel and a glorious record of participation in the Israeli army, started putting pressure on the government to get out of the Shouf area and let things settle there by themselves.

The patrolling of the Beirut area soon proved to be a major burden to the Israeli army. It required stationing of considerable forces, and created easy targets for Palestinian guerrillas. The government could not justify continued Israeli presence in Beirut and the Shouf area after the evacuation of the PLO, because the formal goal of the war was seemingly accomplished.

Politically, the Israeli government started intense negotiations with the newly established Lebanese government under the presidency of Amin Gemayel, Bashir's brother. After long maneuvering, a nonbelligerence agreement was signed on May 17, 1983. The joy regarding the agreement was, however, restricted to a small number of ministers in the government who still wanted to believe that the war had accomplished something. It soon became evident that the agreement was rendered meaningless the moment it was signed. First, the Lebanese government that had signed it had been and continued to be a fiction in a country that has been torn apart by civil war for the past nine years. Second, even the fictional government that had signed the treaty had no intention of abiding by it. Indeed, the Lebanese government announced that the agreement was null and void in less than a year after it had been signed. Against this background, the Israeli dilemma is explained by Yaniv (1987: 184–185):

> By the summer of 1983, . . . Israel was psychologically running out of steam. Although the government understood very well that resolve would be more logical strategically, politically it could not heed its own best judgment. The implication was that disengagement and a gradual lowered profile would quite soon be inescapable. The problem was complicated by the need to choose among three alternatives: withdrawal from the Beirut area and the troubled Shouf Mountains, withdrawal from the Beqa'a Valley where the IDF faced the Syrians, or withdrawal from both places simultaneously. A withdrawal from the Beirut area would extricate Israel from the maze of Lebanese politics and from the area where heavy casualties were suffered. On the other hand, . . . it would most probably doom the May 17 accord, the most tangible consequence of the war so far. . . . staying in Beirut and the Shouf while giving Syria an occasion

to celebrate a victory on account of an Israeli disengagement in the Beqa'a made no sense. Indeed the political stakes for Syria would remain as high as ever while its strategic position would be greatly improved. Thus, between staying in Beirut and the Shouf or staying in the Beqa'a, the latter alternative appeared far more logical.

But what about a complete withdrawal? Such a move would have been greatly welcomed by the Israeli left, including segments of the Labor party. For this reason alone such a move was totally unacceptable for a government led by Menachem Begin which had taken the country into this war in the first place. At the same time, the temptation to overstate this factor should be resisted since strategic logic alone, without any political and personal considerations, advised strongly against a hasty unilateral pullout. Anyone with even the most rudimentary military training and certainly any military historian would readily confirm that a retreat is the single most exacting military exercise. A retreat boosts the morale of the adversary while undercutting that of the retreating party. Whereas casualties and other costs in an advance may make some sense, casualties suffered in the course of a retreat inevitably appear as an unforgivable waste. In fact [retreat] creates nothing less than a built-in danger of collapse, even if the retreat is tactical and certainly if it is strategic.

Seen from this perspective, a complete, abrupt and unilateral Israeli withdrawal would make no sense even if ultimately there was no alternative and even if it was taken for granted that an orderly and phased-out withdrawal would entail heavy casualties. An abrupt, unilateral retreat could be assumed to lead to a dangerous vacuum in the areas to be vacated and subsequently to a return there of precisely those forces that Israel had attempted to drive away. . . . By a simple process of elimination, then, the most attractive (or rather, the least unattractive) alternative was a pullout from Beirut and the Shouf Mountains while maintaining the line in the Beqa'a.

Thus, much like the case of Vietnam, once the government implicitly realized the kind of bind it got itself into, it wanted out. Yet wanting out is one thing; getting out is quite another. The reasons underlying the strategy of gradualism were primarily strategic. But the same strategic logic that demanded gradual retreat was responsible for the intensification of the war of attrition between Israel's forces and the Shi'ite population in southern Lebanon, where from summer 1983 on, most of the Israeli troops were concentrated. The death toll in June 1983 was 345 Israeli soldiers dead, and over 1,500 soldiers wounded. Yet, the struggle to salvage something out of the war was at its peak.

Domestic factors started to play an important role toward the spring of 1983. In February of that year, the Kahan Inquiry Commission published its controversial report on the Sabra and Shatilla massacre. This report led to the forced resignation of the architect of the war, Defense Minister Ariel Sharon. But it also intensified public criticism of the government, putting pressure on it to find ways to end the continued IDF presence in Lebanon. The economic cost of the war could not be ignored. The Israeli presence in Lebanon was costing the country $650,000 a day in direct costs and $1.5 million a day in indirect costs.[10] Public ratings of the government's performance as satisfactory went down from 64 percent in September 1982 to a low of 47 percent in July 1983. Begin's personal popularity declined from 50 percent to 42.1 percent over the same period. Opposition to the government was beginning to be significant, not only qualitatively but quantitatively. Groups of reserve soldiers who had served in Lebanon started demonstrating at the prime minister's office, and increased pressure from within the standing army also became significant, as the army was bogged down in police activities in Lebanon instead of in training activities.

But rapid and general withdrawal would have not only demoralized the army; it would have been a clear admission that this war was a blunder from the start. It would have meant an end to the Likud government and its policies, not only in Lebanon but primarily its preposterous settlement policy in the West Bank. This was clearly a no-win situation for the government. Begin, the heroic and undisputed heavyweight champion of the Israeli right, realized this. But, characteristically, instead of admitting failure, he chose to resign on August 27, 1983, while letting his uncharismatic deputy Yitzhak Shamir take charge of the unpleasant task of cleaning up the mess that Begin and Sharon had created.

On September 4, 1983, Shamir implemented the first phase of the withdrawal, characteristically labeled "redeployment" in celebration of the coming year of 1984. The effect of this withdrawal was that the Shi'ite population in central and southern Lebanon started to concern itself with the seeming Israeli plan to create a strong Christian-dominated militia in southern Lebanon. As a result, Shi'ite resistance to the Israeli forces intensified significantly. The withdrawal from the Beirut and Shouf areas was a green light to a cautious return of Palestinian guerrillas to these areas, and, with the aid of the Shi'ite population in the south, the raids on Israeli targets in Lebanon intensified considerably.

At this point in the game, domestic factors changed the Israeli calculus considerably. A national election was called for May 1984, with the country entering into a political chaos that has tended to characterize recent preelection periods in Israel. This put the government on the defensive even more. Shoving aside growing demands from within the army to withdraw completely, it bitterly resisted any advocacy of rapid withdrawal before the elections. Notwithstanding the constant mounting of casualties, the worsening of the strategic situation in Lebanon (with the addition of the Shi'ites to the long list of enemies that Israel managed to make in Lebanon), the economic cost that became even more acute given the soaring inflation, the rapid decline in the foreign currency reserves, and the increased public criticism of the government, the Shamir administration was digging in its positions.

The 1984 elections led to a national unity government and a new prime minister, Shimon Peres, representing the Labor party. However, the role and weight of virtually all of those ministers who had led Israel into the war in the new cabinet was equal to that of the Labor contingent. As a result, the decision to withdraw completely from Lebanon took another six months, and the actual withdrawal yet another six months. In the interim, more than 150 Israeli soldiers were killed.

Even the decision to withdraw is difficult to explain in terms of strictly short-term rational calculations. In the absence of any assurances that the security of northern Israel would not be jeopardized by such a move, Israel was better off staying in southern Lebanon than withdrawing. Yet precisely because of this short-term strategic calculus, everyone else in the game kept fighting the Israelis. The decision to withdraw was in many ways a long shot. By withdrawing, the Israelis hoped to change the attitude of the Shi'ite population toward the Palestinian guerrillas. The gamble was that the Shi'ites, knowing that the Israelis would return in force if the Palestinians are allowed to return, would limit PLO activities in southern Lebanon. This gamble has worked for two years. Yet, even then, the Israelis kept a small force inside what they call a "security zone" in southern Lebanon that is a source of frustration and limits the effectiveness of the initial arrangement (Maoz and Felsenthal, 1987: 193–196).

## Lessons of the Sunk-Cost Paradox

The Israeli dilemma in the Lebanon war was in many respects similar to the American dilemma in the Vietnam War. It is also possible to show that similar dilemmas characterized the Soviet disaster in Afghanistan. The costs of attempts to recover sunk costs are sometimes greater than the initial costs themselves. And, of course, the harder the effort, the more cost is sunk, the more one is tempted to recover part of it, and the deeper one sinks into the muddy water of senseless warfare. A wide variety of factors contribute to this paradox, some of them external, some of them domestic, and some of them intrinsic to our psychological makeup.

The reputation of the state and the effect that a defeat would have on that image is a key factor in deepening a state's involvement in war far beyond the point of diminishing marginal returns. This is a typical tragedy of states that rely on deterrence of one form or another, because reputation is seen as a key determinant of the willingness and ability of the state to carry out its threat. In the case of Vietnam, the issue was the willingness and ability of the United States to aid a pro-Western ally in its struggle against the dark forces of communism. Because the whole network of extended deterrence is based on a projection of an image of resolve and capability when it comes to protecting weak allies, the United States had to keep the pressure on North Vietnam and find ways to get its ineffective and corrupt ally to defend itself on its own.

The Israelis had a similar problem of protecting a corrupt and ineffective ally in Lebanon, but that was a relatively minor part of the Israeli calculus. Israel's ability to deter its opponents is perceived by its leadership to rest on an image of effective recklessness. This implies a tendency to inflict disproportionately sharp and painful blows in reaction to small-scale provocations. The Israeli strategy of combating terrorism is an embodiment of this logic (Yaniv, 1986: 225–227). This was maintained by a constant notion of invincibility. The Israeli perception was that the first crack in that image was going to destroy or severely damage the effectiveness of its deterrent threat. The image of invincibility suffered a severe blow in the Yom Kippur war despite the convincing Israeli victory. This blow was seen by the Israeli leadership in 1982 to have a direct effect on the Syrian entry to Lebanon in 1976, and on the placement of Syrian antiaircraft missiles in the Beqa'a valley in the summer of 1981. This was one of the main incentives for attacking the Syrians in 1982, certainly for the destruction of their SAM missile sites during the war (Yaniv and Lieber, 1983). By the same token, the cease-fire agreement with the PLO in the summer of 1981 was seen as a major source of damage to Israel's deterrent reputation. When things started going sour in the conduct of the Lebanon war, calculations of the damage to the Israeli image of invincibility played a key role in the effort to recover sunk costs. The temptation to stay in the mess was particularly strong because of the clear advantage Israel had in capabilities. Yielding to the guerrilla pressure would mean that low-level combat could gradually erode Israeli resolve. This would lead to repeat performance of the PLO in other areas of the conflict, especially in the occupied territories.

The Soviet losing battle in Afghanistan displays almost identical patterns of behavior aimed at recovering sunk costs due to a deterrence posture vis-à-vis the East European states. While the strategic signifi-cance of Afghanistan to the Soviets is questionable, a reputation of resolve and invincibility was important if the Soviets were to deter efforts by their Eastern European allies to turn to the West. This policy of intervention had worked twice in the past: Hungary in 1956 and Czechoslovakia in 1968. However, in Afghanistan the Soviets met, for the first time in the history of the communist regime, with determined guerrillas. And in their case too, the confrontation proved too much.

In Vietnam and in the Lebanon case, domestic factors had a dual impact on the government's effort to recover sunk costs. It was the public that proved to be the smartest in the confrontation with the government: the antiwar movement in the United States and the antiwar movement in Israel were the first to realize that these wars could not be won. The more extreme factions of these two movements also realized that rapid unilateral exit from the mess would—in the long run—be a far better strategy than gradual disengagement because the latter strategy would lead to the same outcome at a higher cost. Undoubtedly, the pressure these movements put on their respective governments was instrumental in bringing about final exit from the conflicts. Yet, the activities of antiwar movements caused further entrenchment of the governments in their positions. The fact that success or failure in the war was identified with the success or failure of the government caused the government to justify the blood that had already been shed by gaining some of the stated aims of the war; in doing this, more blood was shed, and there was even more to justify. The criticism of the government, which grew sharper with time, had the effect of increasing entrenchment.

Finally, the people who made the decisions were thinking in terms of personal stakes that they had in the outcome of the conflict. Nixon and Kissinger, who were given a war they knew could not be won, came into office with the stated goal of finding an "honorable solution" to the conflict. The commitment to this goal was not only national, prompted by calculations of U.S. credibility, but also personal. To abandon this goal meant admitting that it had been preposterous all along. Ariel Sharon started the Lebanon war with only limited consensus; certainly, the expansion of the war beyond the 40-kilometer zone was not accompanied by widespread support, even in Begin's cabinet. Sharon had a lot of people whom he had to prove wrong, and their number grew as time went by. When Sharon resigned as minister of defense and Begin resigned as prime minister, Shamir's problem was similar to that of Nixon: he had to get the nation out of the losing battle started by his predecessors. However, in contrast to Nixon, Shamir also had a problem of split personality: he could not deviate sharply from the policy of his predecessors. First, Shamir had been a leading member of the cabinet that had started and expanded the war. Second, Shamir's own belief system made Begin's hawkish views appear moderate in comparison. A rapid withdrawal not only would have damaged Shamir's standing within his own party, it would have contradicted his deepest convictions. It takes extremely confident and powerful people to admit they were wrong. Neither of the leaders discussed above was brave enough to face the consequences of a drastic policy shift.

What this paradox really shows is that a state may become trapped by its own commitment to such a point that it loses not only the war, but—in the final analysis—also its credibility. Is there an escape from this paradox? The simplest way out seems to be to quit as fast as one gets the chance to move. The impact of this move is that one must incur short-run costs in order to gain long-range benefits. This policy, which Elster (1979) calls precommitment and Schelling (1984) calls self-command, involves short-term irrational behavior (in which the costs outweigh the benefits) that causes long-term rational behavior that would not have been possible if the irrational path were not taken in the first step. Unilateral termination of hostilities or withdrawal from occupied territories without any reciprocation by the opponent may seem stupid in the short run, because a little more effort and determination could lead the opponent to pay some price for the same move. However, beyond the effect such a policy has on the overall costs of the conflict, it has the effect of better serving the very same goals that policies of gradual disengagement are supposed to serve.

Unilateral exit from war forces an actor to look for alternative ways to reestablish credibility and an image of resolve and invincibility. Continuation of the war to preserve those images causes an actor to put all its eggs in one basket. It also causes more damage in the long run, especially if in the long run the actor ends up losing anyway at the same price (or worse) it is afraid to pay at present. Not only is the image of resolve apt to be damaged, but so is the image of military effectiveness which may be closely linked to credibility.

## The Loser's Fortune

Losing is bad for national health. At least this is the conventional wisdom; otherwise, it is hard to explain why nations fight in the first place. Defeats on the battlefield are usually accompanied by political and diplomatic humiliation. The defeated nation typically enters a dark era, a period of low morale, desperation, and—in many cases—feelings of revenge. During this era, a lot of national energy is spent crying over spilled milk (dealing with issues of who is or what factors are responsible for the defeat) rather than on rebuilding what was destroyed during the war.

But sometimes defeat can be a springboard for major national accomplishments. In fact, defeat in war can cause major improvements in a nation's social and political systems that could not have been accomplished without the defeat. In many ways, these benefits are unique to losers of war; they typically do not occur following victories. The loser's fortune paradox deals with two aspects of national change following defeat: economic growth and political development.

## The Phoenix Factor:
## War as a Cause of Rapid Economic Growth

Organski and Kugler (1980) have coined the term "phoenix factor" to describe this paradox. The phoenix factor describes how the loser of the war, like the legendary bird that rises from the ashes, exhibits rates of economic growth following defeat in war that are not only faster than its own prewar rates of growth, but also faster than those of the winner. Figure 10.3 shows a hypothetical example of this trend.

As is evident from this figure, the years of war are indicated by a decline of the GNP for both the winner and the loser. The projected

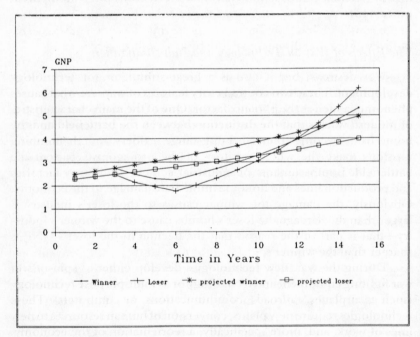

**Figure 10.3**   The Phoenix Factor

*Source:* Organski and Kugler (1980). Figures are hypothetical.

lines for both actors show how fast their economies would have grown if there had been no war. Following the war, for reasons that will be discussed below, both the winner and the loser experience accelerated growth rates that are significantly higher than the prewar growth rates. So war may have actually affected the rate of growth of the two national economies. What is surprising, however, is that the loser, whose loss in war is indicated by a much steeper drop in GNP during the war period, experiences a growth rate faster than not only its own prewar rate but also that of the winner. The loser is the first to overtake its own projected growth rate and soon overtakes the growth rate of the winner.

West Germany and Japan in the post-World War II period are the two most obvious examples of the phoenix factor. Explanations of this phenomenon must simultaneously address two questions: (1) Why is the growth rate of both winners and losers faster following wars than it had been before the war? (2) Why do losers grow faster than winners? Two complementary explanations are offered here to account for this phenomenon. The first explanation focuses on the effect of war on technology and industrialization. The second explanation stresses the role of national resolve and determination in economic development processes.

## The Effects of War on Technology and Industrialization

War destroys, but it also is a great stimulator for technology development. These two contradictory features of wars are what causes phenomena such as the phoenix factor. One of the main characteristics of modern wars is that the distinction between the battlefield and the home front becomes blurred. Long-range artillery and air bombing missions make the whole territory of the protagonists part of the battlefield. Bombardments of industrial centers do destroy factories and production lines and do some immediate damage to the economy. Obviously, the damage the winner causes to the loser's industry is larger than the damage the loser's bombs cause to the winner's industry—that is part of the reason that the decline in the loser's GNP is sharper than the winner's.

During the war, new technologies develop either as spin-offs of war fighting equipment and technology or as multipurpose technology (such as airplanes, railroads, communications, or computers). These technologies require new plants, conversion of human resources to new lines of work, and, more specifically, a reorientation of the economy. Following the war, the parties start rebuilding their industries, and during this process they absorb the new technologies, which tend to be more efficient than prewar technology. Factories are rebuilt or replaced and new factories are equipped with newer and more efficient production lines. That explains the faster postwar growth rates of winner and loser alike. However, by the same logic, the loser, which suffered more destruction than the winner, has much more to replace and rebuild. As a result, the modernization of equipment and reorientation of workers is far more thorough and general for the loser. The winner continues in many areas to work with prewar equipment and technology, and the rate at which it absorbs new technologies is much slower simply because it experienced less damage. The effects of technological change are common to winner and loser; in this respect both parties "benefit" from the destruction caused by war. However, for the same reason, the loser benefits more from the greater destruction it has incurred.

A related factor that explains the differential winner-loser growth rates is that of the constraints imposed on the loser's production of military equipment by the winner. If the victory in the war is sufficiently one-sided that the winner can impose economic conditions on the loser's production schedule, the winner may be interested in severely limiting the kind and quantity of war-fighting equipment production of the loser, for obvious reasons. This forces the loser's government to find new sources of employment for a substantial number of people. These new sources of employment tend to be more effective in inducing subsequent growth in the GNP than military production in a postwar era. The winner must maintain a large army and worry about keeping its military equipment up to date. Therefore, it continues to invest in military production far in excess of what is justified. Hence, its growth rate is slowed down by military production, much of which is done according to old standards.

## Defeat and National Mobilization

Some claim that most first-generation millionaires came from poor and broken families. Also, there is a well-known phenomenon that families whose houses have been burned down or destroyed by some natural cause (flood, earthquake) build new houses that are larger and fancier than those that were destroyed. The same phenomenon occurs in the wake of disastrous wars to some states. And the reason for all these outcomes is the same: disaster causes a common sorrow and a feeling of communality that leads to a high motivation to rebuild the society. All the frustration that is caused by the damage of war is channeled into a wish to rebuild what was destroyed during the war. The nation pulls together, continuing the wartime tightened-belt economy, which is characterized by low rates of consumption and high rates of production, only now production is devoted to consumption goods rather than to war material and equipment. Savings turn into investments, which lead to rapid development of new projects and result in accelerated rates of growth.

Because war causes damage and destruction in both the winner's state and the loser's state, the increased motivation to rebuild and the pattern of economic activity that causes accelerated growth is identical in both. However, because the destruction is more extensive in the loser's state, national mobilization is more pronounced there than in the winner's state. Another thing that works to the loser's advantage is the set of constraints imposed on it by the winner. In many cases, winners limit the loser's army to a size that will not threaten the winner in the future. Even without such external constraints on the size of the loser's army, since the winner gains territory and the loser loses territory, the size of the army needed to defend the national territory is smaller than it had been before the war for the loser and larger than before the war for the winner. Finally, the loser invokes sympathy from rich and powerful allies, sometimes even from the winner itself. This sympathy is often converted into economic aid. On the other hand, the poor winner, because it won the war, even if the costs for doing it were excessively high, gets no aid at all, or only limited aid because its damages were less extensive than those of the loser. Taken together, the combination of increased national will, external or internal constraints on the size of the army and on nonproductive expenditures to military and security affairs, and external economic aid leads to rapid economic growth that causes the loser to overtake not only its prewar rate of growth, but also that of the winner.

## The Phoenix Factor in History

All of the elements described in the above two sections are eminently present in the cases of post-World War II Germany and Japan. But since Organski and Kugler (1980) have explored these cases in detail, I will not dwell on them. Rather, the unexplored miracle of Jordan might be more interesting to examine here. Jordan lost 26 percent of its arable territory to Israel during the Six Day War, as well as 29 percent of its population.[11] This loss was particularly painful to Jordan because it was dragged into this war by the false pretenses of the Syrians and by Egyptian fairy tales of unprecedented victories. In addition to the loss of the territory, Jordan encountered yet another flood of refugees from the West Bank (estimated at about 300,000, or about 18 percent of its population). All these people were thrown into refugee camps located at the outskirts of the main cities.

The loss of territory and people, not to mention the humiliation of the defeat, became, however, a springboard to a major process of economic development that has made Jordan the most prosperous non-oil-producing Arab state. After the war, the Palestinian activity from Jordan, especially the repeated infiltrations to Israel, led to massive Israeli shelling of the eastern Jordan valley, the largest area of arable land in the East Bank of the Jordan river, including the Ghor Canal project, a major project of irrigation. The northern part of the Jordan valley was evacuated by most of the inhabitants. To add fuel to the fire, the Palestinian guerrillas started establishing a state within a state, hampering much of the recovery process. In the period prior to the Six Day War, Jordan's GNP was growing at an average annual rate of 7 percent. During the 1967–1974 period, the growth rate averaged 5.4 percent per annum.

King Hussein expelled the Palestinian guerrillas following fairly violent struggle in September 1970, with repeat performances in November 1970 and July 1971. This move angered many Arab states, which had been giving Jordan significant foreign aid. However, after a short interlude in the inflow of aid, the Arab states renewed economic aid. Indeed, from the year 1974 on, Jordan's GNP grew at an average annual rate of 14.4 percent. Figure 10.4 documents this trend.

How was this miracle accomplished? Several factors explain this trend. First, the defeat led to considerable increase in foreign aid to Jordan from the oil-rich Arab states. Foreign aid to Jordan increased from 26.57 million Jordanian dinars (12.8 percent of the GNP) in 1964 to 289.56 in 1983 (about 16 percent of the GNP). However, the figure in 1983 is far below the 1967–1980 average of 25.8 percent of the GNP, with the peak year being 1975, when foreign aid reached 37.2 percent of the GNP (Hammad, 1987: 15).

Second, just as the West Bank spelled nothing but trouble for the Israelis following the 1967 war, it spelled nothing but trouble for the Hashemite regime prior to the war. The Palestinian population in these territories had been highly mobilized and active in anti-Hashemite struggles in the 1950s and 1960s. In addition, infiltrators from the West Bank across the Israeli border caused numerous Israeli retaliation raids. All these factors forced Hussein to maintain large numbers of troops in the West Bank, the primary task of which was to police the area rather than to defend the border with Israel. The loss of the West Bank rid Hussein of a pain in the neck without really reducing the economic benefit accrued from the region. Due to the Israeli policy of open bridges, a de facto peace has developed between the two states, with open

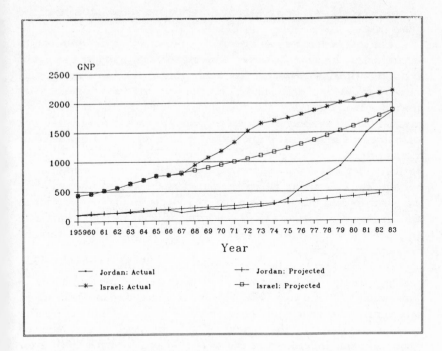

**Figure 10.4**  Jordanian and Israeli Economic Growth Rates, 1959–1983

*Sources:* Berglas (1986), SIPRI (vols. from 1970–1988), Hammad (1987), Kanovsky (1976), and Khader and Badran (1987).

*Note:* Israeli GNP figures have been divided by six to allow comparison. This does not bias the analysis because what is analyzed here are growth rates rather than raw GNP figures.

boundaries and almost unlimited movement of goods, services, and people across these borders. As a result, Jordan still benefited from the goods and services oroginating in the West Bank with only minimal investment in the area, while the Israelis were making heavy investments in the security of the region.[12]

During the 1973 war, Hussein refused to convert the Jordan river valley into a third front. Instead, he sent the 40th armored brigade to fight alongside the Syrian army in the Golan Heights. As a result, Hussein qualified as a contributor to the war effort and was eligible for generous foreign aid from the new bankers of the Arab world, the Saudis.

All this shows that Hussein was able to convert the worst defeat in the short history of his state into a springboard for major economic development. This level of economic development is reflected not only in terms of GNP. It is converted into a relatively modern network of educational, social, and medical systems that outperforms many of its counterparts in the Arab world.

## The Paradox of Democracy

There is a widespread popular belief that governments start conflict when they face considerable trouble at home. This belief has not received overwhelming support in the empirical and quantitative literature on international conflict, but it has some firm believers, nonetheless.[13] The idea is that governments try to rally the mob around the flag by finding some common adversary or external cause to invoke patriotism in the hope of causing people to forget domestic troubles. Whether or not this theory has some empirical foundation is not at issue here. For the sake of the argument I shall assume that it has, at least in those few cases that are candidates for the paradox of democracy.

This paradox goes as follows. A totalitarian government finds itself in domestic trouble; the economy is bad, people are mad at the government on the one hand and terrified by it on the other. If they have not started rebelling already, the government fears that they are likely to do so in the near future. The government may also feel that it is losing ground in those sectors that provided it with the narrow basis of legitimacy it may have had thus far (the army, the aristocracy, rich businessmen, major landowners, and so on). So, a little conflict might divert national attention from the domestic problems. People will be called to the flag in the name of the national interest, honor, and the like. The government hopes that, in the face of an outside enemy, people will be converted to fanatic supporters of the government. What follows is the initiation of a little conflict. But, once the conflict is under way, the domestic pressure is such that the government cannot back down, even if it realizes that it is fighting a losing battle; it may be driven by its own rhetoric to its demise. The conflict escalates into a general war; the nation is defeated.

At that point, the people turn against their government. Not only did they have major grievances against the government before the war started, the government failed them in war, adding a humiliating defeat to its brutal and corrupt handling of the economy and social affairs. The totalitarian government loses its traditional bases of legitimacy and is overthrown by the disappointed masses. Because people turn against the regime, not only against the specific government that got them into the war, the new regime becomes the opposite of the previous one. Hence, because the nation lost the war, it gains freedom. Had it won the war, the regime would have at least gained some breathing time, benefiting from the spirit of elation following the victory.

This phenomenon is not a property only of inefficient totalitarian regimes that get themselves into foreign policy problems in addition to their domestic ones; it can happen to democratic regimes when the popular support for the incumbent government is diminishing. But if this happens to a democracy it is not a paradox, because, in addition to losing some tangible assets in the war, the people lose their freedom if the army overthrows the democratic regime.

The extent of causal effect that defeat in war has on the emergence of democracy is unclear. Because the conflict was initiated to divert attention from domestic problems, the defeat in the war may merely accelerate the downfall of a corrupt, inefficient, and brutal regime that had no widespread support in the first place. It is difficult to prove that it was the defeat in war that caused the regime change. The logical exclusiveness condition may be difficult to satisfy in this case, but the defeat in war may have at least a contributing effect on the downfall of the government. It strongly affects the speed with which the government falls.[14]

## *The Sweet Defeat:*
## *The Falkland War and Argentina's Return to Democracy*[15]

Virtually all experts admit that domestic considerations were one of the chief incentives for the Argentinean invasion of the Falkland islands on April 2, 1982. The Galtieri government, which had overthrown the Viola government on December 11, 1981, came into office with a laissez faire economic plan and an ambiguous attitude about redemocratizing Argentina, which had been under military rule since 1976. The Argentinean economy was in deep trouble. During the years 1979–1981, Argentina experienced negative economic growth, peaking with a 7.9 percent drop in GNP in 1981 (Wynia, 1986: 145) and an inflation rate averaging 178 percent per annum over the 1976–82 period (Pion-Berlin, 1987: 225). Popular opposition to the military government was emerging from all over the political and social spectrum in Argentina. The military regime had established its rule by brutal suppression of opposition, with thousands of people suspected as members of the opposition having disappeared, and many others simply thrown into concentration camps without trial. By 1982, the erosion in the support of the government spilled over to the military itself. The invasion of the Falkland islands gave the military a cause it could pursue (Pion-Berlin, 1987: 221). Likewise, Galtieri had hoped that the occupation of the Falkland/Malvinas islands would rally popular support for the government (Mandel, 1987: 88).

Unfortunately, the regime miscalculated the ability and willingness of the Thatcher government to fight, it overestimated the army's ability to defend the islands, and it committed numerous military blunders during the war. With the Falkland invasion, the Galtieri government dug its own grave. Interestingly enough, it was not public protest that brought down the military regime in Argentina, but rather a feeling of defeat and paralysis within the military junta that replaced the Galtieri government that led to a decision to call for national elections in October 1983 (Wynia, 1986: 26–27). The defeat intensified public demands for civilian rule and a simultaneous erosion in the military's belief that it was capable of solving Argentina's economic problems with any kind of policy that was not backed by popular support.

The elections were a renewed experiment in democracy in a state with a complex social and political structure and a history that was a long tale of coups d'état and successions of military and civilian governments of all shapes and colors. With skyrocketing inflation of over 400 percent per year (averaging a 25 percent price increase per month), negative growth, a foreign debt of $46 billion, and a legacy of devastating defeat for a—by and large popular—national cause, the problems facing the newly elected president, Raul Alfonsin, were seemingly insurmountable (Hirschman, 1987).

While it is clearly too early to make any assessment of the experiment in democratic problem solving in Argentina, certainly for someone who is not an expert on this country, the first reviews seem, on the whole, quite positive. It took the Alfonsin government more than six months to devise a strategy. On June 11, 1984, Alfonsin announced a radically new economic package designed to stop the economic decay of the country. The package consisted of several steps. First, the government stopped printing money. Second, a new currency was announced. The austral equalled 1,000 pesos and the government was committed to freezing its exchange rate vis-à-vis the American dollar. Most important, the government announced a freeze on wages and prices. Initial figures show that the program changed many things around in Argentina's economy. Most important, inflation went down to two-digit rates for the last four years. Growth was restored, albeit at slow rates, with the GNP rising at an average of 2 percent per year during the 1985–87 period.

In foreign policy, the Alfonsin government staged another small coup, solving its problems with Chile on the control over the Beagle Channel Islands, with the (October 1984) acceptance of the Vatican plan calling for granting Chile sovereignty over the islands. Following major difficulties in the parliament in ratifying this treaty, Alfonsin again outmaneuvered his opposition the democratic way, by calling for a plebiscite on the treaty. The plebiscite, held on November 25, 1984, featured 73 percent of the eligible voters overwhelmingly supporting ratification (by a majority of 77 percent). While no progress has been made on the Falkland/Malvinas issue, the relaxation of tensions with Britain and the turn inward have left much room for hope.

## Conclusion

In this chapter I have shown that defeat in war can be both more bitter than it should and more sweet than it normally is taken to be. This in itself makes for an interesting paradox, which I will not explore here because I have covered enough paradoxes for one book. What the loser's paradoxes imply is that one should not view defeat in war as the end of the world, because from the strong can come the sweet. Just as the winner should be careful about what it does with the fruits of victory, the loser must be able to explore the seemingly hidden advantages of defeat. More important, defeat in war carries some major advantages to the nation because it may create major opportunities for economic and political development. Hence, when one realizes that one is going to lose the war, it is important not to try to cut down losses by prolonging the war. This not only has the effect of actually increasing losses, but also may cause the disappearance of existing opportunities. Just as the winner must know how to optimize victory, the loser must learn how to optimize defeat.

Both the winner's paradoxes and the loser's paradoxes may well be of the veridical kind, in that they are susceptible to "double flip" solutions. In the case of the winner's paradox, cutting down the size of the achievement may sometimes cause a greater willingness of the loser to accept the postwar status quo, where a maximization of gains may cause the loser to defy any status quo. The Israeli victory in the 1973 war was followed by a concession of virtually all the territories that Israel had gained during the war on both the Egyptian and the Syrian fronts and some territories that Israel had occupied during the 1967 war. This brought about two disengagement agreements and started a process that culminated in the Egyptian-Israeli peace treaty of March 1979. As a result, the two borders have not seen a single military casualty since 1974. And 14 years of quiet borders is a major achievement in the Arab-Israeli conflict.

In the case of the paradox of sunk cost, precommitment—which itself is a clear case of paradoxical behavior—seems to be the obvious solution to another kind of paradoxical behavior, the effect of which is to cause an actor to sink deeper into the mess in order to recover sunk costs. If one adds to it the loser's fortune paradox, they sum up to a reversal of the whole means-ends linear logic of war.

It is very important to caution against jumping to general conclusions from what has been discovered in the last two chapters. These paradoxes occur with an extremely low frequency. In fact, it has been shown that the magnanimity in victory principle, which seems the kind of "double flip" solution to some of the winner's paradoxes, does not in general work in international politics. But when the circumstances showing that paradoxes of the sort documented herein are at work, the solutions generally apply. This can certainly be said with confidence with regard to the sunk-cost paradox.

The loser's fortune paradox is a difficult case to deal with on a normative basis. Because defeats might be extremely costly not only in terms of national morale and human and material losses of war, they might divorce the state from major resources essential to its recovery. Yet, what this paradox does suggest, and I believe this is an implication of major importance, is that a nation can recover from the pit of defeat if, instead of putting its energy into the meaningless business of avenging the losses of the last war, it focuses on building its economy and society such that the next war will be rendered unnecessary.

## Notes

1   It really does not matter whether we start out this model with two, three, ten, or a hundred people in the auction. The game always converges into a two-person affair. Whoever has the good fortune of becoming the third-highest bidder can drop out without cost, should do so, and almost always does at the first available opportunity (Teger, 1980).

2   Of course, this possibility should have been discussed early on in the game. But we need not concern ourselves with the problem of why it was not considered, for we shall see in a moment that even if this were a feasible course of action at the start of the game, it is not necessarily rational to use it.

3   An interesting problem similar to the one introduced here is the centerpid paradox, due to Nimrod Megido (Auman, 1988). This game is as follows. There is a sum of $10.50 on the table. Bob can choose to take $10.00, leaving the 50 cents to Alice. If he does that, the game ends. However, if he passes, the sum on the table is multiplied by ten. Now there is $105.00 on the table, and it is Alice's turn. Alice can pick up the $100.00, leaving $5.00 to Bob, or she can pass. If she chooses to pass, the sum is multiplied again by ten, making $1,050.00. Now it is Bob's turn again. Bob can pick up $1,000.00, leaving $50.00 to Alice, or pass. If he passes, the game ends there and then, and neither gets anything. It is easy, if somewhat surprising, to show that the *only* rational solution—no matter how one turns and twists it—is for Bob to pick up the $10.00 in the first round. The reason I did not present this game as *the* model of the sunk-cost paradox is that the reasoning process is the inverse of the one given below, though the results are just the same.

4   A related problem is discussed by Rubinstein (1982) in his analysis of asymmetrical bargaining costs of players. The solution he devised is that if one player pays less for a given move than the other, he should get the whole pie, which requires division at the first round of offers.

5 See Janis and Mann (1977) for an analysis of the effects of cognitive conflict on decision making.

6 This war does qualify, however, as a case to demonstrate another paradox that has to do with the relations between beliefs about victory that might cause a nation to lose the war.

7 This section is based on Isaacs (1983), Kolko (1985), Gelb and Betts (1979), Kissinger (1979), Tuchman (1984), and Pillar (1983).

8 The extra 8,000 fatalities include those missing in action whose bodies were subsequently recovered, fatalities endured between the official cease-fire and the withdrawal of American troops, and wounded soldiers who later died from their wounds.

9 This section is based on the same sources used in Chapter 8, particularly, Schiff and Ya'ari (1984), Yaniv (1987, 1986), Maoz and Felsenthal (1987), and Dupuy and Martell (1986).

10 This figure is based on the estimates of the total cost of the war given in Yaniv (1987: 314, fn. 81). The estimates of the economic costs of the war range from a low of $1.5 billion to a high of over $5 billion. This suggests that the daily costs (direct and indirect) ranged from $1.4 million to $4.5 million.

11 Sources for this discussion include Kanovsky (1976), Mazur (1979), and Khader and Badran (1987). These figures are from Schliephake (1987: 63).

12 King Hussein kept close ties to the West Bank up until August 1988. The Jordanian investment in the West Bank was in the form of payment of salaries to some 21,000 educational, judicial, municipal, and religious civil servants. In addition, the lower chamber of the Jordanian parliament was composed of West Bank representatives. On August 1, 1988, the king announced that he was severing his ties to the West Bank, stopping the payment of salaries, and closing the lower chamber of the parliament.

13 There is a vast body of literature on this topic. For two good reviews, see Stohl (1980) and Levy (1989). Levy examines both quantitative evidence and historical evidence, and shows that the two types of evidence clash: the historical evidence tends to support the "scapegoat" hypothesis persistently.

14 Stein and Russett (1980) show that all of the losers in interstate wars in the twentieth century underwent regime changes, whereas none of the winners of these wars did. This provides at least some evidence for this paradox.

15 This analysis is based on Hirschman (1987), Wynia (1986), and Pion-Berlin (1987).

# 11
# *Paradoxical Lessons from Paradoxical Wars*

The difference between a wise person and a smart one is that the former knows how to avoid traps that the latter knows how to escape from. (old Jewish proverb)

It is time to draw some general lessons from this tour of perversities in the initiation, management, and termination of war. These lessons are of two types. The first concerns the theory and practice of war and strategy. The second concerns other processes that are inflicted by the tendency to generate unintended consequences from intentional behavior. In addition, it is time to explore the feasibility and generality of various solutions to these paradoxes of war.

This chapter is organized as follows. First, I provide a brief summary of the findings of the book. Second, I explore and respond to possible objections to the approach and the methodology used in this study. Third, I examine the lessons that can be derived from the paradoxes explored here with regard to theory and practice of war and peace. Fourth, I explore the implication of paradoxical logic for the study of other problems of contemporary world politics. Finally, I offer some suggestions for future research along these lines.

## Summary of Findings

It is difficult to talk about "findings" in a book in which the focus is primarily on the exceptional or irregular aspects in the conduct of war. The reader is cautioned not to take what follows as regular aspects of war, but rather as potential commonalties among seemingly exceptional cases of war. Yet, the diversity of the wars examined here suggests one of the central themes of this study:

*While each of the paradoxes discussed in this study is an exception, rather than the rule, in international war, there are quite a few paradoxical aspects of war. Hence, most of the wars in the modern era (if not all of them) are afflicted by at least one of these paradoxes. And quite a few wars contain compound paradoxical aspects.*

This suggests that a pattern recurs in those aspects of most—if not all—wars that are not susceptible to explanations that rely on straightforward linear logic. This pattern makes the approach employed herein a significant contribution to the understanding of war. The following points represent some of the common themes that have been discussed in the preceding chapters.

(1) *Policies that are designed to stabilize a hostile relationship between states may actually cause a flare-up of war, even when policymakers display a high degree of caution.* Arms races initiated and maintained out of defensive intentions may create incentives to fight due to fear of falling behind the opponent. They may also be associated with increased perceptions of hostility and thereby lead to preventive wars. Deterrence policies may provoke opponents into believing that the deterrer actually prepares for a first strike. The relationship between prudence and provocability in deterrence may be—contrary to conventional wisdom—positive: policies that are thought to be prudent can be interpreted as provocative by those whom they are intended to pacify.

(2) *Initial success may cause eventual disaster in the management of war.* This emerges both from the paradox of attrition and from the paradox of surprise. Success in the initial stages of the fighting may cause carelessness in subsequent stages. Initial success might lead to unanticipated problems of logistics and strategy that stem from the fact that planning for war had been characterized by worst-case assumptions that were thought to cover less severe cases. Finally, initial successes may cause the opponent to switch its strategy in an unanticipated manner that turns the tables on the initially successful actor.

(3) *Military capabilities are a double-edged weapon in international politics.* This finding is most pronounced in paradoxes of power, but it also stems from the analysis of arms races and of deterrence. This suggests that the law of "more is better" is seriously challenged by the present study. And the reasoning behind the challenge is not that of inefficiency, waste, and opportunity cost. Rather, three essential findings warn against a "more is better" notion in military affairs. First, more in the name of stability might be more likely to cause instability. (This follows from the para bellum paradox and the paradox of successful deterrence.) Second, extra capabilities might

cause loss of control over outcomes in war. This argument is of particular importance because war is presumably where capabilities are being tested. (This follows from the power paradox.) Third, acquisition of resources that are seen to contribute to a nation's capability, such as territorial growth, might actually cause social and strategic problems that would not have existed otherwise. And the net result is that a nation might be less secure due to more resources. (This follows from the winner's paradoxes.)

(4) *International commitments might cause entrapment.* This emerges from the ally's paradox and from the sunk-cost paradox. Commitments can cause entrapment in that allies may drag an actor into wars it does not want. Commitments may also cause entanglement in wars far beyond the point of diminishing marginal returns.

(5) *Marginality may be a deadly logic.* This emerges from the two paradoxes that are based on the Dollar Auction game: the paradox of unintended escalation and the sunk-cost paradox. It is also related to the finding about the damaging effects of prudence. Behavior that is based only on immediate gains and losses may result in costly messes, even if each choice seems eminently rational. Marginality causes actors inadvertently to enter into wars they did not want, and it also causes them to delay the termination of wars they cannot win.

(6) *Sometimes it is not so good to win a war, and sometimes it is not so bad to lose one.* These are the findings that emerge from the chapters on winners' and losers' paradoxes. The significance of this finding is that it casts serious doubt on the instrumentality of war in forwarding national goals. This finding also challenges seemingly obvious notions about the relationships between strategy and politics (where the former is treated as an instrument of the latter).

Do these findings come together into a meaningful bottom-line thesis? I think they do. What they suggest is that when dealing with issues of war and peace, a careful inspection is warranted of the whole logic on which certain recommended courses of action rest. One must examine not only if the premises are sound, if assessments of friends and foes stand close scrutiny, and if general notions about means-ends relations are valid, but also if the fundamental soundness of this logic in general does not doom the recommended actions from the start.

More fundamentally, these findings put the realpolitik logic that dominates decision-making processes in foreign and security affairs on a tentative basis. This analysis suggests that it is quite legitimate and quite necessary to question not only the premises of realpolitik thinking, but also its means-ends logic. Realpolitik logic gives rise to quite a few conclusions that depart from the accumulated conventional wisdom in more than the simple surprise-revealing sense. Several of the counterintuitive findings discussed above amount to an argument that the weaknesses of the straightforward "realist" thinking are not that it fails to account for many "things" that have important impact on the outcomes of national choices (Mansbach and Vasquez, 1981; Keohane and Nye, 1977). Rather, the weaknesses of the paradigm might lie within it because it gives rise to results that are contradictory to its own expectations, and because these contradictions cannot be resolved within its own logic.

Finally, this book generally argues that war is a bad idea, because it may well turn out to be detrimental precisely in terms of the objectives that had made this option look appealing at the outset. First, there are no good guys or bad guys in international politics—no heroes or villains. And nobody is immune to adverse consequences even if the whole theoretical and practical setup on which war was predicated seemed foolproof at the time. An actor may lose even if it wins the war, and may win even if it loses. It may lose control of events just when it is convinced it is in full command. If it is true that no modern war has been without its paradox(es), then actors can never know what kind of surprise is going to be sprung on them when they start one.

## Possible Objections

I do not expect the ideas and analyses contained in this work to go unchallenged. Much of what I have been arguing throughout this book goes against a conventional wisdom that has been accumulated over centuries of research and practical "experience." Besides the interesting (amusing or sad) aspects of these problems, there is little to worry about for two reasons: (1) they do not happen very often, and (2) if they do, there is little that can be done about them. In this section I address some potential objections to the approach, methodology, and substantive findings.

### Objections to the Approach

(1)   The conceptualization of problems is all wrong. It is aimed at irregularities in war, hence, it creates an incorrect impression that everything about war is paradoxical. This constitutes an impediment to cumulative knowledge about war. The paradoxical approach creates an erroneous impression that much of what we know about war is inadequate. If followed, it may actually lead to abandonment of knowledge that is the result of much experience and research.

The premise of this approach is that there is considerable knowledge about war, and that much of it is valid and relevant. All of the general approaches to the study of war that are briefly reviewed in Chapter 1 have generated important findings about the causes, courses, and consequences of war. The purpose of this book was not to recount these findings, but to add to them. Since most works on war started out with the aim of finding regularities, I accepted these known regularities as given and started out in an effort to discover patterns in the exceptional cases, those that do not seem to fit conventional wisdom explanations. In order to do that, I could not rely upon the conventional linear logic, because if I did, I would have doomed the analysis to failure. I think that the importance of the approach is embedded precisely in its effort to use a different logic to highlight the unexplained aspects of war.

The paradoxical approach serves two purposes. First, it shows that a number of features in international politics represent contradictions between expectations and the consequences of reasoned behavior. Second, and more important, it explains why these contradictions arise. The real problem with the approach is that it does not establish the precise conditions that give rise to these contradictions. I have not tried to develop a general theory of paradoxes of war, simply because there is no need to. The same theories that account for regularities in peoples' behavior prior to, during, and following wars also account for these contradictions. These explanations call our attention to the fact that precisely a carefully thought-through scheme, one which, on average, works very well, might work contrary to expectations.

Another advantage of identifying and explaining irregularities in terms of paradoxical logic is that these paradoxes have profound ramifications. The significance of the study of deviant behavior is the social ramifications of such behavior. Likewise, the paradoxes of war highlight aspects of international politics that are of major significance in terms of the issues and tangible costs involved. In fact, each and every one of the paradoxes discussed in this book deals with aspects of war that are central to its conduct. Awareness of these paradoxes, while not generally sufficient to suggest quick and easy solution, might be a first step toward a remedy.

Finally, the study of paradoxes of wars has a heuristic value. The severity of the problems raised by these paradoxes may stimulate thinking along new paths that might enrich our understanding of the phenomenon. The philosophical and social paradoxes I have discussed in Chapter 1 have yet to be solved in a satisfactory manner. Yet, the research they have inspired has made numerous contributions to the disciplines wherein these paradoxes have arisen. I hope that something similar may emerge in the study of war.

(2)   The way the two explanatory models have been used throughout this book does not make sense. The rational and cognitive models are mutually exclusive at their basis. It is impossible that they would account equally well for the same phenomena. The approach is defective in that it consistently refuses to choose between the two explanatory models. In fact, it vacillates between the two explanations throughout the book, sometimes leaning toward one explanation, and in other cases leaning toward the other.

I will not spend much time on refuting this argument, simply because I have done so at considerable length elsewhere (Maoz, 1989). The key point of this criticism simply does not hold water. The rational and cognitive models cannot be mutually exclusive simply because each of them deals with aspects that the other takes as given. For example, the rational model does not deal with the factors that cause people to have one set of preferences rather than another. The cognitive model deals at great length with the processes by which preferences are formed. Utility-maximizing choice may result, as we have seen in the para bellum paradox, from irrational preference-formation processes. Moreover, since these explanations emphasize sometimes different factors that give rise to a given paradox, it is not inconceivable that both rational factors and cognitive factors operate simultaneously to produce these phenomena in both the abstract example and—more important—in the real world.

But at a more profound level, the level of their implications, these models are different. Because I intend to devote special space to this topic, I defer discussion of this issue to a later section.

(3)   The approach is ad hoc beyond the general focus on the paradoxical aspects of war. There is no theoretical spinal cord that connects the paradoxes of war to one another. A different set of explanations is tailored to each of these paradoxes. An explanation that fits one paradox is abandoned when another paradox is discussed. The end result is that one does not know what to make of the findings because they have not emerged out of a consistent theoretical framework.

This criticism is also not grounded in profound understanding of the approach. The essence of the approach is not that it focuses on paradoxes of war, it is *how* these paradoxes are studied. The systematic nature of the approach stems from several of its key features. First, the view of paradoxes as a *causally induced* contradiction between expectations and the consequences of behavior based on them forces us to account for a sequence in causal terms. This enables a relatively clear differentiation between a true paradox and a solvable puzzle (Zinnes, 1980b). The demanding definition imposes a need to show that a candidate paradox indeed constitutes a significant break in our conventional way of thinking. The effort to show that a paradox exists in the abstract cannot be done ad hoc in that it must rest upon rational choice logic.[1] Moreover, because of the causal sequence involved, explanations are required, and the same two models systematically explain the various paradoxes.

The different explanations of the models across paradoxes result from the fact that the paradoxes represent different kinds of problems, that is, they result from different kinds of causally induced contradictions. Nonetheless, in all the paradoxes that rest on choice-related approaches, the explanations provided stem from the same two general models. Because the models tend to complement rather than contradict one another, the emphasis placed on them is proportional to what I believe to be the relative contribution of each model to the overall account, and, therefore, to the documentation of the historical cases.

(4)   The problem of the approach is that it is unit-based. That is why it makes such a big deal out of paradoxes of war. Had this study been based on a systemic perspective, many of the paradoxes would have become comprehensible, because, as Waltz (1979: 107) argues: "[Systemic] structures cause actions to have consequences they were not intended to have. Surely most of the actors will notice that, and at least some of them will be able to figure out why. They may develop a pretty good sense of just how structures work their effects. Will they not then be able to achieve their original ends by appropriately adjusting their strategies? Unfortunately, they often cannot." Systemic theories also explain why awareness of contradictions between expectations and consequences of purposeful behavior does not eliminate them. "So long as one leaves the structure unaffected it is not possible for changes in the intentions and the actions of the particular actors to produce desirable outcomes or to avoid undesirable ones. . . . The only remedies for strong structural effects are structural changes" (Waltz, 1979: 108). This sounds like a superb explanation for virtually all the paradoxes discussed in this book, especially when taken to be problems in rational logic. What systems theory does is show that within an anarchic structure in which each actor is out to get the most for itself, and in which there exists no mechanism for enforceable social choices, paradoxes are bound to arise. In fact, paradoxes of war are but one small aspect of more general paradoxes that prevail in world politics, but their treatment in terms of choice-related perspectives obscures the larger systemic picture.

This is probably the most serious criticism of the approach, because it seemingly is based on an understanding of the notion of paradox and of the properties of the paradoxes, and—more important—it is based on an understanding of the limits of these explanations. What constitutes a paradox at one level constitutes a natural feature of a higher level of analysis. This is illustrated in the rational explanation of all the paradoxes, if one considers the system structure to provide the rules of the various "games" used to demonstrate the paradoxes.

Perhaps the best illustration of this point is the case of the power paradox introduced in Chapter 8. The acquisition of extra resources by one actor causes it to lose control over outcomes because other actors perform a classical "balancing" maneuver that is the standard balance-of-power response to an apparent rise of an actor to near-preponderant status. Hence, what seems an unpleasant outcome from the perspective of the unit is a perfectly reasonable exercise in maintenance or restoration of systemic equilibrium. Moreover, an actor who becomes aware of the adverse consequences of the extra control over resources cannot alter its behavior to avoid the loss of control over outcomes. This is perfectly consistent with a balance-of-power theory under a security dilemma, wherein each actor must act to maximize its power.

Although this criticism has some validity, it is misguided for at least three principal reasons. First, most of these paradoxes are driven by the preferences of the actors and their strategies. While these preferences and strategies are constrained by the environment in which states interact with one another, and the anarchical system serves to make the menu of choices available to actors somewhat narrow, it is not obvious that this structure necessarily makes for paradoxes. For example, if all account holders in a bank claim their savings, the bank will collapse. Of course, nobody intends for the bank to go bust, but if everyone is afraid that this might be the case, everybody will make a run for his or her money, causing this result. Further, knowing that this is the case does not alter people's behavior. This may be a paradox, but the question is why it does not happen all the time. The answer, of course, lies in people's expectations. As long as nobody expects the bank to go bust, the number of people closing their accounts on any given day does not risk the fluidity of the bank. The key question is what particular combination of expectations produces behavior that causes paradoxical consequences. As long as system theory focuses on capabilities rather than on preferences as determinants of structure, systemic explanations of paradoxes will be of limited validity. Where they are most useful is in pointing out that the anarchic structure of the international system may give rise to a wide variety of paradoxes. Beyond this argument, systemic approaches cannot say which paradoxes would arise, when they would arise, or even what their implications would be.

Second, from the perspective of the poor actors who are entangled in a paradox, whether or not their actions had been influenced by systemic forces is of secondary importance. What is of primary importance is that most of the paradoxes described above show how they get hurt. Hence, awareness of the potentially adverse consequences produced by a given behavior creates incentives to change it in a manner that would cause less harm. Systemic perspectives are useful in that they highlight the difficulty of doing so. But even within the constraints imposed by the structure of the system, which defines the rules of the game, actors can act to manipulate those rules to their advantage. For example, self-binding commitments in cases of alliance politics, resource accumulation, or international negotiation represent one kind of manipulation of rules of the game in a way that cannot be seen within a systemic perspective (Maoz and Felsenthal, 1987; Schelling, 1984; Elster, 1979). Unless one looks at the unit-level causes of the paradoxes of war, one cannot see the incentives to manipulate structures. When paradoxes are due to fundamental misperceptions and other kinds of cognitive errors, awareness of the paradoxes may alter the expectations that produced them and they would disappear.

Third, at least some of the paradoxes introduced herein have little or nothing to do with the structure of the system at large. The paradox of crisis escalation, the paradox of attrition, the paradox of surprise, and some of the winner's and loser's paradoxes are simply consequences of choice behavior. For example, the paradoxes of attrition and of surprise occur within a war that is under way. I do not know of any system-level explanation for the aspects these paradoxes describe. The most that system-level theories have to say about the management of war is that some wars are prone to expand while others are not. But apart from that, how wars are managed is something that is beyond the scope of such theories. The same applies to the sunk-cost paradox. There is nothing in system theories that suggests that national governments prolong wars because they must prove to their constituencies that those who had died had not died in vain.

Having said all this, it is important to stress that system-level theories do provide an appropriate context for the rational choice explanation of many of the paradoxes. System structures describe those "rules of the game" that set the stage for the paradoxes—at least the rational aspects of some of the paradoxes. Most prominent among those are the para bellum paradox, the paradox of successful deterrence, the ally's paradox, and the paradox of power. The implications for solution (or, more precisely, lack of solution) of these problems should also be seen in the context of system structure. So, while I have chosen to cast these paradoxes as choice dilemmas, the systemic background is significant to their explanation and—as I shall soon argue—a major impediment for their resolution.

## Objections to the Methodology

(1)　The methodology is twisted. Although two models are applied to explain paradoxes of war, no effort is really made to explain these phenomena as mere puzzles that have actually straightforward explanations. In fact, many of the phenomena that are termed paradoxes in this study are explicable using simple linear-logic principles. The bias is inherent in the methodology of paradoxes, which views everything as unintended consequences. Had this logic been confronted with linear logic, many of the so-called paradoxes would have disappeared.

This criticism misunderstands the whole point of the cognitive model, which is a linear-logic model par excellence. The cognitive model attempts to explain away the causal link between expectations and contradictory outcomes by blaming it on human error. The implications of this model—which will be discussed in greater depth below—are that virtually all paradoxes in which cognitive factors play a role can be resolved through awareness and learning. Hence, the contrast between the rational model and the cognitive one is really an ironic feature of the study: the rational model is usually taken to be synonymous with linear logic, but here it is used as a model of paradoxes that attempts to preserve, rather than explain away, contradictions. The cognitive model is that which represents linear logic by trying to account for paradoxical aspects of war choices as consequences of error and bias. Hence, the use of the two models is not only a contrast between two perspectives of choice behavior; it is a contrast between a linear logic and a dialectical one.

Moreover, in many cases, I have mentioned various explanations that attempt to account for various paradoxes of war by other factors. In the case of arms races, there are explanations that stress domestic factors rather than security concerns as underlying national mobilization policies. Presumably, the link between arms races and war could be extended through a Machiavellian notion that those arms have to be used, or else national decision makers may decide that a nation has all the arms it needs. At most, wars are side effects of arms races. In the case of deterrence failures, most conventional explanations focus on weakening of commitments, ambiguity of threat, or the defective communicability, credibility, or feasibility of the threat. In the case of power paradox, I discussed explanations that focus on alternative measures of power, resolve, aid from allies, suitability of resources, and so on. I stressed the fact that all these factors are valid in that they account for many cases that might have been solid candidates for paradoxes.

The historical cases I have selected to demonstrate para bellum, deterrence, or power paradoxes are ones that suggest the inadequacy of all these other explanations. In both cases used to demonstrate the para bellum paradox, there was no domestic production of weapons. All states concerned had to import the weapon systems they thought they needed. Moreover, the governments involved monopolized the import business, so there was neither a military-industrial complex nor a military-arms merchants complex to speak of. In the deterrence cases, I tried to show that there was nothing ambiguous, noncredible, or infeasible about the deterrers' threats. I have tried to document the fact that the challengers were both aware of the threat and impressed by it. In the power paradoxes, I tried to show that neither resolve nor aid from allies transformed the resource ratios. The point of all this is that both in theory and in history, paradoxical explanations were constantly confronted with linear ones. And I believe that—by and large—the former explanations emerged as not less, but perhaps equally convincing as the latter.

(2) The case study approach is limited in terms of its generalizability. Even so, there is an obvious case selection bias. Hence, one does not really know what to make of the findings. The historical demonstration of the paradoxes, even if it is convincing in those cases examined, is merely of heuristic value. It certainly does not warrant the kind of conclusions drawn in the present chapter. Nor do these cases really make the case for the analysis of important international problems via paradoxical logic.

The first part of this critique is well taken, but the last part does not necessarily follow. The rationales for the case study method and the deliberate case selection bias were given in Chapter 1, and there is no sense repeating them here. Yet, the fact that I have tried to demonstrate each of the paradoxes in more than one case suggests that they might be more general than established in this study. Further, it suggests that they may recur even if the cases I have examined are the only examples of such paradoxes. The principal value of the approach is, indeed, heuristic. Yet, it is a very important value because all the lessons I have summarized above are cautionary in nature. They suggest that paradoxes might happen and that, when planning a move, a nation might do well if it spends some time thinking about the unintended consequences of such a move. They also suggest new ways of thinking about problems that traditionally have been analyzed strictly through linear binoculars. Finally, I hope that the paradoxes I have discussed above—especially the less known ones—would provoke people into thinking in terms of solutions, because some of these paradoxes carry very important implications for strategic and political planning.

(3) This study shoves under the rug the systematic aspect of the paradoxes. In other words, it does not even attempt to discuss the

specific conditions that give rise to the various paradoxes. Saying that paradoxes of war are the exception rather than the rule is an elegant way of ducking the real issue: When and under what conditions are specific paradoxes to be expected? All that can be inferred from this study is that paradoxes might happen. It is just like saying that rain might come sometime; no weather forecaster would be able to make a living with this kind of prediction. Science requires not only the identification of problems; it requires saying when, why, and how they might arise. Unless one is able to answer such questions regarding paradoxes of war, it is impossible to accept these findings as having some scientific significance.

Each of the explanations of the paradoxes attempted to discuss the conditions that give rise to the emergence of contradictory outcomes. The common factor that runs through all the paradoxes that have something to do with free choice of policy by actors is the structure of expectations. The nature of expectations, or, in some cases, the combination of expectations and other factors such as resources were seen to make for fatal combinations. The conditions under which one case would be paradoxical while another would not are to be found in each of the models that discuss the paradox. This is as specific as one can be in a book whose professed aim is to identify and illustrate paradoxes of war. A scientific study of the paradoxes will have to start with those explanations and will attempt to examine whether the conditions they specify as giving rise to paradoxes stand up under empirical scrutiny of a more rigorous nature than that given here.

For example, in the para bellum paradox, an arms race can breed either stability or war. The different outcomes of arms race processes depend on the risk propensities of the protagonists. They also depend on the valuation of the two intermediate outcomes: continued stability through arms races and war. If one or both actors become risk-averse, and if their valuation of the two intermediate outcomes increases, war becomes increasingly likely. This is an eminently testable implication of the analysis. A similar argument can be made regarding the testability of the power paradox. I have argued that it is not the increase in resources of the actor that is responsible for the ganging-up process leading to its demise, but the combination of increased resources and the perception of inferior actors regarding what purpose might be served by these resources that determines whether a paradox of power will arise.

The fact that the paradoxes were not tested in a manner that would satisfy any serious scientifically oriented scholar does not imply that they cannot be tested in such a manner. If readers are sufficiently provoked by the contents of this study, they are more than welcome to examine whether these paradoxes go beyond the examples discussed in the book.

*Objections to the Findings*

(1)  What this study is trying—successfully or unsuccessfully—to do is to invert the whole logic of war and peace, a logic that has evolved over centuries of practical experience and research and has yielded a tremendous amount of knowledge. The substantive findings are not only counterintuitive, they are meaningless because they run against everything we know about war, strategy, and politics. When it comes to refuting such a coherent body of knowledge, the burden of proof is on the paradoxical approach. And the evidence presented in the current study, even if plausible, is simply not sufficient to render the substantive findings credible.

This is a valid criticism of the findings. Because of its limited nature, this study does not cast doubt on the linear logic of strategy. The problem is that this is not the only study of its kind; there are quite a few studies that suggest similar findings. First and foremost is Luttwak's (1987) important book on strategy, which challenges many conventional wisdoms in this field and shows many other truisms to have little validity. Second, many of the paradoxes discussed in the present study are not new; they have been known to baffle scholars, military strategists, and politicians (in that order of importance) for years, so that challenging the significance of the para bellum, deterrence, or crisis-escalation paradoxes means, precisely as the critical argument goes, challenging a long-standing body of knowledge.

I do not wish these findings to be interpreted as more than food for thought. Yet, because these findings emerge in a setting wherein linear logic has been most prominent, and because they all imply reconsideration of the logic of war, they appear more revolutionary than they really are. The next critique addresses just this point.

(2)  The findings are not all that counterintuitive. Most of the points reiterate well-known warnings about the initiation, management, and termination of wars. We have known all along that arms races may lead to war, that deterrence may fail, that swift attacks may run aground, that allies can be treacherous, that strong states might lose wars, and that getting out of wars can be very difficult. It is unclear what this study has revealed that we have not known all along.

This is the opposite of the previous critique, and both cannot be correct. But both points can be overstated, and that is precisely my line of defense. The issue is not whether the findings are radically different from conventional wisdom. Some of them are and some of them are not. What matters is that they all emerge from what are, to me and other observers who have been cited along the way, puzzles. What matters is also that once these puzzles have been shown to involve true paradoxes, they cannot be brushed aside.

(3)   The problem with this study is that its focus is on both genuine problems of war and its use of paradoxical logic to account for them. Consequently, the findings point out real problems of unquestionable importance. Yet, many of these problems seem to have no solutions. So what is the good of that new knowledge if all it does is cause despair?

This, I think, is the major problem with the findings. Luttwak's (1987: 231–236) discussion of the practical implications of his theory displays a similar difficulty, for he is very vague on how his ideas can be converted from a descriptive theory to a prescriptive one. I defer discussion of this issue to a later section because I think it requires exploring the practical implications of the two explanatory models used throughout the book.

## Implications for the Study of War

In the first chapter I discussed very briefly three approaches to the study of war: the strategic approach, the decision-making approach, and the systemic approach. This section examines how the present study relates to those three approaches.

### Paradoxes and the Strategic Approach to War

The present study reinforces Luttwak's (1987) conclusion about strategy being a dialectic art in which opposites constantly meet because war is a duel of wills and of wits. Beyond this, the present study contributes a political dimension to this conclusion because it emphasizes the political rather than the military aspects of this dialectic.

Since nuclear strategy was not discussed herein, it is useful to ask whether the approach, methodology, or findings of the paradoxical aspects of conventional war carry over to the nuclear realm. I think the answer is decidedly yes. If nuclear weapons have anything to do with contemporary international politics, their effects can be better understood through a dialectical approach whose emphasis is on paradoxes. If nuclear deterrence theorists are correct, then superpower stability is maintained primarily due to the destructive potential of nuclear weapons. Others contend that *because* the nuclear threshold is so clear and unambiguous, states display considerable adventurism at lower levels of conflict (Gochman and Maoz, 1984: 586).

The seemingly special features of nuclear weapons and the lack of historical evidence about how they have affected war require understanding of the kinds of paradoxes that have emerged in other times and in different settings. It requires exploring potential parallels to these paradoxes in nuclear settings. And one can observe quite a few candidates for the study of nuclear paradoxes. For example, the performance of nuclear powers in conventional wars has been all but successful. In many ways, the possession of nuclear weapons has constrained their behavior in such a manner that they were prevented from accomplishing victory. Given the stability of general deterrence, one of the most plausible scenarios for the outbreak of a nuclear war is through an inadvertent escalation of a local conflict between clients of the two superpowers.

An increasing number of studies examines superpower management of local crises and war (e.g., George et al., 1983; Bar-Simantov, 1987). Yet, one has yet to examine the unintended effects of superpower involvement in local conflicts on the likelihood of their escalation. Sadat's bet on the reaction of the superpowers to a war between their clients ignited one of the most severe superpower crises in the post-World War II era. The dilemmas facing the major powers in such settings are paradoxical because of the fact that they play simultaneously at least two types of strategic games: a game of Chicken vis-à-vis their primary rival, and a primarily cooperative game with their minor allies (in many cases the outcome of the second game affects the perception of the credibility of the major power by other allies). Both the rival superpower and the minor power wish to exploit this kind of entanglement in order to advance their goals (G. H. Snyder, 1984). So it may well happen (and some might argue that this does happen all the time) that the tail wags the dog: minor allies of major powers have led their patrons into major messes despite the will of the latter.

Of even more significance to the analysis of nuclear strategy is the methodology of the present study. Despite ample speculation, we know very little about what a nuclear war might look like because—fortunately or unfortunately—there are no historical precedents. The vast majority of the propositions about nuclear strategy are sheer speculation because the principal evidence for them is of a "dog that did not bark" nature.[2] Because data about nuclear war are unavailable, logical analysis monopolizes nuclear strategic thinking. Under such circumstances, the impact of linear logic is tremendous because one cannot detect empirical breaks in this logic. (Some of the key propositions of this logic in the nuclear setting are such that they can be disproved only if nobody will be around to acknowledge their refutation.) Thus, the principal challenge to those propositions is that the only way they can be delimited is through a mode of analysis that focuses on logical breaks in this logic, a mode of analysis that focuses on the perverse and unintended consequences of behavior that employs this kind of logic.

## Implications for Decision-Theoretic Approaches to the Study of War

The two models I have used to explain the paradoxes of war throughout the study differ from each other in many respects. Yet, in many other ways, they complement each other rather nicely. Both explanations show that people may be trapped in a system of beliefs that they set for themselves even if most aspects of that system seem quite reasonable. The primary difference between the two models is that they attribute to national decision makers different abilities, and hence the implications of the two models depart sharply from each other.

The cognitive model has a mixed view of political leaders. Unlike some more popular depictions of political leaders as slightly stupid people who unwittingly act contrary to the national interest (Tuchman, 1984), this model is centered on the fears, motivations, and biases under which such people operate almost all the time. These factors sometimes serve to distort reality, invoke erroneous expectations, or breed erroneous notions regarding the relations between expectations and rational behavior. Hence, they cause actions to have the opposite consequences of those intended. Because people are susceptible to these biases and cognitive pitfalls, even the smartest politicians can commit stupid mistakes under certain circumstances. And war situations, by the nature of the pressures they exert on national elites, are precisely those situations in which reasonable people are most likely to become victims of their own cognitive fallibility.

Yet, by the same token, the cognitive model is very hopeful with respect to the implications of knowledge. Awareness of these cognitive traps and the circumstances under which they arise may lead political leaders to devise countermeasures that would either prevent national entrapment or—if such entrapment has already taken place—minimize its adverse effects on national goals. Knowledge is important in that it helps save people from the consequences of their cognitive imperfection. Stated more generally, the principal implication of the cognitive model is that paradoxes can be avoided, or their adverse ramifications can be minimized, if proper care, based on sound knowledge and rational behavior, is taken. The merit of works that focus not only on paradoxical effects of human behavior but on less severe forms of deviations from rationality is that they can serve as learning material for future choices.

When President Kennedy was at the height of the Cuban missile crisis, he remarked that he had read Barbara Tuchman's then recent book, *The Guns of August*, about the outbreak of World War I. He told associates that he realized the danger of uncontrolled escalation that might take place during intense international crises. This may have had a major effect on how the crisis was handled. Policy-relevant theory of the sort advocated by George and Smoke (1974) and by George (1980) wishes to make use of this kind of knowledge in order to find remedies to those problems. And it appears to have some interesting recommendations for the organization and rationalization of foreign policy decisions.[3]

The rational model gives a lot of credit to national decision makers. It envisions them as calculating, clear-minded, and smart people. The principal reasons for the conflicts nations get into are the fact that states operate in a system wherein the outcomes of their choices are based on the choices of other states and the fact that actors lack influence over the rules of the games they are playing. The key implication of the rational model is that, in many cases, political wisdom is not sufficient for avoiding paradoxes of war, nor is political wit enough for escaping traps one was not smart enough to avoid.

This is a very pessimistic conclusion. First, it suggests that knowledge may not be of much help. Second, it implies that, in the context of paradoxical aspects of national behavior, scholars have very little to contribute to policy-making because the cures for paradoxes of war cannot be found in improvement in decision making. If decision makers are rational expected-utility maximizers, then they must already be doing the best they can do. It is the "circumstances" that cause actions to have unintended consequences. Unless one can change those circumstances, paradoxes of war cannot be avoided.

The rational model requires satisfaction of the solvability-through-awareness criterion. This means that awareness of the unintended effect of some action cannot lead to the resolution of the paradox. Now, if parties wish to avoid a paradox, they must look for solutions at levels on which their control is extremely limited. In fact, it appears that in many of the cases we have examined in this study, the Alexander method is the only viable solution for the paradox. This method requires changing the rules of the system within which the paradoxical games are being played. As long as that cannot be done, the rational model essentially tells us that we must put up with the contradictions inherent in international politics in general, and in the art of war in particular. This sounds highly counterintuitive in that the conclusion of a seemingly scientific model is that we must accept those contradictions that it revealed, as long as the fundamental structure that had formed these paradoxes remains unchanged. It also seems to be a highly pessimistic result in that it implies that learning can only cause increased frustration.

Anyone familiar with rational choice theory would hardly be surprised by such an implication, for the theory is fraught with paradoxes. Yet, this—I would argue—is one of its principal strengths. Because it is a theory that recognizes its own problems, it is one that is constantly driven by challenges. Paradoxes of rational behavior are primary stimulants to the development of new schemes that are designed to solve these paradoxes. Some of these schemes suggest that the pessimistic outlook of the rational model may be both premature and misleading. Although I have no intention of discussing at great length recent developments in rational choice theory, two such schemes are worth mentioning.

The first scheme involves a new definition of rationality. This definition differentiates between short-term (or myopic) rationality and long-term rationality. Some of the most interesting paradoxes of rationality arise as contradictions between these two types of rationality, and they can be fairly easily solved using a double-flip approach. Perhaps the most prominent example of myopic rationality is the Nash equilibrium concept in game theory. This principle suggests that a state of affairs is Nash-stable if no actor has an immediate incentive to depart from it. The notion of immediate incentive is taken to mean that the payoff an actor gets immediately after departing from that outcome is *strictly* valued more than the outcome the actor obtains by staying where he or she had been. Myopic rationality requires from actors that they look ahead only one step. As such, it adds empirical plausibility to the assumptions of the model in that the number of possible outcomes that an actor must examine to make a sensible choice is significantly smaller than the number of possible outcomes he or she would have to explore if his or her horizon were larger (Kilgour, 1985).

On the other hand, nonmyopic rationality is behavior that maximizes the final (or total) payoffs of an actor. A behavior is nonmyopically rational if it leads to optimal end results, even if it involves bad intermediate outcomes. Accordingly, an outcome is nonmyopically stable if no actor has a long-term incentive to depart from it (Brams and Wittman, 1981). The Dollar Auction is perhaps one of the most acute examples of a contradiction between myopic and nonmyopic rationality.

Historical hindsight reveals that actors who got entangled in unintended processes of escalation would have been better off had they avoided the first step in the crisis. Such hindsight also reveals that, once in a war that drags on without end in sight, sometimes short-term humiliation is more than outweighed by the saving of long-term costs of war as well as long-term humiliation. While Monday-morning quarterbacking is a deplorable practice, it is indispensable if next Sunday's game is to be won. The benefit of knowledge is that it can help reveal the problems of the previous war in order to avoid repeating them the next time around, even if one can understand the rationale that led states into the first kind of mess. The significance of the paradoxes studied herein is that they reveal such contradictions and show that expectations can be manipulated so as to alter behavior in a manner that resolves these paradoxes.

The notions of precommitment (Elster, 1979) and self-command all represent examples of how knowledge of inherent problems of rationality can lead to ways of overcoming them. Analyses such as these can teach politicians to devise schemes that would prevent them from making short-term rational decisions that contradict their long-term interests. This does not entail changing rules of the games they are playing. However, it does require looking at the games from a different angle. The task of the analyst is to examine different definitions of the situation and test whether they reveal such a solution that cannot be seen by the decision maker who is grappling with the problem of the moment.

Another aspect of the rational choice analysis is the examination of the ways in which the seemingly unalterable "rules of the game" can be manipulated in ways that would solve paradoxes of war. Examples for manipulation of rules of play are notions of self-binding commitments or other tactics leading to the foreclosing of options. The problem with the Nash equilibrium is not only that it is based on a shortsighted notion of rationality; it is also that it is based on a marginal improvement rule rather than on indifference notions. A move, according to this notion, would not be made if the outcome of that move is the same as the outcome of a previous move. Yet, even according to shortsighted notions of rationality, there is no harm in moving from one outcome to another as long as one is not hurt in the process. This is especially true in cases where this move induces a subsequent move of the opponent that eventually improves the payoffs of all actors. Maoz and Felsenthal (1987) have shown that even in seemingly hopeless situations where actors have no control over the rules of the game, they can manipulate them at the margin in a manner that is both counterintuitive and mutually beneficial. Their analysis of the Sadat 1977–78 peace initiative and of the Israeli unilateral withdrawal from Lebanon suggests that double-flip resolutions of paradoxes of cooperation are both feasible and effective. However, it takes some doing to realize that such solutions exist, and it takes some courage to apply them, because they all involve numerous uncertainties and short-term costs.

What all this sums up to is the theme that choice-related approaches focusing on the paradoxical aspects approach are important because they can yield potentially surprising findings and unconventional solutions to seemingly insoluble puzzles.

## Implications for Systems Analysis of International Politics

This analysis suggests that the major changes in the structure of the international system, the distribution of power within it, and its principal rules of operation may be unintentional consequences of intentional choices. Waltz's notion of the "tyranny of small decisions" may be more twisted than even he intended it to be. Some of the major system transformations may have begun without anybody wishing them to happen. Since war is seen as the great transformer of international systems, and since major wars can be unintended consequences of processes designed to prevent them, this should not be surprising. If students of the crisis of July-August 1914 are to be taken seriously, then the war that terminated a hundred years of relative tranquility under a balance-of-power system is a first-rate example of system change that nobody wanted.[4]

Likewise, the outcomes of wars can be responsible for the creation of structures that may have been unplanned and unintended. The rise and decline of international actors may be contrary to the plans of the designers of the new order following major wars. For example, following the Napoleonic Wars, the conservative European powers established the Holy Alliance, whose professed aim was to repress national liberation movements in Europe and secure the monarchical status of the major European states. No sooner had the Greek revolution broken out than the major European states found themselves, for tactical reasons, supporting a national liberation movement. Following World War II, the plan, as reflected by the Yalta agreement, was to set up a new international order consisting of the United States, the Soviet Union, Great Britain, and France, which would jointly supervise the reestablishment of the political and economic systems in Europe and the Far East. However, due to the costs of victory, Great Britain and France quickly faded into the background, with the United States picking up most of the slack. Of course, the bipolar system that has developed has no clear intentional documentation. Yet, the systems that have not developed have ample intentional documentation.

The implication of all this is that when looking through systemic binoculars at the changes that have occurred or may still occur in international politics, it is important to examine how intentions of actors have affected change and stability in international politics. Elsewhere, I have discussed a theory of international processes that shows that both stability and change in long-term international processes can result from short-term and highly parochial interests (Maoz, 1989). If one wishes to predict how the contemporary international system will evolve over time, it might be useful to consider the structural factors that shape system-level changes; but it might be also useful to examine how intentions play a role in that process.

## Paradoxes of Peace:
## Features of Contemporary International Politics

International war, though a pathological feature of an anarchic system, may well fade into the background in terms of the threat it poses for humankind. If nuclear weapons make large-scale war senseless, and if the fear of uncontrolled escalation checks the behavior of the superpowers such that either intentional or unintentional war becomes limited, then the key threats for humankind might be due to the nonviolent activity of people and states. Some of these peacetime threats are worth mentioning because, in many ways, they represent social paradoxes.

(1) *The depletion of natural resources:* As more energy and effort is put into construction and less is put into destruction, more resources are used, more people are born, more people live longer, and the pace of decline in the natural resources of planet Earth is stepped up.

Because competition in times of peace is concentrated in production and markets rather than on destruction, there is a strong incentive to grow rapidly. Much like military might, economic power is relative in nature. Hence, performance is measured in comparison to the performance of key competitors, and the trick is to beat others in the economic growth game. The more growth, the more resources are required, and the faster they need to be extracted. Peacetime growth is also associated with population growth, at least in developing states. But more population means more mouths that need to be fed, and more food sources are required. Both the limits on arable land and the drive toward an industrial edge actually slow down food production. Malthus's nightmare becomes all the more viable in peacetime than in wartime. We bring children into the world so that they can bring their own children, who might starve to death.

(2) *Environmental risks:* Industrialization makes life easier and more comfortable—no doubt about it. It is easier to move around, there is more leisure time and more choices for spending it. Yet, not only does industrialization bring progress, it may bring about an environmental holocaust in the long run. And the steeper the competition among industrial powers, the faster this holocaust is to come about. Pollution, waste dumping, and alteration in the atmospheric structure and its climatic consequences are all human-made risks.

(3) *Complexity and international management:* The more developed the world becomes, the more intertwined the problems that units confront, and the more difficult it is for each state to solve its problems on its own. The tremendous degree of interdependence that characterizes contemporary international politics is both extensive and

intensive. Not only is one nation's fate a function of other nations' fate; the outcome of one type of national goal is increasingly a function of the performance of the state on another dimension. All this calls for increased efforts for international coordination. But it is this increased complexity that makes international cooperation and coordination more difficult because of the increased divergence of national interests on multiple issues. Optimal international solutions are more difficult to devise because the concerns of states over different management problems differ, and as the number of issues on the agenda grows larger, the difficulty of realizing a prominent solution to all these problems is more pronounced.

I have brought up these issues because they are all dilemmas of social choice. Nobody wishes these problems to linger on and on, because everybody is going to suffer in the long run. Yet, the structure of the problems, the interrelations among them, and the lack of significant progress toward their resolution suggests paradoxical features. It is typically assumed that some form of supernational regulator might solve the paradoxical features of these peacetime problems, but it is generally agreed that such a regulator is unlikely to emerge. So substitutes are being sought in the form of international institutions, which soon turn out to be largely ineffective in solving the problems.

The difficulty of finding rational solutions to paradoxes of war is analogous to the efforts at solving paradoxes of peace. But the logic of those solutions that have been shown effective in the case of the former paradoxes can be extended to the search for potential solutions of the latter paradoxes. The answers to these problems might be more productively found in mechanisms that use the rules of anarchy to produce cooperation, rather than in attempts to apply Alexander-type schemes that seek to change the rules of anarchy. Axelrod's (1984) work on the evolution of cooperation, and Maoz and Felsenthal's (1987) self-binding commitments notions may prove more fruitful approaches to collective choice problems in noncooperative settings than the attempted transformation of the settings into cooperative ones.

## Future Research

Three potentially fruitful lines of inquiry follow from the present investigation of paradoxes of war: systematic analyses of the conditions under which these paradoxes arise using quantitative methods, analyses of potential solutions to these paradoxes, and the expansion of the methodology and approach to the choice-related explanation of the paradoxes of peace.

Systematic analyses of the various paradoxes of war should start by converting the qualitative explanations of the paradoxes into precise hypotheses that are amenable to quantitative analyses using available data on international war or short-of-war conflict. These hypotheses can establish both the validity of the explanation and the significance of the paradoxes in terms of relative frequency. We have seen that some of the paradoxes discussed herein have some prima facie evidence that goes well beyond the interesting anecdotal case nature. This applies particularly to the para bellum paradox, the paradox of surprise, and the power paradox. The empirical examination of these paradoxes will establish if the various explanations developed in the book seem to account for the facts in those cases. An additional feature of systematic analyses of paradoxes is the ability to examine the nonparadoxical cases to see whether those factors emphasized by the two models as contributing to paradoxical outcomes were absent.

Some very interesting examples of solutions to some of these paradoxes that were used by states in ancient history have seemingly been forgotten in modern times. They have been replaced by naive institutional arrangements that prove to be of dubious value. One of these examples is the custom of exchanging hostages in the Greek city-state system as a mechanism for preserving agreements. Instead of devising elaborate institutions whose function was to monitor treaty violations, the ancient Greeks made the violation of a treaty costly for themselves. They tied their hands in a way that would make treaty violation impossible.

For example, the credibility-provocability trade-off in deterrence could be solved by imposing on the deterrer costs that are incurred only if it initiates a first strike, but not if it retaliates to a first strike of the opponent. One scheme that can be developed in the nuclear deterrence context is some sort of automatic mechanism that causes total destruction of the initiator's second strike capability if it launches a first strike. For example, a neutral power possesses information about the precise location of all the nuclear submarines of both superpowers. If one of them launches a first strike, this information is automatically entered into the targeting mechanisms of the opponent's missiles. Those can be fired before they are hit and leave the initiator totally disarmed. This can assure that an initiator of a nuclear exchange will always lose it, hence making initiation self-defeating for whatever reasons it was contemplated. This is the kind of double-flip logic that solves this kind of paradox by devising a scheme for how a deterrer can make its threat both effective and nonprovocable by deterring itself. The notion of double-flip solutions to the paradoxes of war can prove a fruitful ground for the search for ways to prevent states from hurting themselves while acting to benefit themselves.

Finally, the previous section has merely scratched the surface in terms of the potential benefits of extending the framework used herein to nonconflictual settings. Because the fundamental structure of peacetime paradoxes is no different from that of wartime paradoxes, their explanation and potential solutions may be sought within a scheme whose focus is on the unintended consequences of intentional behavior.

## Notes

1   In fairness, not all of the paradoxes were established as contradictions between rational choice principles. But (1) most paradoxes were seen to rest on choice-related logic, and (2) those that did not were seen to create real puzzles in related terms.

2   The reader should be reminded of the paradox of existence I have briefly discussed in Chapter 1. Since nuclear war or the use of nuclear weapons in conventional war has only one example, we do not know what a nuclear war is, how and why it may break out, how it would be managed, or what its outcomes and implications would be. Yet to establish what cannot (or must not) exist, we have to establish how and why it might break out, how it is going to be managed, and what its outcomes and implications might be, which is a contradiction.

3   For similar notions coming from social psychologists, see Kahneman and Tversky (1982), Fischoff (1982), Nisbett et al. (1982), and Wheeler and Janis (1980).

4   Gilpin (1981) asserts that a system changes if at least one of the key powers becomes sufficiently dissatisfied with the prevailing order that it feels it can gain more from changing it than from maintaining it. Yet, the evidence regarding the intentional nature of the process leading to World War I is more than sketchy. It is unclear that the major actors saw this as more than a balance-correcting exchange. Most of them were thinking in terms of a brief, decisive war on the battlefield, but they did not think about the outcomes of the war in terms of major political changes in the European power structure (Blainey, 1988; Levy, 1988b).

# Bibliography

Abdulghani, J. M. (1984). *Iraq and Iran: The Years of Crisis*. London: Johns Hopkins University Press.

Abel, T. (1941). "The Element of Decision in the Pattern of War." *American Sociological Review*, 6(4): 853–859.

Achen, C., and Snidal, D. (1989). "Rational Deterrence Theory and Comparative Case Studies." *World Politics*, 41(2): 143–169.

Ajami, F. (1981). *The Arab Predicament*. Cambridge: Cambridge University Press.

Alexander, B. (1986). *Korea: The First War We Lost*. New York: Hippocrene.

Allan, P. (1983). *Conflict Bargaining and the Arms Race*. Boston: Ballinger.

Allison, G. T. (1971). *Essence of Decision: Explaining the Cuban Missile Crisis*. Boston: Little, Brown.

Allison, G. T., and Halperin, M. H. (1972). "Bureaucratic Politics: A Paradigm and Some Policy Implications," pp. 40–79 in R. Tanter and R. Ullman, eds., *Theory and Policy in International Relations*. Princeton, NJ: Princeton University Press.

Allon, H. (1980). *Countering Terrorism: An Analysis of Israeli Policies and Countermeasures*. Santa Monica, CA: Rand Corporation.

Allon, Y. (1970). *Curtain of Sand* (2nd ed.). Tel Aviv: Ha'Kibbutz Ha'Meuchad. (in Hebrew)

Altfeld, M. (1984). "The Decision to Ally: A Theory and a Test." *Western Political Quarterly*, 37(4): 523–544.

Apostel, L., et al., eds. (1972). *Negation*. Louvain: Nauwelarets.

Aron, R. (1966). *Peace and War*. Garden City, NY: Doubleday.

Arrow, K. J. (1951). *Social Choice and Individual Values*. New York: Wiley.

Ashley, R. K. (1984). "The Poverty of Neorealism." *International Organization*, 38(2): 225–286.

Auman, R. J. (1988). "Irrationality in Game Theory." Paper presented at the Conference on Economic Theories of Politics, University of Haifa, June 22.

Axelrod, R. (1984). *The Evolution of Cooperation*. New York: Basic Books.

——— (1979). "The Rational Timing of Surprise." *World Politics*, 31(2): 228–246.

Azar, E. A. (1972). "Conflict Escalation and Conflict Reduction in an International Crisis: Suez, 1956." *Journal of Conflict Resolution*, 16(2): 183–202.

Baldwin, D. (1979). "Power Analysis and World Politics." *World Politics*, 31(2): 161–194.

Baram, A. (1980). "Saddam Hussein: A Political Profile." *Jerusalem Quarterly*, 17(3): 115–144.

Barnds, W. J. (1972). *India, Pakistan, and the Great Powers*. New York: Praeger.

Barnett, C. (1963). *The Swordbearers: Supreme Command in the First World*

*War*. Bloomington: Indiana University Press.

Bar-Simantov, Y. (1987). *Israel, the Superpowers, and the War in the Middle East*. New York: Praeger.

―――― (1983). *Linkage Politics in the Middle East*. Boulder, CO: Westview.

―――― (1980). *The Israeli-Egyptian War of Attrition, 1969–1970: A Case Study of a Limited War*. New York: Columbia University Press.

Beard, C. A. (1948). *President Roosevelt and the Coming of the War, 1941: A Study of Appearances and Reality*. New Haven, CT: Yale University Press.

Beer, F. (1981). *Peace Against War*. San Francisco: Freeman.

Ben-Gurion, D. (1968). *The Renewed State of Israel*. Tel Aviv: Po'alim. (in Hebrew)

Ben-Zvi, A. (1976). "Hindsight and Foresight: A Conceptual Framework for the Analysis of Surprise Attacks." *World Politics*, 28(4): 381–395.

Berglas, E. (1986). "Defense and the Economy," pp. 173–191 in Y. Ben-Porath, ed., *The Israeli Economy: Maturing Through Crises*. Cambridge, MA: Harvard University Press.

Betts, R. K. (1978). "Analysis, War, and Decision: Why Intelligence Failures Are Inevitable." *World Politics*, 31(1): 61–89.

Bialer, S., ed. (1984). *Stalin and His Generals: Soviet Military Memoirs of World War II*. Boulder, CO: Westview.

Blainey, G. (1988). *The Causes of War* (3rd ed.). New York: Free Press.

Blechman, B. (1966). "The Quantitative Evaluation of Foreign Policy Alternatives: Sinai 1956." *Journal of Conflict Resolution*, 10(4): 408–426.

Bond, P., and Alexander, M. (1986). "Liddell Hart and De Gaulle: The Doctrines of Limited Liability and Mobile Defense," pp. 598–623 in P. Paret, ed., *Makers of Modern Strategy: From Machiavelli to the Nuclear Age*. Princeton, NJ: Princeton University Press.

Borg, D., and Okamoto, S., eds. (1973). *Pearl Harbor as History: Japanese-American Relations, 1931–1941*. New York: Columbia University Press.

Bose, A. (1977). *Political Paradoxes and Puzzles*. Oxford: Clarendon.

Brams, S. J. (1985). *Superpower Games*. New Haven, CT: Yale University Press.

―――― (1976). *Paradoxes in Politics: An Introduction to the Nonobvious in Political Science*. New York: Free Press.

Brams, S. J., Felsenthal D. S., and Maoz, Z. (1987). "Chairman Paradoxes Under Approval Voting," pp. 223–233 in G. Eberlein and H. Berghel, eds., *Theory and Decision*. Dordrecht, Holland: D. Riedel.

Brams, S. J., Felsenthal, D. S., and Maoz, Z. (1986). "New Chairman Paradoxes," pp. 243–256 in A. Diekman and P. Mitter, eds., *Paradoxical Effects of Social Behavior: Essays in Honor of Anatol Rapoport*. Vienna: Physica Verlag.

Brams, S. J., and Kilgour, D. M. (1988). "Deterrence Versus Defense: A Game-Theoretic Model of Star Wars." *International Studies Quarterly*, 32(1): 3–28.

Brams, S. J., and Wittman, D. (1981). "Non–Myopic Equilibria in 2 × 2 Games." *Conflict Management and Peace Science*, 6(3): 39–62.

Brecher, M. (1980). *Decisions in Crisis: Israel, 1967 and 1973*. Berkeley: University of California Press.

―――― (1979). "State Behavior in International Crises." *Journal of Conflict Resolution*, 23(3): 446–480.

―――― (1974). *Decisions in Israel's Foreign Policy*. New Haven, CT: Yale University Press.

Brecher, M., and James, P. (1986). *Crisis and Change in World Politics.* Boulder, CO: Westview.

Brito, D. L., and Intrilligator, M. D. (1985). "Conflict, War, and Redistribution." *American Political Science Review*, 79(4): 943–957.

Brockner, J., and Rubin, J. Z. (1985). *Entrapment in Escalating Conflicts: A Social Psychological Analysis.* New York: Springer Verlag.

Brodie, B. (1973). *War and Politics.* New York: Macmillan.

Brown, J., and Snyder, W. P., eds. (1985). *The Regionalization of Warfare.* New Brunswick, NJ: Transaction.

Bueno de Mesquita, B. (1985). "The 'War Trap' Revisited: A Revised Expected Utility Model." *American Political Science Review*, 79(1): 156–173.

—— (1981). *The War Trap.* New Haven, CT: Yale University Press.

—— (1980). "Theories of International Conflict: An Analysis and an Appraisal," pp. 360–386 in T. R. Gurr, ed., *Handbook of International Conflict.* New York: Free Press.

Bull, H. (1977). *The Anarchical Society.* New York: Columbia University Press.

Bullock, A. (1952). *Hitler: A Study of Tyranny.* New York: Harper & Row.

Burke, S. M. (1973). *Pakistan's Foreign Policy: An Historical Analysis.* London: Oxford University Press.

Burrowes, R., and Muzzio, D. (1972). "Aspects of an Enumerative History of Four Arab States and Israel, 1965–1967." *Journal of Conflict Resolution*, 16(2): 211–226.

Butow, R. J. C. (1962). *Tojo and the Coming of the War.* Princeton, NJ: Princeton University Press.

Choucri, N., and North, R. (1975). *Nations in Conflict.* San Francisco: Freeman.

Churchill, W. (1948). *The Gathering Storm.* Cambridge, MA: Houghton Mifflin.

Clark, A. (1970). *Operation Barbarossa.* Tel Aviv: Ma'arachot. (Hebrew translation from English, S. Gafni)

Clausewitz, C. V. (1966). *On War* (Anatol Rapoport, ed.). New York: Penguin. (Original work published 1832)

Coombs, C. H., Dawes, R. M., and Tversky, A. (1970). *Mathematical Psychology: An Elementary Introduction.* Englewood Cliffs, NJ: Prentice-Hall.

Correlates of War (COW) Project (1986). *Military Capabilities 1816–1980.* Ann Arbor: University of Michigan.

Coser, L. (1957). *The Functions of Social Conflict.* New York: Free Press.

Crampton, R. J. (1983). *Bulgaria, 1878–1918: A History.* Boulder, CO: East European Monographs (distributed by Columbia University Press).

Dakin, D. (1972). *The Unification of Greece, 1770–1923.* London: Ernst Benn.

Dayan, M. (1976). *Story of My Life.* New York: William Morrow.

—— (1966). *Diary of the Sinai Campaign.* Tel Aviv: Am-Ha'Sefer. (in Hebrew)

Deakin, F. W. (1962). *The Brutal Friendship: Mussolini, Hitler, and the Fall of Italian Fascism.* New York: Harper & Row.

Dedijer, V., et al. (1974). *History of Yugoslavia.* New York: McGraw-Hill.

De Rivera, J. (1968). *The Psychological Dimension of Foreign Policy.* Columbus, OH: Bobbs-Merrill.

Deutsch, K. W. (1969). "The Point of No Return in the Progression Toward War," in D. G. Pruitt and R. C. Snyder, eds., *Theory and Research on the Causes of War*. Indianapolis: Bobbs-Merrill.

Diehl, P. (1983). "Arms Races and Escalation: A Closer Look." *Journal of Peace Research*, 20(3): 205–212.

Diplomatist [anonymous] (1915). *Nationalism and War in the Near East*. Oxford: Clarendon.

Dupuy, T. N. (1978). *Elusive Victory: The Arab-Israeli Wars, 1947–1974*. New York: Harper & Row.

Dupuy, T. N., and Martell, P. (1986). *Flawed Victory: The Arab-Israeli Conflict and the 1982 War in Lebanon*. Fairfax, VA: Hero.

Eban, A. (1977). *Abba Eban: An Autobiography*. New York: Random House.

Eckstein, H. (1975). "Case Study and Theory in Political Science," in F. I. Greenstein and N. E. Polsby, eds., *Handbook of Political Science* (Vol. 7). Reading, MA: Addison-Wesley.

Elster, J. (1985). *Making Sense of Marx*. Cambridge: Cambridge University Press.

——— (1979). *Ulysses and the Sirens: Studies in Rationality and Irrationality*. Cambridge: Cambridge University Press.

Farquharson, R. (1969). *Theory of Voting*. New Haven, CT: Yale University Press.

Farrar, L. L., Jr. (1973). *The Short War Illusion: German Policy, Strategy, and Military Affairs, August-December, 1914*. Santa Barbara, CA: ABC-Clio.

Feis, H. (1950). *The Road to Pearl Harbor*. Princeton, NJ: Princeton University Press.

Feldman, H. (1972). *From Crisis to Crisis: Pakistan, 1962–1969*. London: Oxford University Press.

Felsenthal, D. S., and Maoz, Z. (1988). "A Comparative Analysis of Sincere and Sophisticated Approval and Plurality Voting." *Behavioral Science*, 33(2): 116–130.

Fischoff, B. (1982). "Debiasing," pp. 422–444 in D. Kahneman, P. Slovic, and A. Tversky, eds., *Judgment Under Uncertainty: Heuristics and Biases*. Cambridge: Cambridge University Press.

Friedlander, S. (1967). *Prelude to War: American-German Relations, 1939–1941*. New York: Knopf.

Ganguly, S. (1986). *The Origins of War in South Asia*. Boulder, CO: Westview.

Garthoff, R. (1953). *Soviet Military Doctrine*. Santa Monica, CA: Rand Corporation.

Gazit, S. (1986). *Egyptian-Israeli Peace Efforts, 1971–1972*. Tel Aviv: Ma'arachot. (in Hebrew)

Geist, B. (1974). *The Six Day War: A Study in the Setting and Process of Foreign Policy Decisions Under Crisis Conditions*. Unpublished Ph.D. dissertation, Hebrew University, Jerusalem.

Gelb, L. H., and Betts, R. K. (1979). *The Irony of Vietnam: The System Worked*. Washington, DC: Brookings.

George, A. L. (1984). "Crisis Management: The Interplay of Military and Political Considerations." *Survival*, 26(5): 223–234.

——— (1980). *Presidential Decisionmaking in Foreign Policy: The Effective Use of Information and Advice*. Boulder, CO: Westview.

—— (1979). "Case Studies and Theory Development: The Method of Structured, Focused Comparison," in P. G. Lauren, ed., *Diplomacy*. New York: Free Press.

George, A. L., et al. (1983). *Managing U.S.-Soviet Rivalry: Problems of Crisis Prevention*. Boulder, CO: Westview.

George, A. L., Hall, D. K., and Simmons, W. (1972). *The Limits of Coercive Diplomacy*. Boston: Little, Brown.

George, A. L., and McKeown, T. J. (1985). "Case Studies and Theories of Organizational Decision Making." *Advances in Information Processing in Organizations*, 2(1): 21–58.

George, A. L., and Smoke, R. (1974). *Deterrence in American Foreign Policy: Theory and Practice*. New York: Columbia University Press.

Geyer, M. (1986). "German Strategy in the Age of Machine Warfare, 1914–1945," pp. 527–597 in P. Paret, ed., *Makers of Modern Strategy: From Machiavelli to the Nuclear Age*. Princeton, NJ: Princeton University Press.

Gilboa, E. (1987). *American Public Opinion Toward Israel and the Arab-Israeli Conflict*. Lexington, MA: Lexington.

Gilboa, M. (1968). *Six Years, Six Days*. Tel Aviv: Am Oved. (in Hebrew)

Gilpin, R. (1981). *War and Change in World Politics*. Cambridge: Cambridge University Press.

Gochman, C. S., and Maoz, Z. (1984). "Militarized Interstate Disputes, 1816–1976: Procedures, Patterns, and Insights." *Journal of Conflict Resolution*, 28(4): 585–615.

Goulden, J. G. (1982). *Korea: The Untold Story of the War*. New York: Times Books.

Green, P. (1964). *Deadly Logic*. Columbus: Ohio State University Press.

Grey, I. (1979). *Stalin: Man of History*. Garden City, NY: Doubleday.

Grummon, S. R. (1982). *The Iran-Iraq War: Islam Embattled*. New York: Praeger.

Halperin, M. A. (1974). *Bureaucratic Politics and Foreign Policy*. Washington, DC: Brookings.

Hammad, K. (1987). "The Role of Foreign Aid in the Jordanian Economy, 1959–1983," pp. 11–31 in B. Khader and A. Badran, eds., *The Economic Development of Jordan*. London: Croom Helm.

Handel, M. I. (1987). "Deception in War," in Z. Offer and A. Kober, eds., *Intelligence and National Security*. Tel Aviv: Ma'arachot. (in Hebrew)

—— (1982). "War Termination: A Critical Survey," pp. 40–71 in N. Oren, ed., *The Termination of Wars*. Jerusalem: Magness.

—— (1976). *Perception, Deception, and Surprise: The Case of the Yom Kippur War*. Jerusalem: Leonard Davis Institute of International Relations.

Harkabi, Y. (1983). *The Bar Kochbah Syndrome: Risk and Realism in International Politics*. New York: Rossell.

—— (1978). *On the Guerrilla*. Tel Aviv: Ma'arachot. (in Hebrew)

—— ed. (1969). *Arab Lessons from Their [1967] Defeat*. Tel Aviv: Am-Oved. (in Hebrew)

—— (1964). *Nuclear War and Nuclear Peace*. Tel Aviv: Ma'arachot. (in Hebrew)

Hart, J. (1976). "Three Approaches to the Measurement of Power in International Relations." *International Organization*, 30(2): 299–305.

Heikal, M. (1975). *The Road to Ramadan*. New York: Ballantine.

Helmreich, E. C. (1969). *The Diplomacy of the Balkan Wars, 1912–1913.* New York: Russell & Russell.

Helms, C. M. (1984). *Iraq: Eastern Flank of the Arab World.* Washington, DC: Brookings.

Hempel, C. (1965). *Aspects of Scientific Explanation.* New York: Free Press.

Heradsveidt, D. (1979). *The Arab-Israeli Conflict: Psychological Obstacles to Peace.* Oslo: Universitetforlaget.

Herbig, D., and Herbig, C. (1982). "On Military Deception," pp. 3–30 in D. Herbig and C. Herbig, eds., *Strategic Military Deception.* New York: Pergamon.

Herken, G. (1987). *Counsels of War.* New York: Oxford University Press.

Hermann, C. F. (1969). *Crises in Foreign Policy: A Simulation Analysis.* New York: Bobbs-Merrill.

Herzog, C. (1975). *The War of Atonement.* Boston: Little, Brown.

Hirschman, A. O. (1987). "The Political Economy of Latin American Development: Seven Exercises in Retrospection." *Latin America Research Review*, 22(3): 7–36.

Holsti, O. R. (1979). "Theories of Crisis Decision Making," pp. 99–136 in P. G. Lauren, ed., *Diplomacy: New Approaches in History, Theory and Policy.* New York: Free Press.

——— (1972). *Crisis, Escalation, War.* Montreal: McGill Queen's University Press.

——— (1962). "The Belief System and National Images: A Case Study." *Journal of Conflict Resolution*, 6(2): 244–252.

Howard, M. (1986). "Men Against Fire: The Doctrine of the Offensive in 1914," pp. 510–526 in P. Paret, ed., *Makers of Modern Strategy: From Machiavelli to the Nuclear Age.* Princeton, NJ: Princeton University Press.

Huth, P., and Russett, B. M. (1988). "Deterrence Failure and Crisis Escalation." *International Studies Quarterly*, 32(1): 29–45.

Huth, P., and Russett, B. M. (1984). "What Makes Deterrence Work: Cases from 1900 to 1960." *World Politics*, 36(4): 496–526.

Hybel, A. R. (1986). *The Logic of Surprise in International Conflict.* Lexington, MA: Lexington.

Ikle, F. C. (1971). *Every War Must End.* New York: Columbia University Press.

International Institute of Strategic Studies (IISS) (1966–1985). *The Military Balance.* London: Author.

Intrilligator, M. D., and Brito, D. L. (1984). "Can Arms Races Lead to the Outbreak of War?" *Journal of Conflict Resolution*, 12(1): 123–128.

Isaacs, A. R. (1983). *Without Honor: Defeat in Vietnam and Cambodia.* Baltimore: Johns Hopkins University Press.

Ismael, T. (1982). *Iraq and Iran: Roots of Conflict.* Syracuse, NY: Syracuse University Press.

Israeli, R. (1985). *Man of Defiance: A Political Biography of Anwar Sadat.* London: Widenfeld & Nicolson.

Janis, I. L. (1982). *Groupthink* (2nd ed.). Boston: Houghton Mifflin.

Janis, I. L., and Mann, L. (1977). *Decision Making: A Psychological Analysis of Conflict, Choice, and Commitment.* New York: Free Press.

Jervis, R. (1985). "Perceiving and Coping with Threat," pp. 13–33 in R. Jervis, R. N. Lebow, and J. G. Stein, eds., *Psychology and Deterrence.* Baltimore: Johns Hopkins University Press.

—— (1984). *The Illogic of American Nuclear Strategy*. Ithaca, NY: Cornell University Press.

—— (1979). "Deterrence Theory Revisited." *World Politics*, 31(2): 289–324.

—— (1978). "Cooperation Under the Security Dilemma." *World Politics*, 30(2): 167–214.

—— (1976). *Perception and Misperception in International Politics*. Princeton, NJ: Princeton University Press.

—— (1970). *The Logic of Images in International Politics*. Princeton, NJ: Princeton University Press.

Jervis, R., Lebow, R. N., and Stein, J. G., eds. (1985). *Psychology and Deterrence*. Baltimore: Johns Hopkins University Press.

Job, B. L. (1979). "Grins Without Cats: In Pursuit of Knowledge of International Alliances," pp. 39–64 in D. A. Zinnes and J. D. Singer, eds., *Cumulation in International Relations* (Monograph Series in World Affairs). Denver: University of Denver.

Kahneman, D., and Tversky, A. (1982). "Intuitive Prediction: Biases and Corrective Procedures," pp. 414–421 in D. Kahneman, P. Slovic, and A. Tversky, eds., *Judgment Under Uncertainty: Heuristics and Biases*. Cambridge: Cambridge University Press.

Kahneman, D., and Tversky, A. (1979). "Prospect Theory: An Analysis of Decision Under Risk." *Econometrica*, 47(2): 263–291.

Kainz, H. P. (1988). *Paradox, Dialectic, and Reason*. University Park: Pennsylvania State University Press.

Kanovsky, E. (1976). *The Economy of Jordan*. Tel Aviv: Tel Aviv University Publishing Projects.

Kaplan, M. (1957). *System and Process in International Relations*. New York: Wiley.

Kelley, H. H., Beckman, L. L., and Fisher, C. S. (1967). "Negotiating the Division of a Reward Under Incomplete Information." *Journal of Experimental Social Psychology*, 3(2): 361–398.

Keohane, R. O., ed. (1986). *Neorealism and Its Critics*. New York: Columbia University Press.

Keohane, R. O., and Nye, J. (1977). *Power and Interdependence: World Politics in Transition*. Boston: Little, Brown.

Kerr, M. (1967). *The Arab Cold War* (2nd ed.). Oxford: Oxford University Press.

Khader, B., and Badran, A. (1987). *The Economic Development of Jordan*. London: Croom Helm.

Kilgour, D. M. (1985). "Anticipation and Stability in Two-Person Non-Cooperative Games," pp. 26–51 in U. Luterbacher and M. D. Ward, eds., *Dynamic Models of International Conflict*. Boulder, CO: Lynne Reiner.

Kirkpatrick, I. (1964). *Mussolini: A Study in Power*. New York: Hawthorn.

Kissinger, H. A. (1979). *White House Years*. Boston: Little, Brown.

Kolko, G. (1985). *Anatomy of a War: Vietnam, the United States, and the Modern Historical Experience*. New York: Pantheon.

Kugler, J., and Domke, W. (1986). "Comparing the Strength of Nations." *Comparative Political Studies*, 19(1): 39–70.

Kuhn, T. (1970). *The Logic of Scientific Revolutions* (2nd ed.). Chicago: University of Chicago Press.

Lacoture, J. (1971). *Nasser*. New York: Simon & Schuster.

Langer, W. L., and Gleason, S. E. (1953). *The Undeclared War, 1940–1941*.

New York: Harper & Row.

Lanir, Z. (1983). *Strategic Surprise in the Yom-Kippur War*. Tel Aviv: Am Oved. (in Hebrew)

Laqueur, W. (1976). *Guerrilla: A Historical and Critical Study*. Boston: Little, Brown.

Lave, C. S., and March, J. G. (1975). *Introduction to Models in the Social Sciences*. New York: Wiley.

Lebow, R. N. (1985). "The Deterrence Deadlock: Is There a Way Out?" pp. 180–202 in R. Jervis, R. N. Lebow, and J. G. Stein, eds., *Psychology and Deterrence*. Baltimore: Johns Hopkins University Press.

—— (1981). *Between Peace and War: The Nature of International Crisis*. Baltimore: Johns Hopkins University Press.

Leinfellner, W. (1986). "The Prisoner's Dilemma and Its Evolutionary Iteration," pp. 135–148 in A. Diekman and P. Mitter, eds., *Paradoxical Effects of Social Behavior: Essays in Honor of Anatol Rapoport*. Vienna: Physica Verlag.

Leininger, W. (1987). "Escalation and Cooperation in International Conflicts: The Dollar Auction Game." Mimeographed, University of Bonn.

Leites, N. (1981). "The Soviet Style of War," pp. 185–224 in D. Leebaret, ed., *Soviet Military Thinking*. London: Allen & Unwin.

Leng, R. J. (1988). "Crisis Learning Games." *American Political Science Review*, 82(1): 179–194.

—— (1980). "Influence Strategies and Interstate Conflict," pp. 124–160 in J. D. Singer, ed., *The Correlates of War, Vol. II: Testing Some Realpolitik Models*. New York: Free Press.

Leng, R. J., and Wheeler, H. (1975). "Behavioral Indicators of War Proneness in Bilateral Conflict," pp. 191–226 in P. G. McGowan, ed., *International Yearbook of Foreign Policy Studies* (Vol. 2). Beverly Hills: Sage.

Levi, A., and Tetlock, P. E. (1980). "A Cognitive Analysis of Japan's 1940 Decision for War." *Journal of Conflict Resolution*, 24(2): 195–211.

Levite, A. (1987). *Intelligence and Strategic Surprise*. New York: Columbia University Press.

Levy, J. S. (1989). "The Diversionary Theory of War: Quantitative and Historical Evidence," in M. I. Midlarsky, ed., *Handbook of War Studies*. Boston: Unwin Hyman.

—— (1988a). "Quantitative Studies of Deterrence Success and Failure," in R. Axelrod, R. Jervis, R. Radner, and P. Stern, eds., *Perspectives on Deterrence*. New York: Oxford University Press.

—— (1988b). "The Role of Crisis Management in the Outbreak of World War I." Paper presented at the annual meeting of the American Political Science Association, Washington, DC, September 1–4.

—— (1987). "Declining Power and the Preventive Motivation for War." *World Politics*, 40(1): 82–107.

—— (1986). "Organizational Routines and the Causes of War." *International Studies Quarterly*, 30(2): 193–222.

—— (1984). "The Offensive/Defensive Balance of Military Technology: A Theoretical and Historical Analysis." *International Studies Quarterly*, 28(2): 219–238.

—— (1983). *War in the Great Power System*. Lexington: University Press of Kentucky.

—— (1982). "Historical Trends in Great Power War, 1495–1975." *International Studies Quarterly*, 26(2): 278–300.

Levy, J. S., and Forelich, M. (1985). "The Causes of the Iran-Iraq War," pp. 127–143 in J. Brown and W. P. Snyder, eds., *The Regionalization of Warfare*. New Brunswick, NJ: Transaction.

Liddell-Hart, B. H. (1967). *The Strategy of Indirect Approach*. Tel Aviv: Ma'arachot. (Hebrew translation from English, Col. Elhanan Oren)

—— (1930). *The Real War, 1914–1918*. Boston: Little, Brown.

Lijphart, A. (1971). "Comparative Politics and the Comparative Method." *American Political Science Review*, 65(2): 682–693.

Litwak, R. S. (1987). "Iran," pp. 116–138 in S. F. Wells and M. A. Bruzonsky, eds., *Security in the Middle East*. Boulder, CO: Westview.

Luard, E. (1986). *War in International Society*. New Haven, CT: Yale University Press.

Luttwak, E. N. (1987). *Strategy: The Logic of War and Peace*. Cambridge, MA: Harvard University Press.

—— (1976). *The Grand Strategy of the Roman Empire*. Baltimore: Johns Hopkins University Press.

Luttwak, E. N., and Horowitz, D. (1975). *The Israeli Army*. New York: Harper & Row.

Mack, A. (1975). "Why Big Nations Lose Small Wars: The Politics of Asymmetric Conflict." *World Politics*, 28(2): 175–200.

Maersheimer, J. J. (1983). *Conventional Deterrence*. Ithaca, NY: Cornell University Press.

Mandel, R. (1987). *Irrationality in International Confrontation*. New York: Greenwood.

—— (1986). "The Effectiveness of Gunboat Diplomacy." *International Studies Quarterly*, 30(1): 59–76.

Mansbach, R., and Vasquez, J. (1981). *In Search of Theory: A New Paradigm for Global Politics*. New York: Columbia University Press.

Maoz, Z. (1989). *National Choices and International Processes*. Cambridge: Cambridge University Press.

—— (1985a). "The Evolution of Syrian Power," pp. 69–82 in M. Maoz and A. Yaniv, eds., *Syria Under Assad*. London: Croom Helm.

—— (1985b). "Game Theoretic and Decision Theoretic Models in International Conflict," pp. 77–111 in U. Luterbacher and M. D. Ward, eds., *Dynamics Models of International Conflict*. Boulder, CO: Lynne Reiner.

—— (1985c). "Foreign Policy Decision Making: A Progress Report." *Jerusalem Journal of International Relations*, 7(4): 28–63.

—— (1984a). "Games and Decisions in International Conflicts." *State, Government, and International Relations*, 23(1): 50–84.

—— (1984b). "The Expected Utility of International Conflict: Some Logical Traps and Empirical Surprises in 'The War Trap.'" Mimeographed, University of Haifa.

—— (1984c). "Peace by Empire? Conflict Outcomes and International Stability 1816–1976." *Journal of Peace Research*, 21(3): 227–241.

—— (1983). "Resolve, Capabilities, and the Outcomes of Interstate Disputes, 1816–1976." *Journal of Conflict Resolution*, 27(2): 195–225.

—— (1982a). *Paths to Conflict: International Dispute Initiation, 1816–1976*. Boulder, CO: Westview.

—— (1982b). "Crisis Initiation: A Theoretical Exploration of a Neglected Topic in International Crisis Theory." *Review of International Studies*, 8(4): 215–232.

Maoz, Z., and Felsenthal, D. S. (1987). "Self-Binding Commitments, the Inducement of Trust, Social Choice, and the Theory of International Cooperation." *International Studies Quarterly*, 31(2): 177–200.

Maoz, Z., and Yaniv, A. (1989). "Game, Supergame, and Compound Escalation: Israeli-Syrian Crises, 1948–1984." Mimeographed, University of Haifa.

Marr, P. (1985). *The Modern History of Iraq*. Boulder, CO: Westview.

Maydole, R. (1987). "Superpower Paradoxes." Mimeographed, Davidson College.

Mazur, M. P. (1979). *Economic Growth and Development in Jordan*. Boulder, CO: Westview.

McClelland, C. A. (1968). "Access to Berlin: The Quantity and Variety of events," pp. 159–186 in J. D. Singer, ed., *Quantitative International Politics: Insights and Evidence*. New York: Free Press.

Meir, G. (1975). *My Life*. New York: G. P. Putnam's Sons.

Midlarsky, M. I., ed. (1989). *Handbook of War Studies*. Boston: Unwin Hyman.

Miller, W. (1966). *The Ottoman Empire and Its Successors, 1801–1927*. London: Frank Cass.

Millett, A. R., ed. (1978). *A Short History of the Vietnam War*. Bloomington: Indiana State University Press.

Moore, B. (1989). "Nasser's Decision-Making in the 1967 Middle East Crisis: A Multi-Staged Game Model." Mimeographed, New York University.

Morgan, P. (1977). *Deterrence*. Beverly Hills: Sage.

Morrow, J. (1987). "Capabilities, Uncertainty, and Resolve: A Limited Information Model of crisis Bargaining." Paper presented at the annual meeting of the International Studies Association, Washington, DC, April 14–18.

Naor, A. (1986). *Cabinet at War*. Tel Aviv: Lahav. (in Hebrew)

Nisbett, R. E., Krantz, D. H., Jepson, C., and Fong, G. T. (1982). "Improving Inductive Inference," pp. 445–462 in D. Kahneman, P. Slovic, and A. Tversky, eds., *Judgment Under Uncertainty: Heuristics and Biases*. Cambridge: Cambridge University Press.

Nisbett, R. E., and Ross, L. (1980). *Human Inference: Strategies and Shortcomings of Social Judgment*. Englewood Cliffs, NJ: Prentice-Hall.

Nonneman, G. (1986). *Iraq, the Gulf States, and the War: A Changing Relationship, 1980–1986 and Beyond*. London: Ithaca.

Nutting, A. (1972). *Nasser*. New York: E. P. Dutton.

O'Ballance, E. (1978). *No Victor, No Vanquished: The Yom Kippur War*. San Rafael: Presidio.

Offer, Z., and Kober, A., eds. (1987). *Intelligence and National Security*. Tel Aviv: Ma'arachot. (in Hebrew)

Olson, M., and Zeckhauser, R. (1966). "An Economic Theory of Alliances." *Review of Economics and Statistics*, 48(2): 266–279.

O'Neill, B. (1986). "International Escalation and the Dollar Auction." *Journal of Conflict Resolution*, 30(1): 33–50.

——— (1985). "The Dollar Auction as a Model of International Escalation," pp. 220–226 in U. Luterbacher and M. D. Ward, eds., *Dynamic Models of International Conflict*. Boulder, CO: Lynne Reiner.

Oren, N. (1982). "Prudence in Victory," pp. 147–163 in N. Oren, ed., *The Termination of Wars*. Jerusalem: Magness.

Organski, A. F. K., and Kugler, J. (1980). *The War Ledger*. Chicago: University of Chicago Press.

Paret, P., Craig, G., and Gilbert, F., eds. (1986). *Makers of Modern Strategy: From Machiavelli to the Nuclear Age*. Princeton, NJ: Princeton University Press.

Peres, S. (1970). *David's Sling*. London: Widenfeld & Nicolson.

Petrovich, M. B. (1976). *A History of Modern Serbia, 1804–1918*. New York: Harcourt Brace Jovanovich.

Pierre, A. J. (1982). *The Global Politics of Arms Sales*. Princeton, NJ: Princeton University Press.

Pillar, P. (1983). *Negotiating Peace: War Termination as a Bargaining Process*. Princeton, NJ: Princeton University Press.

Pion-Berlin, D. (1987). "Military Breakdown and Redemocratization in Argentina," pp. 209–230 in G. A. Lopez and M. Stohl, eds., *Liberalization and Redemocratization in Latin America*. New York: Greenwood.

Pipes, D. (1983). "A Border Adrift: Origins of the [Iran-Iraq] Conflict," pp. 3–26 in S. Tahir-Kheli and S. Ayubi, eds., *The Iran-Iraq War: New Weapons, Old Conflicts*. New York: Praeger.

Popper, K. R. (1968). *Conjectures and Refutations: The Growth of Scientific Knowledge*. New York: Harper Torchbooks.

Posen, B. R. (1984). *The Sources of Military Doctrine*. Ithaca, NY: Cornell University Press.

Quattrone, G. A., and Tversky, A. (1988). "Contrasting Rational and Psychological Analyses of Political Choice." *American Political Science Review*, 82(3): 719–736.

Quester, G. (1966). *Deterrence Before Hiroshima*. New York: Wiley.

Quine, W. V. (1965). *The Ways of Paradox*. New York: Random House.

Rabinovich, I. (1985). *The War for Lebanon, 1970–1983* (rev. ed.). Ithaca, NY: Cornell University Press.

Raiffa, H. (1982). *The Art and Science of Negotiation*. Cambridge, MA: Harvard University Press.

Rapoport, A., Guyer, M., and Gordon, D. (1976). *The 2 × 2 Game*. Ann Arbor: University of Michigan Press.

Ray, J. L. (1987). *Global Politics* (3rd ed.). Boston: Houghton Mifflin.

Ray, J. L., and Vural, A. (1986). "Power Disparities and Paradoxical Conflict Outcomes." *International Interactions*, 12(4): 315–342.

Raz, S. (1985). "The Iran-Iraq War as a Protracted War." *Ma'arachot*, 298: 6–11, 30. (in Hebrew)

Rice, G. (1986). "The Making of Soviet Strategy," pp. 648–676 in P. Paret, ed., *Makers of Modern Strategy: From Machiavelli to the Nuclear Age*. Princeton, NJ: Princeton University Press.

Riker, W. H. (1982). *Liberalism Against Populism: A Confrontation Between the Theory of Democracy and the Theory of Social Choice*. San Francisco: Freeman.

Rosen, S. (1972). "War, Power, and the Willingness to Suffer," in B. M. Russett, ed., *War, Peace, and Numbers*. Beverly Hills: Sage.

Rothenberg, G. E. (1986). "Moltke, Schlieffen, and the Doctrine of Strategic Envelopment," pp. 296–325 in P. Paret, ed., *Makers of Modern Strategy: From Machiavelli to the Nuclear Age*. Princeton, NJ: Princeton University Press.

Rubinstein, A. (1982). "Perfect Equilibrium in a Bargaining Model." *Econometrica*, 50(1): 90–109.

Russett, B. M. (1983) *The Prisoners of Insecurity: Nuclear Deterrence, the Arms Race, and Arms Control.* San Francisco: Freeman.

—— (1972). *No Clear and Present Danger: A Skeptical View of the U.S. Entry into World War II.* New York: Harper Torchbooks.

—— (1967). "Pearl Harbor: Deterrence Theory and Decision Theory." *Journal of Peace Research,* 4(2): 89–105.

Sabrosky, A. N. (1975). "From Bosnia to Sarajevo: A Comparative Discussion of International Crises." *Journal of Conflict Resolution,* 19(1): 3–24.

Sadat, A. (1978). *In Search for Identity.* New York: Harper & Row.

Safran N. (1969). *From War to War: The Arab Israeli Conflict.* New York: Pegasus.

Sahliye, E. F. (1986). *The PLO After the Lebanon War.* Boulder, CO: Westview.

Sainsbury, R. M. (1988). *Paradoxes.* Cambridge: Cambridge University Press.

Schelling, T. C. (1984). *Choice and Consequences.* Cambridge, MA: Harvard University Press.

—— (1966). *Arms and Influence.* New Haven, CT: Yale University Press.

—— (1963). *The Strategy of Conflict.* Cambridge, MA: Harvard University Press.

Schiff, Z., and Ya'ari, E. (1984). *Israel's Lebanon War.* New York: Simon & Schuster.

Schliephake, K. (1987). "Jordan: The Geographic and Economic Potential," pp. 62–92 in B. Khader and A. Badran, eds., *The Economic Development of Jordan.* London: Croom Helm.

Seale, P. (1965). *The Struggle for Syria.* Oxford: Oxford University Press.

Seaton, A. (1976). *Stalin as Military Commander.* New York: Praeger.

Sella, A., and Yishai, Y. (1986). *Israel: The Peaceful Belligerent, 1967–79.* New York: St. Martin's.

Sharett, M. (1978). *The Personal Diary of Moshe Sharett.* Tel Aviv: Am-Oved. (in Hebrew)

Shazli, S. (1980). *The Crossing of the Suez.* London: Widenfeld & Nicolson.

Shigenori, T. (1956). *The Cause of Japan.* New York: Simon & Schuster.

Shirer, W. L. (1960). *The Rise and Fall of the Third Reich.* New York: Simon & Schuster.

Shlaim, A. (1976). "Failures in National Intelligence Estimates: The Case of the Yom Kippur War." *World Politics,* 28(3): 348–380.

Shlaim, A., and Tanter, R. (1978). "Decision Process, Choice, and Consequences: Israel's Deep Penetration Bombing in Egypt, 1970." *World Politics,* 30(4): 483–516.

Singer, J. D. (1984). *Deterrence, Arms Control, and Disarmament* (2nd ed.). Lanham, MD: University Press of America.

—— (1969). "The Incompleat Theorist: Insight Without Evidence," pp. 63–86 in K. Knorr and J. Rosenau, eds., *Contending Approaches to International Relations.* Princeton, NJ: Princeton University Press.

Singer, J. D., Bremer, S., and Stuckey, J. (1972). "Capability Distribution, Uncertainty, and Major Power War, 1820–1965," pp. 19–48 in B. M. Russett, ed., *Peace, War, and Numbers.* Beverly Hills: Sage.

Singer, J. D., and Small, M. (1972). *The Wages of War, 1815–1965.* New York: Wiley.

Singer, J. D., and Small, M. (1968). "Alliance Aggregation and the Onset of War, 1815–1965," pp. 247–286 in J. D. Singer, ed., *Quantitative*

*International Politics*. New York: Free Press.

Siverson, R. M., and King, J. (1979). "Alliances and the Expansion of War, 1816–1975," pp. 37–49 in J. D. Singer and M. D. Wallace, eds., *To Augur Well*. Beverly Hills: Sage.

————— (1980). "Attributes of National Alliance Membership and War Participation, 1815–1965." *American Journal of Political Science*, 24(1): 1–15.

Slaatte, H. A. (1982). *The Pertinence of the Paradox*. Washington, DC: University Press of America.

Small, M., and Singer, J. D. (1982). *Resort to Arms: International and Civil Wars, 1815–1980*. Beverly Hills: Sage.

Snyder, G. H. (1984). "The Security Dilemma in Alliance Politics." *World Politics*, 36(4): 461–495.

————— (1961). *Deterrence and Defense*. Princeton, NJ: Princeton University Press.

Snyder, G. H., and Diesing, P. (1977). *Conflict Among Nations*. Princeton, NJ: Princeton University Press.

Snyder, J. S. (1984). *The Ideology of the Offensive: Military Decision Making and the Disasters of 1914*. Ithaca, NY: Cornell University Press.

Sokolovsky, V. D. (1975). *Soviet Military Strategy* (H. F. Scott, ed.). New York: Crane, Russak.

Staudenmaier, W. O. (1983). "A Strategic Analysis of the Iran-Iraq War," pp. 27–50 in S. Tahir-Kheli and S. Ayubi, eds., *The Iran-Iraq War: New Weapons, Old Conflicts*. New York: Praeger.

Stein, A. (1979). *The Nation at War*. Baltimore: Johns Hopkins University Press.

Stein, A., and Russett, B. M. (1980). "The Consequences of International Conflicts," pp. 399–422 in T. R. Gurr, ed., *Handbook of International Conflict*. New York: Free Press.

Stein, J. G. (1987). "Deterrence and Reassurance." Paper presented to the Committee on the Contribution of the Behavioral Sciences to the Prevention of Nuclear War, National Research Council.

————— (1985). "Calculation, Miscalculation, and Conventional Deterrence," pp. 34–88 in R. Jervis, R. N. Lebow, and J. G. Stein, eds., *Psychology and Deterrence*. Baltimore: Johns Hopkins University Press.

Stein, J. G., and R. Tanter (1980). *Rational Decision Making: Israel's Security Choices, 1967*. Columbus: Ohio State University Press.

Stephens, R. (1971). *Nasser: A Political Biography*. New York: Simon & Schuster.

Stockholm International Peace Research Institute (SIPRI). (various years, 1965–1988). *World Armaments and Disarmament: SIPRI Yearbook*. Cambridge: MIT Press.

Stohl, M. (1980). "The Nexus of Civil and International Conflict," pp. 297–330 in T. R. Gurr, ed., *Handbook of International Conflict*. New York: Free Press.

Sun Tzu (1983). *The Art of War*. New York: Delacorte. (Original work written sixth century B.C.)

Tahir-Kheli, S., and Ayubi, S., eds. (1983). *The Iran-Iraq War: New Weapons, Old Conflicts*. New York: Praeger.

Tanter, R. (1978). "International Crisis Behavior: An Appraisal of the Literature." *Jerusalem Journal of International Relations*, 3(2–3): 340–374.

Teger, A. (1980). *Too Much Invested to Quit*. New York: Pergamon.

Tevet, S. (1972). *Moshe Dayan: A Biography*. London: Widenfeld & Nicolson.

Toland, J. (1970). *The Rising Sun: The Decline and Fall of the Japanese Empire, 1936–1941*. New York: Random House.

Toms, E. (1972). "The Paradox of Existence," pp. 3–31 in L. Apostel et al., eds., *Negation*. Louvain: Nauwelarets.

Trotsky, L. (1980). *The Balkan Wars, 1912–1913*. New York: Monad.

Truman, H. S (1964). *Memoirs: Years of Trial and Hope*. Garden City, NY: Doubleday.

Tuchman, B. (1984). *The March of Folly: From Troy to Vietnam*. New York: Knopf.

—— (1962). *The Guns of August*. New York: Macmillan.

Tversky, A., and D. Kahneman (1973). "Availability: A Heuristic for Judging Frequency and Probability." *Cognitive Psychology*, 5(2): 207–232.

Ulam, A. (1974). *Expansion and Coexistence: Soviet Foreign Policy, 1917–1973* (2nd ed.). New York: Praeger.

U. S. Arms Control and Disarmament Agency (1978). *World Military Expenditures and Arms Transfers, 1967–1976*. Washington, DC: Government Printing Office.

Van Creveld, M. (1985). *Command in War*. Cambridge, MA: Harvard University Press.

—— (1983). *Supplying War: Logistics from Wallenstein to Patton*. Tel Aviv: Ma'arachot. (Hebrew translation from English, S. Gonen)

Van Dam, N. (1979). *The Struggle for Power in Syria*. London: Croom Helm.

Vasquez, J. A. (1983). *The Power of Power Politics: A Critique*. New Brunswick, NJ: Rutgers University Press.

Vaughan, C. E. (1915). *The Political Writings of J. J. Rousseau*. Cambridge: Cambridge University Press.

Wagner, A. (1974). *Crisis Decision Making: Israel's Experience in 1967 and 1973*. New York: Praeger.

Wallace, M. D. (1982). "Armaments and Escalation: Two Competing Hypotheses." *International Studies Quarterly*, 26(1): 37–56.

—— (1980). "Some Persisting Findings." *Journal of Conflict Resolution*, 24(2): 289–292.

—— (1979). "Arms Races and Escalation: Some New Evidence." *Journal of Conflict Resolution*, 23(1): 3–16.

Waltz, K. N. (1986). "Reflections on Theory of International Politics: Response to My Critics," pp. 322–346 in R. O. Keohane, ed., *Neorealism and Its Critics*. New York: Columbia University Press.

—— (1979). *Theory of International Politics* (5th ed.). New York: Random House.

Ward, M. D. (1984). "Differential Paths to Parity: A Study of the U.S.-Soviet Arms Race." *American Political Science Review*, 63(2): 297–317.

—— (1982). *Research Gaps in Alliance Dynamics* (Monograph Series in World Affairs). Denver: University of Denver.

Wayman, F., Singer, J. D., and Goertz, G. (1983). "Capabilities, Military Allocations, and Success in Militarized Disputes." *International Studies Quarterly*, 27(4): 497–515.

*Webster's New Twentieth Century Dictionary* (1980). Unabridged (2nd ed.). New York: Simon & Schuster.

Weede, E. (1980). "Arms Races and Escalation: Some Persisting Doubts." *Journal of Conflict Resolution*, 24(2): 285–288.

Weizman, E. (1975). *Yours Is the Sky, Yours Is the Land.* Tel Aviv: Ma'ariv. (in Hebrew)

Wheeler, D. D., and Janis, I. L. (1980). *A Practical Guide for Making Decisions.* New York: Free Press.

White, R. K. (1970). *Nobody Wanted War: Misperception in Vietnam and Other Wars.* Garden City, NY: Anchor.

Whiting, A. S. (1960). *China Crosses the Yalu.* Stanford, CA: Stanford University Press.

Wilkenfeld, J. (1973). *Conflict Behavior and Linkage Politics.* New York: McKay.

Wittman, D. (1979). "How a War Ends." *Journal of Conflict Resolution,* 23(4): 743–763.

Wohlstetter, R. (1962). *Pearl Harbor: Warning and Decision.* Stanford, CA: Stanford University Press.

Wright, Q. (1965). *A Study of War.* Chicago: University of Chicago Press.

Wynia, G. W. (1986). *Argentina: Illusions and Realities.* New York: Holmes & Meier.

Yaniv, A. (1987). *Dilemmas of Security: Politics, Strategy and the Israeli Experience in Lebanon.* New York: Oxford University Press.

———— (1986). *Deterrence Without the Bomb: The Politics of Israeli Strategy.* Lexington, MA: D. C. Heath.

———— (1985). "Syria and Israel: The Politics of Escalation," pp. 157–178 in M. Maoz and A. Yaniv, eds., *Syria under Assad: Domestic Constraints and Regional Risks.* London: Croom Helm.

Yaniv, A., and Lieber, R. (1983). "Personal Whim or Strategic Imperative: The Israeli Invasion of Lebanon." *International Security,* 8(2): 117–142.

Zagare, F. C. (1987). *The Dynamics of Deterrence.* Chicago: University of Chicago Press.

Zhukov, G. K. (1982). *The Memoirs of Marshall Zhukov.* Tel Aviv: Ma'arachot. (Hebrew translation from English, S. Gonen)

Zinnes, D. A. (1980a). "Theories on the Causes of War," in T. R. Gurr, ed., *Handbook of International Conflict.* New York: Free Press.

———— (1980b). "Three Puzzles in Search for a Researcher." *International Studies Quarterly,* 24(3): 315–342.

# Name Index

# Subject Index